ANOTHER
COUNTRY

ANOTHER COUNTRY

Journeying toward the Cherokee Mountains

CHRISTOPHER CAMUTO

The University of Georgia Press / Athens & London

Published in 2000 by the University of Georgia Press
Athens, Georgia 30602
© 1997 by Christopher Camuto
Printed and bound by Creasey Printing Services

The paper in this book meets the guidelines for
permanence and durability of the Committee on
Production Guidelines for Book Longevity of the
Council on Library Resources.

Printed in Canada

04   03   02   01   00   P   5   4   3   2   1

Library of Congress Cataloging-in-Publication Data

Camuto, Christopher.
Another country : journeying toward the Cherokee
Mountains / Christopher Camuto.
    p.   cm.
Originally published: New York : Henry Holt, 1997.
Includes bibliographical references and index.
ISBN 0-8203-2237-7 (pbk. : alk. paper)
1. Great Smoky Mountains (N.C. and Tenn.)—Description
and travel. 2. Appalachian Region,
Southern—Description and travel. 3. Cherokee
Indians—North Carolina—History. I. Title.
F443.G7 C34   2000
976.8´89—dc21

                        99-057974

British Library Cataloging-in-Publication Data available

Originally published in 1997 by Henry Holt and Company, Inc.

Grateful acknowledgment to The Museum of the Cherokee in
Cherokee, North Carolina, for permission to quote from the
Fading Voices interview series, and to the Newberry Library,
Chicago, Illinois, for permission to quote from the Payne Papers.

for *Canis rufus gregoryi*
perfect walker
far traveler

and

in memory of
James Mooney
who listened

The health of the eye seems to demand a horizon.

—RALPH WALDO EMERSON

Contents

Acknowledgments

Thanks, again, to William Strachan, who supported the idea and evolution of this book. Mitchell Byrd of the College of William and Mary and Keith Watson of the National Park Service gave me access to the hacking of peregrine falcons at Shenandoah National Park in the summers of 1991 and 1992, an experience that was, in many respects, the genesis for what follows. Christopher Lucash and Barron Crawford, both of the United States Fish and Wildlife Service, allowed me to closely observe their work with red wolves at Great Smoky Mountains National Park from 1991 to the present. Gerald Schroedl of the Department of Anthropology at the University of Tennessee and James Bates and Robert Morgan of the United States Forest Service showed me the archaeology being practiced at the Chattooga Town site in South Carolina in the spring of 1994. Claire Newell of the University of North Carolina, Chapel Hill, and Dale Holder of the United States Forest Service let me tag along on their botanical studies in the Joyce Kilmer–Slickrock Wilderness during the summer of 1994. Mary Kelley, then of the Western North Carolina Alliance, and Dan Pittillo of Western Carolina University guided my understanding of southern Appalachian flora, particularly the biodiversity of old-growth forests.

Thanks also to Joan Greene, archivist at the Museum of the Cherokee in Cherokee, North Carolina; Betsy Brittigan and Yolanda Warren of the Leyburn Library at Washington and Lee University; and Linda Lester, Heather Moore, and Pauline Page of the University of Virginia's Alderman Library. I am inspired by the intelligence, curiosity, and natural sympathy of the youngest members of my clan—Cheryl Bilinski, Katie Bilinski, Alyssa Bilinski, Elizabeth Dubovsky, Michael Dubovsky, and Kevin Dubovsky. I am particularly indebted to Ms. Alyssa Bilinski for information on bears. Special thanks to Eve Richardson and James Rosen, who helped me see the sounds with which this book begins.

ANOTHER
COUNTRY

Prologue: No Heaven, No Hell

Skepticism, Melville complained, is the curse of modern travel. The novelist's ship had put in at Malta and he had trouble imagining the solitary, first-century presence of St. John in what had become one of the most crowded places on earth. While noting that fact in his journal, Melville's subconscious must have taken another turn toward fiction, where what he later called true places might be preserved forever. Apparently, even in the mid-nineteenth century, modernity seemed to be not only crowding every landscape with commerce and congestion but also pushing the significance of the past beyond the mind's eye.

In a landscape as injured by the cyclops of growth and development as the southern Appalachians, it is as difficult to visualize the Quaker botanist William Bartram greeting the Cherokee chief Attakullaculla alongside the Nantahala River in the spring of 1775, or the British lieutenant Henry Timberlake witnessing the eagle dance at Citico one winter night in 1762, as it was for Melville to imagine an evangelist meditating in sublime isolation on bustling Malta. Harder still to imagine Hernando de Soto's ominous incursion through these mountains in the spring of 1540 and the lost world of precontact North America—its thoughts, stories, and songs.

Much that was real is now nearly unimaginable, and what once was imagined in these mountains may already be, in spirit, beyond reach.

In the shadow of the cyclops, the possibilities of genuine enchantment continually recede. True places, and with them part of the truth, disappear daily. The much-descried destruction of nature—especially the logging of forests, the damming of rivers, the pollution of air and water, and the overdevelopment of rural landscapes—leads, among other disadvantages, to the erasure of history. You only have to approach the Great Smoky Mountains from Sevierville, Tennessee, through Pigeon Forge and Gatlinburg, perhaps the ugliest stretch of road in eastern North America, to see the deep past and immediate future juxtaposed in a very confused present moment, a weird snarl of traffic and herd consumerism foregrounding one of the most magnificent landscapes on earth.

In the southern Appalachians, beautiful as they still are, it gets harder each season and each year to imagine a more luminous world, especially the nature and culture of life in these mountains before the troubling rumor of de Soto's approach came through the woods—the dances and councils, the hunting and war, the horticulture and tool-making, the fashioning of gorgets and polishing of birdstones, the trading of soapstone pipes and sheets of mica, the hafting of spearpoints with animal sinew and the crafting of atlatls, the magic and healing as well as the beliefs and stories that upheld sanity and enabled survival amid much uncertainty and danger— not to mention the mythic time before those unrecorded centuries when, in the mind of the Cherokee, animals and plants held council and pondered the problem of man.

No one calls them the Cherokee Mountains anymore. The anachronism harkens back to the first white traders among the Cherokee, a literal-minded group of widely varying character who came out from Charles Town in the late seventeenth century plying the deer trade. The convenient usage persisted at least through the eighteenth century, as the Cherokee themselves became increasingly inconvenient to the material progress of American culture. In his *History of the American Indians,* published in 1775, James Adair tells us that "the Cheerake mountains look very formidable to a stranger, when he is among their valleys, incircled with their prodigious, proud, contending tops: they appear as a great mass of black and blue clouds, interspersed with some rays of light." William Bartram used the term in his famous *Travels,* published sixteen years later. But after the forced removal of most of the tribe from the East in 1838, the name must have fallen rapidly out of fashion, its loss of no particular moment to the Cherokee, who had their own words for things.

The most recent use of the phrase I have come across is as a caption to a photograph in the *Nineteenth Annual Report* of the now-defunct Bureau of American Ethnology. The photograph, a densely forested landscape of hardwoods and tulip poplar framing an indistinct horizon of mountains, was taken by Bureau ethnologist James Mooney in North Carolina in 1888, fifty years after the removal, and used as the frontispiece for his *Myths of the Cherokee,* which made up the bulk of the Bureau's annual report for 1900. The caption reads simply: "In the Cherokee Mountains."

Mooney draws the historic realm of the Cherokee as "the whole country from the Savannah to the Ohio," a breathtaking reach if you visualize what the phrase embraces—all the country between Atlanta and Cincinnati from well east of Asheville, North Carolina, to well west of Nashville, Tennessee. By treaty, the Cherokee ceded nearly 120,000 square miles of land between 1721 and 1835, when the fraudulent Treaty of New Echota was imposed on the tribe prior to their removal. This great square of land, which included hunting grounds in Kentucky north to the Ohio River and westward to its confluence with the Cumberland River, constituted a country more than twice the size of England and immeasurably richer in natural resources. If Mooney's population estimate of 22,000 Cherokee before the first recorded smallpox epidemic is correct, there were nearly five square miles of land per person in this realm. Whatever the hardships of life in precontact North America, the Cherokee nonetheless lived with an enviable relation to unspoiled natural space, a world of great visual breadth and imaginative depth.

Of course, there is no way to quantify the psychological and spiritual relation of people to land. The Cherokee never imagined their country the way it appeared pieced out on treaty maps, where unnaturally straight survey lines cut across rivers and mountains with no regard for the lay of the land and the proper use of it.* Without buying or selling an acre, they exercised cultural stewardship over vast, fluid resources, the great variety of flora and fauna on which they based their lives and from which their ethics,

---

* These conflicting geographies can best be seen on Charles Royce's 1884 Map of the Territorial Limits of the Cherokee Nation of Indians, part of the Bureau of American Ethnology's *Fifth Annual Report* (1887).

philosophy, and art flowed, a way of life that fused the material and non-material worlds in ways we can now but dimly understand.

Mooney depicts the Cherokee heartland in historical times as being

> the entire Allegheny region from the interlocking head-streams of the Kanawha and the Tennessee southward almost to the site of Atlanta, and from the Blue ridge on the east to the Cumberland range on the west, a territory comprising an area of about 40,000 square miles, now included in the states of Virginia, Tennessee, North Carolina, South Carolina, Georgia, and Alabama. Their principal towns were upon the headwaters of the Savannah, Hiwassee, and Tuckasegee, and along the whole length of the Little Tennessee to its junction with the main stream. Itsati, or Echota, on the south bank of the Little Tennessee, a few miles above the mouth of the Tellico river, in Tennessee, was commonly considered the capital of the Nation.

In contemporary terms, the remnants of this other country are centered along the summit-line border of North Carolina and Tennessee, where the southern Appalachians reach their greatest height and their most impressive breadth and where rivers older than the mountains sweep through them against the grain of the Appalachian orogeny. In those places where you can get an uninterrupted view of it, this fundamental topographic tension between taut, hard-flowing rivers and steep, darkly forested mountains still has the power to suggest a broader, deeper world than we generally have left ourselves. And the southern Appalachian summit region, more biologically diverse than Europe, remains a refuge and showcase of Holocene life, harboring cove forests of staggering ecological complexity where tropical and boreal species comingle; toothy summits of spruce-fir forest, rock outcrops, and windswept balds where Arctic species give testimony to periglacial cold; as well as a variety and density of wildlife that reminds you how empty the rest of eastern North America has become. This coincidence of a variegated landscape, natural diversity, and the complexity of precontact Cherokee culture is, of course, no accident.

But getting back is a problem. To get to the Cherokee Mountains now, you can work your way southwest from Virginia as the Cherokee themselves might have done thousands of years ago, following the narrow crest of the Blue Ridge until it buckles into the dark crescent of the Black Mountains and then splits through the jumble of the Craggys and Balsams. You can approach as Bartram did, from the coastal plain and piedmont of South

Carolina across the gentle coruscation of the southern Blue Ridge into the valley of the Little Tennessee—née Cherokee—River and then up the abrupt rise of the Nantahalas. Or trace what now seems likely to have been de Soto's dark route from Asheville along the French Broad River as it sweeps west through the Blue Ridge just north of the Unakas, as the Great Smoky Mountains were once known. Or, perhaps better, wander among the strange buffalo backs of the Yellow Creek, Cheoah, and Snowbird mountains, which graze peacefully around the old Middle Settlements, finally crossing the Cheoahs to follow the voluble Tuckasegee along the haunting landscape line of the Alarkas. The Alarkas guard mythic *Kitu'hwa,* the sacred place where the Cherokee came out of the earth and where much of the eastern band of the tribe remains, largely hidden behind the tragicomic mask of the tourist trade in the town of Cherokee, North Carolina, a mirror image of the Pigeon Forge–Gatlinburg strip that reflects the current mythology of endless consumption and deflects attention from the sacred things preserved in the surrounding hills.

All these ways lead toward the Cherokee Mountains, which exist now principally as a picturesque mirage wavering in the face of the intense pressure of what Edward Abbey called industrial tourism, the final cutting blade of the machine in the garden. The fragments of quiet backcountry preserved to some extent in Great Smoky Mountains National Park and to a much lesser extent in the adjoining national forests—the Pisgah, Cherokee, Nantahala, and Chattahoochee—coincide with the backbone of the old Cherokee territory and provide the best potential points of access to that other, older world where not that long ago the sacred was real and culture and nature were two aspects of a single practice, a fabulous horizon that asserts itself now only when no one is looking.

Beyond a physical eagerness to explore the southern Appalachians and curiosity about the diversity of life they still encourage, this book has its origins in two things Cherokee—James Mooney's classic collections of Cherokee mythology and the restoration of *Canis rufus,* the red wolf, to Great Smoky Mountains National Park in the fall of 1992.

Years ago I came across the Charles Elder Booksellers reprint of Mooney's *Myths of the Cherokee* and *Sacred Formulas of the Cherokees* in the National Park Service bookstore at Linville Falls, North Carolina, a spectacular break in the Blue Ridge Mountains once within the unstated borders of Cherokee lifeways. I was busy with other work but this odd book, like much else about the mountains, was a powerful distraction, especially its glossary of Cherokee words, strange verbal shards that gave a glimpse not just of another language but of another way of looking at things. If to understand a language is to understand a way of life, there was much in the life of the rivers and mountains I thought I knew well locked away in the unfamiliar words and unfathomable grammar of Cherokee as well as in the myths and stories Mooney had collected. Here was a chunk of the "wild and dusky knowledge," the "tawny grammar" Thoreau had written of when pondering the question of our proper relation to wild life and wild places.

The persistent, self-taught Mooney had been hired as an ethnologist for the Bureau of American Ethnology by its first director, John Wesley Powell, in 1885. Powell is best known as the charismatic veteran of the battle of Shiloh who led the first expedition to run the Colorado River through the Grand Canyon in 1869. He was, among many other things, a student of Native American culture, and his principal mission at the Bureau was to oversee a belated attempt to rescue aboriginal American languages and thought from oblivion. Mooney, who had to pester Powell mightily for the job, became an invaluable part of that effort.

Mooney did his seminal fieldwork among the Eastern Cherokee during the summer of 1887 and 1888, the summer and fall of 1889, and briefly in the summer of 1890. His first major work, *Sacred Formulas of the Cherokees,* was published as part of the Bureau's *Seventh Annual Report* in 1891. *Myths of the Cherokee* followed in 1900, as part of the *Nineteenth Annual Report.*

Three hundred fifty years after the first significant contact with Europeans, Mooney found living remnants of an uncontaminated oral tradition reaching back into precontact Cherokee thought and imagination, part of it preserved in written Cherokee by the last great generation of the tribe's medicine men—Gatigwanasti, Ayun'ini, Awanita, Tsi'skwa, Dagwatihi, Gahuni, Ina'li, Yanugulegi, Duninali, Aya'sta, A'gansta'ta, and others.*

During his visits, the oldest medicine men and women of the tribe decided, one by one, to reveal to Mooney aspects of Cherokee culture of which earlier travelers among the Cherokee were left unaware. The lives of Mooney's informants reached far into the past. In 1890—the year the U.S. Census Bureau was unable to find a western frontier—there was still a

---

* Belt, Swimmer, Young Deer, Bird, Catawba Killer, untranslated, Black Fox, Climbing Bear, Tracker, Spoiler, and Groundhog Meat.

sanctioned eagle-killer among the principal people of western North Carolina, a man schooled in the arcane rituals surrounding the acquisition of feathers for the eagle dance. The oldest woman of the tribe had "carried a scalp in the scalp dance in the Creek war 75 years before." The tribal memories of Cherokee elders reached even farther back and included not only knowledge of ancient rites of purification but of the worldview that underwrote such practices and their attendant myths and prayers. On the brink of the twentieth century, Mooney found, in short, that the old ways were still being practiced in the shadow of the Cherokee Mountains. Even informants who were practicing Christians—one was a Methodist minister—cherished the myths and sacred formulas the anthropologist rescued from oblivion.

In his introduction to *The Sacred Formulas of the Cherokees,* Mooney recounted his first, awestruck confrontation with the contents of the Ayun'ini notebook, the so-called Swimmer manuscript that was one of his principal sources:

> Here prayers, songs, and prescriptions for the cure of all kinds of diseases—for chills, rheumatism, frostbites, wounds, bad dreams, and witchery; love charms, to gain the affections of a woman or to cause her to hate a detested rival; fishing charms, hunting charms—including the songs without which none could ever hope to kill any game; prayers to make the corn grow, to frighten away storms, and to drive off witches; prayers for long life, for safety among strangers, for acquiring influence in council and success in the ball play. There were prayers to the Long Man, the Ancient White, the Great Whirlwind, the Yellow Rattlesnake, and to a hundred other gods of the Cherokee pantheon. It was in fact an Indian ritual and pharmacopoeia.

Mooney was blunt in his assessment of Cherokee medical practice, which he did not think held up under scientific scrutiny, but he immediately perceived the underlying value of what he had found: "It is impossible to overestimate the ethnologic importance of the materials thus obtained. They are invaluable as the genuine production of the Indian mind, setting forth in the clearest light the state of the aboriginal religion before its contamination by contact with the whites. To the psychologist and the student of myths they are equally precious."

Mooney was not paying lip service to the primitivism of the noble savage or succumbing to the Romantic charms of his exotic material. He recognized a *literature* in the tattered notebooks reluctantly brought forward from the cabins of the Qualla Boundary, the principal reservation of the Eastern Cherokee in western North Carolina. He had unearthed the primary ideas and modes of expression of a practical but profoundly imaginative culture. In what Mooney called sacred formulas and the foundational myths from which they derived authority can be found extraordinary language and unique genres, an earthbound spirituality as well as a transcendental geography, all drawn from an uncannily compressed history of thousands of years of direct relationship with what Emerson, searching for a purchase on natural history, called the primary forms—the sky, the mountain, the tree, the animal.

Despite the fragmentary state of the material he collected, Mooney rightly inferred there was "a wonderful completeness about the whole system which is not surpassed even by the ceremonial religions of the East." In those notebooks of unadulterated Cherokee thought Mooney perceived and admired what he called consistency of theory, particularity of ceremonial, and beauty of expression.

Mooney also recognized that the Cherokee mind was not proto-Christian, as some tried to portray it, but was cast in entirely different categories: "The language, the conception, and the execution are all genuinely Indian, and hardly a dozen lines of the hundreds of formulas show a trace of the influence of the white man or his religion." "It is evident from a study of these formulas that the Cherokee Indian was a polytheist and that the spirit world was to him only a shadowy counterpart of this. All his prayers were for temporal and tangible blessings—for health, for long life, for success in the chase, in fishing, in war and in love, for good crops, for protection and for revenge. He had no Great Spirit, no happy hunting ground, no heaven, no hell." Mooney describes a tragic view of life and history in the underlying psychology of the Cherokee mind: "death had for him no terrors and he awaited the inevitable end with no anxiety as to the future." He compared the "linguistic value" of the Cherokee formulas to that of the sacred texts of the Maya and repeated D. G. Brinton's observation of the impossibility of adequately translating the aboriginal tongues of the Western Hemisphere into European languages—because the "flow of thought" was so different and the metaphors so strange.

Powell's concern about the Ghost Dance revival among western tribes interrupted Mooney's work among the Eastern Cherokee. In December of 1890 Mooney was en route to the Indian Territory to investigate this resurgence of Native American spirit when the massacre at Wounded Knee occurred on the Pine Ridge Reservation of the Sioux. Before coming back east, he made a brief visit to the Western Cherokee in Oklahoma to add to his knowledge of their language.

Mooney did not return to the Eastern Cherokee until 1911, when he found most of his original informants dead, many rituals in disuse, and much changed among the Cherokee of the Qualla Boundary. He was drawn, his able biographer L. G. Moses reports, to those "who still prayed to the water at new moon, and put out fires at the death of a kinsman." He returned again in the summer of 1913, when he was deeply moved upon witnessing the ceremony of Cherokee "going to water" for purification before eating the first corn of the season. Although he was no longer a stranger among the Cherokee, who had done him the honor of giving him a name, he unconsciously echoed James Adair's impression of the haunting otherness of the Cherokee country: "It was very impressive in the open air with the mountains all around, with tops hidden in heavy mist while the [Indians] stood in line looking steadily into the water." He came again the following summer, with his sons, and for the last time in the summer of 1916, with the Easter Rebellion—throes of another colonial disorder—heavy on his Irish mind. A generation later, *Nun'da* was still fondly remembered by the people to whose stories he had listened with attention and respect.

If you travel the southern Appalachian backcountry, eventually you wonder not only about native plants and animals but about native ideas and images, particularly what ethics, spirituality, and art evolved in such a hard, beautiful place. Mooney's work is the key. A scholar in the best sense, his interest in native thought was not academic. He knew words and myths thrived, like wildflowers and wolves, in situ: "as with other tribes and countries, almost every prominent rock and mountain, every deep bend in the river, in the old Cherokee country has its accompanying legend. It may be a little story that can be told in a paragraph, to account for some natural feature, or it may be one chapter of a myth that has its sequel in a mountain a hundred miles away. As is usual when a people has lived for a long time in the same country, nearly every important myth is localized, thus assuming more definite character."

After encountering Mooney's work, I shaped my travel toward those places where old words and things were fused in the precontact Cherokee mind—trail crossings and river bends that had some transcendental life in them. Many, of course—most, really—have been obliterated, but it is still possible to read the fragmented southern Appalachian summit region through the fragments of precontact culture James Mooney salvaged from a beleaguered people. This is to see through a glass darkly, but history has not left much to go on. What follows is, in part, an attempt to follow a landscape line, to borrow that phrase again from Mary Austin, from the present to the past, to catch glimpses of the Cherokee Mountains behind the veil of the southern Appalachians.

I want to emphasize that I pursued the old soul of this landscape as an outsider, that is, as a non-Cherokee, and I hope with proper respect. In my reading and in my traveling I tried to use what in Zen Buddhism is called *shoshin*—beginner's mind—in this case a native curiosity about the place where I feel most at home. Whenever I refer to precontact Cherokee culture, or to "the Cherokee mind," I refer only to my own evolving understanding as a student of these things. The Cherokee, of course, speak for themselves.

Originally, I wanted to include Cherokee voices in this writing. But I am well aware that the final theft of colonialism is the theft of ideas and art, and I came to understand the reluctance of most Cherokee, particularly the dwindling number of native speakers who seem tired of being prodded by the world beyond their thoughts, to talk about the sacred things.

During a tape-recorded interview conducted by Cherokee folklorists for the Fading Voices Program in 1987, then seventy-two-year-old Bessie Jumper, a member of the Deer Clan, the *Ani'Kawi'*, announced with clarity and dignity that she would tell her stories for the last time: "I don't want to repeat again what I have told. I do it only for one time." The density of her memories makes them seem fragmentary, partly because of the literalness of the translation and partly because the implied wholeness of her thoughts does not fully emerge into our fragmented world. Bessie Jumper was one year old that last summer James Mooney visited the Cherokee. She remembered being born outside, near a large poplar and some walnut trees. She remembered being brought into the house in her mother's apron. She remembered being taught to face east when praying and that the dead were to be buried facing east. She remembered communal scenes from her childhood—men and women hoeing in a cornfield, gathering wood, cooking. She remembered men gathered outside after dinner "in the shade telling of the past and what is to happen in the future after they were gone." She remembered being forbidden to speak Cherokee at Mission School. She remembered the old ones saying that everything was different and that everything would disappear. "That what they said. It true. . . . They told a lot of different thing. To know the meaning, you had to listen—what they were saying."

The silence of those Native Americans who are still rooted in their past—like the silence of the deer and bear and now wolves that roam these mountains, as well as the silence of the mountains themselves—is one of the most important sounds in the backcountry. I hope I heard it right. I have, for reasons of my own, walked thousands of miles in these mountains and canoed hundreds of river miles during the last twenty years. After a while you do begin to wonder what the animals and trees and rocks were saying before man brutalized nature here. As the poet and essayist Gary Snyder suggests, the only hope now is for each of us to try to become, by the trial and error of our own practice of the wild, native American. If we are to have a future more interesting and more generous than the current materialism, we will, individually and communally, have to work out some actual relation to the wildness Emerson, Whitman, Thoreau, and Dickinson long ago suggested might keep America from becoming a purely material place.

When I was ready to begin work on this book, wildness was at hand. On November 5, 1991, I heard Dr. Ronald Nowak's passionate address to the Southern Appalachian Man and Biosphere Conference in Gatlinburg, Tennessee: "For the first time in history," the soft-spoken U.S. Fish and Wildlife Service biologist told a rapt audience of several hundred wildlife management professionals, "a large predatory mammal, thought to have been totally eliminated in the wild, has been restored to a part of its natural habitat. Wolves, born and raised in captivity, have been conditioned to subsist, socially interact, rear young, and hunt in the wild just as did their prehistoric ancestors. . . . I think it is an expression of hope that this animal, that came down to us from the early ice age almost to disappear before our eyes, may yet return in its original form to its natural environment."

Nowak was inspired by the successful reintroduction of *Canis rufus,* the red wolf, to the Alligator River Wildlife Refuge in eastern North Carolina and by the pending experimental release of red wolves in Great Smoky Mountains National Park, also once part of the wolf's historical range. The reintroduction of the gray wolf, *Canis lupus,* to Yellowstone National Park in 1995 would attract much more attention than the red wolf project in the East, but *Canis rufus,* which may be the only extant New World wolf, was the first North American wolf species to step through the opened gate of an acclimation pen into what is left of the wild. When the Endangered Species Act was passed by Congress in 1973, *Canis rufus* was the most endangered mammal in North America.

The day I heard him speak, Nowak also had been energized by renewed attacks against the taxonomic status of the red wolf, which had become a problematic animal to classify. Particularly galling to Nowak, an authority on the evolution of North American canids in general and on the red wolf in particular, were assertions that the red wolf had either been hybridized out of existence before it was rescued by the recovery program or, worse, that it had never been anything more than a coyote–gray wolf hybrid. "The red wolf," Nowak warned in 1991, "which survived five hundred years of human persecution, the near destruction of its environment, and this critical problem of genetic swamping, may yet be done in by biologists."

At the time, this seemed to be a purely scientific dispute. But although neither Nowak nor anyone else in the audience could have known it in 1991, the Endangered Species Act would itself become endangered in a few years, and the taxonomical classification of species and subspecies would become a political football in a game played by cynical rules that had little to do with science.

By the fall of 1992, when the permanent release of red wolves into the Great Smoky Mountains took place, I found myself holding the threads of a complex story, a story that led to the heart of what was left of the old Cherokee country. The wolf is the principal clan animal of the Cherokee and figures prominently in the tribe's most important foundational myth. In American history, the wolf embodied a diagnostic cultural difference between New World and Old, between Cherokee and European. The former was forbidden to kill a wolf, the latter could not let one live.

In fact, wolves and Indians were associated in the European mind, and the extermination of the one was intimately related to the genocide of the other. Mooney himself noted the association: "The Indian was regarded as an incumbrance to be cleared off, like the trees and the wolves, before white men could live in the country." Both practices were, of course, quickly obscured by the myth that American culture and the American character were formed by conquering the wilderness. Now this nearly conquered animal, sacred and profane, was going to be released back into the Cherokee heartland, a modernist gesture with deep time overtones.

. . .

There is no question that *Canis rufus* deepened the woods. It was not possible to observe wolves continually in the backcountry, the way you could set about watching black bear foraging in the fall, but if you hiked or backpacked within their newfound territory, you might hear them howl or come across tracks, or a lone print, or a pile of scat. Humble work. Anywhere a wolf might be was suddenly wolf country—that was the important thing. Tangible possibilities had been created. Even when I was a hundred miles from where the wolves probably were—watching for peregrine falcons at Linville Gorge or searching out stands of old growth in the Nantahalas—*Canis rufus* was out there somewhere along that fabulous tangle of mountain ridges, and I don't think it was an exercise in belated Romanticism to believe that was important. In any event, for several years I spent more time in wolf country than at home. As Aldo Leopold put it: "There are some who can live without wild things, and some who cannot."

But the wolves also sharpened my awareness of how small and fragmented wolf country was, because even in the half-million-acre Great Smoky Mountains National Park, which was the only place they legally had a right to be, a wolf with any talent for travel quickly ran out of room. Despite the heroic genetics of the animal—which hard-wired it for the hunting skills and kinship ties the Cherokee had long admired—their shifting fortunes were tragicomic from the beginning and raised the nagging problem of the fate of wild life in a tame world.

I knew the southern Appalachians well and had no illusions about wild places strangled by interstates, bordered by polluted rivers, and doused with acid rain and snow, or about a "wilderness" backcountry where you had to make reservations for campsites and where the water in the most remote stream was not safe to drink. And I had my doubts about the future—natural and political—of the red wolf, but its presence put heart back in these ancient uplands and I was not going to miss the pleasure of it. When the first free-ranging wolf howls stung the air, I imagine that Bear as well as Deer lifted their heads with interest and that Raven remembered the unique break of the sound. In any event, the release of wolves in Tennessee intrigued me—this reassertion of wildness in the eastern woods.

The attempt to restore a permanent, self-perpetuating population of red wolves in Great Smoky Mountains National Park began on October 9, 1992, when the so-called Cades Cove wolves were released. Two months later a second family of wolves, the Tremont wolves, was freed. By the onset of winter a hopeful play of contradictions had been set in motion. I let the unfolding success and failure of these wolves dictate the real-time narrative that underlies, in varying degrees, the following essays and set about exploring the parallel problems of being a wolf on the cusp of the twenty-first century and a writer drawn to the continually shrinking southern Appalachian backcountry.

Having read Mooney's work, I knew that the restoration of the principal familiar spirit of the Cherokee could not be unimportant. *Canis rufus* became for me a moving, for the most part invisible, center, one that drew me across many boundaries—from the present into the past, from science into mythology, and from the material toward the transcendental. About halfway through the work for this book, I understood that although I had set out to write about place, I was forced, at almost every turn, to write about time and that *Canis rufus*—as an embodiment of the idea and practice of restored wildness—had led me, in a series of circles, from one vanishing point to another.

I have given this writing as much narrative continuity as those vanishing points would support. Fragmentation, for obvious reasons, is thematic on several levels, and this book's structure reflects in part a concession to that fragmentation and, in part, an attempt to order the fragments in a meaningful way without violating the facts of time and place. What follows are essays on horizons—ecological, historical, mythological—ordered against this occasion of wolves—horizons that are still visible from one vantage or another, in certain seasons or kinds of weather, in the fragmented archipelago of wild places left in the southern Appalachians.

The first problem I encountered when I began work on this book remains unsolved—that of practicing the wild in a tame world. I worried all along that this practice may be only a literary affectation, a use of words to fill the unnatural vacuum we have created around us. And I worry about that still. I am not sure what the goals of nature writing can be at this point in the history of the destruction of North America, but I think that American writers have never been less entitled to creative epiphanies or to use nature for purely literary purposes.

In the southern Appalachians, beautiful as they still are, metaphors are as scarce and elusive as wolves.

Winter 1997
Highland Farm
Rockbridge County, Virginia

I

WOLF COUNTRY

In the beginning, the people say, the Dog was put on the mountain and the Wolf beside the fire. When the winter came the Dog could not stand the cold, so he came down to the settlement and drove the Wolf from the fire. The Wolf ran to the mountains, where it suited him so well that he prospered and increased.

—James Mooney, "Myths of the Cherokee"

Mind on a Wolf

*Only the mountain has lived long enough to listen
objectively to the howl of a wolf.*

—Aldo Leopold, "Thinking Like a Mountain"

*The spaces between the mountains, empty for a hundred years, are now
occupied by the howling of wolves. Not the chesty baying of gray wolves or
the throaty singing of coyotes, but a high-pitched, two-note riff that has
just enough timbre to echo well. Piercing from a distance, especially in
daylight; deeper, more resonant at night when you hear it from beside your
fire. At once formal and intimate. A subjective sound for the mountains to
ponder, ridge to ridge.*

*A long time ago, the howl became a word, a name. Wa'ya to the Chero-
kee, to whom the mountains also listened in the old time. Son of the wind;
companion to Kana'ti; father of the Ani'-Wa'ya, the Wolf people, principal
clan. Familiar spirit to hunters. Perfect walker. Far traveler. Revenge taker
and altruist. Unseen shape between the trees. Shy shadow from the long
past. Rufous flicker in the mind of god.*

*For centuries, red wolf skirted the smoke of history. To the European
settlers of eastern North America, who killed nearly all of them, the name
of the wolf was unimportant. Whatever it was, they learned to howl the
creature up and track it to its den, the predator easy prey to the newcomers*

who did not observe the old taboos. To taxonomists, the animal underwent numerous incarnations—Lupus niger, Canis lupus, Canis niger, Canis rufus—leaping with mythic prowess from taxon to taxon under their belated scrutiny, creating confusion. Under any name, a hunter and provider for three-quarters of a million years; as mate, parent, and sibling a strong-minded kin. As finely wrought a form of forest sentience as ever lifted nose to the breeze, curled against the cold, or turned head to watch daylight fade. Indigenous vestige from the middle Pleistocene, a hunter's hunter, its track a sign of hope, its absence a warning. Brother both to the dire wolf, alpha canid, and to the dog, whose loyalty to man is perhaps man's greatest accomplishment.

From these mountains, red wolf smelled the meat cooking in de Soto's camps and heard the clinking mail of the absurd, greedy men stumbling through the southern wilderness. Red wolf heard the constant thock of axes and the little thunder of guns, saw the forest disappear, watched the beef and mutton eaters come, watched the soft-walking daughters and sons of the old people melt like spring snow. Not like the first hunters, these new men. They destroyed the world around them so they could eat more easily and built many houses for their things. Settlers. As time went on, the settlers came to hate the hunters who kept hunting—mountain lion and wolf most among them—with a visceral, libidinal hatred. Red wolf left the mountains, drifting west and south, watched itself vanish from a vanishing world until there was almost nowhere to howl and the last vivid forms of its pure spirit prepared themselves to leave this earth.

Just before red wolf leapt into nonexistence, it was trapped out of the wild, taken in cages from the thickets of coastal southeast Texas where it had been driven by history, left to prowl at night, scavenging mesquite beans and cactus fruits.

For generations there was no far traveling. The unseen walls of lost habitat became the chain link of breeding pens. The great skills went unused. Sharp sight, keen hearing, shape-changing stealth. Great endurance, silent speed over forest litter, tolerance of the deepest cold. A boreal, mountainous heart. Generations without a hunt, without the joyous chase and the muzzle-bloody dance around the wide-eyed deer.

Generations without a proper den. The young knew nothing of the world. Had no wildness in their hearts, no weather in their fur. Did not know the proper seasons—the short, staccato southern winter, the long soft spring, the muggy summer, and the invigorating autumn. The wind-bare fall. Musk of oak leaf litter and rotting poplar, tart scents of spruce and hemlock, reindeer moss and cinnamon fern, perfume of persimmon and grape, the funky trace of raccoon and fox in the air, the squeal of a rabbit and the tender flavor of fawn. Where was all that? How to pass that on to the fast-growing young confined in cages? And where were the odd, dark shapes of the mountain ridges? The rocky defiles that led to the streams? The secret, game-rich coves? The cold sinews of the Long Man? The narrow paths of the Cherokee? The ghosts of the ancients alongside whom one had once hunted and howled? Where was the eastern mountain moon?

After three generations, all the old ones were dead and there was not a wild red wolf in the world. Only shadows of wolves. Pale flames of red wolf spirit licked the cages. The soul of the old wolf nursed her last young from afar. The wolf clan keened. Hunters wandered. Ravens held aloof. Even black bear turned their great heads to listen to the final silence.

Then red wolf was returned to the old places, freed.

To Horn Island, where they had troubled the sleep of shipwrecked Spaniards. To Alligator River, where they had serenaded the Roanoke Islanders from the bald cypress and black gum swamps. To Bull Island, along the coast where Catesby and Lawson had heard them.

On the Atlantic and Gulf coasts, red wolves smelled black water and salt air again, hunted and slept through the open seasons, explored fragments of the lost world. Wherever they went, life shifted around them until there were wolf-shaped spaces on the land and an edge in the night like a scimitar. Hunted, prey quickened or died. Red wolves feasted on squirrel and rabbit and deer, their intestines wrapping the shattered, marrow-sweet bones in fur. They jumped coots, slashing out of marsh grass tall enough to conceal a panther, ferreted cotton rats out of mud banks at low tide, scavenged beached dolphins, sleek with ocean, rested and slept listening to the moon pushing waves on shore. They watched hurricane, passionate father, great howler. When an alligator devoured a red wolf, an ancient circle was restored, an old appetite and an old alertness was reborn and great possibilities begun again. The order of the carnivore was restored.

Red wolves courted and bred, dug dens. Wild pups yawned.

And then freed in the southern mountains, casting a shadow again on the oldfields and medicine places, drinking from streams, padding through forested clouds.

The settlers were sleeping in their graves, prone beneath barely legible headstones. The unmarked bones of the old people sat upright, listening.

.   .   .

Tsiya'hi, *otter place.*

Even in the predawn darkness, you can feel the unusual shape of this space, a broad oval of level pastures and hilly woodlots, several miles long and a mile wide, surrounded on all sides by an abrupt rise of forested mountains. There is a satisfying balance between earth and sky here, a fit and mutual fullness that is pleasing to the eye, even in the dark. You can feel it, especially in autumn, a well-wrought play of figure and ground that ends in the air. From the vantage of the telemetry truck, wolves come, invisibly, out of this air, each an abstraction, like a mathematical point.

Six A.M. I'm riding with Barron Crawford, a National Park Service biologist who is working for the U.S. Fish and Wildlife Service on red wolf restoration. He's got the headphones hung around his neck with the gain up high and his arm out the window so he can crank the directional antenna mounted on the roof.

"Let's see who is where. . . ."

The heater and blower are barely keeping up with the cold air drifting in through the open window. A fine-grained rain hisses on the leaves, as if an extension of the static through which the wolves should appear. Night hunting is over and although daylight will be delayed another hour by the rim of mountains, it's not hard to imagine wet wolves feathering their movements away from the obvious edges and settling down in the predawn darkness.

"Unh."

He hands me the headset. "Here. You can't dance to it, but it's pretty cool to listen to."

A steady beep at, maybe, one-second intervals. Nothing wolfish about it. The same sound you could hang around the neck of a coyote or a bear, or implant in the belly of an otter.

"538M. That way. On the other side."

One of the male pups, up Whistling Branch maybe. Six months old. Three weeks in the wild.

The beep continues, steady in the dark. I listen, holding the headset to one ear, trying again to imagine a wolf in the woods, feel a wild heart beating in the neutral electronic tone.

The pup 538M is one of a litter of six wolves born in captivity, four of which survived to adolescence, one of the first litters of red wolves to be born in captivity in Great Smoky Mountains National Park, which sits on the border of western North Carolina and eastern Tennessee. This litter and its parent wolves was selected to begin the establishment of a permanent, self-perpetuating population of *Canis rufus,* a native canid extirpated from the mountains around the turn of the century.

The signal weakens and then breaks up, slipping through an understory of white noise. I hand the headphones back and Crawford interprets.

"He's gotten behind something . . . there . . . no . . . gone. One of these." Tapping with a pencil point at a knob of contour lines on the topographic map that lies between us.

The radio collars these wolves wear make it possible to keep track of them, one of the essential conditions of the release, but, like an electron, a wolf is not exactly where you last fixed it, and Crawford is never dogmatic about where a wolf is or what he thinks it is doing. Laconic and soft-spoken when he does speak, he seems conservative by temperament and training, not prone to jump to conclusions or to begin spinning theories. He knows wolves are controversial and that interest in them is volatile. To a biologist, the flow of red wolves through these mountains is something new, an old unknown.

We drive from one listening post to another along a blacktop road that is a busy tourist loop during the day. The rain eases as daylight emerges from the chill dark. Crawford cranks and listens, switching frequencies, taking bearings, triangulating wolves.

We set up for a while on a knoll across from the foothill drainages the wolves currently favor. Then 538M comes back into range, padding down Wildcat Branch, having come through Whistling Gap, where it shed its signal in a tangle of dense vegetation and edgy terrain.

"Here's another one."

A second male pup.

The restlessness of a wolf, which changes the direction and strength of the signal we listen to, and the intervening landforms, which play tricks of signal bounce with it, give the identical beeping wolf signals some character. You can visualize movement from the shifting source, infer curiosity and hunger as well as spatial relationships among animals whose sense of kinship is as strong as their extraordinary individuality. Their lives, in fact, will describe a series of ellipses drawn around those two foci.

Crawford takes notes and switches frequencies until he finds the adult female and the other two pups, a male and a female. They are strung out along a stream that flows toward the acclimation pen from which they were released. Only the adult male is missing.

We turn down a dirt road that dead-ends in a mile, passing quite near the acclimation pen, which is hidden by the woods. This is Forge Creek Road, part of what was once Ekaneetlee Path, a Cherokee trail that led south over the mountains down Eagle Creek to the Little Tennessee River, which flows along the southern border of the park.

The wolves are all around us, though you wouldn't know it without the radios. It's a rather dreary late-autumn morning in the mountains, with a ground fog shredding itself through the surrounding woods and Forge Creek flowing hard but clear alongside the road. But since I know the wolves are out there, it's not hard to imagine a silent flicker of tails and a tawny rushing in the woods, lithe bodies flowing over logs and slipping down stream corridors, then lying flat along mud banks, ears twitching like mice, sharp faces watching upwind.

"Not much going on today. Some mornings they're more spread out."

Although they were now free-ranging wolves, their former chain-link home has a *gravitas* that keeps pulling them back. The adult male and female spent almost two years there, pacing and waiting. They mated in the pen. The young were whelped, weaned, and socialized in the open-air cage. And of course they were fed there—deer and boar carcasses mostly—and handled during medical checkups. For better or worse, the acclimation pen was now a wolf place in the new lore of the clan, and the time spent in captivity there, and elsewhere over the years, not just an interregnum in the evolutionary history of *Canis rufus* but a test of its spirit, a leap through man's hands. It would be some time before the wolves would lose interest in it. Some would never recover from the effects of being cared for.

Crawford drives back to the loop road and, as the cove brightens, white-tailed deer clarify in the light rain and thin fog, browsing like livestock. In the chilly half-light of an indifferent day, October falls toward November in the Great Smoky Mountains.

"I watch the deer too."

At the moment these seem unconcerned, clustered in small groups of mostly does and yearlings, with sentries posted here and there, sniffing and head turning and tail-flicking a bit, but no more than usual for an animal that, even unhunted, raises nervousness to an art.

By 7:00 A.M. the road is opened to the public. An unsteady line of cars makes its way from deer sighting to deer sighting, often stopping just to watch the cows that also graze the park's pastures. Millions of people drive this road every year looking for something. Before the loop gets busy with the day's traffic, Crawford sets up in the center of the cove to get a last set of bearings. The adult male is unaccounted for, as is the one coyote in the area that still has a functioning radio collar.

Around us I watch *Tsiya'hi* appear and disappear behind the veil of ground fog that drifts through woodlots and hangs in pastures. Full day-light reveals an ashen front stuffed into the surrounding mountains and brightens the cove only for the most unappealing kind of day. In precontact Cherokee, there was no word for gray. Pressed for the color, the Cherokee mind offered "blue, faded." This surprises me, since there are so many days like this in the southern mountains, days when a foggy neutrality hangs on everything and the picturesque horizon remains obscured. It is on such days that the old truths in this landscape might move across your limited field of vision, like wolves drifting back into place.

The coyote turns up on the opposite side of the cove from the wolves, keeping its distance halfway up the mountainside. Crawford had collared the coyote himself during a two-year study of the park's coyote population. Migrants from the West, coyotes have been drifting east for thirty years and entered Great Smoky Mountains National Park around 1985. Crawford estimated that between 52 and 160 coyotes used the park at least some of the time, with Cades Cove having the highest density. They were obviously occupying the niche for canids left vacant by the extirpation of wolves from these mountains. Nature abhors even a man-made vacuum. Crawford's skill in locating wolves among the signal bounces and static, as well as his ability to interpret patterns of canid land use from long-term data, owed quite a bit to the education *Canis latrans* had given him. He learned the tricks of radio tracking from the trickster himself, and he seems to retain an unsentimental affection for the wolf's less glamorous cousin.

"The most misunderstood animal in North America," he mutters as he logs the coyote. This may be quoting someone or just repeating something he has said many times before. He has already seen enough media fawning over "the return of the red wolf" to be skeptical about that species' current celebrity.

The signal from the missing wolf, the adult male, finally comes in from a ridge above the wolves' favorite drainage. Crawford nods his head a bit as he talks, as if he likes what he hears.

"Very interesting. Where he's at. 341M. Maybe he's found something to eat. Or killed something. Somewhere along in here."

The pencil point circles a cul-de-sac at the head of a stream, a thin blue line that doglegs into the mountains.

"That's good he's up in there. Out of trouble."

341M has been a problem. Three weeks after release, the wolf's behavior still sparked like a shorted wire, a double helix of wolf DNA with its insulation frayed by contact with man. Whatever urged a wolf to retreat from the presence of humans, a predatory wariness programmed to err on the far side of invisibility, failed badly at times in 341M. The adult male often traveled the loop road in broad daylight and was tolerant of people and vehicles. When approached, he would stand on the asphalt, obviously confused, acting more like an abandoned dog than a predator freed in the wild.

341M had been born in a zoo in Syracuse, New York. Like most of the breeding adults, he was three and four generations removed from his last wild ancestors, the animals that had been rescued from the Texas–Louisiana Gulf Coast by the Endangered Species Act and the U.S. Fish and Wildlife Service's captive breeding program. 341M had spent nearly three years in a zoo and apparently had too much exposure to people. Its flight distance was much shorter than that of a wild animal, and when it was spooked by the presence of humans or their vehicles, it tended to run off, only to reestablish that distance. Then it would stop and stand there looking back, as if it were tethered to something. It didn't, according to Crawford, "run into the woods and disappear the way a wild animal would."

But whatever its shortcomings, 341M carried the code, a unique chunk of the rare and endangered genetic material from seven of the founding fourteen red wolves in the captive breeding program. The tension between that narrow ancestry and the profound influence of captivity seemed to freeze 341M at the edge of its new possibilities. If wolves have something like a racial memory, a tribal sense of their totemic self—the platonic genes on which the gens was founded—that consciousness was clouded in this animal. Nothing reflected this so much as its affinity for a road and its tolerance of people.

Much Cherokee mythology is concerned with the origin of animals and constitutes a kind of mythopoeic evolutionary biology. Some stories are fanciful, folktales more or less, woven to amuse and entertain, light as basketry. But others have the lineaments of cultural fictions fashioned in the most remote past, carefully molded in strips like clay pots, pressed with uncanny designs, and fired for long use. Only fragments of these ancient narrative vessels remain. The shards that tell us something about the original nature and status of the wolf are among the most intriguing.

Dine'tlana a'nigwa—soon after the creation—we are told, the wolf was the revered watchdog and hunting companion of *Kana'ti,* a Paleo figure with one foot in myth and one foot in history. It could be argued that it was history itself for which the wolf was set to watch.

Kana'ti and his wife, *Selu,* did not live in a paradisal garden. They lived in a modest clearing at the edge of a great forest, until fairly recently the situation of man and woman in eastern North America for at least 14,000 years. *Kana'ti* and *Selu* are figures from the deepest past, simultaneously prehistorical and pretemporal. They and the stories associated with them are truly mythic, rooted in that time before time, along the oldest part of the border between memory and imagination. Figuratively, they often are taken to be the first man and woman, but although they are an intimate part of the southern Appalachian landscape, they enter history only as magic presences, attendant spirits of hunting and agriculture.

Kana'ti hunts and *Selu* produces crops, a primary division of labor that conferred equal status on man and woman and on which was founded the essential balance between wild and cultivated in diet and every other aspect of life. Before history, however, hunting and agriculture are ideal pursuits, more ritual than labor.

In fact, the hunt of *Kana'ti* nearly defies the meaning of the word. All game is hidden in a cave, a common motif in Native American mythology. *Kana'ti* must fashion arrows from river cane and fletch them with bird feathers. He must make a bow from yellow locust and draw a bow string from bear gut. *Kana'ti* also must have acquired the skills of a hunter. He must shoot quickly and accurately, making a clean kill, and carry the game, in its highest form a heavy male deer, home for *Selu* to clean at the edge of their stream.

But *Kana'ti* does not have to hunt in its primary sense. He does not have to search for his game. He does not hunt in history. He rolls a stone from the mouth of the cave, a buck bounds out, and he shoots, making the kill on the strength of having followed the proper formulas. He never fails.

For *Selu,* agriculture is equally successful and no less formal. Corn and beans to supplement wild meat are supplied by ritual and magic, a stylized reenactment of the origins of agriculture. The prelapsarian Cherokee economy is simultaneously real and ideal and is based on a magically maintained balance between culture and nature.

For the Cherokee, time and history begin not with intellectual ambition and sexual transgression, as in the Judeo-Christian fall, but rather with the inevitable appearance of the guilt of the hunter from the blood of the game washed in that stream, a guilt in which *Selu,* as food preparer, is implicated as much as *Kana'ti* the hunter. From that guilt emanates the resistance of nature to man—manifested in the occurrence of disease and the difficulty of obtaining food.

The wolf is present for the dawn of man's realization of the guilt of the hunter, the guilt of culture, keen awareness of which structures the Cherokee's tragic view of history. The wolf *must* be the critical figure, since at the time of man's evolutionary ascendance the wolf was the most numerous, widespread, and successful hunter on earth. The animal remains the best hunter nature ever made.

It happens in this complex founding myth that the young unnamed son of *Kana'ti* and *Selu* takes to playing with another young boy who "comes out of the water and calls himself my elder brother. He says his mother was cruel to him and threw him into the river." *Kana'ti* and *Selu* understand instantly "that the strange boy had sprung from the blood of the game which Selu had washed off at the river's edge." This is *I'nage-utasun'hi*, "He-who-grew-up-wild," the Wild Boy, artful and disruptive spirit of the blood of the game.

The Wild Boy is the agent of the great changes that initiate history, the fall into time, work, and mortality. He leads the natural son of *Kana'ti* and *Selu* to help him release the animals from the cave: "The deer came running past until the last one had come out of the hole and escaped into the forest. Then came droves of raccoons, rabbits, and all the other four-footed animals—all but the bear, because there was no bear then. Last came great flocks of turkeys, pigeons, and partridges that darkened the air like a cloud and made such a noise with their wings that Kana'ti, sitting at home, heard the sound like distant thunder on the mountains."

Kana'ti has no power to retrieve the animals and knows that true hunting has begun: "Now you have let out all the animals, and after this when you want a deer to eat you will have to hunt all over the woods for it and then maybe not find one." Then the boys return home, discover the secrets of *Selu*'s magic horticulture, and slay her for being a witch, a sacrifice that prepares the ground for historical agriculture and all the vicissitudes of raising crops for food.

So history begins. "After Kana'ti's boys had let the deer out from the cave where their father used to keep them, the hunters tramped about in the woods for a long time without finding any game, so that the people were very hungry." From that moment on hunting was difficult and agriculture full of uncertainty. All that was balanced—the food on the table, the relations between men and women, between parents and children, between humans and animals—will teeter precariously.

Before he recedes from view, to join *Selu* at the end of the world where they will dwell apart from history, *Kana'ti* addresses the Wolf People in council and asks them to kill the boys—to stop this process. They readily agree to do so after a ritualistic wait of seven days. This is not the human Wolf Clan, which does not yet exist, but rather the mythological race of wolves. The seven-day wait works to the advantage of the boys, who use the time to prepare their own magic for the coming of the wolves. The Wolf People fail in their assault on the Wild Boys, and through this defeat of the wolves the boys begin to become men, a process that is depicted as simultaneously heroic, arrogant, and foolish. The mythological order of wolves is largely destroyed by the Wild Boys' deft use of a circular fire. The few that escape, defeated, found the historical races of wolves. All the wolves in the world, we are told, have their origin here.

Although the boys seem to be, in part, figures for the emergence of a troubling and troublesome human nature, the Wild Boys do not literally become human. Eventually they are reassociated with *Kana'ti* in his guise as Thunder. As the Sons of Thunder they disappear into the southern Appalachian landscape from which they emerge from time to time to aid and hinder man in unpredictable ways.

According to the Cherokee, man and wolf hunted together at the beginning of history. In fact, their lore suggests that the historical wolf taught man to hunt the game that was now free to flee him, which at least ameliorated some of the harm done by the Wild Boys. The reputation of wolves was unequivocal: "They are good hunters and never fail." But somewhere early in time the wolf and man part company forever, which leaves a trace confusion about what is wild and what is domestic and underwrites the essentially uncanny relation in the Cherokee mind between man and wolf and between what is civilized and what is wild. The dog substitutes itself at man's side for the wolf, and the order of wolves, through this reversal, comes to be associated with the very wildness—disruptive and enabling—with which the tragicomedy of history began.

As the wolves ran into the mountains for the first time, a thin veil of what came to be called wilderness closed around them, not the heart of darkness Europeans projected onto North America but the attractive, unfathomable otherness of nature the Cherokee assumed to be sacred. Since that separation of man and wolf, no true wolf watches itself be watched. The wolf you see is not a wild wolf.

So at night, when the tourists were gone, Crawford and his boss, Chris Lucash of the U.S. Fish and Wildlife Service, hunted the recalcitrant, unwild 341M with radio-tracking equipment and night-vision goggles, firing shotguns loaded with cracker shells at it, trying to reinstill a fear of man, remind the wolf of the changed order of things.

Eventually 341M would figure it out, remember something, or forget, or simply become frightened, which is a kind of degraded wildness. Its flight distance would improve as the nature of its ancestry blew through the memory of its captivity and its old mind flamed for hunting and winter. But three weeks into the release, 341M was still wavering, like much else, between the forces of evolution and the forces of history.

In any event, Crawford seemed pleased this morning that the wolf was preoccupied with something in the Smoky Mountain backcountry, miles from any road.

The adult female of this first family of wolves, 378F, was a better wolf. Like her pups, she had been born in captivity in a wild setting, in an acclimation pen on Horn Island, off the coast of Mississippi. When two months old, she had been released with her parents and littermates to spend a year living freely in Gulf Coast habitat that also had been part of the historical range of *Canis rufus*. Hunting rabbits, raccoons, and nutria, the Horn Island wolves quickly adapted to life in the wild, asserting their territorial imperative and establishing the patterns of an unfettered family and social life.

Although she was eventually drawn back into the captive breeding program, 378F had experienced a run of wild life that nurtured her hunting and social instincts and reduced her contact time with man. When released again in the Smokies, she was much less visible than her mate and a good influence on her pups. She was more like the original idea of a wild wolf, something you glimpsed, a distinct blur.

Back on the loop road, we stop to take a look at a road-killed copperhead, a brightly colored sliver of the forest floor mashed the previous evening, a few weeks shy of denning, its tire-flattened body one indication among many that we are not in some primeval wilderness. As the head of the day's parade of cars reached us, I thought Crawford was going to toe the snake off the road. Instead he stepped aside and kept talking, nodding up toward the side of the cove where the wolves were holed up.

"The best thing we can do is leave them alone. See what happens."

Tracking the tentative movements of newly released red wolves that were still orbiting their old acclimation pen was hardly a vantage on life in the wild. But each dawn's telemetry data caught *Canis rufus* at an old edge of night and day and gave Fish and Wildlife another set of coordinates in the red wolf's escape from man's influence, its readaptation to life in the mountains away from man's fire. But it wasn't clear, as the curious traffic made its way around Cades Cove that morning, whether *Canis rufus* had been restored to the wild or whether it was supposed to bring the wildness back with it.

However the attempted restoration worked out, in the winter of 1993 there would be wolves out there defining themselves—red wolves—and their return to the blue faded landscape, so awkward and prosaic in its details, so diminished a gesture in such a compromised place, put a vibrancy into the air, as if a tuning fork had been struck on bedrock.

Bedrock, of course, defines the place.

In full daylight the foot of the mountains draws the horizon close at ground level, while the ridges they rise to are a half day's walk away. The foreground is laced with corridors of sycamore and alder that cling to the banks of the winding cut-bank streams that give direction to the surrounding pastures and woodlots. The flat limestone surface of the valley braids those streams into a chalky creek once full of trout and the otters for which the place was named.

At the foot of the cove, the creek spreads through a swamp and then pulls itself together before it makes a pronounced loop around a knot of unbreachable resistance buried in a ridge of Precambrian sandstone. A topographic map reveals that loop to be shaped like a hammerstone pointed downstream toward where the creek, loud with boulders and rushing water, loops again and then falls out of the mountains. The creek becomes a river in the fall, filling a large stone bowl before continuing west through riffles and pools for a few miles until another frozen wave of sandstone turns it south, directing it into a broad expanse of still water above Chilhowee town.

The path from Chilhowee town back up the river to the empty wolf pen in Cades Cove is an old one. In fact, ancient paths reach out in every direction from this place—south over the mountains to Ekaneetlee Gap, east toward Oconaluftee, north across the Little Pigeon River toward the hunting grounds of the Shawnee and the distant settlements of the Iroqouis. These ways are cold. If there is a ghost life at *Tsiya'hi*—drumming from the eagle dance, laughter from smoky councils, or the tense silence of men hunting—it does not show. And although the swollen ridges still uphold a wild profile—that great give-and-take of earth and sky—and although the chalky creek still falls loudly toward the sacred places below Chilhowee Town, the broad oval valley is quite tame and has been for a long time. You might trace two histories from this place. At their intersection you will find the wolf.

There were wolves here when the first white settlers arrived in 1818, descending a Cherokee path that curled down the steep slope of the mountain that defines the north side of the valley. This was John Oliver, Lurena Oliver, and their infant daughter, immigrants from Carter County, Tennessee, a hundred miles to the north. Representatives of the future. They came unexpectedly and late in the season, when the hardwood beauty of October flares before the open grayness of late fall. They were a family intent on staying, not long hunters drifting through, and their arrival must have caused discouraged talk around Cherokee fires, where illusions flickered dimly if at all.

For a Cherokee, autumn was the most powerful time of the year, when leaves filled the hard-running streams, and this was one of the last good places left to be a Cherokee, an enclave still beyond the Watauga settlement, which was spreading south across the Nolichucky and French Broad rivers toward the Little Pigeon River, northern edge of the mountainous Cherokee heartland, the bulky highlands that divided and united the principal settlement areas of the historic Cherokee—the Out, Valley, Middle, and Overhill towns.

But by the fall of 1818, the Cherokee's long attachment to this land was doomed. With the arrival of the Olivers and other American settlers in this coveted mountain cove, a long historical process was coming to an end.

Sporadic Cherokee military resistance to the American Revolution persisted long after the British had cut and run from North America, but in 1792 the Cherokee chief Eskaqua—Bloody Fellow—traveled to Philadelphia to petition George Washington for aid even before a formal peace was signed: "Game is going fast away from us. We must plant corn and raise cattle, and we desire you to assist us." That assistance came at the cost of nearly everything.

No tribe was more adaptable than the Cherokee to the demands of acculturation, the Jeffersonian carrot held out for a time until the Jacksonian stick of removal came down on them. Land cessions came in relentless waves. For the Cherokee, every treaty site was a burial place, and the names of treaty places made a dark list.

The dignified language the Cherokee brought to the centurylong farce of negotiation is an important, neglected genre in American literature.

David Corkran, the superb historian of eighteenth-century Cherokee affairs, refers to the "moving forest oratory" of Cherokee chiefs. This poignant holophrastic rhetoric, still largely buried in colonial records, was the means by which Cherokee leaders attempted to convey some sense of their people's transcendental attachment to the land within the narrowly rational and legalistic language of treaty negotiations. Beyond their obvious material dispossession, the Cherokee were stripped of a necessary geography their adversaries could not or would not comprehend. Loss of land meant loss of *place* and the profound disorientation that preceded their eventual homelessness, an unimaginable condition before the contact.

As land was taken, cultural practices and concepts collapsed. In 1794 the peace treaty with the Americans abolished the Cherokee's right to wage war. Even ritual forays to count coup on one's enemies were forbidden. Young men who could not become warriors through intertribal skirmishing stole horses and cattle to prove themselves of worth. Crime became a substitute for honorable fighting. Warriors who could not become young chiefs tugged at the ground, shamefaced, with government mattocks or raised sheep and pigs while women, who had cultivated the earth with great skill for thousands of years, carded wool and wove, not looking at the men. Blood revenge—the fundamental principle of the Cherokee legal system and a principle that had been sanctioned by the wolf—was restricted and eventually outlawed. Without the practice of clan revenge, the authority of the clans unraveled. Matrilineal inheritance was abandoned and the rights of women eroded. The ballplay and the dances were destroyed by alcohol. Diseases burned like fires. Towns dissolved. Mission schools forbade Cherokee children from speaking their parents' language and encouraged them to shun the old beliefs in favor of an incomprehensible religion. Then in 1801 Little Turkey, principal chief of the Cherokee, gave up the winter hunt, claiming he was too old but implying that it was time for the hunt itself to end. When 10 million acres of the old hunting grounds between the Tennessee and Cumberland rivers were sold in 1805 and 1806 for a tenth of a penny an acre, the Cherokee were left traumatized and confused.

North America had been discovered by hunters. The Cherokee were descendants of that great hunt, the only true confrontation with wilderness that ever took place on this continent—the prehistoric migration across the broad plains of Beringia toward a now-unimaginable otherness of land and wildlife bathed in periglacial light that still glows faintly from the recesses of Native American mythology. The traditional hunting grounds in the Allegheny Mountains were an essential part of the back of the Cherokee mind, a psychological as well as a cultural space essential to individual identity and communal spirit. The young chiefs killed the old man who sold them—the full-blood Doublehead—but the hunting grounds were gone.

Some loaded their lives into canoes and drifted down the Tennessee River with Saulowee and The Bowl in the winter of 1810. Others trekked overland to Arkansas and Texas hoping to continue a hunting life but found only bitterness with the Osage and the Quapaw. A few joined with the inflamed young Creek and danced the fevered Ghost Dance that Tecumseh brought from the Shawnee in 1811. And some hung on here in the mountain coves like a mist that would not dissipate, protesting that the earth could not be divided in these new ways, against the ancient lines, and that the place of the Cherokee in a quadripartite universe was in the East: "We want the ancient lines yet to stand. . . . We do not want to go towards the setting sun. We want to remain toward the rising sun." So protested the Valley Town chiefs in 1816.

The importance of these mountains and rivers in the Cherokee mind cannot be overestimated, both as the most enduring part of the precontact landscape and as a critical social, psychological, and spiritual horizon. The attachment of the Cherokee to them is neither aesthetic nor sentimental. One of the first formal agreements between the English and the Cherokee, the *Articles of Friendship and Commerce Proposed by the Lords Commissioners for Trade and Plantations, to the Deputies of the Cherokee Nation in South Carolina, by his Majesty's Order, on Monday, Sept. 7, 1730,* bound the tribe to serve the English "as long as the Mountains and Rivers shall last, or the Sun shine."

This was neither rhetoric nor cliché but an unusually perceptive recognition on the part of the English of where, for the Cherokee, ultimate authority lay: "The Articles were drafted by Sir Wm. Keith, then in England, who was called on in order that the document might be phrased in the imagery to which the Indians were accustomed. . . . 'In uncommon style; it is such as is best understood by them.' " When, years later in 1810, the tribal council at Ustanali declared that the Cherokee had been left with a tract of land "barely sufficient for us to stand on," the elders were speaking literally and metaphorically.

As the pressure for removal west of the Mississippi grew in the first decades of the nineteenth century, these mountains did, in fact, turn out to be the ultimate landscape of the Cherokee spirit. As mainstream Cherokee culture adapted to non-Cherokee ways, the most conservative members of the tribe retreated into the less hospitable highlands. The mountains, which had been the source of their culture, were its last refuge. In the face of the final encroachments, an "alternative for many Cherokees was to withdraw to the most remote regions of the Cherokee Nation, the high hills and hidden valleys of the Great Smoky Mountains of western North Carolina. . . . In the Great Smokies life was difficult, but here the old customs could be continued, English was seldom spoken, and the festivals of the changing agricultural seasons were honored. There was a tendency among those who moved to these outlying areas of the nation to believe in the myth of racial separation. The Great Spirit had not meant the red man to adopt the white man's ways and cease to be a Cherokee. In these areas, the Cherokees adopted from white culture only the minimum they needed to survive."

In the decades preceding the arrival of the Olivers in Cades Cove, the eastern mountain Cherokee spoke their native language and danced the Green Corn Dance, carried the fire and went to water, practicing the sacred formulas that were the center of the tribe's knowledge. They donned the strange masks and stomped the awkward steps of the Booger Dance, a rude psychological antidote to the relentless invasion.

In 1811, at the height of the Ghost Dance revival, some listened hopefully to The Elk relate his apocalyptic vision of a return to the old ways and waited for the tide of history to turn against the insatiable white men. They saw the comet that summer and dreamed dreams of new warriors come to the people attended by black wolves. And when the New Madrid earthquake shook the eastern United States near the end of that year, the old ones knew an *Ukte'na,* a great snake, was rousing itself and that profound changes, beyond the control of even the whites, were at hand.

But although the sinuous aftershocks persisted through the first plantings that spring, nothing came of all the portents. In 1812 mainstream Cherokee fought with the Americans against the Creek, in the vain hope of winning acceptance as citizens of the new nation. But the ruthlessly acquisitive culture represented by men like Jackson and Calhoun could not comprehend, or care, that land in Arkansas or Oklahoma was not like the land here. In 1818 the chief Pathkiller wrote in vain to the government agent McMinn, "It appears to me that you want to dispossess us of our habitation . . . but I will hold my country fast. . . . I love my country where I was raised. I never will find such another Country."

Here in Cades Cove, the Olivers reenacted the American Genesis story. Arriving far too late in the year to plant any crops, they hastily built a cabin by a spring on high ground and proceeded to starve until some Cherokee gave them enough food to get through the winter—dried pumpkins, local history has it, a useful staple in game-poor winters.

This act of charity might have galled John Oliver, who had watched Andrew Jackson use Cherokee warriors to help massacre the Red Stick Creek at Tohopeka, at the horseshoe bend of the Tallapoosa River in the recent war. It might have galled Lurena also, who was reputed to fear and hate Indians after the uncompromising east Tennessee custom. But in the winter of 1818–1819, on land that had not yet been ceded by treaty, John and Lurena Oliver took the food that saved their lives and on which they founded their family from Cherokee hands. When they had gotten a hold on themselves and a purchase on the rich, productive land, they would help to drive away the few remaining Cherokee as well as the wolves that embodied what their descendants would later insist they had found a "howling wilderness."

That winter a new treaty was signed—the last, the tribe was once again led to believe—and by it the Cherokee lost the right to live north of the Little Tennessee River. This treaty made the Olivers legal settlers and left the Cherokee to ponder the meaning of a river that had, for them, only one bank. With the land so terribly divided and the Cherokee pushed south of their ancestral river, the old ways were almost gone, like the buffalo and elk, the lion and the wolf.

To the Olivers and the other early settlers of Cades Cove, Cherokee and wolves were equally disturbing, not so much a danger as an affront to the idea of settlement. A year after they founded their church, John Oliver and his neighbors helped to round up the lingering Cherokee for the brutal federal removal of the tribe to Oklahoma in 1838, Andrew Jackson's cold repayment for the debt incurred at Horseshoe Bend. Local legend has it that the sound of the forge hammer for which Forge Creek was named had already driven the last wolves from Cades Cove in 1827, and that this in itself had been the final discouragement for a people who had fashioned their largest and most influential clan after the idea and spirit of that animal.

For the red wolf, the bloom of iron in the forest was undoubtedly the beginning of the end of its natural existence in the mountains. The Ekaneetlee Path had become Forge Creek Road, the cove lowlands were drained, game driven off, the land cleared. Trees fell like treaties. And for the Cherokee, the dwindling of the wolf did indeed foreshadow their near extirpation from mountains that had shaped their founding myths and underwritten their prosperity for as long as they remembered.

Now, not far from where that forge had stood, and within a few miles of the graves of John and Lurena Oliver, there was a wolf pen with its gate ajar.

Geologically speaking, the Cades Cove valley is a window, an exposure eroded through a layer of rock thrust-faulted over younger rock. Normally, you go back in time as you go down through strata. The deepest layer is the oldest; the uppermost layer, the most recently formed. But the underlying structure of the southern Appalachians is as rumpled as its human history, folded like some stony cortex whose subconscious occasionally sends old thoughts to the surface. So the surrounding mountains cast Precambrian shadows on Cambrian pastures. Rock from the heyday of red and green algae overlooks rock from the advent of the first fish, inventors of gills and bone. Which is to say that time is well shuffled here—as sandstone and limestone, Cherokee and settler, wolf and not wolf—and that unexpected cards often turn up. Now there were wolves again.

I wanted to see what a red wolf was, so that autumn and into that first winter of wolves I watched, serving a self-imposed apprenticeship in some undefined trade. In fact, I haunted wolf country.

After that morning with Barron Crawford, I spent days skirting the woodlots and pastures of Cades Cove, keeping an eye out for wolves and trying to find a point of access into the renewed significance of this place. I was out each day from dark to dark, watching the uneventfulness of woodland dawn and dusk, noting how those sandstone mountains moved against the changing daylight and reshaped themselves in the volatile autumn weather, shrinking under warm brown sunlight one day, enlarging themselves in the purple glow of their own hoarfrosted slopes the next.

I was, at first, too self-conscious about the wolves, still burning off a Romanticism I did not want to lose entirely, and looked for a drama that wasn't there. I threaded myself through the corridor of trees that grew along Abrams Creek and its small tributaries, trying to become a creature of the edge. I eyed wolf-high pasture grasses beating to windward and sat among the half-tame deer in woodlots, posting my attention parallel to theirs, hoping to see something happen.

But what had happened in Cades Cove? Does a wolfish flickering through ranks of trees at the edge of a field revive a dusty engram in the brain of prey twenty generations removed from its last contact with the source of that image? Does the thought *wolf* leap across the consciousness of deer? Does the cursorial lope, or a musty scent, dishearten them, or only throttle their attentiveness up a notch? Or is the image of the wolfish gleam at the edge of the woods a human projection, a way we have of thinking about such things that has nothing to do with the practical relations between predator and prey?

The wolves showed themselves some evenings in the pastures, within sight of the road, but their appearance in fields where people slung Frisbees during the summer months deflated their significance. Within the loop road, they appeared within the frame you can't keep out of the picture when nature is kept in parks, however large, and history is arranged in mute exhibits, a neat array of cabins and churches swept clean of contradictions. Standing in a pasture, the wolves looked as if they hadn't been released yet, as if Cades Cove itself was one large acclimation pen, which of course it was. In effect, the wolves were held in thrall by the very edge that had driven them toward extinction in the first place, that troubled border between nature and history where wildness is either tamed or destroyed.

When I became disillusioned with the domesticity of Cades Cove, I started cruising the surrounding forest. I would walk one of the well-groomed Park Service trails until it crossed an interesting creek and then bushwhack up the creek into the backcountry. I was hunting the hunter, or so I thought, following edges toward centers with a sense that I was getting closer to something. Wolves, I suppose. As I walked, I threw my sight into the half-shed October understory, looking for a blur or a still pattern of wolf color. I listened to every forest sound, every bird and rustling animal and the wind. I studied everything as if it were a sign, taking this occasion to relearn the woods. But a wild wolf was, by definition, invisible, at most a sound—the beep in the headphones, the howl in the settlers' howling wilderness, the barbaric yawp the Cherokee and Creek understood to be a name. Eventually I understood that a wolf in the wild was not something you saw but something you wanted to see.

Dressed in soft, dun-color clothes, I moved up and along each stream as carefully as I could. I did not try to be more silent than the murmuring woods, which is impossible, but walked flat-footed and even shuffled quietly where that might mask my two-footed tread. Every form of stealth generates a pattern of sound, and nothing sounds so artificial as a man walking carefully in the woods. So I tried to make the unapologetic noises a deer or a bear might make, and when this alarmed squirrels, I took up the squirrel chatter and moved on.

The idea was to be present and unseen, to rely on hearing and peripheral vision, to drift from tree to tree with a motion so slow and irregular it made me breathless. When I wasn't moving well, I'd stand against a shoulder-wide poplar or sit in the shadows under a hemlock until my sense of myself diffused and my senses became keener. In the southern Appalachians, autumn broadly mimics spring, making a gradual transition along a convoluted border where there is still much to explore every year, even without wolves—the warp and woof of the year where the birth and death of things is shuttled together so tightly that you cannot quite pick up the thread of the difference.

It was not hard to walk up on deer, short strings of does and yearlings browsing the game trails woven into the woods. But when I came on deer, I knew there were no wolves about. And more often than not it was a misstep of my own that would spook them, some stumbling they mistook for a predatory lunge. When I moved well, I tripped grouse from underfoot, reddish-brown birds that held their ground until they couldn't stand it and then materialized out of the damp leaf litter, forming themselves loudly in flight but disappearing before they resolved into a clear image.

I got closer and closer to things. One day I slid around a tree and came face to face with a pileated woodpecker. I remember flecks of sapwood clinging to its bill and the rust stain under its eye, white feathers bled scarlet at their tips like the petals of Indian paintbrush. Instead of its usual harsh cry, I got a silent, deeply startled stare before its scalloped flight, a kind of iambic in the air, took it away. The bird came to a standing stop against a tree trunk twenty feet away, its black wings flaring to take in momentum, flashing white signs to the woods behind it, and then folding in a motion too quick to see, leaving it again in its characteristic posture casting a profile so strong it suddenly looked two-dimensional.

Mostly I cast my eyes down and looked for the print of a wolf's paw in the mud at likely stream crossings, some sure sign that this was wolf country. A red wolf print is a subtle exaggeration of the familiar, the impression of a dog's paw too large and rounded to be a dog's paw, too large to be a coyote. Years ago, while deer hunting near home in Virginia's Blue Ridge, I came across the splayed, three-toed print of a male wild turkey in snow for the first time, a familiar shape drawn larger than life, a difference in degree that stretched the common form of a bird's foot into a riveting new sign. I watched for something like that.

As I explored up each watershed, I hid behind the sound of its stream where I could, especially along those stretches of boisterous water that covered my scrambling over boulders as I grabbed slick arms of alder and ironwood to hoist the next stretch of woods into view. But I knew that the noise of the white water fell away downstream behind me, and I learned not to stumble forward into the abrupt silence of still pools at the tails of which small trout waited, trembling like strung arrows.

There was a time I could not walk along such watercourses without casting a fly on every likely pane of still water where a trout might be. But fly fishing taught me only that I was not a sportsman, and now I was fishing for the river itself, casting for the wild, wolfish spirit in these relentless Appalachian cascades, something stream-born trout once shared with forest-born wolves, a force freeform as whitewater, edgy as quartz.

To the Cherokee, no river or stream was inconsequential; flowing water was a sign, bright and dark by turns, a descending expression of the land's ascent, a ceaseless murmur about the birth of mountains and the passage of time, a surface play of something deeper. These mountain streams were, the Cherokee knew, important seams in the world, and there was nothing fanciful in the fact that water pouring over bedrock produced an animation that compelled attention. A standing wave holds the eye, creating space in the mind. You naturally stop and stare at pools. A Cherokee went to water before gathering medicine, or going to war, or falling in love. You were required to bathe in a stream in the predawn darkness before being allowed to hear an important story.

As you walk along such streams, the sound of water constantly eroding rock gets in your head and stays there as an echo of deep time. Not historical, treaty-making time, but mountain- and forest-making time. Where the vegetation is dense on both banks, the stream itself is the only path and, knee deep in cold, rushing water, that feeling of being eroded, of moving against the grain of things is quite distinct. A quarter mile of this wet shuffling and hoisting yourself from ledge to ledge is tiring, and you will stop before long feeling as if you had been walking through molten stone. But the function of *Yun'wi Gunahi'ta*—the Long Man—is, after all, to slow and direct your progress in this landscape, to force you to ford the density of things and cross paths with something other than your own intentions. The Puritans feared the pathless woods and imputed much evil into wild nature's instructive tendency to balk human progress. The Cherokee derived a religion from that fact.

When you do stop to rest on the bank of a stream, your heart beating

wolves hunting wild boar

hard, you tend to listen more closely to the loud water, as if that were what you were walking against, the *sound* of something in the woods, a speech you did not understand, strange words for all the things in the forest you did not know. When I first heard the rising contours and pronounced junctures of spoken Cherokee—a liquid but emphatic language full of voicelessness—I knew I had heard right those first days and weeks when I went fishing for rivers hoping to cross paths with a wolf. If there was something left of the old life in the mountains, it would show itself in and around such streams.

For the biologists, who had the benefit of their radios, there was little mystery about the general whereabouts of the Cades Cove wolf family during those first weeks after release. The wolves ranged throughout the valley and made forays into the surrounding mountains. They traveled alone and in groups of varying sizes and combinations, ranging as far as three or four miles from the release site. The resident coyotes were displaced by the wolves, a predictable reassertion of canid hierarchy and behavioral evidence that the red wolf and the coyote were distinct in their habits and character.

Two facts stand out from the first month. Near the end of October, the adult wolves stalked, chased, attacked, and killed a seventy-pound wild boar, the first verified hunt of large prey by the wolves and undoubtedly a valuable lesson in cooperative hunting for the four pups. Equally significant was the fact that the wolves had no immediate designs on any of the 250 head of Angus cattle grazed, by special lease with the Park Service, in Cades Cove. Given a choice between wild food and hamburger on the hoof, the wolves chose haute cuisine.

In short, *Canis rufus* had slipped back into the mountains as if it belonged there.

Of course, I frequented Whistling Branch, which led me from the busy cove toward the wilder mountains across the shifting range of new wolves. Followed upstream, this pasture creek curved back through a screen of planted white pines at the head of a pasture toward wind-sown hemlocks and squirrel-set hardwoods—the maples, hickories, oaks, and walnuts with which the woods were built. The creek secreted itself for stretches under dense banks of rhododendron, broke open shoulders of bedrock in places and in others flowed slowly through level woods.

There was promising sign along Whistling Branch—scat and scrapes that may have been wolf, musty bits of skunk flesh and fur that just as likely were a fox's capture. There were gleaming buck rubs and black piles of seedy bear shit, much birdsong as well as the silent testimony of the life of the woods into which the wolves had insinuated themselves. Details rose and overlapped, repeating themselves until an ancient narrative surrounded me, a story full of natural objects so vivid they seemed to have just stopped moving.

Patterns and colors caught my eye at every glance—a spiky yellow wild-flower still blooming out of a thatch of emerald sphagnum, an eruption of polypody and wood fern, boulders sheathed in mats of cushion moss so thick you could sleep on them, dark red slabs of hemlock varnish, desic-cated shafts of last spring's squawroot, orange and ivory fingers of coral fungi that cast marine suggestions across the forest floor. The strange life of things far older even than the idea of a wolf. Still, mute expressions of forest life.

Every time I stopped and sat down something fine came into view. Once it was a juvenile snake, six or seven inches long. Glossy tan head sheathed with hexagons, black eyes and neck patches, basketweave back of cream and brown, gleaming white belly, and a dark, finely tapered tail. The small snake moved without apparent effort, testing the air with its scarlet tongue. Another hunter. I watched it slowly make its way over dead leaves and hemlock needles. When I leaned over, it stopped hunting and curled in my shadow, tightly wound in a miniature coil, not much larger around than a silver dollar. I reached down and passed my hand back and forth in front of it, which forced its shapely head to shift about uncertainly in the air. But the glistening reptile would not strike, and its refusal, with my soft palm nearly touching it, broke the undeniable spell of even its diminutive threat display.

A mile or so into the mountains Whistling Branch disappeared under-ground. In its place there was a braided bed of sand and gravel where I found wolf tracks. One wolf, apparently, had crossed there recently, the fat pads of its paws cleanly impressed into the damp streambed, enlarged a bit by the weight of the animal settling into the sand. Deer, too, had leaned to the ribbons of clear water that filtered up, clean as rain, through the sand where the creek started. They left deeper prints, angled into the wet earth in their direction of travel, some prints pooled with water at the toe end. You could see the idea of the animal in the way it set all its weight down so narrowly, a structure that gambled on a bounding escape, just as you could see the silent, well-balanced poise in the frank impress of a wolf's paw.

The first time I came on this sandy spot, I thought it was the head of the stream, but the dry impression of a streambed continued up the cove, and in a hundred yards a narrow leaf-strewn flow of water reappeared in the woods, small pools for salamanders and water striders, hunting ground of crayfish and raccoons. In another half mile the watershed ended at a wall of bedrock exposed along the steep foot of a ridge. The true head of the creek fell along a rocky crease formed by this dead end, cascading quietly over mossy stone slabs to which stunted red maples and rhododendron clung. Each time I visited this spot, I'd climb on all fours halfway up this final reach, leaving a bear path of disturbed leaves and soil behind me, pull myself to a flat rock perch, and watch the stage below.

This gloomy hollow was not a wilderness, but it was a wilder place. Crows occasionally flapped overhead, and I took their nagging flight calls to be the voice of settlement, a sign that I had not gotten far. But each time I ascended the stream woodlots became forest, a modest resurgence of now-undisturbed hemlock and poplar, oak and hickory, maple and buck-eye and magnolia that overshadowed the impressions of logging roads that lay along the slopes like faded contour lines.

The late October canopy is mostly yellow at those altitudes where pop-lar predominate, brushed in the midstory with the red and orange of ma-ples and the russets of oaks, which collectively distribute a well-seasoned glow into the air overhead, as if a spring and summer of sunlight had been aged in the wood of the trees. In late autumn the sun angles off, day by day, as the leaves fall, and the quickly passing minutes reveal themselves in long, shifting shafts of gray light split by tree trunks and branches. Each after-noon this fractured light reaches a bit farther for the forest floor.

When dusk began to darken the way downstream, I would rouse myself, slide back down the leaf-slick slope, and move along the way I had seen deer move, knowing that twilight was my best chance to cross paths with a wolf. Halfway down the mountainside there was a bog where I would watch dusk thicken. I'd sit up on an old chestnut log and mark the wide turn the year makes in fall, cutting a broad path through a generous lati-tude of season that slowly winnows living things from dead things, thresh-ing the woods as it were, for the grain of the year.

Warm evenings and cold evenings alternate in late October and early November, pulsing according to the meanders of the jet stream. Colder nights at the bog seemed wolfish; you could almost feel fur thickening when a wind blew through the canopy, or imagine the coats of deer turning from brown to grizzled gray, as if deer, too, were deciduous. The bog was full of migrant birdsong and the odd, promising odor of rot. Screech owls shiv-ered the air with Cherokee—*wuhulu . . . wuhulu . . . wuhulu.* Some evenings the fluting of a veery would mesmerize the failing light and hold it in the canopy for a few moments. Other evenings the superfluous autumnal drumming of grouse suddenly would darken the woods.

Despite the almost constant rain of leaves, the year still seemed to be growing. And even in the dark, the leaves on the forest floor were bright with their life in the air. Beech leaves, especially, seemed to hold a residual quantum of bronzed sunlight at my feet. I sat through a dozen evenings there, on that bench of chestnut, waiting for the shape or shade or sound of a wolf. Cold nights the nearby stream seemed loud, warm nights I could barely hear it. The woods were full of real illusions, and I knew there were wolves about again.

I never saw a wolf at that bog or anywhere along Whistling Branch, but when I think of all the time I spent there that first fall, all I remember are wolves.

Fire in the Path

*The wolves, which are not like those in Germany,
Poland and Lapland (because they fear men and do
not easily come near) give us such music of six different cornets, the like of which I have never heard in
all my life. Several brethren, skilled in hunting, will
be required to exterminate panthers, wolves, etc.*

—The Moravian Bishop Spangenberg, entering the
Cherokee country in autumn of 1752

Above *Tsiya'hi*, to the south, the main ridge of the Unakas runs southwest to northeast, part of that crest of Precambrian stonework buried in the
ground from Georgia to Newfoundland and uplifted in the Permian, long
before the earth thought of wolves. Two hundred fifty million years of
percussion have given the southern Appalachian summit that monumental
if weathered look we vaguely associate with permanence but that we know,
on reflection, is the shape of change. These mountains revealed themselves
by eroding and continue to come into being, like wolves, in the act of
disappearing.

In early November, mountains and wolves did in fact disappear into the
weather, moving behind the blind of raw, squally days that drives visitors
from roads and leaves the backcountry in relative peace for half the year. If
you watch them closely, day after day, the mountains take on an added
nobility in late fall, an effect both of longer shadows cast into the lower
slopes and hazeless air bathing their summits. The relief of the landscape
deepens, as if the grain of the underlying rock had tightened. The shape of
each ridge becomes more distinct, and the idea that these mountains are
ancient storehouses and council places for animals seems not so fanciful.

The grizzled pelage of the mountains in the middle distance may well be the flank of something sentient.

When, except for the tenacious oak and beech, the trees have shed their leaves, longer views of the landscape open up, an invitation to longer thoughts. Words emerge, each stark as a gray buck lifting its antlered head in bare timber to watch you, old signs with spirit of place in them.

Words for where you are and where you are going: *tsa'gi,* upstream, a way you often walk in the mountains, exploring, searching for a source; *ge'i,* downstream, the direction going home, the way not to be lost. *Nunna'hi,* for the path itself and, as it widens in space and time, the trail, the road. Words for patterns in the landscape that are also images: *gadalu'tsi,* fringe standing erect, the serried ranks of bare hardwoods on ridge crests you notice in the high country. This stark fringe relates the earth to the sky and filters the shifting light of shortening days. Looking west—*wude'ligun'yi*—at sunset, the trees are black and seem to move against the gold glow.

There were archaic, stony nouns for shapes in the land—*nugatsa'ni,* a high ridge with a long gradual slope—as well as for a man's passing or habitual relationship to that land—*gunun'dale'gi,* one who follows the ridge. And there were names for the agents of forest experience: the Homeric *nunyu'gunwani'ski,* for instance, rock that talks, which tells you the source of the voices you hear, that matter-of-fact, uncanny chatter that prompts dreams when you sleep by a stream in a forest. And now, once again, there was *wa'ya,* the howling of red wolves.

I was camped on Anthony Creek the first time I heard them, a few miles into the backcountry at a place where I started many a circular trek through wolf country. Opening my eyes before the second, longer note trailed off, I knew instantly what it was. I sat up in my sleeping bag and looked at my watch: 4:00 A.M. The wolf that woke me seemed to be across the stream and well above camp but clearly on my side of Anthony Ridge, a wedge that points toward the east end of Cades Cove, two or three miles downstream.

What woke me was a two-note ascending howl that lasted maybe three seconds. Perhaps there was more than one of these, the earlier phrases buried in my sleep. Then the wolf seemed to be moving about on the ridge, giving out test patterns of yips and barks with only an occasional howl. Twenty minutes of this. Then silence and sleep.

At five thirty, a wolf on that ridge again, very likely the same animal, giving a sustained howl, a bark rising to a howl, and another sustained howl. All the same duration, about three seconds. I propped myself up on an elbow, groped for a notebook and pen, and stuck a small flashlight in my mouth. I made up a crude notation in which to record what I was hearing—the kind of sound and its relative duration: yip, yip, bark, pause, yip, yip, bark, the animal seeming to test or hold the dark air for itself. I thought it might be one of the juveniles trying to get the hang of a locator call. Then a set of strong, clear phrases pitched high enough to sound plaintive were there not so much apparent syntax in the vocalization: bark rising to the type howl, another such howl, then a howl descending to six barks and a bark rising to the two-note sustained howl.

After ten minutes of this, there was a response from downstream in a similar voice with more economy of phrasing: a bark rising to the sustained howl, bark rising to a shorter howl, another bark and the short howl.

Then the wolf on the ridge: bark rising to howl; bark, pause, bark, long pause, single note howl; then four widely spaced barks, a pause, and a final rising howl.

Two sustained rising howls rang out from the second wolf and reverberated into a silence that kept me awake until dawn. Not *like* anything else. Like *red wolves howling*.

I moved on the next morning, carried into a cold, blue November day buoyed by the cry and response of wolves. I doubt that we will ever understand the grammar of animals, the structure of consciousness that shapes their vocalizations. But open communication between two free-ranging wolves was, I thought, a mark of an improved world. This dialogue I had overheard and absurdly transcribed seemed a valuable addition to things.

The woods were bare now, the understory open and the canopy leafed only in daylight. But the leaves on the ground had not yet faded and gave the impression of bright paths leading everywhere. On the trail, the effect was of a snakeskin, imbrication of copperhead or timber rattler rendered in scales of oak and maple, sassafras and sourwood, poplar and hickory, birch and magnolia. The best of our language, I often think when I walk the mountains, is in our names for things, unadorned by any adjectival need for beauty and unused by verbs. When sunlight got overhead, a redolence was released from underfoot, a spicy odor faintly laced with something of spring and summer, liberated by my heavy steps into the chill air, where it disappeared on the breeze around me.

I far more expected to see black bear than wolves. Even before the first wolf release in October, it had been a great year for bears, or rather for seeing bears, since the animals themselves were hard-pressed by a mast

failure that took hold across much of the southern Appalachians, a consequence of late frosts the previous spring. First soft mast failed to materialize
in summer—blueberry, blackberry, grapes fruited poorly—and then the
woody meat of hard mast hung undeveloped in the nut-bearing hardwoods—the oaks, hickories, and buckeyes did not produce. That sent *Ursus americanus,* long-suffering omnivore of the eastern woods, down from
the more remote places in the mountains to the lower slopes in search of
food. By late fall you could not turn a bend of trail without catching at
least a glimpse of a bear, usually a female with a cub or two.

Backcountry black bear, at least where they are no longer hunted, are
not especially wary. If you are walking into the wind and not making much
noise, you can, intentionally or unwittingly, raise a bear's head from its
business grubbing under a log or snuffling for acorns. If there are cubs
about, they are softly grunted off without much ado and seem to understand which direction they are to take, usually uphill over the nearest ridge.
Then the female slowly quarters uphill toward where its young had disappeared, as if she were drawing a diagonal across the slope. What I remember most clearly from such encounters is the silhouette of each retreating
animal as it tops the ridge and briefly stops, as almost every one of them
does, to turn that solemn Slavic face alongside its near shoulder to make
sure I am not following.

Before the possibility of wolves slipped back into these woods, it was
seeing bears that took you back in time. Bear enlarged the woods in a way
deer did not and reminded you of the old fullness here. Black bear, like red
wolves, seemed to appear and disappear through a rift in time that you
might encounter along the silent trails that wound around these mountains,
trails that were so fine to walk in the cold months when a constructive
solitude lay on the slopes and time seemed to hang still over the brown
glow of the forest floor.

But I moved no bear that morning, only solitary high-country deer
whose startled attention, when they saw me watching them, reminded me
of the wolves. I howled where the trail made its final bend away from
Anthony Creek, thinking one of the wolves might still be up in the head of
the watershed, and howled again along Bote Mountain Road for the pleasure of it, but got no response in either instance. I walked the modest
summit of wolf country south for a few miles enjoying the way the big gray
ridge underfoot tacked to one side or another of the trail, opening stupen-
dous views into North Carolina and Tennessee. The stunted beech, yellow
birch, and chestnut oak were spare and oriental in their beauty, each

shaped like an elder gnarly with experience of many summers and winters, hard forms won from the extreme weather on the narrow summit.

I had the shelter at Russell Field to myself and that evening probably howled more than any wolf in the mountains. Wolves were well known to respond to such invitations to give voice, and I had gotten over my initial self-consciousness about doing this. Gray wolves, in fact, were more prone to answer a human voice imitating a wolf howl than a recording of an actual wolf. Their ability to make the discrimination is not as striking as their preference for real voice, even one tinged with human intentions.

People who fear wild animals or who hate them for economic reasons imagine they are everywhere. But even in wolf country wolves would prove to be scarce. The howling that morning had spoiled and misled me. As I hiked along, I assumed I was going to be listening to wolves all winter, that as long as I stayed in the backcountry I would have a sustained opportunity to learn their language. But it was, in fact, a long time before I heard them again, and, in retrospect, I was very glad I had risen, half conscious, out of my sleeping bag that morning on Anthony Creek, propped myself on an elbow, and scribbled down, as best I could, exactly what I heard.

That night there was nothing for me except a cold wind and a starry sky. I kept a small, disheveled fire of kindling and log ends going in front of the Appalachian Trail shelter until the gusting wind thrummed the ground so hard the stars shook and it got too cold to stay out. The wolf's ancient associations here with the wind and cold, with the Milky Way itself, were not lost on me. To the Yuchi, the wolf was one of the four lost sons of the wind, never where you thought it was. And silence, too, was a virtue of wolves, the most prized skill of hunting and war. The Creek answered the wolf's stealth with their own and forbade themselves even to utter the animal's name. Now that wolves were free, that dark, starlit silence within the gusts just might be the silence of wolves—not the final muteness of extinct beings, but the close counsel of animals that could be present beyond the ragged circle of the campfire, a transcendental rather than a political silence, an Emersonian silence, unvoiced echo of something that might call out.

What was left of the old mythologies was like the mountains themselves—like red wolves themselves: an old resistance that was hard to read—a mystery or a truth, a shape, a trace. I suspect I had already heard far more wolf howling than I would ever understand.

The red wolf was as elusive in books as it was in the field, having left few distinct impressions in the pages of early American writing. The best of these is found, not surprisingly, in William Bartram's luminous *Travels.* Here is Bartram crossing Alachua Savanna, in northern Florida, in the spring of 1774:

> We continued some miles crossing over, from promontory to promontory, the most enchanting green coves and vistas, scolloping and indenting the high coasts of the vast plain. Observing a company of wolves (lupus niger) under a few trees, about a quarter of a mile from shore, we rode up towards them, they observing our approach, sitting on their hinder parts until we came nearly within shot of them, when they trotted off towards the forests, but stopped again and looked at us, at about two hundred yards distance; we then whooped, and made a feint to pursue them, when they separated from each other, some stretching off into the plains and others seeking covert in the groves on shore; when we got to the trees we observed that they had been feeding on the carcase of a horse. The wolves of Florida are larger than a dog, and are perfectly black, except the females, which have a white spot on the breast, but they are not so large as the wolves of Canada and Pennsylvania, which are of a yellowish brown colour. There were a number of vultures on the trees over the carcase, who, as soon as the wolves ran off, immediately settled down upon it; they were however held in restraint and subordination by the bald eagle (falco leucocephalus.)

This is the only sustained observation of red wolves in the early American archive, covering perhaps a minute or two in 1774. The moment is instructive, in part because of Bartram's attention to detail but also because of the historical moment through which he was traveling. Bartram reached the Cherokee country forty years before the arrival of the Olivers in Cades Cove, but the botanist missed seeing an undisturbed aboriginal landscape by more than two centuries. He had encountered wolves elsewhere in his travels, but they were already part of a retreating edge. With his father, John, he had heard what were probably red wolves howling along Florida's St. Johns River in January of 1766. He notes that "the tyger, wolf, and bear hold yet some possession" on the Georgia coast in his day and that wolves were "numerous enough" in the interior of Georgia, above Augusta. Along with the great forest, the wolf, bear, and mountain lion were the heart of eastern wilderness, but in Bartram's time they were already in rapid decline. North American nature was receding quickly in front of the settlements. Beneath the pre-Romantic surface of his prose, which Coleridge and Wordsworth admired, there is a chilling modernism, a continuous encounter with places haunted by absence, loss, and destructive change. This is not wilderness, where red wolves raise their heads to watch Bartram and his party approach, but the shrinking no-man's land between the wild and the settled, the critical ecotone of American history romanticized as the frontier. A good deal of what Bartram wrote about was already on the verge of disappearance.

What Bartram called *lupus niger,* the black or Florida wolf, came within his purview because it was scavenging a dead horse. In fact, every form of wildlife in this scene is held in place by that carcass of European origin—the bald eagle that waits on the wolves, the vultures that wait on the eagle. Bartram came to Alachua Savanna through a radically changed landscape. Herds of cattle grazed near herds of deer. Orange groves intermingled with mature forests of magnolia, red bay, and beech "of incredible magnitude, their trunks imitating the shafts of vast columns." The savanna—a complex system of wetlands, grasslands, and wooded hills—was still intact, filtering and draining a biologically profuse land, but the Alachua themselves, a race of people, were gone.

The richness of Bartram's prose often obscures the fact that he sometimes vividly describes what isn't there, in the following case a native town superimposed, through the agency of a trader's tale, on overgrown native old fields: "it was the ancient Alachua, the capital of that famous and powerful tribe, who peopled the hills surrounding the savanna, when, in days of old, they could assemble by thousands at ball play . . . over those, then, happy fields and green plains; . . . almost every step we take over those fertile heights, discovers remains and traces of ancient human habitations and cultivation."

The Alachua, a famous and powerful tribe, like the tribe of red wolves, about which we know almost nothing. Then the company of wolves appears in Bartram's narrative, wary but curious, as if their flight distance already had been eroded by the confusion created by vanishing habitat.

No one records as detailed a view of the appearance and behavior of the red wolf as William Bartram did that day on Alachua Savanna. What is now called the red wolf, *Canis rufus,* was historically and prehistorically a wolf of southeastern North America, an animal thought by its principal students to have evolved in the region and adapted as an opportunistic hunter of deer and small game to coastal wetlands, piedmont savannas, and river bottoms as well as to the forests and mountains of the southern

Appalachians. *Canis rufus* may be the only extant wolf to have evolved independently in North America and may represent a primitive evolutionary stock, the last living vestige of New World wolves. Its historic range overlapped with the eastern variety of the gray wolf, *Canis lupus lycaon,* and, in the West, with the coyote, *Canis latrans.*

Many other travelers, before and after Bartram, reported wolves in the Southeast, but more often than not never saw them, or offered no detailed description. A wolf was a wolf, and there are very few conclusive accounts of red wolves within their historic range. Every student of the animal makes the same point: Almost nothing is known about the red wolf's natural history. The first scientific study of the animal in the wild was not made until two hundred years after Bartram, when it was already on the brink of extinction and no longer living a normal existence. What is now an important but problematic distinction between the Eurasian gray wolf and the North American red wolf was lost on settlers who had carried the blind European hatred of any wolf to the New World.

The historical record is intriguing but vague. On Roanoke Island, the failed Grenville expedition of 1585–1586 reported *"Wolves* or *wolfish Dogges"* in the wild and living among the natives. At Jamestown, John Smith claimed "their Dogges of that country are like their Wolves, and cannot barke but howle, and their wolves not much bigger than our English Foxes." In 1709, in his *A New Voyage to Carolina,* explorer John Lawson gave a general account of coastal and piedmont wolves:

> The Wolf of *Carolina* is the Dog of the Woods. The *Indians* had no other Curs, before the Christians came amongst them. [This is untrue.] They are made domestic. When wild, they are neither so large, nor fierce, as the *European* Wolf. They are not Man-slayers; neither is any Creature in *Carolina,* unless wounded. They go in great Droves in the Night, to hunt Deer, which they do as well as the best Pack of Hounds. Nay, one of these will hunt down a Deer. . . . When they hunt in the Night, that there is a great many together, they make the most hideous and frightful Noise, that ever was heard.

In 1731, in *The Natural History of Carolina, Florida, and the Bahama Islands,* naturalist and painter Mark Catesby repeated Lawson's account of what may be the red wolf, adding a few details: "The wolves in America are like those of Europe in shape and color, but are somewhat smaller; they are more timorous and not so voracious as those of Europe; a drove of them will fly from a single man, yet in very severe weather there has been some instances to the contrary. . . . The wolves in Carolina are very numerous, and more destructive than any other animal; they go in droves by night, and hunt deer like hounds, with dismal yelling cries."

Smith, Lawson, and Catesby (who did not paint one) may not have seen wolves firsthand—none offers a convincing description—and Catesby may well be aping Lawson, or they both may have been working from the same source. For those interested in the original distribution and natural history of the red wolf, the critical detail is not the obligatory "hideous and frightful Noise" and "dismal yelling cries" of these early accounts but the fact that Smith, Lawson, Catesby, and William Bartram each asserts the distinctively smaller size of the eastern wolf, compared to the gray wolf, with which Europeans were familiar. To the present day, the intermediate size of the red wolf—smaller than a gray wolf, larger than a coyote—is its most observable and controversial feature.

What many consider to be the little-known native wolf of the Southeast probably will always be an enigma, its nature and identity a victim of history. U.S. Fish and Wildlife Service biologist Ronald Nowak has spent a lifetime studying the elusive animal: "Although the red wolf, in unmodified form, seems to have survived in the lower Mississippi Valley through the 1920s, the species had been under heavy human pressure throughout most of its range. . . . Wolves disappeared from Pennsylvania, Maryland, West Virginia, Virginia, North Carolina, South Carolina, Tennessee, Kentucky, Ohio, Indiana, and Illinois without specimens having been saved which would have enabled us to determine their systematic status." This is the historical heartland and hunting grounds of the Cherokee, as James Mooney defined it.

In colonial times, many eastern wolves, large and small, were blackish, and the red wolf cannot be distinguished by color or by size alone. Bartram noted elsewhere in the *Travels:* "I have been credibly informed that the wolves here [Florida and coastal South Carolina] are frequently seen pied, black and white, and of other mixed colours. They assemble in companies in the night time, howl and bark altogether, especially in cold winter nights, which is terrifying to the wandering bewildered traveller." Charles Darwin himself was aware of the intriguing variety of wolves in eastern North America and commented on it in *The Origin of Species.*

For a time Bartram's account of the animals on Alachua Savanna was taken as the type description of the species that is now known as the red wolf, even though it was called the black wolf throughout much of man's historical contact with it. Bartram's binomial, *Lupus niger,* was first over-looked and ultimately rejected during the complex evolution of North American canid taxonomy, a subject that remains controversial and fluid. Through the years the red wolf has been pelted with scientific names: *Lupus niger, Canis lycaon, Canis lupus ater, Canis lupus rufus, Canis ater, Canis rufus, Canis floridanus, Canis rufus rufus, Canis rufus floridanus, Canis rufus gregoryi.*

It is now thought that there were, historically, three subspecies of red wolf. Bartram saw *Canis rufus floridanus,* the southernmost and eastern-most of the subgroups, often called in casual literature the Florida or black wolf. This animal is extinct, the last having survived in the Okefenokee Swamp into the early twentieth century. The westernmost subspecies of the red wolf, *Canis rufus rufus,* a wolf that John James Audubon painted, vanished as a valid subspecies when its last representatives hybridized with the coyote as the latter moved east into Missouri and Arkansas in the 1940s. Audubon identified his specimen, which looks very much like a coyote, as *Canis lupus (Var. Rufus)* and called it the red Texan wolf. What is now designated as *Canis rufus* was known colloquially as a "red wolf" only in east Texas and Arkansas. The wolf that was afield in the Great Smoky Mountains, *Canis rufus gregoryi,* was the only surviving subspecies of red wolf, the least well known of the three.

The fossil record for *Canis rufus* is also sparse and controversial—a handful of maxillaries, mandibles, and skull fragments from a canid too large to be a coyote and too small to be the familiar gray wolf of Eurasian origin. This evidence marks a range from Florida north along the Atlantic coast to southern New Jersey, west across southern Pennsylvania, Ohio, Indiana, Illinois, and Missouri through eastern Nebraska, Oklahoma, and Texas down to the Gulf Coast near the Mexican border.

The heart of the red wolf's range, reconstructed from fossil evidence, is the southern Appalachians and the southeastern Atlantic and Gulf states. Red wolf fossils associated with archaeological sites occur at the northern and southern limits of historical Cherokee territory as well as in their win-ter hunting grounds in what is now Kentucky and southern Ohio. What are possibly red wolf jaws that have been carefully fashioned into spatula-shaped objects have been found in the mouths of tribal shamans at Adena sites in Kentucky. These are thought to be ritual masks with which honored dead were buried. A maxilla found at a prehistoric and historically occu-pied Cherokee site near Franklin, North Carolina, has been identified as belonging to a mature red wolf. Another jaw fragment, recovered from the

Citico Mound, an Overhill Cherokee site, also may be evidence of the presence of *Canis rufus*. Nine specimens of red wolf have been unearthed in Alachua County, Florida, where William Bartram saw the species.

From colonial times to the present, the red wolf suffered the fate of wolves generally. Natural wolf populations in the East declined rapidly in the face of deforestation. Stanley Young and Edward Goldman, authors of the 1944 *The Wolves of North America,* had noted the association: "Wolves . . . seemed to disappear more rapidly with the establishment of settlements than any of the other wild animals . . . due to the cutting of the forests." John Harlan Shaw, who was both the first and last person to conduct a sustained study of the red wolf before its removal into the U.S. Fish and Wildlife Service's captive breeding program, also asserts that "logging has probably been the most severe form of habitat change within most of the red wolf's original range since the arrival of technological man."

With the loss of deep-forest escape habitat, wolves were fairly easy game for bounty hunters. Hunting and trapping wolves in southwestern Virginia, western North Carolina, and east Tennessee persisted throughout the nineteenth century, especially after an apparent increase in the wolf population during the Civil War. But except for hair-raising accounts of an outsize wolf "bounding along on my track, with long flakes of yellow foam streaming from his mouth, and eyes like two balls of fire," there are few useful details in this fatuous lore about the appearance or behavior of these animals.

The travel writer Charles Lanman encountered a hunter in the mountains of north Georgia in 1848 who routinely distinguished between the black (red) and gray wolf and who encountered both in the southern Appalachian backcountry. In an extensive trip through the Blue Ridge and Great Smoky mountains, Lanman himself heard a wolf only once and came across one print of a wolf's paw between north Georgia and Asheville. Fifty years later, sign of a wolf of any variety was an even greater rarity.

The last bounty hunters farmed the few remaining animals, killing pups in the den each spring for the price on their pelts but leaving the adults alive to breed another doomed litter the following year. Gideon and Nathan Lewis, "the great wolf hunters of Ashe county [in North Carolina's Blue Ridge] . . . would follow the gaunt female to her den, and while one waited outside, the other brother crawled in and secured the pups, from six to ten in each litter, but allowing the mother to escape. The young were then skalped, the skalp of a young wolf being paid for the same as that of the mature animal. For each skalp the county paid $2.50."

Two centuries after Bartram, the red wolf was long gone from the southern Appalachians, living *in extremis* elsewhere. In his 1975 study John Harlan Shaw found that although "most of the red wolf's original geographic distribution fell within southern forests. . . . yet the animal survives only in coastal prairies and salt marshes." The list of the extermination of the last known wolves of any species in the Southeast charts the tail end of this centuries-long process: 1905 in North Carolina, 1908 in Georgia, 1920 in South Carolina and Florida, 1921 in Tennessee.

Despite the long-standing pogrom against the animal, it was assumed that the red wolf survived in viable populations in the most impenetrable portions of bottomland forests in east Texas and parts of the deep South, refuges that were, however, rapidly degrading. The popular outdoor press occasionally mentioned a unique race of southern wolves, more as an oddity than a nuisance, but always adding another layer of ambiguity to the problem of the animal's identity. *Forest and Stream* for February 3, 1906, notes "a gray wolf, a black wolf, and a red wolf" in east Texas and distinguishes between the coyote and "the common red wolf," by which it seems to refer to *Canis rufus rufus,* Audubon's "Red Texan Wolf." The magazine also notes "vague reports of a small wolf occurring further east on the coast prairie even to the border of Louisiana," which might well have been the surviving population of *Canis rufus gregoryi* that became the basis of the captive breeding program and restoration. In the pages of *American Forests* Stanley Young wrote of the persistence of this population of what he called the Texas red wolf (*Canis niger rufus* at that time) as late as 1968 but took an overly optimistic view of their status in the wild: "There will still remain large areas in which this red wolf can live and breed in no direct conflict with man, and where its presence may be tolerated and even encouraged."

In fact, the only surviving variety of red wolf, *Canis rufus gregoryi,* was barely hanging on in the scrub oak, juniper, mesquite, and chapparal where it was said to be making its last stand. In 1962 Howard McCarley of Austin College in Sherman, Texas, raised the alarm about the species after determining that most of what were thought to be red wolves were actually coyotes and that the population of true red wolves was much smaller than Young had thought. The species was in danger of hybridizing itself out of existence. When two Canadian researchers, Douglas Pimlot and Paul Joslin, went looking for the red wolf in 1964 and 1965, they found only a few ragged packs left on the Texas–Louisiana border. The red wolf was federally listed as rare and endangered in 1965. Ronald Nowak tried to clarify what was known and not known about the red wolf in the pages of *Natural History* in January of 1972, noting that "the native wolf population of the Southeast has become nearly extinct" and that the red wolf may well "disappear entirely before their taxonomy and life history are known." After passage of the original Endangered Species Act in 1973, the U.S. Fish and Wildlife Agency began capturing any canid it thought might be a red wolf in order to cull them and rebreed true red wolves in captivity.

That the red wolf has nearly always been an unknown, from Bartram's day to the present, has come to be its central characteristic. The scientific and political confusion it has caused, and continues to cause, is grounds for meditation as well as study. Whatever happens to it now, *Canis rufus* symbolizes something important about native wild nature in North America. When the Endangered Species Act became law, the red wolf was the most endangered mammal in North America. Like much else, it barely had made it through the seine of history.

William Bartram made three other observations of the red wolf—once in art, once in ceremony, and once more in the field. Visiting the disease-stricken Atasi, he noted the image of the wolf among the sacred hieroglyphs decorating the pillars and walls of their principal square. These were caricatures of men with animal heads, metamorphs or maskers, and animals with human heads, fantastic images freely crossing species boundaries, which Bartram understood to be an important aspect of indigenous consciousness, "designs . . . not ill executed, the outlines bold, free and well proportioned." These may well have been something like what was found at the Adena sites in Kentucky.

The night before, Bartram had been entertained in the largest council house he had seen in his travels. He watched a spiral fire of dried river canes burn clockwise round the center pillar through the night, a singular mystical fire arranged as a brilliant imitation of the circuit of the sun. After the seats had been filled with warriors, arranged with great particularity as to age and rank, carved soapstone pipes and ornately decorated animal skins full of *Nicotina rustica*—old tobacco—were distributed. Finally a large conch shell full of cassine was brought round to the company with great ceremony. As the shell bearer, a chief posing as a slave, presented the drink, he howled. Bartram attempted to describe the sound, which led him to a rare abandonment of language: "the slave utters or sings two notes, each of which continues as long as he has breath. . . . These two long notes are very solemn, and at once strike the imagination with a religious awe or homage to the Supreme, sounding somewhat like a-hoo–ojah and a lu–yah"—the ascending two-note howl, I can't help now but believe, of the red wolf.

And then traveling through west Florida in what is now Montgomery County, Alabama, Bartram recorded a red wolf in the field for the last time: "Early next morning, our guide having performed his duty, took leave, returning home, and we continued on our journey, entering on the great plains; we had not proceeded far before our people roused a litter of young wolves, to which giving chase we soon caught one of them, it being entangled in high grass, one of our people caught it by the hind legs and another beat out its brains with the but [sic] of his gun."

Destroying the unknown creates confusion.

Diga'kati'yi: "place of setting them free." Once a site on the Tuckasegee River where the Cherokee released their prisoners of war, now the word could be used to refer to the backcountry acclimation pen for the Tremont wolves.

Wolves seem to have a prejudice that they do not belong in pens. When watched from out of sight, they do nothing, or very little. They sit, walk about, feint at each other in spiritless adumbrations of dominance and submission, eat when food comes with no memory of having hunted, defecate shyly like dogs. There is no drama in captivity. Wolves don't howl and hurl themselves at the chain-link fence. Suspended from real action, the mind of this creature designed for constant engagement retracts, coiling not like a snake but like an overwound spring.

When you approach a wolf pen, the wolves slowly panic, stirred not by fear but from lack of choice. The closed geometry of captivity turns flight into a neurotic motion. The juveniles race half circles together, running an arc through the mud and shit in front of the corner opposite the gate where the humans are gathering. This creates a constant pounding that is unaccountably loud. The wolves change direction without apparent effort or motive, their uncharacteristically pointless behavior driven by some tic that will not serve them well in the wild. Intellectually, these young wolves know that they should not be near humans. But captivity forces them to entertain a contradiction, not something for which the animal mind is grooved. Occasionally one of them will stop and shyly pull a gape into a half snarl, vaguely assaying its power, careful not to fix its eyes on any of the men or women who are now entering the pen. Ears back, the wolf will lock its forelegs, which are spread defensively, involuntarily raise a ridge of hackle between its hunched shoulders, and tentatively clamp its tail down in the tense semaphore of threat display. But even the elaborate communication system of wolves is no match for the ambiguity of this situation.

The adult wolves stand aside, wasting no energy, eyes sliding back and forth across the humans gathered now on the inside of the gate. They keep as much distance as possible, moving distinctly a little over and back to this spot or that, like knights in chess. They do not bark and snarl as captive feral dogs will. They watch and think.

Despite the disclaimers in the technical literature, the wolves *are* red, some more than others—laced through the back of the ears and neck and splashed through their shoulders and haunches and legs. Not bloodred, *gi'gage'i,* but *wa'dige'i,* the brown-red color of certain animals like the copperhead and the grouse, a forest red that easily darkens to brown or black in a wolf's shoulders and across its back and flanks, or bleeds into the ruddy yellow that fades to the pale fur of its underbelly. What a connoisseur of trout fly hackle would call furnace, or like the tawny blend of a cross-phase fox or of a fox squirrel in winter. Red in the signature way that a red-tailed hawk is red. Red as a point of departure. A red quickly hidden in the flowing motion of a running wolf, when the animal turns darker, almost black, not red at all.

Once we are in the middle of the pen with an odd assortment of gear piled around us, the adults join the juveniles in their pointless race around the inner perimeter of the enclosure, effortlessly accelerating and decelerating, dancing the dance of the dispossessed. This is too much even for them. The family runs bunched up, stumbling over one another in a way they never do in the wild, stopping in the corners where they literally hang their heads and create a collective stare that is as intense and centerless as the strange sound of their running. Then they run again, silent ahead of the galloping sound, intent on their half circuits, as if they might create space with motion.

The gathering of those faces in the corner of the pen, ancient images hovering in front of the gleaming chain link, is what I remember most vividly. I remember one face—the face of the red wolf—and different faces—these six red wolves that I would come to know as two generations of numbers: 337F, 357M, 520M, 521M, 522F, 525M. I liked that they were named with numbers. It made the subsequent narrative of their lives austere, almost abstract. The numbers protected them from human emotions, which is the only thing that can harm them. In history and mythology, red wolves had suffered from either too much love or too much hate.

The numbers allied them with the other side, with *Kana'ti* and *Selu* and with the ancient Wolf People who failed to stop the Wild Boys from starting history. Whatever the taxonomists eventually decided, *Canis rufus* was one of the race of wolves that had made it into time. And here it was, about to be released into one of the fragments of that original world.

The face of the wolf is one of the extraordinary masks of being—a triangle in a circle, a blend of bear and fox—a dense totemic look, a forest visage. The medial line of raised fur that divides a wolf's face is one of the great edges in nature, keen diameter of perfectly balanced predatory senses. The bilateral symmetry of a wolf's face comprises one of those rare, finished images of creation, something that could be improved no further. Another 10 million years of evolution and not a hair would move—no more than the shape of sharks will ever change. The wolf's face, like the face of the bear and the mountain lion, is not so much a mask as nature's embodiment of the idea of the mask, something final, like the form of salmon or falcons.

The face of the red wolf is a further refinement of the idea of a wolf—the snout elongated, the eyes more narrowly set than those of a gray wolf and tilted more steeply, the ears almost dainty. There is a foxlike quality to the look of this wolf, but drawn heavier and bolder than a fox, as if the idea of a wolf had been whittled down to the idea of a fox and then molded back into a wolf as a finer form stained with new shades of fur. There must be at least a dozen colors in the swirling pelage of a face nearly lost to extinction and still shadowed by an uncanny hatred from which wildlife management alone will not rescue it. The juveniles have more white around the muzzle and larger patches of grizzled fur above their eyes. They have not earned their colors. The faces of the adults are darker, redone in those shades of bled umber that take red into black and brown over the underfur of gray and cream, an art that makes a red wolf in dense vegetation no more visible than a grouse on the forest floor.

Eight people have entered the Tremont pen to witness or assist in the preparation of these animals for release: Chris Lucash of the U.S. Fish and Wildlife Service, who is in charge of the Smoky Mountains red wolf reintroduction; his assistant Barron Crawford, then of the National Park Service; Lucash's boss, Gary Henry, a veteran of endangered species work who oversees the project from the Asheville, North Carolina, office; two student volunteers; and two cameramen from a Knoxville television station. Lucash directs the work, but all the principals know what they have to do.

The first time I walked into Chris Lucash's office, a government-issue house trailer planted near the Cades Cove Ranger station, he was on the phone haggling for cattle carcasses produced by a tractor-trailer accident on I-40 east of Knoxville, an unexpected bonus for the wolf program, which was always looking for roadkill. And Lucash was, first and foremost, a pragmatist who was well aware of the obvious contradictions of trying to manage wildlife and of the supreme irony of trying to manage wolves. But his job was not speculative. A windfall of wolf chow might not make the pages of the *Journal of Mammology,* but here in the Great Soggies, it made life a little easier.

With an undergraduate degree in zoology, Lucash had worked his way up through the ranks in the wolf business, first in Minnesota with David Mech's gray wolf project and ultimately for the U.S. Fish and Wildlife Service. From 1986 to 1990 he was one of the backcountry biologist-caretakers at Alligator River National Wildlife Refuge in coastal North Carolina, site of the first permanent reintroduction of red wolves and a breeding source for some of the animals he was handling now.

Fish and Wildlife sent Lucash to the Smokies in October of 1990 to test the feasibility of red wolf reintroduction there while Crawford was doing his study of the park's coyote population. A year of experimentation with free-ranging wolves in Cades Cove convinced Lucash that the red wolf could survive in the mountains without undue controversy and simultaneously convinced Fish and Wildlife to put Lucash in charge of that effort.

When I first talked to him in 1991, Lucash told me so emphatically that he wasn't a "wolf groupie" I assumed that he once had been. Tried it in college, perhaps, but hadn't inhaled. But if this dark, wolfish-looking mid-westerner had brought any Romantic feelings about wolves east with him, he had worked through them during his tour of duty at Alligator River while living in a dank houseboat moored to a mosquito swarm from which he sallied forth to poke gingerly—there *were* alligators at Alligator River—around blackwater swamps radio tracking *Canis rufus* through the cypress, cedar, blackgum, and sawgrass.

By the time he had gotten set up in the Smokies, the thirty-something Lucash was seasoned and all business. Except for defending their significance as a unique North American canid, he never expressed any feelings about the animals under his care. And he seemed to pride himself on how well his operation took care of its wolves without coddling them. His acclimation pens were well-run, minimum-contact staging areas, not zoo exhibits. The whole point was to prep the animals to leave and never voluntarily come near humans again. With an animal as psychologically sensitive and socially complex as the wolf, quality of captivity was critical.

I grew to appreciate Lucash's clarity of purpose more and more as time went on. He and Barron Crawford knew exactly what they were—and what they weren't—doing. They were neither practicing science nor dancing with wolves. They were physically delivering an apex predator, a major North American carnivore, to what was left of eastern mountain wilderness—right under the nose of the twenty-first century and flat in the face of American history.

The pen is the standard fifty-foot chain-link square surrounded by an electrified fence. Two roofed plywood boxes serve as rudimentary shelters. A few trees have been included within the perimeter to provide shade in summer, but the ground has been churned into a barren, muddy yard. There are water troughs and the black-haired carcass of a wild boar that has been eaten down to its nose, a delicacy that even here didn't pass muster. When the wolves are not running, you can hear a stream tumbling through the foggy woods. This pen is maybe a dozen miles and half a dozen headwater drainages from the Cades Cove acclimation pen. The big spine of mountains, heart of the Smoky Mountain backcountry, rises abruptly to the south, which explains why the small stream runs so hard.

The site is remote enough to have made it necessary to helicopter the fence sections into what was once a logging camp, the last in the area where, in a final spasm of greed, the Little River Lumber Company destroyed a watershed of old-growth forest that had made it to the brink of preservation before handing the stumps over to the federal government to make a national park out of in the 1930s. Skidder cables and other rusty junk still lie strewn through the second growth of mixed oak, hickory, and maple where, with a little forebearance you might have seen trees twenty feet around whose roots reached back to the contact. The surrounding woods are as lean as the wolves, which are themselves a kind of second growth.

The idea is to release another family of red wolves here—at a backcountry site where the prey base is smaller and more widely scattered and where the terrain is rougher than at Cades Cove. To see what wolves off the tourist route will do. As a release point, the Tremont pen comes as close to what is now called wilderness as it is possible to get in the southern Appalachians, which is to say we're a few miles into some quiet woods visited only by the occasional backpacker and trout fisherman.

Lucash is clearly enthused about this release although somewhat daunted by the prospect of having a dozen wolves at large. But keeping track of the Cades Cove wolves had already become routine, and by December the project needed a few new wrinkles. And the Tremont release was intended to have less predictable, more interesting effects. If these wolves stayed in the backcounty, they would be much harder to track but they would give Lucash and Crawford a better idea of how red wolves used mountainous terrain and the great variety of vegetation zones for which the Smokies were famous.

The home range of the Cades Cove wolves was unusually small and their movements perhaps less complex than they would have been without the centralized prey base provided by the woodlots and pastures. The movements of the Tremont animals should provide better information on the red wolf's relation to deep-forest habitat where apparently it had once thrived. That readaptation was essential to the red wolf's long-term survival, since the edge was, even within a national park, not the best place to be. And beyond national parks, there is nothing *but* edge. It's quite likely that massive deforestation made the wolf, and many other North American animals, much more creatures of edge habitat than they were naturally. Fish and Wildlife needed wolves that, like the surviving population of black bear, were inclined to stay in the mountains.

Unlike the Cades Cove wolves, which were a natural family, the Tremont wolves were a makeshift arrangement, not unusual in captive breeding programs—for wolves or other species—where candidates for release are often in short supply. But given the importance of early emotional bonding in wolves—between parents and offspring and among siblings—the adoptive status of three of the juveniles raised questions about the bonding within this composite wolf family, which had been pacing off the dimensions of its pen since summer.

The four-year-eight-month-old female, 337F, was born at Alligator River, where she had a run of ten weeks in the wild before being paired with the three-year-eight-month-old male, 357M, which had been born at the Texas Zoo in Victoria, Texas. They mated and then bred in April of 1992, producing 525M and three other wolves that died soon after birth. Around the same time, a large litter of seven pups was born at Alligator River to a pair of red wolves out of the Horn Island, Mississippi, and the Bull Island, South Carolina, facilities. Three of these pups—two males (520M and 521M) and a female (522F)—were transferred at two weeks of age to the Tremont pair. Adoption in the wild was not unknown among wolves, so this strategy had some precedent.

In any event, Fish and Wildlife couldn't afford to be too picky; the Red Wolf recovery program was still racing to escape the narrow genetics of the founding population of wolves. At the time of the Tremont release, in early December of 1992, the original band of fourteen red wolves had increased to several hundred animals, a small but increasing fraction of them wild born. Most of the captive-born wolves were at least born in open-air acclimation pens in wild settings, which exposed *Canis rufus* to the sights and sounds of a portion of its historical habitat. But the relatively small size of the red wolf population left considerable genetic overlap among the wolves available for release—and even within a given wolf's ancestry—a breeding density that was an afterglow from the species' brush with extinction on the Texas–Louisiana Gulf Coast in the 1960s.

The last of the original red wolves died in 1988. The Tremont female was two and three generations removed from that founding stock, closer than most wolves in the program. The male's bloodlines went back three, four, and five generations to the last free-ranging wolves. Between them, they shared seven of the fourteen founders. Of the female's twelve ancestors in the program, all but one also appear in the male's family tree. Within the male's ancestry, four wolves showed up in both its maternal and paternal lines of descent, with two of those animals also shared within its maternal line.

You did not have to be a geneticist to see that the evolution of *Canis rufus* was starting over. Twenty-five years after the species was first listed as endangered, the people at Fish and Wildlife who were piloting the genetic recovery were staring at some dangerous if slowly improving readings on their instrument panel—distribution of the founders' alleles, survival of founding genomes, retention of wild heterozygosity as well as an inbreeding coefficient they watched as intently as a rate-of-climb indicator during a foggy takeoff. The recovery program's goal was the same as it had been from the beginning: Increase the population and genetic variety of red wolf stock and expose as many animals as possible to the shaping forces of natural selection within their historically known range. With any luck, the Great Smoky Mountains would have two litters of wild-born wolves in the spring of 1993, and the natural history of *Canis rufus,* never studied under natural conditions in any part of its historic range, would begin to unfold as it had in and around the blackwater swamps at Alligator River.

The cage in the woods was history, the eye of the needle.

The work in the pen is routine. The student volunteer approaches the racing wolves with the kind of long-handled net used to boat salmon or steelhead. When she has a wolf singled out, she intercepts it along the fence, trapping it with a lunge and instantly snapping the net mouth to the ground. As the wolf surges in the net, rocking the net handler about, Crawford grabs the animal's head from behind while simultaneously kneeling on its body, the aluminum rim of the net helping to turn the glaring teeth away. The wolf struggles until it exhausts its options and senses it is pinned. Then it idles, mixture rich, breathing hard and straining in a controlled way, cycling its muscles through a continuous test of the possibilities of escape.

The mesh is pulled back enough to enable Lucash to tie a strip of cloth around the middle of the wolf's snout as a temporary muzzle, at which point the net is pulled out of the way. Crawford shifts his weight about like a wrestler to keep control over the animal's head and back so that it can neither bite nor jump upright. A nylon muzzle is exchanged for the cloth noose. The wolf is now all eye—black and amber outrage—but struggles only if the pressure on its neck or hindquarters is eased. Then it will surge against the opportunity and try to free its head and get to its feet, which are soon loosely tied together.

The wolf is inspected for injury, vaccinated, and then weighed. Finally the animal is fitted with a radio collar. The crew works methodically but quickly. All this takes about ten minutes but seems much longer, as if in the presence of wolves, wolf-time takes precedence. Lucash is keenly aware of the dangers of contact time. Not the danger to the handlers, which is minimal, but to the wolves, which is enormous. Then the legs are untied, the muzzle is removed, and the wolf, unhanded, springs away without a sound and stands off with its mates, distinguished now by the thick, brightly colored collar.

Despite all the handling, intimate in its way, there doesn't seem to be any contact between man and wolf in this exchange. There is no oohing and aahing over these beautiful animals. No one says *anything* to calm the wolf being handled, as you would to a dog at a vet. The animal is rarely alluded to in what little instrumental conversation goes on. The wolves have not been given pet names, as was once the odd fashion in wolf research, and although their numbers will take on character and narrative significance once they are released, in the acclimation pen the studbook designations are merely a bookkeeping convenience, tags to each animal's genetic ancestry and medical history that now are pegged to a radio-tracking frequency. This intense work goes on in an emotional vacuum with the tacit hope that the necessary handling, all the better for being perfunctory and a bit rough, will not ruin the prospects of release.

The adults are the last to be prepped and collared and are noticeably harder to deal with, partly because they are twenty pounds heavier than their young but also because of their stronger emotional, or psychological, reaction to this contact. That intransigence is a good sign, since both are well traveled and have been handled before. Good wolves never get used to this.

Not surprisingly, the Tremont male is the most difficult. For a zoo-born wolf, 357M is assertive. He wants no part of what is happening to him and cannot be handled in the open. Eighty pounds of healthy, independent-minded red wolf doesn't make for a docile patient, and shouldn't. If the proponents of the red wolf are correct, this bristling canid represents the wildness descended from all those red wolves lost in history.

Somehow 357M is driven into the three-foot-square plywood kennel, the sliding door of which is quickly closed. Perhaps he just dives into it to escape the net handler's futile moves. Once in, 357M settles down. This is escape, not aggression. The wolf is seeking space he can't find, a wolf's fate.

When the roof is slid off, the Tremont male seems stunned to find itself confronted from above. The animal looks trapped but not frightened. It has no moves to make in this man-controlled world. Crawford gets a long-handled noose on the wolf, and Lucash lowers himself into the box to pin the animal with his knees. The noose is the last straw. The Tremont male bares its teeth for the first time in this struggle, a silent, neck-twisting, eye-bulging snarl, momentary flash of gleaming dentition—that ridgeline of incisors, canines, premolars, and molars archaeologists love to find—a New World tool that can be traced back to the Irvingtonian, when the idea of canine predation hereabouts was refining its resourcefulness in a real-life diorama of *Smilodon* and mastodon, ground sloth and tapir. The wolf in the box has come a long way, its slashing jaws the working edge of a timeworn wildness.

Crawford controls the animal from above with the noose while Lucash does his work—cloth noose, nylon muzzle, inoculations, radio collar. The juveniles suffered the indignity of being hog-tied and hung upside down for a moment from a large spring scale. The big wolf's weight is guestimated. The animal is covered with mud and shit, as is Lucash. But this muddy, shitty, cold, and bloody work—Lucash has cut himself with the knife he's using to trim the excess length off the radio collar—is how wildness gets back into the world. A man and a wolf wrestling in a plywood box. It's come down to that—this unruly inheritance from the Wild Boys.

Lucash is done and out in ten minutes. Crawford releases the noose and the kennel door is opened. The Tremont male bounds out and reoccupies the netherworld of the perimeter where it has taught itself to wait. Its posture is neither submissive nor aggressive. The young wolves watch the elder wolf closely. Judging from its neutral body language, 357M seems psychologically unharmed.

Physically, the Tremont male or any of the wolves could have pounced on the human intruders and taken a piece out of someone, but there was no suggestion of any such possibility. There is so much natural separation between man and wolf, this intrusion is accomplished quite casually. Wolves, too, observe taboos, adhere to a rational nature when they are allowed to do so. The animal is a predator, but predation is not the same as violence. No one who knew wolves would think of bringing a weapon into a wolf pen. The danger is all on one side. Except for what history has done to them, these wolves have come through the prep unharmed. All they need now is to be allowed to take their numbers into the woods they have been observing with great interest for half a year. They watch us with intense indifference.

The prep is done in an hour. The gear is gathered up and we troop out, backs to the wolves. Someone stops to chain and padlock the gate. The gap in the electric fence is restrung and the juice turned back on. This is not to keep the cunning, rapacious beasts at bay, in case they should pick the lock, but to protect them from humans for one more night.

Last I saw of them, the mud-spattered Tremont wolves stood together on the opposite side of the weird enclosure staring obliquely at us through a dismal grain of sleet. I remember the filthy boar's head and the hull of muddy ribs and that the wolves looked more like lean, offbeat survivors in a Beckett play than sweaty heroes in a Jack London story. But *Canus rufus* had run the gauntlet. Six wolves were headed home.

As we moved down the trail single file, I realized that except for that eerie pounding of their paws on the frozen mud, the wolves had not made a sound. All the language, all the vocalizations I had heard that morning on Anthony Creek, they kept that to themselves.

When, on the way back down to the vehicles, I asked Lucash when he would consider the reintroduction a success, the pragmatist threw an un-wittingly Emersonian answer over his shoulder.

"When wild-born wolves give birth in the wild."

Then he stopped and we stood aside and let the others troop by with the nets and gear.

"When we've got wolves out there that don't remember this shit. Then we might have something going."

The next day, exactly two months after the release of the Cades Cove family, the gate on the Tremont acclimation pen was left open and the backcountry wolves were free to leave. The crew from WBIR had mounted a video camera over the gate hoping to capture the moment on film. Whoever opened the gate turned the camera on. That afternoon the first winter storm of the season settled into the mountains, and the recovering forest slowly filled with snow. Some time after the videotape ran out, the Tremont wolves stepped into the woods to begin, in private, a recovery of their own.

"Happy families are all alike," Tolstoy writes, "every unhappy family is unhappy in its own way." So it is with wolves.

That December the Cades Cove wolves continued an orderly life in the relatively small home range centered by Abrams Creek and its pastures. But the Tremont wolves split up as quickly as the Cades Cove animals had settled down, and split, not surprisingly, along man-made lines.

After they had finished with the deer carcasses left near the pen, the adults ranged the backcountry, as did their offspring, the male pup 525M. But the adopted juvenile males took the nearest trail down to the nearest road, ran through every permutation of edge trouble they could devise, and spent December and January yo-yoing in and out of captivity.

521M started out by hanging around the ranger station at the foot of the drainage, transfixed by a playful black Labrador retriever. The feckless wolf indulged in some boot- and bowl-stealing antics that would have made a warm and fuzzy moment in a Disney movie but didn't say much about its potential as a free-ranging wolf. He was captured in a culvert trap, normally used for bear, held in the Tremont pen for a few days, and then released again.

About the same time, a thin and gimpy 520M turned up outside the park boundary cruising paved roads and stopping to stare at honking cars near the community of Townsend. Lucash and Crawford pursued and darted it. The wolf had a fractured toe and had lost eight pounds.

As 520M was convalescing, 521M wandered out of the park in the same area. On Christmas eve, it scavenged ham scraps off someone's back porch and was seen wandering back roads at night. Lucash and Crawford succeeded in hazing the animal off roads, but that made it difficult to get close enough to dart it. After a few days of woods chess, they tricked it into a rubber-jawed leghold trap and returned it to the Tremont pen for a short time for rerelease with 520M a few days later. This would be 521's third release. The call of the wild seemed pretty faint for this animal, and Fish and Wildlife was getting tired of catch-and-release wolf restoration.

Another deer carcass held the two juvenile wolves in the backcountry for a few days, but after that they were seen frequently on one of the park's main roads. Like the Cades Cove male, they were confused by vehicles but didn't flee from them. The shotguns and cracker shells might drive them off, but they did nothing to unseat whatever was driving their behavior. Six weeks into the release, the future of both wolves was questionable.

The adopted female, 522F, did better. The only Tremont wolf to be seen in contact with the Cades Cove wolves, she spent a week and a half within their home range and was known to be with them on three occasions, once during a group howl, a strong sign that she had been afforded at least temporary acceptance, perhaps because she was a potential mate. 522F eventually left Cades Cove to continue ranging on her own, following the trail down along Abrams Creek and stopping just outside the park to feed off a deer carcass. She escaped from one leghold trap but eventually was caught and brought back to the Tremont pen.

All of this activity was predictable for a wolf release under these conditions. In any kind of captive breeding program, you don't know what kind of animal you have until release. In fact, release behavior is the only indicator of what happened to an animal during captivity. And although Fish and Wildlife was required to retrieve any animal that left the national park, and was vigilant about doing so, it was natural for wolves to explore, and, of course, they had no way of knowing where the park ended and the other world began. A wolf without curiosity about its new habitat might be easy to manage, but it wouldn't be much of a wolf. If, like other wild animals, the wolves kept shy of man-made things, that instinct would keep them where they belonged. In that respect, the travel of the juvenile female looked like wolf behavior; the travel of the juvenile males was a sign of trouble.

Less was known about the Tremont adults, which was encouraging. As expected, radio tracking the backcountry was harder than triangulating wolves off the Cades Cove loop road. It wasn't easy to get a second bearing on a wolf in the narrow headwater drainages, and signals often were blocked for days when a wolf went over a ridge. Then, too, Fish and

Wildlife didn't want to be pushing the animals needlessly around the mountains just to get a temporary fix on them. Something like the Heisenberg uncertainty principle applied at wolf level: If you track too aggressively, you create the effect you measure and plot the movements of wolves trying to get away from you. You end up with coordinates on human rather than canid intentions, a nice map of the tendencies of radio trackers. Lucash and Crawford knew when to back off. Aerial reconnaissance, weather permitting, would always find the big wolves.

The important thing was that the Tremont adults were not seen on roads, and their offspring, 525M, was much less visible than the other juveniles. The Tremont male mostly kept to the high country, exploring the rugged terrain south of the release point. He would stay tucked away for days in narrow coves that rendered his radio collar ineffective. The wolf seemed to be readapting without hesitation or confusion to the half-million acres of wild land around him. The female, too, stayed in the backcountry, often moving independently of the male, doing her own reconnaissance. She eventually ran the main ridge overlooking Cades Cove south to Gregory Bald, a magnificent site that was also visited by the Cades Cove wolves. 337F went so far as to go down the Gregory Ridge trail, which led it to the head of Forge Creek Road and the area of the Cades Cove acclimation pen, Plymouth Rock for the Smoky Mountain wolves. She undoubtedly crossed much territorial scent marking by the Cades Cove wolves before retreating back up into the mountains that were quickly coming to be laced with wolf travel.

It wasn't clear how much time 525M spent with either of its parents, but the ruddy juvenile was much less visible than its adopted siblings and was not prone to get into trouble. Young wolves learn largely by imitation, and the native son of the Tremont animals undoubtedly was picking up good travel and hunting habits from its parents, or at least benefiting in some indirect way from their example. As in other higher mammals, instinctual tendencies and learned behavior overlap in wolves in complex ways. For wolves, as for man, hunting is an art. Research shows that although juvenile wolves are born with a playful instinct for hunt/search behavior, they must be taught to kill. So despite the radio collars, which marked the wolves as, in part, man-made, considerable education was taking place in secret, an education that freed them from their captive past. A bit of natural history had come back into play, and the wildness of red wolves, whatever that was, was slowly working itself out.

By midwinter, a useful picture was emerging. There were too many artificial influences on the animals to draw any scientific conclusions about what might be natural behavior in red wolves, but anecdotal differences among individual wolves and between the two families were beginning to reveal the dimensions of *Canis rufus*'s readaptation.

I visited Lucash one dismal day in late January, and we talked while a steady rain drummed the tin roof of his trailer.

"The wolves in Cades Cove pretty much hang around together. They'll move independently for a day or so, one may range away for a week even—one of the female pups was up on Rich Mountain alone for a week—but then they group back up. There's some sort of bonding there, a structure. I've seen three or four wolves actually very tight together, and it's not unusual to see one of the juveniles leading the adults and another juvenile around."

We stood in front of the large topographic map that hung in the hallway outside of his office, a great square of mountains and rivers that could be scored now, in the mind's eye, for a dozen wolves.

"We're not seeing anything like that out of the Tremont animals. I don't think they are in any kind of stable social situation right now, anything predictable. I know they are not meeting up with each other every day. There doesn't seem to be any influence at work. It's partly the habitat. They are dispersing more, looking for food. The adults are getting into it—those drainages—and the young ones are sort of bailing out, coming downhill, which leads them into trouble—roads mainly—then they get out of the park and get into residential areas. They get confused around people. Stuck. A million places to hide and they don't run away."

Genetics is one thing. What a wolf does when free to do anything is what counts. In some cases, captivity never ends.

"It's not at all unusual for wolves to use trails and even dirt roads—all those old logging roads—at night, but the adults, at least with this Tremont group, head uphill or stay out of sight. The pups don't get it."

They had, perhaps, lost whatever wildness was. For wolves, it's not literary. Other researchers had noticed this: "Wolves that have not had experience in a natural environment do not feel at home there. Very quickly they will seek out and associate themselves with people, their pets, and their dwellings and remain very close to them." Which confirms, empirically, what Cherokee mythology had intuited—that within the center of their wild detachment, that perfect otherness, is a vestigial kinship with man, or with man as he used to be.

"Anyway, they are not a unit. There's a lot that has to be shaken out.

There's some kind of social structure in the Cades Cove wolves; with the Tremont wolves, it's hard to say. The postrelease behavior is very hard to interpret. In a way it's not significant. They are not wolves yet. I don't know if those pups and adults will ever get back together. And I don't know if the pups will make it. We can't keep playing with them forever."

But he was willing to wait and see. Some wolves, initially confused on release, turn around and make it to the other side. Winter in the park was relatively peaceful, and the harsh weather of February and March was a great educator.

Only one family outing shows up for the Tremont animals in the activity logs. In late December, while 522F was temporarily back in the pen after her jaunt down Abrams Creek, the adults—and perhaps some of the juveniles—dismantled the Tremont camp. Even the reserved Lucash seems a bit amazed at what they had done.

"They tore the electric fence down, chewed up the insulators, tore the canvas caretakers' tent to pieces, even bit the eyelets off it. They ripped the gas lines off the heater, tossed the propane bottles around, shredded the mattresses apart. Got into anything they could find."

Lucash assumed, or guessed, this emotional outburst was frustration at having a wolf penned up inside the chain-link enclosure—even one of the adopted wolves—and that the separation triggered the only destructive behavior he had ever seen in these animals, a kind of righteous violence.

"They were upset as hell."

Clan revenge.

While Lucash fielded a phone call and sat down to pull up something on his computer, I checked out the pile of books on the edge of the desk. On top of the stack was an old hardback edition of Young and Goldman's *The Wolves of North America,* one attempt among many to unravel the tangle of relationships among North American wolves. The first time I saw this book, I was surprised to see two red wolves standing confidently in the small world of the book's frontispiece—*Canis rufus gregoryi,* as luck would have it, the surviving subspecies. Odd that such a rare, little-known wolf was chosen for the place of honor.

I held the picture up for Lucash, who was clicking away at his keyboard, searching for files with the phone tucked under his chin. He shook his head.

"Gary Henry just sent that down."

He reached deeper in to the pile on his desk and handed me the December 1992 *Conservation Biology.*

"And this."

I'd seen it. In 1991, when Lucash and Crawford were setting up their program, new studies by researchers Robert Wayne and Susan Jenks suggested that the red wolf may have originated as a cross between the gray wolf and the coyote—that is, that it had never been and was not now a unique species. Their work was based on statistical extrapolation of mitochondrial DNA characteristics. Two Harvard biologists, Barbara Lawrence and William Bossert, had argued as early as 1967 that the red wolf was possibly a subspecies of the gray wolf, an argument largely rejected based on the small sample used for analysis. But this new challenge to the identity of the red wolf was a more radical and controversial charge and, needless to say, unwelcome news to the red wolf recovery team. The *Conservation Biology* Lucash had handed me contained the most recent volleys in the debate. Once again Ronald Nowak had come to the red wolf's defense.

Nowak, who worked from fossil and physical evidence, was unequivocal in his response to the new charges: "Fossil history does not support this [hybrid] origin for *C. rufus*. The red wolf, in much the same form as now, was present in North America through the Irvingtonian and Rancholabrean ages. . . . It seems to represent an intermediate, surviving stage in the course of wolf evolution from a small coyote-like ancestor to the modern gray wolf. . . . hybridization with the coyote did occur, but only within the last 100 years or so." By statistical analysis of critical diagnostic skull measurements, Nowak found that "The red wolf falls roughly between the coyote and gray wolf, but does not merge with either. The captive and reintroduced red wolf stock has a statistical distribution close to that of the original *C. rufus*." The red wolf was, in this view, a unique animal, a valid species.

The controversy would not end there, but Lucash and Crawford, who had their hands full with the practical side of wolf restoration, were glad *Canis rufus* was holding up to these bewildering new attempts to get rid of it. They were not in a position to split hairs. They had seen enough red wolf–coyote antagonism to doubt the kinship theory. On the level of field observation, *Canis rufus* seemed to be something like what Bartram and the others had gotten fleeting glimpses of—a wolf well adapted to the southern mountains that didn't look, or sound, or act like a coyote or a gray wolf. In fact, the red wolves had driven the resident coyote population out of Cades Cove, which could be interpreted as interspecific aggression. Nowak, who had examined more of the physical evidence than any other scientist in the world, considered the extant red wolf specimens, historic and prehistoric, to be "more than subspecifically different from the gray wolf" and was convinced that the animal Fish and Wildlife had captured, culled, and then bred back to viable numbers in captivity was, without a doubt, the last surviving subspecies of red wolf.

But Nowak had always known that *Canis rufus* was surrounded by unknowns that probably would not be recovered completely from the past: "There may never be indisputable proof that the red and gray wolves did not undergo intergradation in the eastern forests. . . . the slender proportions of the red wolf indicate that its prey averaged smaller than that of the gray wolf, and that its ecological niche may have approached that of the coyote which did not exist in the eastern forests when the white settlers first arrived." What looked to Wayne and Jenks like hybridization between gray and red wolves might represent parallel evolution or simply reflect the well-known close genetic kinship among all canids. In any event, "available early specimens from the southeastern United States can all be separated from known species of *C. lupus,* and seem to represent a different species, *C. rufus.* The exact distribution of *C. lupus* and *C. rufus,* and the extent to which they overlapped in eastern North America, will probably never be known." The intriguing case was Florida, where Bartram saw the red wolf and where there is no evidence at all of the gray wolf.

For Nowak, *Canis rufus* was particularly interesting and valuable, because it closely resembled the extinct *Canis edwardii,* a medium-size Pleistocene wolf that thrived in the Southwest long before the gray wolf migrated into North America, which apparently did not occur until the Illinoian. In Nowak's view, "*Canis edwardii* may represent the first unquestionable appearance of a wolf in North America" and may well be ancestral or related to the red wolf. Both species represented the evolutionary radiation of New World wolves driven by the pressure of Pleistocene glacial cycles. *Canis edwardii* was lost to extinction, outcompeted and replaced by the invading gray wolf. *Canis rufus* survived in the Southeast and remained the only living link to the ancestry of New World wolves. There was enough prehistory and history on the red wolf to call into question any statistical extrapolation that suddenly reduced it to hybrid status in the way that Wayne and Jenks were now proposing.

For Lucash and Crawford, who did the humble Holocene work of tracking and trapping as well as everything from scat collecting to public relations, the heady scientific debates that fueled academic careers were the least of their concerns. Managing real wolves in the real world was full-time, often exhausting, work, and Lucash had little time for the second-guessing that swirled perpetually around the animal under his care.

A half minute after the tan Fish and Wildlife pickup sloshed to a halt in Lucash's yard, the screen door banged and Barron Crawford bustled in with a box of radio collars and the morning's tracking rap sheet—a Rorschach of fuzzy reception—tucked up under his raincoat. As I nodded hello the phone burbled to life and Lucash leaned reluctantly toward it.

"What can I say? The animals we've got are representative of the wolf that was in the Southeast historically. In the old days, no one thought that animal was a gray wolf or a coyote. That's absurd. What was Bartram looking at? What the hell is this?" he asked, holding up the sketch in Young and Goldman.

"What we've got here isn't a coyote and it isn't a gray wolf. You've seen them."

He snatched up the receiver just before the answering machine kicked in.

Lucash knew as well as I did that seeing the wolf didn't settle anything. But I'd read nearly every historical document on the southeastern wolf as well as much of the voluminous technical literature. And I'd heard the distinctive howling up on Anthony Creek and stood in the Tremont pen knee deep in red wolves. I knew what he meant.

Much as I admired the solidarity of the Cades Cove family, it was the Tremont wolves that intrigued me. Standing in the acclimation pen with them that day, I had felt the uncanny distance between man and wolf, a frontier now being quietly reestablished in wolf country. You could destroy every wolf in the world and that polarity would remain, as if it were embodied in the very words—*man* and *wolf*—and determined the grammatical as well as the practical possibilities of their relations. The idea of that tension stayed with me, as much as did their collective stare—those floating, totemic faces that had gotten into my dreaming, their tawny markings that darkened when they ran, and the righteous snarl of the Tremont male in the plywood box, which struck me more and more as an expression of political as well as biological anger. Whatever the motivation, attempts to make the red wolf disappear on paper were as offensive as their violent extirpation in the field.

Having witnessed the Tremont wolves being manhandled and dressed with radio collars did not demystify them in my eyes any more than listening to the Cades Cove wolves through headphones that morning with Barron Crawford had demystified animals I could not see in the rainy dark. *Canis rufus* stood well apart from both the rough and ready concerns of wolf management and the progress, if that's what it was, of scientific research. I was happy to glean what I could from both kinds of interest in wolves. But all of the rumors, facts, and theories about the red wolf and every move in this heavy-handed attempt to transform captive creatures into independent spirits only corroborated everything language and mythology suggested about men and wolves—that they should not touch each other, that they were useful to one another only across a vacuum that there may not be enough wild nature left to sustain.

Like the better half of the Tremont wolves, I was drawn to the backcountry myself. After talking to Lucash and Crawford, I geared up for another weeklong loop through wolf country, filling a large frame pack with a week's worth of coffee and dehydrated food as well as enough wool and Gore-tex to keep me warm and dry. That night the huge drive-in campground at Cades Cove was deserted. Just before dark, a flock of wild turkeys made a stately traverse across the asphalt parking spaces, serenely and absurdly passing the dumpsters and picnic tables on their way to roost. In the morning I got up in the dark, drove the black ribbon of the loop road around the reassuring space of Cades Cove, and parked my truck at the visitor center. Shouldering the pack with a grunt, I walked off into the chill but clear weather that trailed the latest front.

I was back to where I and the wolves had started. Forge Creek ran hard in the dark at my side, charged with days of rain. The rock-strained whitewater foamed as if it were phosphorescent, syruped over logjams, and bulged in long dark pools that couldn't quite still the flow but rapped impatiently at tree trunks along their banks, insistent as tidewater. As I walked along, still patting my pockets for keys, wallet, and notebook, a high, percussive wind bent the canopy upslope, as if to replace whatever the stream was carrying away. The bare crowns chattered and twisted about; the evergreens groaned and rode the predawn bluster.

I walked up the dirt road that was closed to traffic in winter, breath pluming in front of me, pack creaking behind. I took a brisk pace, for warmth, but marched mechanically, like a person who was still half asleep. There was plenty of sleep around me. I knew trout were lodged deep in the cold water, nestled up to boulders that buffered them from the nagging current. Like snakes piled in dens and female black bears about to give birth in their sleep, the metabolism of trout take them out of time in winter. Every form of life in the woods took its own way through the seasons. Mammalian persistence—a man following the idea of wolves that were following the scent of deer and other prey—was the exception, not the rule, an expensive use of energy and imagination for all concerned.

beautiful writing

The road and the river switched sides as they gradually ascended a narrowing hollow until the former dead-ended at that turnaround from which Barron Crawford took bearings the morning I rode with him. From there a well-worn foot trail rose through hemlocks that held the trailing edge of night firmly in the morning woods. The trail rose above the stream, seemed to leave it on an independent tack, then recrossed a slight divide and rejoined first the sound and then the sight of running water, by which time even two-hundred-year-old hemlocks couldn't fend off the breaking day.

This is the way of walking in the southern Appalachians, a studied wandering along a progressively more difficult and beautiful way—a hard-surfaced road, to a gravel road, to a dirt road, to a trail; then up a stream course, over a ridge, unfolding terrain step by step, making the overlapping, foreshortened slopes move oddly before your eyes. You stop frequently, like a hunter, to check the strange motion of the mountains that conceal deer and bear and fox you'll never see, a motion that, before you've fully wakened, seems independent of your walking. But when you stop to see if any other being moved against the still slopes, the ghosting deer or bear or fox stops moving and the woods stand blank. There is nothing there. Then you start walking again, and the surrounding vegetation brushes against the back of your mind as you eye the way the turning trail makes the mountains move again in forest parallax.

The creaking of my pack was apparently masked by that wolfish wind that trailed the passing front, and I flushed a series of solitary winter grouse out of the broods of hemlock seedlings that gathered underneath canopy openings, each startling *thruff* and *whir* waking me another notch. In a half hour, the night wind died and the grouse held their ground or silently walked off at the sound of my approach. Daylight slowly lit the surrounding forest, seeming to issue from the insistent creek rather than from the indifferent sky, first brightening glossy shafts of striped maple and spicebush, which flamed suddenly and coolly like tinder, then warming the trunks of young pale-barked trees—the redbuds and serviceberry—that crackled until the beeches, maples, and magnolias flamed and sent bright columns of daylight along the fluted columns of giant tulip poplar. By the time you stop to admire the way light suffuses through the forms at its disposal here, you notice the boisterous counterpoint of birdsong between the understory and the canopy without being able to remember hearing it begin and realize you have missed the dawn you started out in the dark to see.

These changes seem to issue from the nearby stream, emissary of the earth and of the underworld in Cherokee lore, rather than from the sky, and once full daylight has risen from the ground, even the flooded creek seems less loud, as if the labor of daybreak had cost it something.

Two miles up this trail that daylight reveals remnant old-growth cove forest, a little bit of North America as it was meant to be, a setting where the idea of wolves and of wildness does not seem out of place or anachronistic. And the wildness of wolves is not the only possibility that is important here—the clash of sunlight off the stream, the stubborn darkness under the hemlocks, the mixed flocks of wintering songbirds bursting about, all argue spirit of place. The backcountry is often trivialized as some sort of recreational resource. In winter, it's as solemn as a church. This is where creation, however you want to think of that, still has a hold.

The trail was half above and half below the forest, clinging to a steeply pitched slope wet with spring water. Huge poplars and hemlocks dominated the scene, overshadowing a complex assemblage of northern red oak and beech, sugar maple and red maple and mountain silverbell, magnolia and papaw—a hemisphere's worth of tree species brought together by terrain and weather and time. Forge Creek made a pronounced bend here and stepped, in its graceful turn, up through long, crescent-shape pools dark with the possibility of trout. Somewhere below me, hidden under a dense picket of rhododendron, laurel, and a Triassic assemblage of wild fern, was the confluence of Ekaneetlee Branch and Forge Creek, where an old Cherokee path and this settlers' trail diverged, in fact as well as spirit, one of many vanishing points hidden in this landscape.

In his well-known essay "Walking," Henry Thoreau suggested that whenever we walk, we should set out toward Oregon and away from Europe, that even in a morning or an evening's ramble in Massachusetts or Tennessee, we should let our steps remind us of the underlying geography and mythology of American history. I believe Thoreau, in his heart of hearts, understood that history to be tragic, but he knew the geography and loved the myth as well as any American:

> Eastward I go only by force; but westward I go free. . . . It is hard for me to believe that I shall find fair landscapes or sufficient wildness and freedom behind the eastern horizon. I am not excited by the prospect of a walk thither; but I believe that the forest which I see in the western horizon stretches uninterruptedly toward the setting sun, and there are no towns nor cities in it of enough consequence to disturb

me. Let me live where I will, on this side is the city, on that the wilderness, and ever I am leaving the city more and more, and withdrawing into the wilderness. I should not lay so much stress on this fact, if I did not believe that something like this is the prevailing tendency of my countrymen. I must walk toward Oregon, and not toward Europe.

Of course, Thoreau knew well what his countrymen did not and still do not know, that the geography and the mythology of American culture would ultimately prove incompatible and were so already in his day. He watched wildlife disappear from the woods and fields around Concord, watched those woods and fields themselves disappear. He noted his neighbors' appetite for road building and that the railroad ran hard by Walden Pond, which Thoreau chose as a place for dwelling not because it was a wilderness retreat, but because it was on the terrible edge of what is called "progress," and more bizarrely "growth." We have inherited that edge where the found world disappears into the manufactured world, where something invaluable and irreplaceable is lost forever—a forest, a swamp, a songbird, a wolf, a morning vantage—for some temporary, narrowly construed gain. That edge has, in fact, devoured our landscape to the point where it is far easier to find a theme park or a golf course than a stand of old growth.

In "Walking" Thoreau teases the reader with the myth of the West—the false promise of infinite space and resources—in the hope that the transplanted European mind would evolve in the course of American history. Like his fellow Romantics Thoreau hoped that before American culture reached the Pacific Ocean and turned around to look back on an exhausted, irrecoverable continent, a profound change would have taken place—induced by the land itself—and that the pursuit of happiness would not, in the end, have turned out to be merely the pursuit of wealth.

Like Whitman, whose preface to *Leaves of Grass* should be the national prayer, if we need such a thing, Thoreau dreamed unashamedly of a broadminded culture, hoping that the topography of North America would educate us in genuinely spiritual ways, as it had the people from whom it was taken, who barely survived the theft:

> I trust that we shall be more imaginative, that our thoughts will be clearer, fresher, and more ethereal, as our sky,—our understanding more comprehensive and broader, like our plains,—our intellect

generally on a grander scale, like our thunder and lightning, our rivers
and mountains and forests,—and our hearts shall even correspond in
breadth and depth and grandeur to our inland seas. . . . Else to what
end does the world go on, and why was America discovered? . . . As
a true patriot, I should be ashamed to think that Adam in paradise was
more favorably situated on the whole than the backwoodsman in this
country.

What's left of the backwoodsman's backcountry is still the best place to
be, but in the end Romantic metaphors create only metaphorical space.
With eastern North America as crowded and overdeveloped as the Europe
of Thoreau's day, and the once-panoramic American West looking more
and more like his East, it is clear that rather than be changed by the land,
man simply changed the land.

If, for reasons of your own health and sanity, you practice the art of
walking anywhere in North America now, you walk as I do, in circles, or
you follow narrow corridors being careful to stay within the confines of
what has become the rarest thing on earth—an undisturbed place. In the
East, you stick to these forested mountains like a bear or a wolf, keep the
last good horizon underfoot even if that puts Oregon at your back.

The two paths that diverged below me—one led to sacred *Kitu'hwa* and
the other to a mountain bald turned into a cow pasture—marked a tragic
divergence. I followed the settlers' trail—above the flashing creek, along an
understory with enough evergreen in it to be dense in the dead of winter,
under bare trees leafed in cold daylight, through a true forest where I knew
wolves were at large. In a mile or so I came to the designated campsite
where I intended to stop the first night. A noisy, overused place in summer,
it was fine there out of season—a raised flat of land that overlooked the
creek, with the foot of Gregory Ridge rising behind it. A wild enough place
in winter. I was only four or five miles into the backcountry and it was
barely midmorning, but I was hungry, so I made a makeshift meal and
watched the constancy of the woods and the creek as I ate. Then I pitched
the tent, packed a daypack, strung the food bag between two hemlocks,
and wandered up Forge Creek along a fishermen's trail.

I wasn't looking for anything in particular. Chris Lucash told me early
on that I would never see a wolf in the woods, and I didn't expect to.
Lifelong wolf researchers rarely see a wolf in the wild on foot without
benefit of radios and handheld antennas. But who could walk in wolf country now and not think *wolves* and sense not so much fear or excitement as

a satisfying completion of place? That first fall and winter, when I logged a thousand miles practicing hard the art of walking, it was enough to know there were a dozen wolves at large between the Little Tennessee and Big Pigeon rivers—red wolves—a fresh breeze of wild life stirring the gray coat of the mountains.

By the look of it, wolf country was unmoved. But it wasn't fanciful now to imagine wolves trotting along trails at night and laying up in coverts during the day, to picture in the mind's eye a rendezvous or hunt. And, having seen *Canis rufus* up close, I watched the reddish-brown tones in the woods in a way I never had before. There were wolf-colored blends of brown, red, and black in leaf litter and rotting logs, in rock and shadows. I knew antlered brush and smoke-gray tree trunks mimicked deer so often you stopped seeing deer at all. But that the colors which concealed grouse also concealed wolves was something I had not known. Now I could walk along and not see wolves.

I spent a timeless day exploring the head of the Forge Creek drainage, walking easily through the second growth above the grove of big trees, following each small tributary to an impasse, learning, as I liked to do, the watershed in detail. I turned around in the late afternoon as the warm winter day suddenly cooled and followed the main stem of the creek downslope in the path of receding daylight. The last rays of warm brown sunlight lit the bedrock float scattered through the woods. The sandstone briefly glowed like coals and then went dark. A half mile above camp, I started fishing my way back in this failing light, using a length of fly line with a short leader to which I attached a weighted nymph I had tied from rabbit fur. I short-cast the line without benefit of a rod, dead-drifting the nymph through pools and probing rocky pockets in riffles where I knew trout were. By the time my blue tent came in view—the only alien thing I had seen all day—I had tugged three decent trout out of winter with more relish than regret.

Back in camp, I hung the dressed fish on a hemlock stob and gleaned the slope above me for an armload of dead wood. I grubbed a handful of yellow birch bark for tinder, wool-gathering strips of outer and inner bark here and there from the frazzled skin of standing trees. As I knelt at Forge Creek pumping water through a small ceramic filter, daylight withdrew back into the creek and evening reemerged from under the hemlocks. A brief medley of birdsong beyond the range of the birds I knew reminded me of the morning's longer fugues. Variations on themes in natural language. As I was refilling my canteens for tomorrow's walk, the tag end of evening dissolved into twilight and the day moved west, toward Oregon. When I stood up, knees aching, twilight was gone, the near woods went black, a starlit sky revealed itself beyond the branches overhead, and the sound of the creek brightened in the dark.

I needed a flashlight to find the eight fist-size stones I wanted for a fire ring, but they came to hand without much searching. I hovered over the stone circle until yellow flames curled from the curled flames of yellow birch bark, one form seeming to encourage the other. The thatch of hemlock twigs set above the nest of tinder crackled softly to life, fusing a tall, pencil-thin flame at its center that drew an audible rush of air through the ring of stones as I fed the new fire more branch tips. The flaming pile soon collapsed, seemed to extinguish itself in a resinous puff, but then relit with a *pop* as a smaller, hotter flame that I kindled with care into a proper fire. As strong firelight rose and lit the trunks of my companion hemlocks, Forge Creek quieted down and the starlit winter sky receded a notch.

The Cherokee recognized that the excitement of the hunt might make a hunter forgetful of the prayers and formulas that justified the kill. But to neglect these rituals—the acknowledgment of guilt that propitiated the game you sought for food—was to invite trouble, excite revenge in nature, which, after all, had no use for man. So the hunter who on his way home from a successful hunt remembers that he forgot to address his game properly has one last chance to make amends. Tired and eager as he is to see his wife and home, he stops on the trail and builds a small four-log fire as a tangible sign of his debt to the life that keeps him alive and his regret at having temporarily lapsed in respect. This is called the fire in the path, an act of gratitude and propitiation. It seemed to me that mild winter night on Forge Creek, and it seems to me now, that to return red wolves to these mountains was to light a fire in the path.

I broiled the trout on switches and ate them with my fingers, sliding crescents of pinkish flesh from the delicate ribs and backbone and enjoying each slough of charred, salty skin. I built the fire up with the wood that was left and did what little cleaning up I needed to do, burning the fish bones well so as not to encourage a restless bear to spend the night sniffing around camp. I took my last cup of coffee down to the stream, admiring as I had all day its pure insistence. I watched the dark forest, cocking my head around like an animal at every sound until the descending cold drove me back to camp. I stood and howled before crawling into the tent—good howls, I think—but was not favored with a reply.

The next morning I stayed nestled in my sleeping bag until I saw sunlight on the ground in camp. I had another fair day to work with, so I gave up the Gregory Ridge trail, which switchbacked up the slope behind me, for cross-country travel. I ate, broke camp, and took off up the open slope across Forge Creek. Once I crested that ridge I could descend to Ekaneetlee Branch, which I would follow upstream along the old overgrown manway to the summit ridge where it doglegged into the Appalachian Trail. From that point I could resume my original plan to hike northeast along the main ridge and then descend the Tremont drainage.

I labored up that seemingly open slope, which closed when I got up on it, and struggled with the big pack around deadfalls and bedrock outcrops. By the time I crested the ridge and then quartered the slope on the other side, trending northeast down toward Ekaneetlee Branch, I was growing doubtful about the way I had chosen.

But you find things off trail.

At a damp, rocky cul-de-sac, much like the one at the head of Whistling Branch, I came on a wolf kill. I had seen something bright fifty yards ahead of me, which I thought was one of those odd chunks of quartzite that pop up here and there in the woods and which the Cherokee prized as jewels fallen from serpents' heads. But from twenty yards, I saw the brightness was sunlight glaring off a beautiful eight-point rack.

I ran my hands over the compelling curvature of the antlers when I knelt down to it, looking over each closely, admiring their perfect condition. They were not scarred from last season's rut. No tines were chipped. There wasn't even a toothmark from a wood rat or a deer mouse on them yet. Except for my handling them, they were untouched. There was a thick, rubbery layer of tissue stretched between the exposed pedicels of the antlers, the knurled burrs of which were stained reddish brown from the bloody velvet the deer had scraped off on a sapling sometime last autumn when the rut was coming on and the first wolves were being freed.

Tiny blackflies rummaged the skull. The eye sockets and nose cavity were cleaned out. The mandible was gone but healthy teeth, the crowns whorled black and white, were lodged firmly in the upper jaw. There was only a very faint odor if you put your nose to the skull. A foot and a half of backbone remained attached to it, flecked at the vertebrae with dried blood but picked clean of meat.

The deer lay pointed toward a dead end between a small stream and a rock ledge. The rest of its vertebrae and broken ribs were scattered about. Its left rear leg was still attached to a piece of pelvis but broken through, leaving a triangular eye of marrow at the break. The other three legs were nearby, torn off at their upper joints but intact. There was nothing but bone except for some skin and fur on the lower legs and one hoof and some tail hair. There were wolf tracks in the soft soil, most scuffed, a few distinct, large enough by the measure of the little plastic ruler I habitually carried to satisfy me that this was the work of wolves.

The deer had been either hunted to death or scavenged. There was no way to tell which, but a story lurked in its broken rear leg, the classic point of attack for wolves. A whitetail with a broken leg will be found out fairly quickly in wolf country. A healthy deer surprised here would be at a fatal disadvantage. But it would be unusual for a healthy deer to break its leg without cause. I felt a hunt in the air.

In any event, red wolves had feasted. Predation had played itself out, and wolf country was enlivened by a death. That skeleton surrounded by wolf tracks was one of the finest signs of life I have ever seen in these mountains, and the unnamed tributary of Ekaneetlee Branch was a sacred spot where predator and prey had made their sudden peace with no need of further ritual. In the end, the fleetness of the deer and the fleetness of the wolf are one. I fought back a greedy impulse to take the skull and antlers. In fact, I did take them, then felt so ashamed walking away with them that I turned around and brought the skull and antlers back and set them down. I was not the hunter here and this was not my kill.

I'm glad I put the Ekaneetlee antlers back and that they are not sitting on my desk now rebuking me, but there was something very appealing in the unmarked symmetry of those antlers wolves had brought down to earth. They were, after all, one of the most beautiful shapes in nature: stony but plantlike, vegetative, branched, deciduous. And so oddly posed there, lifelike in death. Promising. The scattered bones still seemed to be a deer, or had been until I disturbed them. The sunlit antlers were ivory still—the thing itself becoming an image of itself in the cold light. The sweep of life was strong in the shape of them and in the way they divided, began to come together, and then left off in the air, as if they held something between them.

The Ekaneetlee antlers were a perfect fusion of nature and art—life become something formal, abstract, objective in death. They were a great sign fallen out the cycle of one being's fleeting awareness into a cycle with a much longer period, the cycle of bedrock and species and myth. Luxury tissue, biologists call it, as if the beauty and truth in things were a luxury. A transcendental shape, I thought, well wrought as a wolf's jaw.

Chalaque

You will not dare to cease following me—at Apalachi, at Cutifachiqui, at Mabilla, turning from the sea, facing inland.

—William Carlos Williams, *In the American Grain*

Juan Ortiz was charged with guarding the temple dead from wolves. He was, so far as we know, the first European to be of use in North America. "Though one Christian might do no good," his Calusa captors thought, "certainly he could no harm." In the spring of 1539, Hernando de Soto found him in Florida and found him useful, because he knew native words for things.

In southeastern North America, words were once as wild and varied as the land. Aboriginal languages and dialects showed much local evolution, as if divergent responses to subtle differences in topography, living connections between nature and culture. There were the Muskogean tongues of the Gulf Coast—Choctaw, Chickasaw, Apalachee, Alabama, Koasati, Hitichi, Mikasuki, Creek, Natchez, Tunica, Chitimacha, Atakapa, Timucua; the Siouan tongues Tutelo, Biloxi, Ofo, Catawba, Yuchi; as well as the Iroquoian Tuscarora and Cherokee. There were extinct, unclassified languages like Cusabo and Yamasee and many others of which not a word survived. In *The Indians of the Southeastern United States*, ethnographer John Swanton lists 173 tribes for the region. This quarter of North America was a world of fabulous languages, its landscape laced with speech strange as birdsong, words as untranslatable as the shapes of mountains and river bends, vocabularies dense as forest vegetation. But de Soto and his followers wanted gold, for which there was no word, and with them a journey began that has in many respects not yet ended.

De Soto had fought with Pizarro in Peru, distinguishing himself for cruelty and rashness and for humiliating Atahualpa, the last Inca ruler, at his capture. Then he cashed in his *cruzados* for *reales* and played at being a rich gentleman in Seville. But his wealth was no match for his greed. When at court he heard Cabeza de Vaca talking loosely of adventures with Narváez, waving a *Relación* in the air—"Here I have seen this . . ."—and intimating great wealth in the unexplored interior of La Florida—"he gave them to understand that it was the richest country in the world"—de Soto was intrigued, his mind long since plundered by what he had seen in South America. And so with him many men "of good condition" who sold their land—the vineyards, wheat fields, and olive groves peasants dream of owning—to go with de Soto and conquer La Florida.

In the winter of 1538 there was a strange muster at Sanlúcar at the mouth of the Guadalquivir. *Extremeños* who had followed their countryman gathered, as did Portuguese and down-at-their-luck Castilians in rusty mail with nothing left to do in the Old World. De Soto eyed their absurd silks, pitted helmets, and poor lances and took the best of the lot—650 men and 330 horses. A handful of priests and friars, some women, two Genoese and a Sardinian who were skilled in building boats and bridges as well as a quantity of chains and collars.

The so-called Gentleman of Elvas, one of the expedition's chroniclers, marks the voyage by high holy days, as if it were a pilgrimage: the Canaries on Easter Sunday, Santiago on the Pentecost. Then across Cuba on horseback while the ships coasted the island—Bayamo, Puerto Principe, Sancti Spiritus, Trinidad, Havana in March 1539.

From Cuba a caravel was sent to reconnoiter the Florida Gulf Coast, a short sail north from Havana and the gateway into the beautiful blank of North America. Two Indians—Calusa or Timucua—were kidnapped and brought back to de Soto at Havana. They told him "by signs" what he wanted to hear: "that there was much gold in Florida."

In May de Soto loaded nine vessels with maize, sweet potatoes, beef, and cacabi biscuits, as well as his stroke of genius—the live swine the conquerors would herd along with them—and sailed north from Havana for the Gulf Coast. A week later, on the feast of Espiritu Santo, land was sighted, and on May 31 1539 the army slogged ashore a few leagues from a town they called Ucita, after the cacique—the chief—there. This was probably a Timucua village near the mouth of Tampa Bay.

Two of the first six natives encountered were killed, a ratio of conquest established. The others escaped, the coastal marsh holding off their pursuers, who would never learn how to deal with the land. From then on the towns were deserted, "for, so soon as the Christians appeared in sight of land, they were descried, and all along on the coast many smokes were seen to rise, which the Indians make to warn one another."

Ucita was comprised of seven or eight log houses covered with palm leaves, with the chief's house—or possibly a communal town house—built on a mound opposite a temple the top of which was graced with a carving of a waterfowl with gilded eyes. Here, we are told, de Soto tarried.

De Soto's tarrying had an edge to it. The *adelantado* lodged himself in the principal house and ordered the rest of Ucita razed, including the temple, where they found only a few brazed pearls. He had the surrounding woods clear-cut for the radius of a crossbow shot, a standard unit of measure on this journey. While the Spaniards and Portuguese were busy with this work, the two Indians who had told them there was much gold in Florida disappeared.

From Ucita, de Soto kindled war, sending out detachments of horsemen and foot soldiers as well as crossbow and gun men. This strange assemblage of medieval and premodern weaponry initially proved no match for the aboriginal bow and arrow wielded in the close, confusing quarters of coastal guerrilla warfare.

Elvas tells us with admiration that the natives were excellent and agile adversaries who never fled farther than an arrow shot. They were stealthy, never presented standing targets, and could get off three or four arrows for every return from a crossbow or shaky blast from an arquebus. Their slender longbows drove the heavy cane arrows with as much force as the bulkier crossbows, and although the sharpened fishbone and stone points often shattered out of their sinew wraps on impact with armor, the splintered cane alone could pierce mail shirts and create ugly wounds.

De Soto's men lost their first battle—a heavy-handed attack on twenty unsuspecting people camped on a coastal creek—but the conquistadors brought back six wounded, one mortally, to Ucita, along with four female prisoners.

It was here, near Ucita, that de Soto stumbled upon Juan Ortiz, who would become his principal if often bewildered interpreter. Ortiz, a native of Seville, was a refugee of the 1528 Narváez expedition, knowledge of which Cabeza de Vaca had used to beguile de Soto in Spain. Ortiz did not know what had become of Narváez and that only a handful of men had survived that venture. He had left the main body of the expedition with the supply ships that returned to Cuba after Narváez moved inland. On his way back to the Gulf Coast, Ortiz was captured by Timucua, who brought him to Ucita, where he won some favor and learned their language. After three years he was captured by a neighboring tribe who spoke a different language and who did not understand Timucuan. De Soto's men found Ortiz sunburned and tattooed, hiding in a thicket. He had great difficulty speaking Spanish and for days used four or five Timucuan words for every one he managed to utter in his native tongue.

At the time of de Soto's arrival, Ortiz said he had not been more than ten or twenty leagues from Ucita in any direction. He knew little, but in 1539 he knew more about North America than any European alive. He had been in country twelve years. When asked about riches, he said there were rumors of fertile corn fields farther along the coast. He knew nothing of gold or silver. But he knew two native languages.

That two mutually unintelligible languages were being spoken within ten leagues of each other on the Florida coast tells us something about the wealth of cultural detail lurking in the large blank spaces that dominated sixteenth-century European maps of North America. But de Soto was not interested in landscape and language. He was determined to drag his titles—governor, adelantado, marquis—across the savannas and through the forests until he found something of value.

The Indians quickly learned the trick of passing him on. Every place the Spanish stopped, Ortiz would ask the same question and get the same answer. De Soto's men marched from Ucita into the tangled interior, to Paracoxi, where they were told, straight-faced, that there was much gold toward the sunset, at a province called Cale. The road broadened toward Cale, but the town was abandoned. They ate watercress and unripened corn. The cobs tasted like wood and so they scraped and pounded the green kernels, sifting the meal through their coats of mail.

To forestall a native uprising there, de Soto sent one of his captains back to Ucita. The captain, disturbed by something, set his greyhounds on an Indian guide, who was torn to pieces and eaten by the dogs. Word of this must have pleased de Soto and put him in the mood. Not long after he had an Indian woman thrown to the dogs because he suspected her of resistance.

The royal historian Oviedo, who knew de Soto personally, tells us that even as a young man soldiering under Pedrárias in Nicaragua he was given to the *montería,* the chase. That is to say that when he wasn't fighting Indians for the king, he hunted them for sport, with greyhounds and Irish wolfhounds trained for the purpose. Infantile and sadistic, he was quite willing to burn his captives to death in order to gain information on the whereabouts of gold. During his career in Central and South America, de Soto was a slave trafficker, a thief, and an overseer of mass murder and mass rape. Based partly on those qualifications, he was charged by the king of Spain with the "conquest, settlement, and pacification" of Spanish North America. Oviedo says bluntly that de Soto returned to the New World "to continue the bloody tactics of times past, which had been his practice."

The army moved on from Cale in August, gathering slaves and extorting supplies as they went, taking local chiefs as hostages, leaving a strange list of place-names behind them: Ytara, Potano,* Utinama, Malapaz, Cholupaha, Caliquen—traces of their misapprehension of native speech and of their own homesickness, Romance names to help them imagine they knew where they were and what they were doing.

They traveled strangely. In a land of lakes, men died of thirst. Their well-trained horses were stampeded by rabbits. Many Indians seemed to follow them, but the towns were empty. Although at war, they were vulnerable to surprise attack. One day a horse and three soldiers of the governor's guard were killed in their very midst. They had set out to destroy a world and seemed taken aback to find its inhabitants "bellicose and indomitable and strong." After all their preparations, they went hungry. After all their plans, they followed rumors. The lay of the land confused them. In a region of broad savannas and pine forests, they spent half their time in swamps, where these Renaissance men feasted like Stone Age hominids on unsalted herbs and roots chased with brackish water.

At Caliquen they were told of the province of Apalachen, where Narváez and his men had met with "continual war." It was the Apalachee who drove the earlier expedition back to the coast, where the survivors hurriedly built boats, and out onto the waters of the Gulf of Mexico, where most of them drowned. The Gentleman of Elvas reports that the Spanish were "depressed at this information, and all counselled the Governor to go back to the port, that they might not be lost, as Narváez had been, and to leave the land of Florida."

---

* Possibly William Bartram's Alachua.

But they kept on, nervously burying supplies behind them as they approached the dreaded Apalachee. The Genoese and the Sardinian engineers built the pine-log bridges to last in case they would be needed again. The Apalachee fought them at every river crossing. At Napetaca, the principal men of Caliquen came to de Soto to ask for the release of their cacique, who was being held hostage to ensure safe passage. De Soto refused. The natives turned on their captors and were massacred. A dark journey darkened.

De Soto perfected his methods as he continued west across the Florida panhandle. A theory of North American conquest emerged in the long-leaf pine forests and palmetto wetlands of north Florida: "Never staying or resting anywhere they went, they made neither settlement nor conquest but caused alteration and desolation of the land and loss of liberty of the people, without making Christians or friends of any of the Indians."

There had been thousands of years of warfare in North America, undoubtedly much of it brutal, but never anything like de Soto's march—an aimless but systematic violence uncentered by the law of clan revenge or by tribal protocols of war. Since it had no purpose, it had no end. Six hundred armed men moved through the landscape like a blind snake. The natives soon understood the theory and, when they could, took to burning their fields and towns before they abandoned them. As the Muskogean peoples torched their homes and crops and sent runners along the coast and inland toward the mountains, native life in southeastern North America began to end.*

Hapaluya. Uzachil. Axille. It was October. Vitachuco, which was in flames. Uzela. And then Anhayca Apalache, the capital, ten leagues from the coast where Narváez had built his boats. Bleached horse skulls and crosses on the trees marked the place. *Bahía de Caballos.*

De Soto prepared to winter at the deserted city, which now is buried under downtown Tallahassee. Unaware of the abandoned Mississippian mounds that cast strange shadows toward him, he sent back word to Espiritu Santo to abandon the beachhead there and sent word to Havana for supplies and reinforcements. His men gathered crops—maize, pumpkins, beans—and ate whatever wild food they could gather, principally persimmons and turkeys.

---

* It is worth remembering that Coronado's incursion across the Colorado plateau to the Zuni (1540 to 1542) took place simultaneously with de Soto's journey.

The Apalachee harassed them unmercifully. Everywhere de Soto's men went they were attacked, and behind the governor's back they admired the spirit and boldness of the natives. "Although the Spaniards pursued them and burned them, never did they wish to come in peace." When the Spanish cut off the hands and noses of captive Indians, they were, their torturers noted, stoic as Romans. "Not one of them denied being from Apalache for fear of death. And upon taking one, when they asked him where he was from, he responded with pride: 'Where am I from? . . . I am an Indian of Apalache.' " Nothing dashed Spanish hopes of an easy conquest of North America as much as those relentless, elusive Apalachee bowmen, as important to American history as the farmers of Concord.

During the winter a captive youth concocted a tale of "gold in quantity" in his homeland called Yupaha, toward the rising sun, "governed by a woman, the town she lived in being of astonishing size, and many neighboring lords her tributaries." In March de Soto gathered new slaves and headed northeast across what is now southern Georgia toward what was then Yupaha. A homesick boy was going home. So went the European exploration of North America.

It was hard going. There was fighting at Capachiqui. At Toalli the houses were roofed with cane instead of grass. There were winter as well as summer houses. These were perhaps Hitichi. One of chroniclers marveled at the fruitful, orderly life of these people, their clothing woven from grasses and the inner bark of mulberry trees and fashioned from supple deer skins dyed vermilion and black, fine as grenadine cloth. He was reminded of gypsies. De Soto moved on unmoved.

Then Achese, where the natives "having had no knowledge of the Christians, plunged into a river" at their approach. But whether their reputation preceded them or not, the Spanish found information less easy to come by in the interior. "They had come through regions speaking different languages" and were far beyond the words that Juan Ortiz knew. Not halfway across Georgia's pine woods and broad rivers, perhaps among the Coweta or the Lower Creek, de Soto's interpreter's interpreter was confused by what he heard. But he reassured the governor that they were on the right path.

They crossed river after flooded river, losing men and horses. They gave the rivers names that were also carried away downstream—river of Guacuca, river of Capachequi, river of Toa. The slaves were unshackled because the Spaniards needed the chains for safety lines. Exhausted, the soldiers slept "in bad order" scattered in pine forests and swamps. When they found natives, they killed them for their food, gorging themselves on turkey and venison when they got the chance.

The land balked the marching army, bedeviling them with sullen swamps and twisted river bottoms. Somewhere they were enchanted by a crystal spring full of fish, and a little farther on, they claimed, women in white appeared with corn tortillas and spring onions "as fat as the tip of the thumb" as well as hides and "blankets of the country" to replace their torn and rotted clothes. Perhaps they were dreaming. Somewhere in the south Georgia woods a messenger from Ichisi, peaceful province of a one-eyed lord, stepped out of the forest and asked them bluntly: "Who are you? What do you want? Where are you going?"

De Soto announced that he was "the child of the Sun . . . and that he was going about the country, seeking for the greatest prince there, and the richest province." He was told to keep going, that the territory of Ocute just up the road held what he wanted, and was given a guide and yet another interpreter to help him on his way. For thanks de Soto had a wooden cross erected at Ichisi and instructed the Indians to worship it.

April: Altamaca and then Ocute, center of a populous country. Two thousand Indians brought food, we are told—rabbits, grouse, maize, bread, a few turkeys, and many dogs. "The Indians never lacked meat," Elvas notes, "with arrows they get abundance of deer, turkeys, rabbits, and other wild animals, being very skillful in killing game, which the Christians were not." Despite their firepower, the Europeans could not hunt and never learned. They rarely ventured into the dark, tangled woods: "They did not dare to turn aside from the paths."

At Ocute, the Indians watched the soldiers of the child of the Sun chase dogs and kill them for food. "On account of the scarcity of meat, the dogs were as much esteemed by the Christians as though they had been fat sheep." Those who were good at catching dogs were thought well of by their superiors, "such was the craving for meat." Besides the dogs, de Soto took 400 men from Ocute.

Next Cofaqui and then the town of the cacique Patofa, who "had heard of the Governor for a long time, and desired to see him." At Patofa, the youth of Yupaha, who was shaping de Soto's steps, had or faked a seizure of some kind, perhaps to free himself and remain in Patofa's fertile country. But de Soto had the devil cast out of him, treatment that cured the young man. The youth then insisted they were only four days' journey from his golden home. The Indians of Patofa said they knew of no such place and suggested de Soto head back inland, northwest to Coca, a plentiful country. The governor was confused.

De Soto followed the young boy's inclinations and took a road that tapered into a trail that gave out entirely on the sixth day out from Patofa. They forded rivers that got larger and swifter, swimming their horses uneasily as much as three crossbow shots from bank to bank. After three days more of slogging through sodden bottomlands, de Soto began menacing the youth, whose golden tale he had embraced without doubt up until now. Now, after six weeks of traveling across uncharted country following his directions, "the youth declared that he knew not where he was." De Soto was enraged. "Fortunately for him, at the time, there was not another whom Juan Ortiz understood, or he would have been cast to the dogs."

The governor was despondent. He had never known where he was but now, somehow, he was lost—in uninhabited country, without food, the men and beasts thin, vulnerable to attack if the natives got wind of his condition. The Spanish had not been living off the land but off the natives' cultivated fields and storehouses. Now they were beyond paths and settlements—probably somewhere on the well-drained South Carolina piedmont—trapped by rivers that rose with the generous spring rains, dragging their armor through the humid southern spring. The governor's secretary writes of the "blindness and rapture . . . of uncertain greed." De Soto released his slaves rather than worry about feeding them and butchered some of his precious swine, herded and bred the whole way, to keep his unworthy men alive.

On the twenty-sixth of April they found a town and some food. They were perhaps among the Yamasee. De Soto placed a letter in a gourd and buried it at the base of a blazed pine tree, telling as best he could of his whereabouts and plans, implying that he needed to be found. Making this pathetic gesture, he must have thought of Seville and Peru and the easy pickings in Darien many years before. Soon after, four Indians were captured. They said only that they knew of no other towns. De Soto offered to burn one of them to death, and another spoke up, revealing they were only two days' journey from Cutifachiqui. To de Soto's ears, this was just another strange name in the litany he had collected from the bay of Espiritu Santo. He had forgotten half already.

But the woman the captive youth had spoken of was waiting for de Soto at Cutifachiqui. In fact, she sent for him, through her lieutenants, who crossed the river in four canoes, for there was a hierarchy at Cutifachiqui, a culture governed by a young, self-assured cacique. She undoubtedly watched the meeting on the far shore of what was quite likely the Wateree River, where her kinswoman saluted de Soto and gave him her instructions: He was to stay put.

When she crossed the river herself, well dressed and well attended, she barely paid the arrogant, bedraggled stranger lip service. Her people showed him some token gifts, a few boatloads of shawls and skins, not the obeisance he expected but the truck of common courtesy in that country.

She knew what he was. He was a wandering cacique, a great lord without a country—which is to say a fool. She would have afforded Quixote more respect. For months she had been receiving intelligence about the zigzagging Christians. She knew what he thought this visit was, but judging from her behavior in the chronicles, the cacique of Cutifachiqui was as disingenuous as she was wise, and de Soto was neither thoughtful nor a good observer. She seems to have had a bleak sense of humor and a notion that rough justice was rough but just. But she also knew that her people were dying and that, even though this brutal fool de Soto was doomed, the future belonged to him and to his servile, brutal men and even to the squealing pigs they drove through the woods because they were not men enough to hunt wild game.

When she drew a string of large pearls over her head and threw them—Elvas's verb—about de Soto's sunburned neck, he eyed the pearls and missed the meaning of the gesture. He did not know that she knew he was on his way to the bitter fighting at Mabilla and then to the Mississippi, where he would be buried in the dark of night, dumped overboard into the broad, indifferent river. The great explorer. Governor of Cuba. *Adelantado* of La Florida. Marquis of nothing. De Soto sleeps here.

But she was fair. She tested him and he failed. She showed him the surrounding country, one of the many jewels of the blank continent—fertile bottomlands well planted with beans, maize, and squash, open groves of walnut, mulberry trees, and spreading live oaks, indescribable forests of pine and oak, sweetgum and cedar, full of wild game and limned by wild streams full of fish. Waterfowl darkened the broad river in spring and fall. Geese and swans wintered at their feet. The sea and all its bounty was only two days downriver. She did not comment on the vacant towns surrounding Cutifachiqui, the houses of the dead disappearing in the tall grasses, the strange diseases that worked liked magic against her people.

Odd details from a vanishing culture embedded themselves in the matter-of-fact chronicles. Although the natives of Cutifachiqui had no cloth, there was much art in their clothing. They went adorned in feathers from waterfowl and furs from game, used the brains of deer to tan deerskins and the juice of berries to dye them. There was nothing unnatural in their artifice. They made figures with freshwater pearls—images of babies and birds, Elvas tells us. There was no gold.

She saw that the Europeans liked shiny things, so she showed him their sepulchers and turned her back while de Soto had his men rob the graves. They loaded 350 pounds of pearls—some pried from the flesh of the dead—onto their horses. She watched this curious man and the curious men who followed orders. The boy from Yupaha announced his conversion to Christ, and they removed his chains and shackles. Since de Soto was interested in religion, she showed the governor some relics of the Christians who had attempted to start a colony on the coast a dozen years before—Biscayan iron axes, a rosary, and a dirk.*

De Soto's men, who were not eager to plunge back into the forest, eyed the women and the land and the pearls for *repartimiento* and proposed to make a settlement there, "but De Soto, as it was his object to find another treasure like that of Atabali'pa, lord of Peru, would not be content with good lands nor pearls, even though many of them were worth their weight in gold." Natives were interrogated and gave the answer they had been giving all along. Yes, yes, there was a greater lord and a richer country farther on. Chiaha, twelve days' march. That way. West. De Soto "resolved at once to go in quest of that country." His men thought he was crazy. Elvas notes he was "an inflexible man, and dry of word who . . . did not like to be opposed. . . . There were none who would say a thing to him after it became known that he had made up his mind."

The cacique of Cutifachiqui was taken as a hostage, along with her attendants. For a hundred leagues, de Soto went unopposed because of her. Although under guard, she gave orders and was obeyed. De Soto thought it was his power. In seven days they arrived at the foot of the mountainous province of Chalaque, somewhere in western North Carolina. Before they entered that rugged country, the cacique of Cutifachiqui disappeared into the woods with her attendants, two of de Soto's men, and a cane box of unbored pearls de Soto had much coveted and sorely missed once he realized she had escaped.

---

* This was the failed colony of Ayllon, near the mouth of the Santee River.

. . .

Tsistu'yi. *Rabbit place*. The broad, bald crest of wolf country. Its wild heart. From here, in late winter, there are nothing but vanishing points, not the least of which is what scholars call the contact.

"Chalaque" was what De Soto's chroniclers heard in the Creek word *tciloki*, "people of a different speech." Neither word meant anything to the Cherokee, who called themselves *Yuñ'wiya'*, "the real people." But they had the forms *Tsa'lagi'* and *Tsa'ragi'*, in their Upper and Lower dialects, for the name by which their Muskogean neighbors knew them. To the Spaniards, this concession became *Chalaque*, a word that migrated through many variants in maps, documents, and journals—Chalakee, Cheerake, Cherakis—before becoming standardized in English as Cherokee by 1708. On some of the earliest maps of North America you see the place-name Chalaque or Chalaqua shifting around uncertainly in the southeastern interior, hovering for a century or so, searching for its referent.

The Creek, of course, knew what they were talking about. The Cherokee were of a different speech. They spoke a divergent form of Iroquois that set them apart linguistically from their neighbors—the Yuchi, Creek, and Catawba—whom they apparently had displaced when they migrated south into the southern Appalachian summit region with which they are historically associated. But the Cherokee were not newcomers. Their language has been separate from northern Iroquoian forms for almost 4,000 years, and in historic times the Iroquois were remembered only as bitter enemies.

There were as many names for the Cherokee in other native languages as there came to be in the languages of the Europeans, names that seem to trace that migration south. The Mohawk name for them suggested they were cave dwellers, or inhabitants of a cave country, which might mark the time they spent in the Alleghenies of western Virginia and eastern Kentucky. Mooney tells us that their Wyandot name implied they were "ridge, or mountain, people," which they probably were from the time they arrived in Virginia, and a Catawba name suggested that they came out of the ground, which was closest to the truth. Like other native North Americans, all of whom lived within a highly articulated poetics of place, the Cherokee moved their sacred fires with them, so that despite what in the long view might seem to be constant migration, in effect they never moved.

Serious-minded people do not wander. Spirit of place moves with them. When the Cherokee arrived in this country, they settled deeply into these mountains, their words and myths falling easily into place along the rocky crags, forested recesses, and foggy riverheads.

An interest in the origin of the name *Cherokee* led me to the chronicles of Hernando de Soto's strange *entrada*. De Soto's route across the southern Appalachians remains a puzzle to scholars, but the work of the contact has been so thorough that it is not necessary to pinpoint where and when the first Cherokee saw smoke rise from his makeshift camps or silently watched his noisy, hapless men pass along the narrow manways that so confused them. The contact doesn't rise to a single dramatic moment, like a scene in a James Fenimore Cooper novel. Knowledge of the Europeans, of their coasting ships and early, fitful landings, would have filtered inland at least since Verrazano's cruising of the Outer Banks in 1524 and probably for much longer before that. Word of de Soto himself would have been in the mountains as much as a year before the Spanish reached them, the winter's hunt darkened by rumors.

The province of Chalaque is vaguely drawn in the de Soto chronicles. We read of 250 leagues of "mountainous country," a way "over very rough and lofty ridges," but see nothing in detail. The people of Chalaque are described as hunters, principally of deer and wild turkey, and dependent in spring on forest edibles. This may have been a band of Cherokee. In any event, they did not impress de Soto, who had gotten used to stealing stores of corn and grain found in the larger lowland villages. He misperceived those hardy mountain people as poor and was unimpressed when one of their warriors presented him with two dressed deerskins, a grudging, expensive gesture, I would guess, of safe passage and good riddance.

Crossing the mountains was so difficult, little beyond the fact of the twelve-day passage made it into accounts of expedition. The southern Appalachians were what all of North America had been described as by Verrazano—"an obstacle of new land." As the first European description of this rugged interior, the de Soto accounts are a disappointment. Since they were searching for gold, de Soto and his men saw nothing. The chronicles mark only the unsurprising fact that in the middle of the sixteenth century, Europe did not know what it had stumbled upon. By the time the expedition arrives in the province of Chiaha—somewhere in eastern Tennessee—where the Spaniards once again could plunder food, they were among Muskogean people, forebears of the Creek perhaps, and narrative detail becomes richer as they fill their bellies and leave the hard mountains—where we are told they ate much dog—behind.

Crossing the southern mountains was the hardest thing the Spaniards had done since fighting off the Apalachee. Later, when they began to talk of their adventures, perhaps the way the mountains resisted and confused them reminded the expedition's survivors of that terrible coastal warfare. Perhaps the association was only subconscious—everything native in the so-called New World resisted them—or perhaps *Appalachian* was, like *America*, a mapmaker's fancy. Eventually the mountains took on a significant misnomer in Old World maps, a word distilled from another batch of verbal guesses—Apalchen, Apalatchi, Apalathean, Apalachean—but a name that makes a fitting memorial to the indurate Apalachee, who knew the difference between a discovery and an invasion and who did their best, as did the mountains named after them, to resist the violent intrusion.

The Spanish left traces in the Cherokee mind as curious as the Oconee bells and bits of Castilian armor that surface from time to time in the southern Appalachians.* There was a Cherokee word, *Skwan'-digugun'yi*, to designate a place on Soco Creek, "where the Spaniard is in the water," that apparently commemorates a skirmish with Spanish soldiers. The Cherokee, who before the contact kept no livestock, eventually took their word for cow, *waka,* from the Spanish *vaca.* Most notably, as James Mooney noted, the Spanish were incorporated into ritual: "Among the Cherokee the eagle killer's prayer was a petition to the eagle not to be revenged upon the tribe, because it was not an Indian, but a Spaniard, who had killed him—an indication of the vivid rememberance in which the cruelty of the early Spaniards was held among the southern tribes."

I come here often—to what is now called Gregory Bald—both to see how the mountains are doing and to look at history, which has left only the shape of the land intact. I'm as far from a hard-surfaced road as you can get now in the southern Appalachians—about ten or twelve miles, a figure that still shocks me. A step in any direction begins to take me out of this vanishing forest interior. The trick here is to remain still and enjoy what space is left to contemplate. It's as if the wild mind of the Cherokee and Creek, Yuchi and Catawba were laid out before me, superimposed on

---

* Scholars of the expedition are uncertain whether or not de Soto made contact with Cherokee. The Juan Pardo expeditions of 1566–67 and 1567–68 clearly did encounter Cherokee speakers in the mountains of western North Carolina.

an even older, wilder scheme of things—the ancient quadripartite universe that once was worshipped here.

To the east, south, and west, mountains fill the horizon, in part a tectonic rumple from the formation of Pangea, deeply dissected now, thickly forested time and space still faintly echoing the silent collision of continents. For every ridge there is a river hidden along its base, a working edge of stasis and change that apparently bore repeating in every direction, as if an artist had found a style here that worked well with these materials.

nice

Looking south, what I can see beyond the snow-covered slopes at my feet is the razorback ridge of the Yellow Creek Mountains in the middle distance fronting the blue bulk of the Cheoahs, beyond which rises a smoky suggestion of the Nantahalas, which in turn merge with a gray stone arch of winter sky that hangs a few thousand feet above the bald. To the southwest, across where the Cheoah River must be, I can see the northern crest of the Unicoi Mountains before they fall abruptly toward the Little Tennessee River, which divides them from the western edge of the Unakas. In the confusing way things are now named here, the mountains divided by the great river of the Cherokee share the same name in different forms—Unicoi south of the great river, Unaka north—from the Cherokee word for *white*. The dark breach in the southern Appalachians was a fitting gateway to the Overhill towns, where Cherokee culture last flowered and last resisted the great changes. Directly west the darkest, coldest stretch of still water in the mountains now rests between them, 4,000 feet below me and out of sight.

To the east a recession of transverse ridges buttresses the Unaka summit that trends northeast, gliding along for miles just above and below 6,000 feet as that boreal island you see in field guides, a remnant ecotone from the late Pleistocene where spruce and magnolia, maidenhair fern and papaw flourish in the same watershed, a range of life that reaches from the Arctic to the equator. There are, quite literally, mountains as far as the eye can see. If I did not know how destructive the mythology of infinite wealth and its cult of consumption had become, I could sympathize with the first Europeans who came upon such vistas unprepared and fantasized about a continent of endless mountains and endless resources.

But fine as the view is, the limits of things here are quite obvious—snowy ribbons of logging roads and patches of clear-cuts beyond the national park, tracts of bulldozed land for condominiums and vacation homes, nets of roads and ganglia of towns in the distance. The only water visible is a blue sliver of Cheoah Lake, one of the many impoundments of the Little Tennessee, which for the most part is a river now in spirit only. And if I turn and walk to the northern side of the bald, the illusion of an original world is shattered as abruptly as the mountains end on the broad floor of the Cumberland Plateau. The approaching edge of a world of unattractive density diced up by endless roads and choked with a weird fetish for redundant commerce meets the eye, putting a distinct limit on any backcountry thoughts about wilderness and the possibilities of wildness here. Directly below me I can see all of Cades Cove at a glance—the pastures and woodlots, the churches and homesteads set out like toys, the mountain the Olivers descended as well as the tourist loop road, tame center of wolf country.

According to the Cherokee, the earth was created in order to make room for life. In that time before time, *Galun'lati,* the realm beyond the stone arch of the sky, had become crowded. Beneath the arch was only water. *Da'yuni'si,* the water beetle, volunteered to search out a new place but found nothing on the surface. Then it dove beneath the water and brought back a bit of mud. The mud grew into an island that was fastened to the sky with four cords. "But no one," we are told, "remembers who did this."

What the Cherokee do remember is that before the earth dried, a great buzzard flew over it to see if it was ready for the other animals. When it reached what would one day become the country of the Cherokee, this progenitor of all vultures grew tired. The tips of its wings struck the earth as they rose and fell, carving behind it the striking sequence of interlocking ridges and narrow defiles we now see, that long view of time space offers here.

Turkey vultures are common in this country at any season. The one above me now must find the cold air unsupportive and, in the absence of any thermals, gathers air speed from the wind, kiting awkwardly from one side of the summit to the other, a passive, earthbound kind of flight. In the dead of winter Gregory Bald is no place for meditation. A sharp wind strikes blows against this summit with air that only a few days ago was honed over tundra somewhere in western Canada. When the gray bruise of sky starts to collapse onto the mountains in the late afternoon, you had best cross the trackless, snow-covered bald and pick up the trail blaze on the other side before you are left without a horizon against which to take your bearings.

Last night I slept at the Forge Creek campsite above where the

Ekaneetlee Path disappears into that stand of old-growth poplar and hemlock. When I approached the trailhead from Cades Cove, I saw the mind of winter layered in well-defined bands on the mountains, which were grizzled and bare for a thousand feet, then thickly hoarfrosted, and finally lost in a low ceiling of cloud within which snow was undoubtedly falling. Camp was below the hoarfrost and snow, but winter was in the woods like a wolf and an aching, Arctic cold had gotten hold of things.

I made camp late in the day and crawled into the tent not long after dark, just to get out of the cold, and fell asleep listening to the intermittent ticking of snow pellets on the tent fly. In the morning the woods were dusted white and had the blue-gray look of Canada. A half-dozen deer drifted through the campsite as if I weren't there, grazing hurriedly, tearing even at leathery rhododendron leaves as I pumped the wavering blue flame of a small gas stove to boil water for oatmeal and coffee.

Forge Creek sluiced hard through a gauntlet of icy bedrock, and the bright sound of it followed me up the trail until the second switchback brought me to another, smaller stream. You get this feeling, walking in the southern Appalachians, of being handed from stream to stream. By the time the trail reached the hairpin turn at the low end of Gregory Ridge, the snow was deep enough to hold my walking stick when I stopped to glass the view that opens to the west there. A ridge wind picked up a variant of the stream sound, buffeting the exposed brow of bedrock that juts out of the earth there like a broken bone.

The trail follows the ridge southwest, ascending steadily into that hoarfrosted realm I had seen from Cades Cove the day before, a snowy avenue of chestnut oak and pine cased with frost, each tree trunk rimed with a stout white vane that could give you an accurate back-bearing on last night's prevailing wind. The trail was glazed with ice along those stretches where it got sun, and I found the walking less treacherous through the powdery snow to either side of it. I felt out of place laboring through that hard, white landscape and stopped so frequently to rest my aching lungs and pounding heart that I felt more like the hunted than the hunter.

A gusting ridge wind no more cuts the silence of the winter woods than the sound of a stream does. It only makes that silence louder. In the extreme cold of late February, when winter takes hold, that compact, well-formed stillness has a register of its own and makes every sound that breaks against it remarkably distinct—the *tck tck* of juncos that move along the trail with you for short stretches, trees creaking against each other or straining against the failing grain of a lightning scar. Each sound carries and stays. The thin *keer* of a passing hawk can fill a watershed for half a day. Even the bark of a squirrel has strong overtones in winter.

I hadn't thought about wolves all morning until I saw the boar. At first I thought they were bear. I had seen many bear in this watershed in the fall, including a hungry mother and three cubs arrayed in the crown of a northern red oak, gleaning it for its green acorns. But these were boar—coming downslope below me, nonnative animals that do much harm to the plant life of the forest floor. Not quite descendants of de Soto's pigs, but close enough. I stood in front of a tree and watched them through binoculars, a sow and two young of the year foraging through the hardest part of a hard winter. Wildlife watching is destroyed by imposing expectations, but the scene looked like something I had read about in David Mech and Adolph Murie and seen in the black-and-white photographs in their books—prey trailing through heavy snow in wolf country. Wolves should appear, fanned out like hunters, in the next frame.

I watched hard but could not make wolves appear. I would have had two quarter off the far slope and charge the pigs toward the thick laurel at the foot of the ridge I stood on and had another wolf or two waiting there. This was perhaps to think like a man, but men probably had learned such tactics long ago from watching wolves or studying their tracks in snow. These things form circles. All the stealthy, weaving moves in sports and war derived, ultimately, from hunting, and one of the least fanciful notions of Cherokee mythology was that men and wolves once hunted together.

But there was no hunt. In ten minutes the boar were below me out of sight, and, for all I know, if wolves were following them, it was my presence that had put them off. But the idea of wolves trailed along behind the boar. That empty, snow-filled cove looked as promising as a forest in northern Minnesota or Ontario, and once again I was glad that there were wolves in Tennessee.

A half mile farther on, the trail curved south as the ridge narrowed. A long view opened up to the north where I could see the fringe of ridge-top hardwoods on the summit—earth and sky filtered through a reciprocal image. *Gadalu'tsi.* The word *summit* always seems to overstate the case in these mountains. But from a distance the southern Appalachians define one of North America's important horizons. You can, I have read, see them from the moon. We would be lost here in the East without them. When you walk into these mountains, you lose that long view of them until you reencounter the horizon underfoot as a coign of vantage of modest height but with considerable depth of field.

A dark, white-tailed buck with a large, oddly canted rack clattered out of its bed as I approached the trail crossing on the crest of Gregory Ridge. Snow flew from the animal's flanks as it disappeared down the North Carolina side of the mountains. The wildest animal spirits cling to this summit in winter. Despite the relative comforts of the lower slopes, it is not unusual to move deer or flush iconoclastic grouse along high country trails in the worst weather. Something attaches a few individuals of almost every resident species to these extremes as securely as the stunted, wind-torn yellow birch and beech and wizened chestnut oaks. Some of these trees have grown so slowly in this harsh environment that you can get your two hands around centuries of growth, their wood tightly wound in the thinnest of annular rings, barest laminations of their years here.

A half-mile west you come to this large grass bald. There is maybe a foot of snow in the woods and piled into the windward side of the heaths that fringe the open crest—the blueberries and flame azaleas that have died back for the season. But parts of the bald are swept clear down to its tan grasses, and much of it is glazed with just a thin crust of frozen snow. Some bedrock is exposed near the center, folded skyward at some impossible angle and pointing southeast, toward Africa. A few blasted yellow birch fidget in the icy wind that stings what little skin is left exposed by my balaclava. This is as wild a place as I can get to, wolfish and unforgiving, beautiful and troubling as an inheritance from a theft.

The first European known to visit the Cherokee after the sixteenth-century incursions of the Spanish had been informed before he started out that the tribe "lived beyond the mountains in a land of great waves." John Lederer, an adventurous but literal-minded German who scribbled a journal in Latin as he crossed the Blue Ridge, expected to find the tribe living on the shores of an inland sea.

In the language of the picturesque, we frequently encounter waves of mountains as well as, at sea, mountainous waves. But I suspect Lederer's native informants were not being metaphorical. There is much we will never understand about the relation between native American languages and the precontact landscape, because too much has been destroyed in the search for gold that de Soto initiated. Not only did no European ever discover North America, no European was prepared to see it as it once was. The genocide of its people and the erasure of their languages and cultures was the beginning of the end of the land. At stake was both the loss of nature and a tragic rupture between words and things, the loss of a 20,000- or 30,000-year-old poetic—half the earth's art and thought, half its words and gods.

So beyond the great waves of mountains you can see from here—the pretty postcard view that keeps the resorts and gift shops humming—there is a difficult horizon to grasp, to understand. It doesn't surprise me that this has also become the heart of wolf country, that *Canis rufus* slips up here frequently, as I do, to measure what's left of the world. Wolves were, I had read, great travelers at any season, and this was a good place to survey what they were seeing of the world. Before man gave up his brotherhood with the wolf and began exterminating it, that boreal, circumpolar species distributed itself over land as freely as did salmon in the world's once-pristine oceans. Wolves wandered from Alaska to New England, from Ireland to Kamchatka. It is not speaking too broadly to designate half the earth as the proper habitat of the wolf, and although the acclimation pens on Forge Creek and Thunderhead Branch were attached to a half-million acres of national park land, the largest brushstroke of preserved land east of the Mississippi, a red wolf in no special hurry could trot across the widest part of this mountainous egg-shape island in a day or two.

The Tremont male lived by the book and traveled more widely than any of the other wolves that first winter. 357M practiced the classic art of the wolf in a way no wolf had done here in many years, and I admired the animal greatly for its energy and range. Late in January he left the high country around Thunderhead Mountain, into which he often disappeared, followed the original route of the Appalachian Trail west to Gregory Bald, and kept going. He was out of radio contact for four or five days, apparently enjoying the folded terrain that eventually led him down to the Little Tennessee River.

But there was no dancing water down there at the foot of the mountains, no broad riffles chattering on to the Overhill towns, cascading over all those contour lines the Little Tennessee had worked its way through during the last 10,000 years. There was no belly-chilling ford to swim, only a silt-choked lake where a wild river should have been and a two-lane blacktop road that led across the ruined river just downstream of Cheoah Dam, an antique concrete wedge jammed between the steep banks of the Little Tennessee just above where the Cheoah River, also dammed, dribbled into it.

If you love free-flowing rivers, there is nothing but bad karma around all that impounded water—a series of soulless, so-called lakes that are drawn down in winter, revealing their unnatural shorelines. And for the Tremont male, ending up back in the world of roads after all that fine backcountry travel, his canine mind carefully mapping what must have registered as the heart of interesting country, was enough to throw a promising wild animal out of sync.

Ridge-running was the most natural thing in the world for a male wolf to do, as was an exploration down toward the river that seemed to organize the surrounding watersheds. But instead of bolting up into the Joyce Kilmer–Slickrock Wilderness above the Cheoah River or backtracking into the Smoky Mountains, the wolf trotted through the hard-nosed company town of Tapoco and on to a small community at the base of the Yellow Creek Mountains. No one bothered the wolf, but the animal had stalled out, confused and in effect captive again—not a howling, elusive ridge-runner but a minor nuisance to the folks on Meadow Branch Road and a major disappointment to Chris Lucash.

"He was walking down the road when we got there."

And even when Lucash and Crawford chased the wolf for five hours trying to dart it, the experienced animal didn't take advantage of the thousands of acres of escape habitat it knew was all around it. Two months in the backcountry had not undone its captivity. The wolf was lost in a landscape that was itself largely lost, and, in a sense, the animal wanted or needed to be brought in, its own wild nature divided against itself along the same lines as the land around it. The struggling wildness of wolves was coming up against vanishing wildness of the land. A wolf walking through a forest, like a man walking through a forest now, was almost always heading back toward the man-made world. There was no wild interior, no longer a center in nature to nurture the old habits and talents.

"He just wouldn't leave that little area, which was what really disturbed me. With people watching, dogs barking, vehicles coming and going. I couldn't believe he had gotten that far—he obviously knew what he was doing on his own in the woods—and then just crapped out around that group of houses back there and wouldn't leave. A good wild animal doesn't face all that commotion and just ignore it, stay there."

Lucash and Crawford spent the night in the truck and caught the wolf the next morning. They put it back in the Tremont pen for a week to settle it down and then released it again, near the favorite haunt of the Tremont female, which would soon be in estrous, in the hopes that the male would give up travel for mating.

That first winter the Tremont male discovered what everyone discovers who walks in nature now—that you can't go far. It's the details along the way that count now. European sailing ships bumping into North America was, Thoreau noted, the easy part of the so-called discovery. The hard part was to see and understand what was at your feet.

So note the sudden appearance of a pair of ravens overhead as you leave the bald. Stop to watch their otherworldly play until they disappear. Note that the whorled leaves of Catawba rhododendron, which hung limp in December and curled against the desiccating cold in January, are now tented with snow. Note the beauty of beech trees in winter and remember that beech bark was the first paper and that *beech* and *book* are cognate. Scour the snow for the signs written there—long bounds of rabbits, distinct steps of squirrels, wing tips of birds. Finally be rewarded with a line of fox paw prints frozen into an icy stretch of trail blown free of snow like a museum exhibit of the straight track of a perfect walker, a talent shared by foxes and wolves but denied to dogs, another natural sign that seems a transcendental image, a strong signifier of wild design and character.

The next evening, back in my snug camper remembering these fox tracks perfectly fossilized for the season in ice on the trail between Gregory and Parsons Bald, I will be reminded by Olaus Murie's fine guide book on animal signs of Thoreau's transcendental observation of a fox track he discovered on Walden Pond one January: "Here," Thoreau wrote, "was one expression of the divine mind this morning."

Be that as it may, some of us are saved by what we see. Searching for wolves in winter, we may well find that fox tracks are enough to lead us on.

There was a designated campsite on a broad saddle of woods at the next trail crossing where I had intended to stay, but that overcast sky was descending quickly and pushing thick wet flakes from the south. I knew what the beginning of a blizzard looked like and that in an hour I would be blinded and buried. I used the time to lose as much altitude as I could down the trail to Panther Gap and made the head of Panther Creek, shedding a thousand feet. The snow picked up, but I was out of the brunt of it and below the whiteout on the summit. Bending the backcountry rules, I made camp alongside the trail, pitching the tiny one-man tent up against some small hemlocks, which doubled as a windbreak and an extra fly. I

the sons of Wind

slept on and off through the windy silence of the storm, glad to be out in it and glad to be in the lee of it. Awake and asleep, I listened to the wind, which I knew was important here.

According to the Yuchi, neighbors of the Cherokee, Wind had four sons, restless young men whose greatest desire was to travel. "Let us go and look at the earth," they declared. One by one the sons of Wind left their father and did not return. "None of them," we are told, "came back."

Wind, which originally had come out of the East, made complex preparations and then traveled west in search of them. He brought a terrapin, a bullfrog, and a joint snake for magic. Across a creek Wind encountered Iron Man, an unnatural being whom he instantly knew had killed his sons. Wind's medicine was stronger than Iron Man's evil, and Wind killed him with smoke from a pipe he fashioned out of his odd kit of creatures.

The wife of Iron Man revealed that the sons of Wind were in a dead tree along the creek bank. With Iron Man's ax, Wind cut the tree down and threw it into the water. His sons emerged, blackened and changed: "They told him they were not under his control any longer."

Wind acknowledged their independence and declared that he would make something different out of each of them. The first spoke too quickly and was passed over. The second declared that he would be a wolf, and Wind sent him into the woods. The third said he would be a crow and the fourth that he would be a raven. Wind sent them into the forest. Only the first son was left.

"I'll be a dog." And so Wind sent him to stay with the wolf, presumably to learn something about the resources of wildness, as the crow, also a creature of the settlements, would learn from the raven.

The principal polarity of the quadripartite universe seems to be established in this story in a way so compatible with Cherokee thought I wonder if they did not share this myth with the Yuchi: four beings—wolf and dog, raven and crow—sharing two versions of the same nature—one wild, one tame—and descended from wind, a primal force. That in this story Being chose first to be a wolf does not surprise me. Nor the fact that the wolf was the son of the wind that howled around me that night up on the head of Panther Creek.

The next morning it must have been near noon before I shook myself out of the tent. I remember waking up at dawn and then falling back into a second sleep. The wind had died down and a bright blue dome had fit itself over the world. Before I broke camp and took on the pleasure of breaking trail, I tore the cardboard back off one of my notebooks and fashioned side shields for my sunglasses.

The head of Panther Creek was frozen and snowbound, held in thrall, promising in its way as spring itself. The beautiful blank of the trail looped away from the creek for a mile or so, and by the time they met again there was a sunken crease of rocky ice water and a sound so soft you couldn't hear it unless you looked hard at the motion that caused it. The play of light off the trickling water, whose barely mobile molecules seemed to click against one another, brought the sound as much to my eye as to my ear. And then I saw them.

Out of the corner of my eye, I saw smoke drift across the stream forty or fifty yards below me. The smoke resolved into three wolves. The trailing wolf stopped to drink at the stream. The other two kept on in a single track. The third wolf pushed along behind them off to one side. Then they were gone, and I stood watching the empty stage of the woods expecting to see something more.

Had I seen them a century ago, or two or three, I would not have had much of a description to offer. It's almost as if you just see the word—*wolves*—and can't construct a sentence that adds very much to the fact of their presence. Just the noun in the woods. When the wolves are gone, details begin to surface from your subconscious without clearly having been part of the scene, and the truth about what you saw becomes as elusive as what you saw and you wonder how you will ever catch up, as a man and as a writer, to these rare receding things:

One winter I saw three wolves in the woods, red wolves. This was in Tennessee. They crossed a stream, walking briskly, heads down. Not hunting. The woods were filled with snow. It looked like Canada. The trailing wolf stopped to drink. The others kept on. Perhaps one of them stopped and turned its head. They were traveling together, quartering downslope, the second wolf walking in the track of the lead animal that plowed snow with its chest in the deep places, its fur bristling with powder, or so I imagine. It was quiet, except for the slightest sound of running water at my feet, a sound mimicked by a nearly silent breeze in my face. The wolves were upwind of me. Perhaps the new snow and the bright hard day had made them careless. They never knew I was there. It looked odd. I wanted to follow them. At first I had thought they were smoke. . . .

I had waited and worked a long time to see them this way, walked far, in circles, to see them, and like the flush of a grouse the event was over in *wild*

the time it took to understand that it was happening. *One winter I saw three wolves in the backcountry, red wolves in Tennessee. . . .*

The study of any wild animal teaches us only that it is not wild and introduces us to another order of things.

If you track the English word *wild* back 1,200 years, you end up where you started. From its earliest recorded uses in eighth-century Old English, *wilde* meant essentially what it means today, an animal or plant in a natural condition as opposed to one that had been tamed or cultivated. The word sprang from an old duality. For the Cherokee, whose word for wild doesn't seem to have the psychological or philosophical overtones of the English word, that duality hearkens back to *Kana'ti*'s cave, where wildness was contained before history began.

In the Western mind, the evolution of the word through Teutonic and Scandinavian languages is obscure. The *Oxford English Dictionary* admits that "the problem of the ulterior relations of this word is complicated by uncertainty as to its primary meaning." It has associations with bewilderment and confusion, with giddiness and going astray, which suggests that the current ambiguity in the idea of wildness was there from the start. What the *OED* calls the ulterior relations of the word are lost in the firelit strangeness of cave paintings and myths. If a wild animal is an animal in its natural state, in what sense is it bewildered or confused, giddy or astray? Or are those connotations traces of the effects of the wildness of animals— the sheer weight of all that intimidating otherness beyond the cave mouth—on the human mind? Or are they a warning of how the elusiveness of wild game leads the hunter on until he is forced to lose himself— like Faulkner's Isaac McCaslin in *The Bear*—to find himself alone on the other side, emboldened and humbled with the joy and guilt of the hunter?

These ambiguities were carried along in the extension of *wilde* to *wildernesse* by the end of the twelfth century. Both words seem to reach back to the Teutonic word for forest, which in the European tradition was early on, perhaps always, an uncanny setting, simultaneously foreign and familiar, easily magical and dreamlike, dangerous and instructive. Today, when true forests and truly wild animals are rare, the two words circle some primary enigma within which is hidden the Möbius logic of man's contradictory, destructive relation to the nature that gave him being.

The more psychologically and socially complex an animal is, the more

wolf pups

captive breeding and rearing may disrupt its original nature, undo that fundamental antithesis between the wild and the tame, an antithesis that Cherokee thought strongly associated with the wolf. In wolves—perhaps the most intelligent, social, and adaptable animals on earth—the effects of captivity are likely to be profound and what we call wildness really only their essential civility. The successful readaptation of an apex predator to a wild condition is the most difficult task in wildlife biology—a scientific attempt to undo history—and depends largely on the animals themselves reestablishing the inherent orderliness of their lives within existing conditions. When they have done that, we may think of them again as wild, but the ambiguity built into the words we use to think about these things is unresolved.

Tsiya'hi. Late May. Back where I started.

Through binoculars I've just watched one of the Cades Cove adults, which carried a limp woodchuck by the neck, disappear into a dark crack in the base of a limestone cliff that overlooks a woody bend of Abrams Creek. There is a cave in the cliff that black bear sometimes use for a den, a cool, clean place that leads to a dark labyrinth where rare bats roost, a magic opening in the earth not unlike *Kana'ti*'s cave. The bats emerge in the evening to compete with swallows and meadowlarks for the swarm of caddis flies that hatch from the stream. This year there is also a litter of red wolf pups in the cave—six-week-old critters, rare as gold. A bit of wild order has been restored and the world here is a bit more civilized, the woodlots and pastures adjacent to the cave taut with the keenness of new wolves. A few miles away, reinforcing this assertion of wildness, three red wolf pups sleep and tussle by turns in the leaves under a rock ledge, wild offspring of the Tremont wolves.

The wolves got through winter playing variations on the themes established during the fall, each family displaying its own peculiar strengths and weaknesses as it tried to readapt its talents to what remained of the land.

The restless, disoriented Tremont young struggled with their freedom, traveling alone, stitching a course in and out of the park boundary, flirting with the edge and getting too familiar with people, roads, and houses. They learned to be less visible than they had been, but they were still stuck, hung up halfway between being nuisances and being wild animals. Lucash and Crawford retrieved them, penned them up, and then let them go again by turns, less hopeful each time about their eventual fate.

The Tremont adults ran the backcountry in high style, sometimes together but mostly alone. The Tremont female, although she roamed the main ridge at least as far as Gregory Bald and sometimes got out of radio range in the backcountry, never left the park. Of all the Tremont wolves, she seemed to have the best sense of what the limits of wolf country were. She was the most elusive of them, perhaps because her maternal responsibilities made her more circumspect. During her travel, she must have been inventorying possible den sites, the final choice of which was a complex calculation that balanced safety—a feature of the interior—with availability of food—a product of the edge.

As 337F approached going into estrous, her peregrinations eventually spiraled down to an area that looked something like a home range with a variety of possible den sites. And so when Lucash rereleased the Tremont male at the end of the first week of February, after his journey across the Little Tennessee River to the Yellow Creek Mountains, he trucked him to the inconspicuous hollow she seemed to have chosen and opened the box there, an attempt to get the pair together during her two weeks in heat. The radio-tracking data showed that they stayed together for twelve days, but Lucash wasn't sure that these far-traveling wolves had mated.

After they split up, the female took the high road to the summit and the male explored down Abrams Creek. Two weeks later they had switched places—the female had come back down to the lowlands and the male was up on Gregory Bald. Something sent 357M west along the summit again. Perhaps he was intrigued by the scent markings he had made there, probably in late January. Perhaps the inviting space and the dramatic fall of the landscape down to the big river just led him on. But he followed his nose or his head or his heart back down to the Little Tennessee River at Deals Gap, where he once again became confused. Lucash found him at Cheoah Dam, the wolf and the river jammed up at the same point, not far from where he had picked him up in late January. Needless to say, the return of the Tremont male to the Tapoco area was a disappointment. Like the juveniles, the big wolf, too, was reaching his limits. By the end of the first week of March, 357M was back in the Tremont pen, as was his mate, who needed a new collar.

This temporary incarceration of the Tremont adults had its benefits. While he had 357M in captivity, Lucash treated infected injuries on his legs. He also had University of Tennessee veterinarian Dr. Linda Munsen check 337F, and she was able to confirm that the Tremont female was pregnant. The two wolves had to wait out a terrible March blizzard in the pen and were released together in April, near where the female had been thought to be scouting dens.

Because of the regularity of their movements, Lucash was confident that the Cades Cove wolves had mated. The family shifted the center of its home range from time to time during the winter, but its patterns of individual and group behavior were stable. The group had well-established resting areas and rendezvous sites and seemed to practice a vigilant opportunism in the cove.

Although less adventurous than the Tremont animals, the Cades Cove family also carried on the work of wolves, which could be pitiless. In late January, five of the Cades Cove wolves ganged up on an emaciated, orphaned black bear cub that, because of the poor mast, had not put on enough fat to hibernate. Some hikers had accidentally flushed the desperate animal out of its hiding place into a pasture alongside Abrams Creek. Wolves normally would not bother a healthy adult bear, but the wolves that happened to be right there quickly surrounded the doomed cub so that it could not tree. One photo of the attack—it can hardly be called a hunt—shows the bear sitting on its haunches waiting to die. Three wolves approach it, tails down, from in front while a fourth wolf approaches, tail up, from behind in what looks like a practiced, well-coordinated end game.

The voraciousness of wolves is nothing more than their natural hunger. Every creature shares it to some degree, man included. For the most part the wolves stuck to legitimate prey. Since their release, they showed remarkably little interest in the cattle grazed in the cove. But they were not above devouring a sick calf that had laid down to die in a field, and they were not above tearing into the animal while it was still alive. What was left of the body was still warm when Lucash found it. He seemed to be impressed with the clinical details of the kill.

"They cleaned it out from the rib cage on down—back legs eaten to bare bone, entrails eaten, most of the meat. An ear was gone and there was a hole in its head, but there were no wounds on the face or nose, no bite marks on the head or neck except for that one missing ear and the hole chewed. I don't think the wolves brought it down and I don't think they would have lit into it if it hadn't been laying there half dead. But they probably killed it before it died from whatever had gotten into it."

Fish and Wildlife paid the market value of a full-grown cow for the lost calf out of its depredation fund and later paid for another calf the wolves took out of an unsecured corral. Lucash knew all along that calving season was going to be a challenge to the wolf program, especially in Cades Cove, where the wolves were deliberately dumped into the middle of a stock-raising operation the Park Service leased to a private rancher. That challenge was exacerbated by a blizzard in mid-March that laid more than two feet of snow in the cove, pinning the wolves in a woodlot about 300 yards from the calving barns. The deep snow made it hard even for wolves to get around. They found tractor tracks convenient to walk in, and of course the ruts led straight to the calving barns.

Five calves were lost to the extreme cold in the aftermath of that storm, and two were either killed or dragged away dead by wolves. Lucash and Crawford found unmistakable wolf tracks and drag marks among the afterbirth and offal at the site. The mothers were still bawling when the men got there. They compensated the stock owner for them and for another calf that disappeared shortly thereafter. The storm clearly had funneled the wolves into the fast food represented by the calves, which were vulnerable, if left unprotected, even in good weather. Part of the legal responsibility of the wolf restoration was to minimize these losses and to make compensation when they occurred. Fish and Wildlife got good marks on both counts, although undoubtedly much public controversy would have arisen had the losses occurred on private land.

By the time a difficult winter melted into spring, Lucash and Crawford were watching both pregnant females circle their final choices for den sites until each of them suddenly stopped moving, disappeared, and whelped.

At the beginning of April the Cades Cove female began fidgeting among a woodlot, a ridge, and an unused hay barn, an arrangement that apparently suited the demanding mother-to-be. The vantage of the ridge seemed important to her, as did the cover of the woodlot. The barn, an unused man-thing, had become a center. The male and the juveniles frequented the area, but they did not enter the barn. This was her show. By the middle of the month she could be seen pulling fur from her belly, and she spent more time in the barn than out of it. Finally, when her time came, she retreated into it altogether.

Wolves show great creativity in their denning. The choice of a den site, along with the choice of a mate, is the most important decision a wolf makes. The unused barn was not visible from the loop road, but the loop road was visible from the ridge. The woodlot and adjacent pasture were relatively undisturbed, although the fine spring weather was bringing more visitors to Cades Cove. The barn was full of hay three and four bales high and was catacombed with tunnels between bales that had been modified by rodents and raccoons and skunks. The presence of a wolf no doubt cleared the barn of its resident rodent population pretty quickly. 378F obviously felt comfortable there, chose or fashioned a tunnel that had a right-angle bend at one end—a classic defensive feature of the tunnel den—and hollowed out a two- by three-foot whelping place at the dead end.

When they missed her for a day or two, Fish and Wildlife left the pregnant wolf alone and waited. She disappeared on a Sunday and was not seen again until Thursday. The following Wednesday morning, Lucash went into the barn while the female was out hunting. She had done her work well. He crawled around for hours—the sunken bales of hay were all tunnel—but could not find the Minotaur.

After she returned to the barn, they used a hand-held antenna to fix exactly where she was. The next morning Lucash went in again. She had made a tunnel along one barn wall, fifteen inches square, one Lucash had rejected the day before as unsuitable. He crawled on his hands and knees for eight feet where the tunnel made a right-angle turn and continued another six feet to the four healthy pups. He estimates they were seven or eight days old when he saw them on April 28, 1993. None of the pups had opened its eyes yet—wildness still literally in the dark. Their world was all musty hay and wolf scent, mother warmth interrupted now, strangely, by man-scent stronger than the faded man-things in the barn. The pups squirmed silently as Lucash gave them an oral dewormer.

The next day Lucash, Barron Crawford, and Gary Henry from the Asheville office used the hand-held tracking equipment to find the Tremont den, a rock ledge at the head of a densely vegetated hollow where they found three healthy pups squirming out of sight under a nest of dried leaves while their parents stood helplessly off to the side. The male and two females were a few days older than their Cades Cove cousins. Two of them were trying to open their eyes.

Seven months into the release, there were fifteen red wolves at large, including seven wild-born. The Cades Cove wolves represented an intact red wolf family with three generations. The Tremont juveniles were now penned up for good, because they were a distraction and probably would be bad influences, but the remaining Tremont family was a natural nuclear unit of parents and wild-born offspring. Both females moved their litters a week or so after whelping, normal precautionary behavior. The Cades Cove pups were moved to the cave on Abrams Creek, which I now had the luxury of watching.

Evening light in spring here is, in and of itself, enough to watch. The essential balance of land and sky is not as deeply drawn as in autumn, but the open clarity of spring air has its advantages. The slopes are pale green, except for gray rivers of late-leafing oaks in the higher elevations and, of course, the dark swaths of hemlocks, which never change but which never look the same because of the kaleidoscoping life around them. The wood-lots were greening, and the pasture grasses were belly high to a wolf.

Not far from the wolf den, on a hill above it, devil's urn and Solomon seal contend for sunlight at the door of the Primitive Baptist Church, a dusty, hollow box of a building and an uninviting sanctuary compared to its spacious, airy surroundings. In back of the church, on a hill overlooking the Cades Cove wolf den, you will find the graves of John Oliver and his wife, Lurena Oliver, and their daughter, Mary Oliver, among others, and a memorial to the "first settlers."

The hunting wolves must flit from time to time through the woodlots beyond the iron cemetery fence. They must know the austere shape of the church with its squat bell tower, a huge black bulk that looms in the woods at night. Their howls must reach the cemetery, if not the ears of the dead, long gone.

I heard that howling last night from the campground at Cades Cove, sometime deep in the night—a peaceful, reassuring sound. A form of mu-sic, I think, that fits the world. And last evening, just after dark, I listened to a family camped a few spots over softly singing what I knew even from a distance were hymns. I did not know the hymns they sang or hear any words, but I knew they were singing to their god by the cadence and devo-tion in their voices. When I crossed paths with the father of this family near the water spigot the next morning, he said he hoped they had not disturbed me. Of course they hadn't, no more than had the wolves.

Beyond the woodlots, white-tailed deer graze in pastures that can easily hide a crouching wolf, but the only wolf I've seen seems to be staking out woodchuck burrows. The bending grasses show the evening breeze. Two deer raise up on hind legs and flail at each other. Crows blow by, trading undulations, looking fine in flight. They are followed by a thick bank of clouds that brings a premature dusk to the cove. The tangled fallen timber at the edge of woodlots looks ominous in the failing light, and I watch closely any deer that wanders near such an edge. There is no movement in or out of the den, and the wolves within are no more a center than the screech owl whinnying from downstream or the stream that rushes past itself indifferently polishing the roots of bankside trees.

Beyond the details of wolf management and wolf watching, it's hard to say what it means to have wild-born wolves in this place again. There are those of us who love all the forms of life that come to us, like the structure of our own cells and bodies, from out of the deep past, and those for whom such things have no meaning. The rancher's life is not made easier by the presence of wolves, but where is it written that the rancher's needs—or the timberman's or the real estate developer's—are to be the measure of all things? And those who are made uncomfortable by the darker side of nature—who like to believe that consumer culture has progressed beyond the primordial tug of life and death—may be made uneasy by the idea and practice of wolves. But perhaps that squeamishness should not be an excuse to erase the past as nature construed it.

Love of wolves and forests and wild rivers doesn't carry debate very far. In the end, as Aldo Leopold suggested, the earth itself will judge—some of us love it first and foremost, some of us love other things more. Frankly, I'd rather live in a culture that patterned itself after the virtues of the wolf than one that had become too devoted to the virtues of the cow, totem of passive consumption and the witless dullness of life tamed. I'm not sure what ratifies man's behavior—my own included—but time long ago ratified the character of wolves, and this spring nothing is so sacred in these mountains, where seven is the most sacred number, as the seven red wolf pups that have just come into a world of daunting contradictions.

The order of the modern carnivore goes back at least to the upper Eocene, when those telltale teeth appeared—canines and carnassials—in the jaws of miacids, martenlike creatures that persisted for an epoch before the true terrestrial carnivores emerged in the Oligocene. The order divided early, over a difference in the structure of a bone in the middle ear the story goes, into two groups, the Arctoridae and the Canoidae, which radiated quickly. The subsequent genera and species distributed themselves widely, filling the world with hunting and shaping the world they filled. The Arctoridae gave us civets, mongooses, hyenas, and cats. The Canoidae expressed themselves as otters, badgers, skunks, weasels, raccoons, bears, foxes, and wolves—the great clans that came down to us from the Cenozoic.

Wolves took the best gifts from their half of the order—large brains that give them extraordinary social intelligence and communication skills and led them toward monogamy and altruism, stereoscopic vision, broad-band hearing and a great nose, the bone structure and musculature of a cursorial hunter, down to their pliant, almost dainty digitigrade feet as well as the dentition and digestive tract of a feast-or-famine meat eater and

the cardiovascular system of a fell runner. You don't have to anthropomorphize to understand that wolves have complex emotions and a great attachment to the things of this earth. It is no wonder man early on conjured
the dog from the wolf and brought those skills, and such a presence,
within the circle of his firelight.

Wolves take us back in time, enlarging our sense of space. Follow the
trails of evolutionary divergence, that fabulous map of the kinship of
things, or the trails of myth, the map of what men remember from the
oldest times, and this busy, overcrowded world suddenly will seem so vast
and unused you will feel the unexplored space it used to lay before the
mind. Stare too long into a backcountry campfire and the ordinary will
begin to seem very strange—that the wind howls like a wolf, for instance—
and the strange will seem ordinary—that ravens follow wolves—and fact
will become as luminous as fiction and the ordinary life of things will glow
like myth until the flames die down.

Cades Cove is getting busy with traffic again, a tight caravan of cars
and motor homes circling about looking for something. Soon the beauty
and significance of this place will disappear for the summer under the
crushing, noisy weight of this attention. But this past winter, *Tsiya'hi* was
larger than it had been for a long, long time.

Thoreau has written, and we often repeat, that "in Wildness is the preservation of the World." That thought, it's worth remembering, brought
wolves to his mind: "The story of Romulus and Remus being suckled by a
wolf is not a meaningless fable. The founders of every state which has risen
to eminence have drawn their nourishment and vigor from a similar wild
source. It was because the children of the Empire were not suckled by the
wolf that they were conquered and displaced by the children of the northern forests who were."

Art and truth run together in Thoreau's prose, but not always side by
side. More down to earth than Emerson, Thoreau was not above letting
the sound of a sentence get ahead of its sense. In North America, certainly—and here in this place—those who held wolves sacred were finally
overcome by those who would destroy any form of life that interfered with
their profit, comfort, or convenience.

Thoreau never quite finished his larger thought on wildness, which has
a difficult, elusive truth in it despite the uncharacteristically jingoistic note
of his analogy. The idea slipped away between the trees into the deepest
part of the woods as American history devoured North America. We have
been trying to track it through a diminishing landscape ever since. Now,

with no deep woods left, there is this nostalgia for the old bright things—wolf and raven, eagle and rattlesnake, forested mountain and mountain stream.

Perhaps wildness was what Emily Dickinson suggested, what we know about nature—feel in our bones—but have not art to say, a sense of the uncanny otherness that set us on our way, which we destroyed beyond repair, and that now furtively watches our belated solicitousness in great confusion. Why *would* a modern culture set wolves on itself, as if it now needed them, of all things—"the wildness whose glance no civilization can endure"—as if it wanted to backtrack to see something it had missed? Something it had not had art or science or spirituality enough to name properly at the first encounter—*Canis wa'ya wa'ya*. As if it wanted to be afraid in the woods again and thereby feel less lonely. As if it missed the old uninterpretable sounds with sky in them, the strange, ancient words with dirt still clinging to their roots.

II

THE CIRCULAR RIVER

*There is another world under this, and it is like ours
in everything—animals, plants, and people—save
that the seasons are different. The streams that come
down from the mountains are the trails by which we
reach this underworld, and the springs at their heads
are the doorways by which we enter it. . . .*

—James Mooney, "Myths of the Cherokee"

Windows

The roots of things are hard to trace, so much is hidden now. It's autumn again. I'm on the great Cherokee River, looking for the Overhill towns.

Linguists were struck early on by the complexity of Cherokee, a polysynthetic language in which words are constructed to convey an intended assertion as well as its context and a host of connotations about the speaker, the action, and the object of the action. In 1852 Hans Gabelentz, a German philologist, noted not only the "great formative ability" of the language but also that it embodied a distinction between nouns "such as express living beings, and such as express lifeless things." A manuscript fragment from the time of the removal makes a similar observation: "It should be observed, that in the Cherokee and other North American languages the Nouns range themselves under two very general classes, one of which comprehends *animated* beings, and the other *inanimate* objects; and the inflections of the nouns and verbs are all made with reference to this fundamental distinction."

Other early students of North American languages noticed this peculiarity and its effect on translating indigenous ideas: "there are many words which it is difficult and sometimes even impossible to render by terms, which convey precisely the same general idea; the Indians being so very nice in their discriminations, and having words adapted to every shade which they wish to distinguish. They are particularly attentive to distinguishing between what is *animate* and what is *inanimate*. . . . The Indians . . . vary their expressions, when speaking of a thing that has life and of one that has not."

The deep structure of Native American languages, including Cherokee, embodied conventions of worldviews lost to the contact and its aftermath. Gabelentz notes many such embedded distinctions in Cherokee, the heart of which was its verbs, any one of which might take on 20,000 forms: "The American languages display the greatest abundance of forms and relations in the verb. This is also the case with Cherokee. Number and person, both in connection with the subject and the object, is indicated through verb forms, quite apart from mood and tense; they express whether the object is animate or inanimate, whether the person spoken of is present or absent, in dual and plural, whether the action of the verb touches on the different objects jointly, or on each separately."

All languages divide the world into words, intuitively grouping them into a finite number of categories that make the rules of sentence formation manageable. Over time, the original taxonomy becomes submerged, parent rock for all the things that need to be said. But traces remain, enriched and confused by the use of the words over time in cultural contexts that add intangible overtones to the tangible distinctions that set the language on its way. What seems to be abstract mirrors what once seemed to be concrete, and a living language thrives between this vibrant, reciprocal reflection. After centuries, what persists from the original classification is the unstated resonance of words and things.

Contemporary linguists identify five categories that determine the forms certain Cherokee verbs take, a classificatory system not found in any other Iroquoian language. More highly articulated classificatory schemes are found in the Athapaskan languages Chipewyan, Navaho, and Hupa as well as in the Penutian Takelma and Klamath. The Muskogean Creek language has a fainter trace of classificatory polarity than Cherokee and may have borrowed from it.

The five categories in Cherokee, each loosely attached to a physical feature, are thought to be vestiges of an earlier stage in the language, one dominated by the names of things. Cumbersome as it may seem, the system invites the speaker to carefully consider the nature of every action, how one thing might be treated with respect to another, as if kinship, philosophically speaking, extended beyond the idea of the clan. So, for example, the form of the verb *to hold* you would use to say that you held an object would depend on the nature of the object—whether it was animate, flexible, long and rigid, liquid, or round, the last a catch-all for anything not assigned to one of the other categories.

The rationale for what remains of the old taxonomy ranges from the obvious to the inscrutable. For example, the system insists on the difference between planting a seed and planting a live plant—a distinction any gardener would appreciate—and extends the category of "long and rigid" from a fishhook to a canoe. A transformed object—a stave of wood fashioned into a bow—may stay in the same category. Historically recent additions to Cherokee culture find their way into the system with varying degrees of whimsy and wisdom—hammers are round, books flexible.

Since the five surviving categories of verb formation are neither all inclusive as a group nor mutually exclusive taken individually, there is much metaphorical displacement at work in a system originally rooted in the literal. Counterintuitive placements may be the most revealing. For example, live plants and animals are classified as animate, but dead animals become—grammatically—flexible, which is also the category for fallen leaves, no matter that they are dry and brittle. Applied to animals and leaves, the category "flexible" takes on an extended sense, suggesting longer thoughts about the reincarnation of animal spirits and the regenerative power of dead leaves, both important concepts in Cherokee thought. Dead animals and leaves are flexible because they are part of cycles. Time, for the Cherokee, often solves apparent contradictions.

But not all contradictions can be solved. These curious vestiges of the original relations between words and things in Cherokee not only make literal distinctions and metaphorical connections, they also identify anomalies and adumbrate taboos. One such taboo was that, except to mark the death of a kinsman, water and fire are not to be mixed together. This taboo is so old and so deeply rooted in the Cherokee mind that, despite the great range and flexibility of their language, there is no grammatical form for combining water and fire. What should not be done cannot be said. In some cultures, some things are inconceivable.

I'm at an east-facing bend of a westerly flowing river, a topographically sacred place in Cherokee theory, caught between an anomaly upstream and a broken taboo that extends a thousand miles downstream through the old Cherokee country.

Upstream there is a lake where a river should be. Not a lake, really, but a reservoir drawn down this time of year for flood control over the winter and spring. The draw down reveals the artificiality of the arrangement—a hundred feet of caked earth exposed between the summer shoreline and the autumn surface of the water, creek bank vegetation left high and dry, false islands turned back into peninsulas, and ugly, barren troughs hundreds of yards wide dwarfing the mouths of the big rivers that stall in muddy channels—ignominious end of the Tuckasegee and Nantahala rivers.

When they take the postcard photos of Fontana Lake, they make sure it has water in it, but half the year it's an ugly, absurd scar on the land, another hideous improvement of what was once one of the most beautiful river valleys in the world, the valley of the Little Tennessee River, by all the old accounts an unimprovable part of the earth.

There's a dam underfoot, of course, a technological wonder of so many cubic feet of concrete and megawatts of electricity according to the beamish promotion doled out at the Tennessee Valley Authority's visitor center, a weird outpost caught in some hydraulic from the Eisenhower administration where you can marvel at a map of ruined rivers that stretch from the Blue Ridge to the Mississippi and purchase Appalachian knickknacks imported from sweatshops on the Pacific rim.

For a dollar you can ride a glass elevator down to the base of the dam and stay ten minutes where there's nothing to do except listen to the hum of the cased turbines and watch a foamy green blast of water shoot out the concrete spillway. The big glass windows are as inviting as a wide-screen television, but people, who seem enormously pleased in some undefined way with what they find here, get bored quickly and start milling around the elevator before it is time to leave.

Fontana Dam was built during World War II and so is draped with a significance that is hard to demystify. In the visitor center there are stunning black-and-white photographs of the dam's impressive construction, showing hard-hatted men and women marching to work or eating in enormous mess halls, crowds of iconic Depression-pinched faces, including more than a few chiseled Cherokee, each face glad to be pulling steady hours at good pay helping win a distant war by working in what were then the remote mountains of western North Carolina. They worked around the clock at Fontana from 1939 to 1942, patriotic music blaring out of speakers nested all over the gargantuan scaffolding, the graveyard shift moving in the high-contrast glare of floodlights that give the site the look of a NASA launch pad. In some photos you can catch a glimpse of the

death of Tremont wolves

broken river running through a diversion channel in the background. Not many people work at Fontana now.

Downstream from this dam three long, thin reservoirs mask the river that wore its way through these hard mountains, a river intent on flowing west. Downstream, three more dams are wedged between the mountains, and so Lake Cheoah, Calderwood Lake, and Chilhowee Lake impound that inclination. And below Chilhowee Lake, sixty river miles from here, is the abomination of the Tellico Dam, which drowned the council fires of the Overhill towns, violating that ancient grammar, injuring spirit here as well as land.

A year after the first red wolf release, I took a brief look at Fontana Lake and then descended what was left of the Cherokee River from the head of Lake Cheoah to Tellico—a moody float, all things considered.

The Tremont male was dead. In the middle of the second week of October 1993, a year and three days after the Cades Cove release, Lucash and Crawford tracked 357M's uncharacteristically stationary signal to a creek not far from the rock shelter den the wolves had used that first spring. The big wolf apparently died hard, aspirating mud while two cups of ethylene glycol crystallized in his kidneys. An autopsy was performed and a Fish and Wildlife investigator looked into the death, which for lack of any hard evidence to the contrary was ruled an accidental poisoning, most likely from antifreeze spilled from a car at one of the roadside pullouts.

This all but finished off the original Tremont group. The Tremont female had died back in June, from injuries sustained in a fight with one or more of the Cades Cove wolves. She had been found near the border between the eastern edge of the well-defined home range of the Cades Cove wolves and the straggling domain of the disorganized Tremont animals, which had edged up to the game-rich pastures the Cades Cove wolves generally considered their own. Both the Tremont female and her mate had been hunting in Cades Cove during the spring, undoubtedly feeling the pressure of providing for the three pups born in April.

Although regrettable, at least the death of the Tremont female could be attributed to natural causes. Conflict between wolves, including fatal combat, was not unknown, and, judging from what was happening at Alligator River, which had five more wolf years on the books than the Smoky Mountain program, the red wolf was extraordinarily territorial. So here was a nudge of natural selection, albeit a costly one. If there was going to be a permanent family of red wolves in Cades Cove, it was going to mark its territory in stronger terms than scent posts, scrapes, and howlings. The reintroduction of wolves put a two-edged sword back in the woods. The death of the Tremont female made sense.

But it also made things hard that summer on the Tremont male, who had three wild-born pups to tend on his own. 357M continued to range, as if he were still mapping terrain, but he didn't travel as far as he had in the fall and winter. After the death of his mate, he spent more time with the pups and, during July, rendezvoused with them on a daily basis, presumably bringing them kills to supplement whatever rodents and small game they might be catching on their own.

Lucash godfathered 357M's efforts by dropping deer and boar carcasses, to ensure the healthy growth of those pups, but the Tremont male's paternal instincts seemed to be intact. Lucash also closed on a decision that had been hanging fire all spring and finally shipped out the problem juveniles from the original Tremont group to breeding pens at Alligator River. Only 525M, the offspring of the Tremont adults, remained in the field with the Tremont male and the wild-born pups that first summer. But the eighteen-month-old, a full-grown wolf, formed no attachment to the new generation and seemed to have moved into Cades Cove on its own while the pups hung around on the safer side of Crib Gap, out of the way of the Cades Cove wolves.

In August one of those pups—594F—was killed by a coyote after its father had been captured to have its vaccinations updated. In the chess game of wolf management, some moves are forced, and it's not always possible to draw the line between an artificial event and a natural one. Coyote-wolf antagonism was not uncommon, with wolves generally but not always getting the upper hand. In the absence of an adult wolf, however, a full-grown coyote can easily take advantage of a four-month-old wolf pup. In this instance, it was notable how quickly the subordinate canid was able to sense the power vacuum and reassert itself. So after it was rereleased in September, the Tremont male had two pups left to rear and one male offspring that seemed to have left the remnant family preliminary to finding a mate of its own.

At the beginning of that same summer, the Cades Cove wolves were perhaps the most promising family of red wolves anywhere. The two adult wolves had steered themselves and their captive-born offspring to independence. They had explored their surroundings and hunted wild game through a hard winter, establishing a home range within which they seemed to return to the natural rounds of their species. They had mated,

death of Cades Cove pups

denned, and bred successfully in the wild and then brought four pups through the first two difficult months of life, two extraordinary months, historically and ecologically, when there were *twelve* red wolves at large in the Cades Cove home range, each generation a little wilder than the previous one.

For the most part, the lives of wolves are secret, their restoration to the landscape an altruistic gesture in which there is little obvious value. Lucash and Crawford got only glimpses of this extended family. Several times in June the four pups were seen traveling with their mother. But by the end of July they were all dead, apparently of parvo virus. This left the Cades Cove wolves back where they started, except that the juveniles were getting older and restless for mates and territory of their own.

So of the seven red wolves born that watershed spring of 1993, only two were alive in autumn, the orphaned Tremont siblings. Black and tawny traces of their parents, alone for the coming winter but wilder than any wolves here in a century.

592M made a bold test of the waters near the end of September and demonstrated that the wild-born generation of red wolves was, from the beginning, far more circumspect than its older siblings or even than its parents. The five-month-old wolf traveled in and out of the park into the Townsend area, where the Tremont juveniles had been sighted so often. But this wolf was seen only once—trotting across a road—in the ten days of its extracurricular travel. It stuck to heavily wooded areas, bothering no one, and came back into the park of its own accord. Fish and Wildlife monitored its peregrinations closely and, although prepared to retrieve it, they were pleased they didn't have to. The theory of the reintroduction was proving itself. The young wolf instinctively knew the rules of the game. The idea of wildness was taking on character and the practice of wildness logging some hours.

Instead of cruising the backcountry again in the autumn of 1993, where I could no longer cross paths with the summit-loving Tremont adults, I paddled a beamy Old Town canoe down the lakes that had swallowed the Little Tennessee, thinking about wolves and rivers, among other things, and keeping an eye on the idea of fall.

You cannot see the summit ridge of the Unakas from the river, but every paddle stroke turns an overlapping succession of lithic shapes along the near horizon that overshadow the water's edge—conical and squarish, rounded and jagged peaks that look like ruins trying to rise above the vegetation that holds them to the foreground. All the way downriver that horizon unfolds, stands and follows, a weathered edge of worked stone off either shoulder, the shape of another time.

The narrowness of the lakes below Fontana suggest the old river, which before construction of the dams made a classic descent through broad sun-lit riffles and cliff-darkened pools, cascading through gauntlets of shattered granite wherever the land put up resistance. The river flooded in spring, of course, but that is what rivers are designed to do and why they have flood-plains. Until recent times, no one was confused by that. Except for the tailrace releases, the only current now was in the transmission lines that looped downstream from tower to tower.

Cheoah Lake doglegs west for ten miles between the Unakas and the Yellow Creek Mountains, the latter a thin ridge not much longer than the lake. The Cheoah Dam was the first on the Little Tennessee, built by the Aluminum Company of America during World War I. Alcoa, formerly the Pittsburgh Reduction Company, reportedly was attracted to the valley of the Little Tennessee River by "cheap water power and docile non-union labor" after the Babcock Lumber Company, also of Pittsburgh, "razed" and "denuded" the surrounding slopes, destroying in a decade a large chunk of one of the richest and most diverse old-growth forests in the world.

So the forest you see now, like the lake, is a bit of a sham, part of a relentless reduction of things. Even on the north bank, which has been protected from logging for more than half a century, that forest has barely begun to restore itself and may never achieve its former grandeur. Summer sunlight burned the life out of whatever soil didn't slough off the moun-tains after the big cuts. The great mounds of silt in Cheoah Lake give mute testimony to all that steep-slope logging.

If there is a paddle stroke along the Little Tennessee River where you can get out of sight of the man-made world, I missed it. As you approach the elbow halfway down Cheoah Lake, you can see the penstock through which water from Santeetlah Lake, the impounded Cheoah River, is di-verted to the Little Tennessee. Then the brick powerhouse and the surge tower come into view. The rough water from the generators keeps you along the north shore, where you are pinned between the occasional drone of a passing car and the constant hum of the machine in the garden.

As I skirted that choppy outflow from the powerhouse, I watched two fishermen in an aluminum vee-hull ease up to the boil as if they were backholing spoons for steelhead the way they do on the big coastal rivers in Oregon. Here they plug for the trout that come out of that deep elbow to glean the churning water.

The hum recedes as you continue downstream, and there's life along the river when you keep an eye out for it—a trout working the trash line, a pair of mallards flushing from a creek mouth, handfuls of minnows popping out of the water when the canoe looms over a school. You can hear tiny rivulets along shore, hidden beneath impenetrable corridors of alder, rhododendron, and hemlock from which escapes only the barest murmur of running water. Opposite the mouth of Twenty Mile Creek, a dark mile of flow rock creates cool enclaves of mosses, lichens, and ferns that may be the only pristine forms of life left here.

October was pleasantly drab, as if a real artist had been at work and not some postcard colorist. There were deft brush strokes on the hills, an oblique use of palette that dulled the blaze of maples in favor of the rust of oaks. The effect was a studied, indifferent rendering of the season that distributed light so evenly the shadowed hills looked as luminous as the sunlit water. There was balance without any perceptible symmetry, a silent revelation that had no preaching in it. The cloying pointillism of spring was redrawn now without the puffy generalized look of flowering and leafing in. Autumn was all edge and motion, paring down at every turn, expressing more with less, until finally the season disappeared, leaving behind the final shapes of things—polished buckeyes and serrated beech leaves, the straight reach of poplar and the ramification of oak, shaggy cables of grape vine moored to the woods for winter.

I pulled out above Cheoah Dam and hauled the canoe and gear up the steep bank and across the road to the head of Calderwood Lake, where I camped for the night. You cannot descend a dead river, and I missed that sense of being carried somewhere, of taking a journey that was inscribed in the land. I missed the surface chatter of riffles and pocket water, the subconscious momentum of deep pools leaning toward the sea, and that satisfying sense that every reach and bend expressed a quality of the earth discovered by the patient, inanimate insistence of the river, wild offspring of the raised horizon receding out of view behind me.

I watched the light from my fire dance in the river that night and thought about the Tremont male, which had crossed near here when it went looking for a lost world last winter. A faint, fading trace of 357M probably lingered in the mountains—in its secret haunts around Thunderhead Mountain, along the contours of its backcountry treks, and in its resting places and hunting grounds. I admired its bold impulse to seek out the unsettling waters of the Little Tennessee River, along whose banks it was once treated, like the river itself, as a sacred, transcendental being.

Next morning I shoved off onto Calderwood Lake surrounded by the wine-colored season, its ruined woods laced with the scent of a wolf, the river silent except for the slur of the paddle, and the shore silent, too, except for a faint percussion of nictitating leaves. Such an oddly reassuring season, animate and flexible, but haunting you all day with that constant, offbeat rain of leaves, an unsettling arrhythmia in the air, as if there were more randomness in death than birth.

Chuckle of a kingfisher, whistle of a hawk. Nothing threatening in the latter, an oddly sweet sound for a predator. Its name in Cherokee derives from the word for lovesick. Lonely hunter.

This is *Tsulunwe'i,* possibly from *tsulu,* that crested, chuckling spirit of the place. The kingfisher is out of sight, but I can see a stocky buteo, white in the sun, hunting for a thermal along a threadbare ridge. And a handful of silent turkey vultures slowly kettling away from the cool, uncertain air over Chilhowee Lake, the next dammed stretch of the Little Tennessee downstream from Calderwood Lake.

An intermittent wind quarters this first broad reach of the Abrams Creek embayment, so that when I lay the paddle across the gunwales in order to jot down notes, I am blown over to the far bank into the cool shade, which prompts me to stop writing and paddle back into the sunlight.

Three feet or so of shoreline is exposed all around this arm of water, from the seasonal drawdown through the raised gates on top of Chilhowee Dam, part of a larger scheme of things the power lines overhead keep tethered to this beautiful place. The gray, silty scar at the hem of the woods gives the game away. I cruise slowly, with deep bites and slow pulls with an ash paddle that can't exercise its spring in the still water, determined to see something here.

The vultures drift through the power lines looking momentarily like notes on a scale drawn in the air, the large ungainly birds threading themselves above and below the thick black wires, as if in another dimension. The shallows are full of common illusions that flash the latent doubleness of things before settling into themselves when you stare long enough to make them give up their other life: stone turtles, snaking branches, beaver heads in bobbing logs, sleek otter backs in wind-dug swells, gray wooden herons only a little less still than the real thing.

Seeing requires recognition of metamorphosis here, capture of an object sliding from one guise to another—a stone pushing itself off a log and paddling down into the green water, an owl resolved into a stob of wood. This is to accept the play of self and other nature invites, an instructive confusion it brings to the mind's eye, the hidden desires of which work sometimes with and sometimes against the grain of things.

So I turn up into Panther Creek to look for panthers, not expecting to see the golden cat, invisible now in this place, but to see the lithe shape of its absence, faded signs of an older arrangement of things—the lionlike intentions of this terrain usurped now by the bobcat, skunk, and bear and by man, strange creature who cannot tolerate the lives of lions.

The Cherokee have a dark story about a hunter who one winter encounters a panther in the woods. Before he shoots the animal, it speaks to him and he understands "there was no difference between them, and they were both of the same nature." They hunt deer together, and, after killing a large buck, the panther takes the hunter through a door in a hill into the underground town house of his clan where the Green-corn Dance, a summer feast, is being prepared. "Somehow," we are told, "it all seemed natural to the hunter," and he joined in this important, joyous ceremony with the panther clan.

But the dance undoes him. Out of season and out of being, underground in winter in a summer world, the hunter has unknowingly devolved, chanced upon a Pleistocene fantasy laced with music from the Pliocene. After a few dances, the hunter senses the pull of time from above, worries that it has gotten late, and expresses a desire to return home.

"So the panthers opened the door and he went out, and at once found himself alone in the woods again, and it was winter and very cold, with snow on the ground and on all the trees." He encounters a search party that has come out to look for him and learns that he has been gone days instead of hours, a little too long for a successful return. The hunter goes back with them to his town but, unable to reconcile the new difference within him—the enlarged sympathy created by his having hunted too far— he dies in a few days, as much panther as man.

I carefully note the missing paw prints on the bar of silt built up opposite a hairpin fold of rock and count that as lion sign in these empty eastern woods. I'm satisfied to see that the delicate hands of raccoons have left cleanly cut impressions around a feast of mussels. Half the bar is covered with dying strands of algae left there by the receding water. Some kind of thick-stemmed grass has already invaded the high ground along with a late-blooming wildflower that offers a drooping yellow raceme to this struggling edge.

The flooded hole between the silt and the rock no doubt harbors the fish of the place—a hundred years ago a two-pound brook trout, then a hatchery rainbow from the logging days, now at best a lip-scarred brown up from the depths of Chilhowee but more likely a bass or sucker.

Around the turn, the canoe scrapes through a sun-warmed flat of frog water and scattering fry, but I can hear the running stream ahead at its shifting mouth of silty rocks and false pools no stream-born trout trust. But sunlight flashes like quivering trout in the moving water, having passed through and picked up the colors of the shedding autumn canopy, a well-turned medley of dogwood and fire cherry, sourwood and sugar maple overhung with walnut and poplar.

Autumn, like sunset, casts a false promise, or misleads by seeming to be the beginning of something, but the charm of these October days was worth the cold, gray world to come. Even sans panthers, Panther Creek looked good there with the year rustling colorfully around it, implying by its healthy rush toward me a mountain in the woods ahead and maybe trout after all in white water and cold pools.

When the canoe stalled against the stream's modest flow, I got out, beached it, and tied it to a rock-hard hornbeam.

There was a fire ring and a campsite next to the first good pool. A modest amount of trash had been left, crowned with a small cairn of beer cans weathered only by a summer. This cache was left not out of carelessness but to mark the place. Like wolf piss on a scent post. Territory. The stream was undoubtedly fished hard in the spring and then again, less hard, in the fall by the same few fishermen year after year, and it was marked for local use, a claim worth respecting.

Panther Creek is a small stream by width, but it reaches far into surrounding watersheds, draining a large, nearly trailless corner of the Unakas. The spates and hard flows it is prone to are visible in the sculpted rock of the lower river, tan humps of sandstone smoothed like well-thrown clay or fluted in clothlike folds Rodin would have admired for their animate softness. Imperfections in the rock surface have been scoured into perfectly circular potholes, each with a handful of drilling stones in it—the hardest kernels from some conglomerate—that whirl like fire when the water rises.

A quarter of a mile upstream I hooked a nice brown trout that tied me up in the debris at the back of a pool and freed itself, as living things like to do, leaving me with a handful of hickory leaves, yellow as the vanished fish, stuck to the ruined fly. Of course, the best spots were fished out, heartbreaking pools below cascades that funnel insects into dancing lines of foam where trout rose recklessly in the spring. But there were still fish hidden in the riffles, dark forms wedged between the dancing slices of light. Before I had gone a mile I had killed and cleaned two trout, neither as fine as the first, and turned back down the vague fisherman's trail hoping no one had cut the canoe loose to test my resourcefulness.

I stopped to rinse the fish again in the last flush of white water, kneeling on the rocks to scrape off the scum and scales and pick out a few more specks of blood and guts from the backbone with the point of my knife. I admired the pearl architecture of the rib cage and the firm, delicate flesh that a river honed in place on those airy bones. I stuffed the body cavities of the fish with wet ferns and tucked them into a moth-eaten canvas creel that I dunked one last time in the cold water.

Then I made my way back to the still-water stretch of Abrams Creek and swung upstream again, enjoying both the silence of the canoe and the way I could turn the woods about with a slight twist and draw of the paddle. I watched the water and the woods and the sky.

A worm or snake appeared in a patch of sunlit water ahead of me. Whatever it was undulated just under the surface, a strand of life a foot or so long, wide as a blade of grass. When I got closer to it, I thought it *was* a strand of grass and that it flexed in such a lifelike way because of the way the water was mixed by the sunlight. As I watched it stir, animate and inanimate by turns, I wasn't sure. I circled until I could get the paddle under it and then brought it to me—some sort of tube worm, free-living or a parasite in search of a host, a thin transparent body filled with yellow light ending in a tiny black head that was featureless to my naked eye.

There was enough of a breeze to keep a constant lapping on the windward shore, but this had become a warm October day, mild as spring at the heart of it. I paddled slowly, savoring the way the woods gradually closed on either side of me, the contours of the land and water beginning to make a better match.

Moving slowly upriver, I approached a heron that was gleaning a strand of silt. Stroking the canoe into a long, silent glide, I feathered the paddle and held myself as still as the bird. The heron was all posture and eye line, ornate in a remarkably functional way. Bluish, mistrustful, it stopped feeding and raised its head when I was still a hundred feet away despite my strategy. Self-possessed and otherworldly, speechless so far as I knew, herons apparently evolved to doubt and keep their distance. How close could I have gotten to it?

One moment it was standing, eyeing the mud, the next it was crossing the still river out in front of me, wing tips almost touching the water, legs dangling carelessly, as if it did not intend to go far. Then it landed, rising to stand at the edge of the woods on the other shore, invisible in the shadows if you did not know to look for it there.

The still-water stretch of Abrams Creek wound right and left, nudged by steep contours, and then curled to the right again in a quiet, leaf-strewn half circle through which the canoe carved a curving, ruffled vee. No craft suits water so well. I paddled kneeling broadly just astern of center, the gear stashed forward to ease the plane. This put my eyes at heron level, the ideal vantage, I assume, and with my weight dug into the hull through my thighs in stillwater the short, light craft tended to track the way I looked, responding when I twisted to see a squirrel jabbering a warning call halfway up the trunk of a red oak or if I turned, startled, when a walnut bulleted into the water.

Before I reached the cliff that turns Abrams Creek left again, I could hear a river around the bend, that inimitable shushing, the working sound that made this place, a speech Cherokee medicine men strove to understand because it was thought to be the sound of the original world talking to men, the generous counsel of *Yun'wi Gunahi'ta,* the Long Man, whose head was in the mountains and whose well-formed thoughts flowed, like water, to make the world habitable and interesting. James Mooney reports that, among the Cherokee, the Long Man was "constantly speaking to those who can understand the message."

I could see whitewater ahead as well as a steady procession of leaves along this last stretch, forest and river well mixed here in the solemn way of fall, one of the enduring signs of good medicine. The bare strip along the water's edge disappeared opposite where the rock-studded pocket water began and the land fit itself properly around the river. As the bottom of the old river came into view, you could see the ledge rock of the original riverbed in the water looking like an abandoned quarry—river-smoothed boulders dusty with silt, the tepid water hung with sunlit bass, the sculpting stopped. I dug hard against the thickening current, enjoying the sound of working water, and threaded the canoe up through the first stretch of boulders until I couldn't go any farther.

Abrams Creek was as broad as what I would call a river, four or five times wider than Panther Creek. This lower stretch had a poor reputation among trout fishermen, but I beached the canoe and wet-waded through an irresistible half mile of pocket water to satisfy myself that there was no well-kept secret here. Beyond the pleasure of being in the river, chilled by the hard rush of it around me, and of letting out long backcasts over all that unobstructed space, I unearthed no surprises.

I roasted the two trout from Panther Creek on the gravel beach where I had left the canoe and ate them with half a jar of marinated green beans and mushrooms, a fine light meal in the open air. Properly cooked and dusted with just salt and pepper, I'm not sure wild trout have *any* flavor. It's the texture you taste, the curved wedges of fish flesh calving apart in your mouth, the crispy skin. I sucked those airy ribs clean and licked my fingers like a raccoon.

When I was ready to leave, I set the canoe in a sluice of whitewater and let the river push me out through the rocks. I got one last firm shove from all the miles of river behind me in the mountains and ruddered the canoe along the dark cliff at the river's mouth. Autumn daylight leaves *Tsulunwe'i* in sections, like rooms going dark, and I could paddle ahead back into the late-afternoon sunlight or hang back in the cool shadows where it was already evening.

Life flared along the river's edge regardless of the light—trilling from warblers hidden in the white pines, fluting here and there from a wood thrush or veery, a woodwind sound that played against the desultory tapping of mixed flocks of small woodpeckers that looped en masse from one part of the woods to another, feeding, I assume, for migration. The trees were unimpressive here, despite the fine color of the woods, second growth—or third or fourth—clinging to eroded slopes, the largest of them too much for their roots, toppled and sledded toward the river.

The heron was gone or hidden, but there was a small blue diver on the water, a beautiful thing I have never been able to identify—gray head with a short dark bill, black chin, and pale short slender neck, a cootlike body with a white-tipped butt and barely discernible tail feathers. A silent creature, like the heron, and it played the heron's game but used the water instead of the air, making long dives whenever I'd paddle toward it. It did not make a splashy dive but simply tipped forward and disappeared—a graceful change of state. Twenty or thirty seconds later it would reappear a hundred feet farther off. I pursued it to a stalemate, which was all it wanted.

The bright stretches of water mirrored the sky and the backlit fringe of trees on the ridge tops as well as the bulk of the ridges themselves, which were darker in the water than they were in the air. The wedge of sky between them looked deeper there below me than it did arching overhead.

The dark water was a window on that underworld where men danced with panthers and rivers flowed freely from the mountains to the sea, a realm out of which schools of bream occasionally silvered in their strange communal motions, briefly reflecting skylight off their scales, and in which the cootlike diver was at home, flying through water as easily as the heron swam through air. With the wind perfectly still, that last dark pane of water looked as if I could reach out and rap on it.

Foreshortening converged the shorelines downstream until I opened the last avenue of water above Chilhowee Lake with a sweep stroke. I passed the mouth of Panther Creek, drifted under the empty transmission lines and then under the highway bridge. The sun was beginning to set downstream over the lower Little Tennessee, toward Citico and Chota and Toqua, scattering a blinding light off Chilhowee Lake.

Downstream of Chilhowee Dam, the Little Tennessee bends around the foot of Chilhowee Mountain opposite the mouth of Citico Creek. Freed from the task of incising the hard rock at the heart of the Unakas, work that kept the river busy throughout the Cenozoic, the Little Tennessee casts itself in broad loops through what was once the valley of the Overhill towns. Before the gates of Tellico Dam were closed and that final stretch of the river lost beneath another featureless mask of still water, students of the river read its twists and turns as well as its abandoned meanders and terraces, inferring from what they found the signature of shifting Quaternary climates.

The living river built nine alluvial surfaces here, in addition to its modern floodplain, a process driven by the rhythm of glacial advance and retreat hundreds of miles to the north. Although glaciers never reached the southern Appalachians, each stadial pushed a finger of cold south along the mountains, creating a peninsula of northern plant and animal species. During the coldest centuries, the lower slopes of the Unakas were covered with jack pine and spruce. An alpine zone of tundra and permafrost took hold above 4,500 feet. The highest peaks were bare, windswept regolith.

During full glacials, the frost action generated by periglacial cold ground the exposed bedrock of the Unakas into unstable debris that eventually sorted itself out into colluvial fans unfolded onto the mountainsides above the river. The interglacials brought rains that washed that rock downslope until it became grist for the river's mill. Eventually the heavy load of gravel, sand, and silt settled out in the river's bed or was deposited on its banks. When sediment loads decreased, the river would abandon its floodplain, which eventually left a landscape of nested alluvial terraces. At some point in the late Quaternary, the river stopped its broad meandering and settled into a more stable, braided flow around persistent islands.

Human beings drifted into the valley 12,000 years ago, about the time the climate eased during the start of the current interglacial. During the early Holocene, another load of frost-churned rock washed off the slopes and the river built the most recent terrace. The boreal climate retreated, withdrawing the life it favored. Tundra and caribou disappeared, as did spruce grouse and most of the spruce. The mountains reforested themselves in response to a warmer, wetter climate with the stunning variety of deciduous trees that survived the Wisconsin glaciation in lowland refugia. Beech, poplar, oaks, hickories, maples, walnut, ironwood, basswood, and elm were waiting in the wings. This new vegetation stabilized the slopes and built soil. The amount of sediment reaching the river decreased once again, and the last terrace was complete. The Little Tennessee abandoned that last terrace for its modern floodplain between 3,000 and 4,000 years ago, about the time the Cherokee language was separating from its Iroquoian parent stock.

The floodplain and lower terraces of the Little Tennessee River preserved a luminous sequence of objects abandoned to time, artifacts that stretch the imagination: from palm-size Clovis and Dalton points of Paleo-Indians, who scalloped their edges with antler tines and thrust them at the trailing edge of Pleistocene megafauna, to the symbolically incised gorgets of the Mississippian people, who taught themselves the dimensions of the quadripartite universe.

Plant-fiber baskets left their weave on the fired clay hearths of the early Archaic, which also stranded notched spear points and chert butchering tools—knives, hammerstones, scrapers, drills, gravers, and cobble net weights—as well as nuts and seeds gathered from forests and savannas.

The middle Archaic made better points, short-stemmed and more easily hafted, refined the lithic tool kit with which meat was butchered, and fashioned cylindrical and crescent-shape stone weights for the throwing stick—the atlatl—which levered a spear with dramatically improved velocity. Cobble weights were notched to anchor fishing nets more securely. Large, broad-stemmed Savannah River points appeared along with grooved axes and celts of the late Archaic. Fragments of steatite bowls confirm the permanent settlement indicated by charred rinds of squash and gourd, the first of a slowly developing sequence of cultigens that shaped civilization here.

Ceramics anchored Woodland period settlements, vessels refined over time by improved tempering mediums—crushed quartzite, sand, limestone. Spear points became arrowheads—small, efficient chert triangles. Stone tools were ground and polished to a beautiful sheen. Mortars and pestles marked an increased use of mast, seeds, and wild plants—maygrass, knotweed, lambsquarters. Trade goods turn up—exotic Adena and Hopewellian ceramics and prismatic blades of Ohio chalcedony acquired for cut sheets of mica and soapstone quarried from the surrounding mountains. Wild marsh elder was cultivated and then maize appeared, the tiny cobs a strange gift from the sun. Wood-structure settlements broadened. Forests were cleared.

Crushed mussel shells tempered Mississippian ceramics. The deadly arrowheads de Soto's men felt were fashioned, along with steatite ear spools, negative-painted effigy vessels, stone and copper plaques. The startling images of the Southern Ceremonial Cult that adorn these things seem to come out of nowhere—bird men and serpents, big thunder and falcons—but a fabulous subconscious had been here all along. Important imaginations lived along this river, imaginations that lent transcendental significance to these material objects. Ceremonial mounds squared the center of large palisaded villages graced with plazas and wood-frame council houses and dwellings of wattle and daub. Within the palisades was kinship and ceremony; beyond the world of hunting, trade, and war.

Then the Overhill towns of the Cherokee occupied these ancient sites:

> Their towns are always close to some river, or creek; as there the land
> is commonly very level and fertile, on account of the frequent washings off the mountains, and the moisture it receives from the waters,
> that run through their fields. And such a situation enables them to
> perform the ablutions, connected with their religious worship. . . .
> They are . . . strongly attached to rivers,—all retaining the opinion

of the ancients, that rivers are necessary to constitute a paradise. Nor is it only ornamental, but likewise beneficial to them, on account of purifying themselves, and also for the services of common life,—such as fishing, fowling, and killing of deer, which come in the warm season, to eat the saltish moss and grass, which grow on the rocks, and under the surface of the waters. Their rivers are generally very shallow, and pleasant to the eye; for the land being high, the waters have a quick descent; they seldom overflow their banks, except when a heavy rain falls on a deep snow.

November now, at Citico, the color failing in the hills. I say Citico, but facing the gray, pockmarked chop of Tellico Lake, I'm not so sure. It's cold and raining lightly. I'm chilled and feeling the weather and tired of searching out things I can't see.

Featureless as the lake is, for a Cherokee, the land here is still well marked. Downstream you can see the great cliff where the *tla'nuwa'*, the great hawks, once nested. "They were immense birds, larger than any that live now, and very strong and savage." In the old time, they wreaked havoc on the people until a medicine man of Citico defeated them, much like Odysseus, by playing one form of negation off against another. He fed their nestlings to the *Ukte'na,* a monstrous serpent that dwelt in the water below the cliff. The enraged hawks pulled the *Ukte'na* from the water and tore it to pieces in the air. The scaly chunks of the snake fell to earth and scarred Chilhowee Mountain, and the hawks departed. Upstream was the favorite haunt of *Utlun'ta,* Spear-finger, a woman clad in stone who fed on human livers.

Despite the myths that add an imaginative dimension to this landscape, I can't get beyond the prosaic. I'm at a well-trashed boat landing where a sign riddled with bird shot warns me not to drink the toxic water or eat any fish from the shapeless lake that now covers the ruined valley of the Overhills.

There was a current from the release at Chilhowee Dam, a mile upstream, but the wind canceled that out, so I paddled easily across the main channel a hundred yards to an island shaped like a fishhook opposite the landing. Huge suckers or carp darted away on my approach, leaving puffs of disturbed silt in the calm shallows along shore. I looked for peach orchards and river cane but saw mostly alder, birch, and willow, the latter holding slender yellow leaves over the water like lures.

Another sign warned me not to steal anything, that this ruined place was now protected. There might be artifacts that escaped the mechanical sluice boxes of the salvage archaeology done here in the shadow of the construction of the Tellico Dam, and there still may be soulless people who come to steal what's left of the past here, but the officious, red-lettered sign seems a bit hypocritical, since the culture that posted the warning also built the dam. As it was, if I had come to steal from Citico, there would have been no one to stop me. But the thieving here—500 years of it—is pretty much done.

When I turn the upstream end of the island, I'm pleased to see two bald eagles perched in the upper branches of one of the drowned snags where Citico was. The golden eagle was the revered bird of the Cherokee, the war eagle whose feathers were sacred objects, but the unmistakable head and tail of its cousin is a heartening sight on eastern rivers, as affirmative as seeing bear or wolves. As long as the great birds don't eat any fish from Tellico Lake, they will be fine.

I paddled closer to the eagles, slowly and obliquely so as not to spook them. A corridor of snags and stumps off to my left marked the old channel of Citico Creek, which had made this an especially desirable place for 12,000 years. I got within fifty yards of the birds and, when they flew off downriver, rousting crows from the shore, I circled their perch, hoping to find a feather. But the taking of eagle feathers is not a casual affair, and there was nothing on the water.

From the base of that tree, I saw the world from what was left of Citico—the broad expanse of water covering what had been the confluence of Citico Creek and the Little Tennessee, the steep rise of Chilhowee Mountain, a large island downstream that would have been part of the town. Underneath me was a world—burials and postholes of homes, middens and gardens, a mound and a council house with a fire burning at the center of a red-clay hearth. A wolf's tooth with a hole drilled in it, as if it had been a pendant, had been found among the ruins.

Lieutenant Henry Timberlake came to Citico in December of 1761, having descended the Holston River from Virginia and then poled his way up the Little Tennessee with bloody, blistered hands, trying not to fall too far behind his Cherokee escort and lose face with the vanquished. The English had tried to use the Cherokee as pawns in their war against the French, but the strategy fell apart in what became an international blood feud. The war between the Cherokee and the English had ended with a treaty signed in November 1761 on the Long Island of the Holston by Timberlake's superior, Colonel Stephens. Timberlake carried the articles of peace to the all-important Overhills, who had requested that an English officer appear in person among them to settle the matter.

After taking in the ruins of Fort Loudoun, the first English fortification among the Overhills, which the Cherokee had captured in August of 1761, Timberlake presented the articles to the war chief Ostenaco at Tomotley and then to the assembled chiefs and warriors at the council house of Chota, center of the nation and keeper of its principal fire. The peace was smoked, following which there was a feast of venison, bear, and buffalo as well as ceremonial dances.

Timberlake then received an invitation to come to Citico,* at the time the most belligerent of the Overhill towns and deeply implicated in the hostilities. They flew two white flags for the Englishman from the top of the council house but received him as a people justified and, in some respects, vindicated by the recent war. Timberlake describes his reception: "About 100 yards from the town-house we were received by a body of between three and four hundred Indians, ten or twelve of which were entirely naked, except a piece of cloth about their middle, and painted all over in a hideous manner, six of them with eagle tails in their hands, which they shook and flourished as they advanced, danced in a very uncommon figure, singing in concert with some drums of their own make, and those of the late unfortunate Capt. Damere."

The unfortunate Damere, along with twenty-five others, had been brutally executed after the successful siege of Fort Loudoun, blood vengeance for the murder of an equal number of Cherokee hostages by the British and one of the last great assertions of the law of clan revenge. This meeting with the English officer at Citico was, therefore, a great moment for the Cherokee, who were still, like the French and English, a nation. The details of it were well etched on Timberlake's mind.

The headman of Citico met Timberlake in front of the town house, "holding an old rusty broad-sword in his right hand, and an eagle's tail in his left." His body was painted red, except his face, which was half black, the visage of war and death, one of the great masks of Cherokee life.

They danced the eagle dance here at Citico for Timberlake and danced it as if they thought all Europe were watching. The violent gestures, pounding dithyrambs, and raucous shouts of the Overhills ended with their chief swinging that rusty sword just over Timberlake's head and striking it with all his might into the ground within inches of the Englishman's

---

* Called Settico in Timberlake's journal.

left foot. While the hilt quivered, he made a short, emphatic speech to the stunned young man—which Timberlake's interpreter told him, tongue-in-cheek I assume, was a hearty welcome. The chief then gave him a string of beads, which was either a peace offering or an insulting talisman for all the cheap trade goods that had undermined the traditional Cherokee way of life and put them on the path to dispossession.

Then it was over.

Timberlake was led as an honored guest into the darkness of the council house, where he was blinded until a circular fire of river cane flared up and revealed the faces of 500 warriors staring at him from an amphitheater of benches. The chief of Citico addressed him again, this time in a tone of friendship, and Timberlake was given another string of beads, this one a true gift, a token of the open-mindedness of these people. Then the eagle dancers entered and finished the dance, which symbolized a manly progression toward peace and reason.

I much wanted to see these things, but they were gone. Citico was gone. And even the place where Citico was—the bank of a river near the confluence of a bold stream—was gone. Strange, this process of erasure, this removal that will not stop.

I turned my back on the empty expanse and paddled through the rain toward the mouth of Citico Creek, losing my way in thickets of cattails that closed in warrior ranks along the shore—Cherokee, Mississippian, Woodland, Archaic, Paleo. A cattail perhaps for every man or woman who had speared a fish or snared a duck here, or who pretended to go for water to meet a lover after dark. Twelve thousand years of North American history so broadly named. You would think that every speck of that deep, intruiging past would have been preserved here, including the shape of this place, that the creek and the river would have been left intact, the old languages honored, and the surrounding forests and mountains treated with respect, if not reverence. Strange. Maybe it was the rain, but the arrogance and the waste in the air was awful. The marsh grasses rattled and I was cold.

I found the creek mouth. The creek was full and still. The sky brightened, the rain eased. It seemed warmer. I heard geese far off on the lake behind me, gabbling as if in response to the changing weather. The creek and the fine-grained rain made the world seem small, as if there were nothing beyond what I could see. There was no wind, just the motion of the quiet surge and drift of the canoe, the hull ticking distinctly against each leaf in its path, the trees beyond the cattails nearly bare, a little bit of everything left—a few leaves, a few birds, the tail end of the year drifting off. I seemed to have found the proper scale of things.

Citico Creek looped gracefully inland, narrow and deep, dark green. Eventually I saw current stream faintly around a sunken branch and a near-perfect thing came alive, flowing. The paddle came to life against the quickening current, the shaft straining at the throat with each deep pull. I flushed two ducks just past the upper end of a small island, slate-blue birds with white showing in the trailing edge of their wings. As I watched the empty air, trying to remember them, a dozen more burst from the opposite bank in a sustained commotion that also ended before I could gather the fact of it in my mind.

I paddled as infrequently and slowly as I could through the vee of sky in the water that separated the image of the closing banks, savoring every nook and moment. The mallards I had flushed reappeared in flight, gaining altitude in a loosely organized chevron of their own. Then a pair of wood ducks broke from behind an overhang of willows. The distinctly shaped and colored male was off first but then stalled in the air, it seemed, as the female took flight from the water behind it and flew past. Then the creek made a sharp turn to the left, narrowed, and the current stiffened until I could make no headway against it. I let the current turn me just below a deadfall of sycamore and drifted back out on the deep, dark water of Citico Creek.

I've not been in a finer place. The richness of life Timberlake described seemed still to fill this quiet corridor. The universe seemed balanced there between water and sky, motion and stillness, expectation and surprise. Time and space eddied in the soft currents of Citico Creek, autumn shorn into fall. Migrant songbirds, oblivious to the rain, hung onto drooping seedheads of marsh grass; pileated woodpeckers cried from out of sight, as if to clear the woods of anything that wasn't going to winter there. The moving water created a direction between the still banks of the known world. Every dead leaf seemed to be going somewhere.

That night I made camp in the rain on the south bank of the great Cherokee River between Citico and Chota. I slept under my canoe like a warrior and dreamed dreams. In the morning I paddled through a mist that danced in sheets on the river like the borealis. Above Bacon's Bend, a raft of what must have been a hundred or more Canada geese suddenly appeared around me, silent as if I were still dreaming. Odd the way they floated there and started their preflight gabbling only after I had paddled through them and then, though I knew it was about to happen, froze my heart with a thunderous communal takeoff that left the river in terrific silence.

I beached the canoe and fell asleep again on the grassy bank until the sun woke me. At Chota you are out of sight of the mountains and surrounded by an open, low-slung horizon befitting a peace town. Chota, too, is gone now, except for a spit of land bulldozed out into the water where there is a halfhearted memorial to the Overhill towns that had been destroyed so many times. A circle of concrete pillars marks the place, one for each Cherokee clan, the remembrance already pitted with weather and acid rain. The pillars are cut obliquely so that the top is an oval on which a clan name is inscribed in English along with a simple image—Deer, Wild Potato, Wolf, Paint, Bird, Long Hair, and Blue. Which is to say *Ani'-Kawi', Ani'-Gatage'wi, Ani'-Wa'ya, Ani'Wa'di, Ani'-Tsi'skwa, Ani'-Gila'hi, Ani'-Saha'ni.* The semicircle of clans is turned south, as is the river for a short stretch, toward peace and Wahala, the White Mountain. In the middle of the clan totems there is an oblong trough, full of rainwater and small stones when I saw it.

The spit of land reaches to the grave of Oconostota, "Great Warrior of the Cherokee," whose bold life from 1710 to 1783 spanned the last victories and the great loss of land. It is supposed to be a great tribute that he was not inundated along with his people. His bones and burial goods were raised and reburied here to spare his grave from the polluted waters of Tellico Lake. He was buried in his canoe, along with his knife, iron cup, siltstone pipe, and eyeglasses. He was given a western gravestone on which is inscribed a prayer stick image of a warrior. Beyond this grave the river bends west again, out of sight, toward *Usunhi'yi*, the Darkening Land, and the ghost country, *Tsusgina'i*, where the spirits of the dead dwell. There were cattails on Oconostota's grave, disheveled by the wind, but I think they had been laid there. I added yarrow, for peace, and a branch of blood-red sourwood.

Downstream of Chota there is nothing really. Ghosts and the ghosts of ghosts. A slight memorial to Chota's sister town Tanase, acknowledging the appropriation of its name for a river and a state out of another comic slippage of syllables—Tanase, Tanasee, Tunisee, Tunissee, Tannassy—none of which the Cherokee ever applied to the river, the indigenous name for which remains uncertain. And then the spiritless suburban world opposite Toqua and Tomotley, a hum of lawnmowers and traffic up and down Tellico River and Ballplay Creek.

And Fort Loudoun, painstakingly reconstructed, and moved to high ground. Some things, apparently, are worth preserving. The fort appears as if the Cherokee had never conquered it—palisade and bastion, face and flank, parade ground and hornwork, glacis and moat. Great care was taken with the reconstruction—the spiked logs of the palisade tilted out at the prescribed fifteen-degree angle and the moat thickly planted with black locust, stiff-limbed and thorny.

The evening I passed by them the water between Fort Loudoun and the Tellico Blockhouse, across the way, was moved only by the evening breeze. There was no Cherokee River. The hearths and graves of Tuskegee lay under water a few hundred yards offshore, invisible. Upstream and down, there was nothing. The Overhill towns were gone: Tallassee. Chilhowee. Citico. Chota. Tanase. Toqua. Tomotley. Tuskegee. Mialoquo.

Sometime just before the removal, a Cherokee patiently tried to explain the sacredness of the placement of these towns and this landscape to a Christian missionary: "The west half of the council house was holier than the other part,—the space about the white seats was still more sacred, but the seventh post and space about it, holiest of all. Mountains were more sacred than low ground. . . . The ground on the banks of rivers and on the sea shore was more holy than that back from the water. But the ground under the water was still more sacred than that on the shore."

Now it was all underwater, but nothing was sacred here.

The Constant Fire, the Old Sacred Things

The hunter prays to the fire, from which he draws his omens; to the reed, from which he makes his arrows; to Tsu'l'kalu, the last great lord of the game, and finally addresses in songs the very animals which he intends to kill. The lover prays to the Spider to hold fast the affections of his beloved one in the meshes of his web, or to the Moon, which looks down upon him in the dance. The warrior prays to the Red War-club, and the man about to set out on a dangerous expedition prays to the Cloud to envelop him and conceal him from his enemies.

—James Mooney, "Sacred Formulas of the Cherokees"

Consciousness is kin to fire, a gift of matter.

Prodding flames within a fire ring, memories fuel impressions, thoughts and feelings flow together around the circle of stones from which those flames cast long shadows across the familiar ridges and strange maria in our minds. Hard to say, some nights in the backcountry, whether those smoky images are real or unreal, what part of us is river and what part rock, whether we are wolf or falcon, tend toward earth or sky.

That fire consumes its fuel is not proof, in the morning, that there was no dancing light, no shadows on the rocks and the solemn trunks of trees. The autumnal fire fading from the leaves on the ground was once in the branches overhead and once, before that, in the sun. The birds that migrate through spring and autumn do not become unreal in winter when they are gone. Even the fossil shapes of things—seashells cast in limestone on mountaintops—and the bones of creatures long extinct—femurs of dire wolves and skulls of short-faced bear hidden underfoot—remind us that time is folded, not stretched out from point to point, that it curls around us like a blue flame around a log end.

The first Englishmen to spend time among the Cherokee noted that they made their most important promises "by ye fire which they adore as theire god." The simile should not be taken literally. The flames the Cherokee held sacred leapt from an earthly, if transcendental, source, not a metaphysical one, a distinction worth exploring.

"In the beginning," we are told, "there was no fire, and the world was cold, until the Thunders (Ani'-Hyun'tikwala'ski), who lived up in Galun'lati, sent their lightning and put fire into the bottom of a hollow sycamore tree which grew on an island. The animals knew it was there, because they could see the smoke coming out at the top, but they could not get to it on account of the water, so they held a council to decide what to do. This was a long time ago."

The humble image of a hollow tree, or hollow log, is a powerful one in many native North American cultures, an old-growth image of the beginning and the end. It is not unusual for a sycamore to have grown near water or that lightning should visit such a place. The dead tree would have lost its puzzled bark and the graceful ramification of its branches, one expression of the relation of earth and sky. Lightning might easily seek out the old snag, striking like a snake, leaving a fire on the island, which is the Cherokee image of the world.

A given lightning strike is both random and inevitable, and this myth, like others, seems to capture an enabling moment in the evolution of things—the two-edged sword of fire brought down to earth in an inaccessible place. Since the charred streak of wood in a lightning-struck tree is to this day considered sacred by the Cherokee, used for medicine and ritual, perhaps randomness and inevitability suggest a distinction without a difference in this realm, the misinterpretation of an outsider whose understanding is divided by categories foreign to these uncanny events. Despite their fragmentation, the roundness of these narratives makes interpretation difficult. Most Cherokee myths seem to record distant facts as well as tell old stories, narratives composed around moments of pure insight strangely compressed into the familiar. Their language, tone, and form suggest that at critical moments there may be only one thing at stake where I tend to see two, or two things where I see only one. Fact and fiction are perhaps merged in the old stories, arranged like a twisting double helix, a ladder that winds around the invisible truth in things. Who knows what the Thunders intended?

In any case, the fire on the island was a difficult gift, if gift it was, and helped shape the character of those beings that responded to it. The three elements—earth, air, and water—were, literally and figuratively, joined by the fourth, and the sacramentalization of the real, spontaneously begun by creation, was completed to the potential benefit of all living things. But the fire on the island presented a boundary problem to the cold animals of the world. An anomalous creature was needed to accomplish the task of acquiring fire, a creature of earth and air or of earth and water. The Thunders, perhaps, wished to make a point.

Birds are strong anomalies, much valued in the North American imagination, which is haunted by bird-men images, especially among the eastern Mississippian cultures, from which the Cherokee selectively drew. To hunting people across the continent, flight was clearly one of nature's perfect ideas, a desperate lunge to escape evolved into the supreme hunting weapon, a metamorphosis of prey into predator. In archaeological digs across the eastern woodlands bird-men images and effigies abound—incised into gorgets, molded into water vessels, hammered into copper plaques. The idea of flying through the air was always recognized as a powerful, fiery idea.

But birds fail in the Cherokee myth of the first fire. The raven, renowned for size and strength, flies easily to the distant island but is confused about what to do with this strange element and so is scorched and frightened and returns without the fire. A fearful raven is no small thing, and this led to much talk. But the failure of the raven is meant, I think, to enhance the idea of fire—its power and strangeness—rather than diminish the status of the great bird, the glossy blue-black sheen of whose feathers was meant as a reward for its attempt, a permanent reminder of its willingness to carry fire.

Then owls tried—the screech owl, the hoot owl, and the horned owl in turn—*Wahuhu', U'guku', Tskili'*—species renowned for constancy, for patient watchfulness and the sagacity that comes from looking and listening in a forest hour after hour. But the owls are overcome by the smoke and ashes drafting up through the hollow tree—their eyes reddened, their faces ringed, their vision changed.

The failure of the raven and the owls discourages the other birds and the task falls to the reptiles, which can move across water and earth. What came to be the black snakes—the rat and king snakes—venture to the island and are also singed in their attempts, acquiring not only their color but that uncanny quickness and unpredictability of movement in close quarters, that seemingly sourceless and centerless power of reptilian locomotion, the most hypnotic motion in nature.

The failure of the racer and the climber renews the confusion among the animals which are caught here for the first time between their fascination with and fear of fire. The coldness of the world—a trace perhaps not only of the original, Archean coldness but of human memory of Holocene glacials—remains a problem that must be solved. But the task of acquiring the fire—the puzzle of the burning at the foot of the hollow sycamore on a distant island—is a different kind of challenge than first perceived. The talents of birds and reptiles will not solve the problem. Mammals are completely at a loss. Even the heroic predators—mountain lion, bear, and wolf—are powerless.

In the end it is not the wolf or raven or a trickster fox or rabbit that solves the problem of the fire on the island. A female water spider carries the first fire for the Cherokee: "at last Kanane'ski Amai'yehi (the Water Spider) said she would go. This is not the water spider that looks like a mosquito, but the other one, with black downy hair and red stripes on her body. She can run on top of the water or dive to the bottom, so there would be no trouble to get over to the island."

The raven might have carried fire in its beak, the owl in its talons. The racer and the rat snake might have coiled themselves around a burning piece of wood. But the water spider, which could glide on the surface of the water or dive beneath it as well as walk on land and hang by a thread in air, had no obvious means of bringing the fire across. At the crucial juncture of many of these myths, the narrative requires a critical adaptation in order to proceed, an evolution.

" 'I'll manage that,' said the Water Spider; so she spun a thread from her body and wove it into a *tusti* bowl, which she fashioned on her back. Then she crossed over to the island and through the grass to where the fire was still burning. She put one little coal of fire into her bowl, and came back with it, and ever since we have had fire, and the Water Spider still keeps her tusti bowl."

By these means a practical and a transcendental problem was solved. Fire entered time.

This is not a folktale. This is a foundational myth that embodies a transcendental vision of the origin of something essential to life—how a useful fire, the constant fire—the most animate of inanimate presences—came into the world. There is no doctrine here, only a vision of things.

Like most crucial events in Cherokee lore, the acquisition of fire took place long before the advent of man. And for the Cherokee, this acquisition is not a Promethean theft that challenges the gods and adumbrates the reckless shape of human heroism. Rather it serves to illustrate the constant, inexhaustible adaptations of life to the conditions of life as well as dramatize how the idea of culture was, in the very beginning, embedded in nature.

The poetics of the acquisition of fire suggest a sensitivity to nature's uncanny connections and relations as well as respect for the unknown processes of natural magic and metamorphosis that weave the forms and functions of life across the eons of deep time and the complex folds of space. The effect suggests the weblike view of cosmos, earth, and mind that have emerged from astronomy, geology, and depth psychology, sciences that validate the power of the oldest myths. What is left of nature marks the ragged, living edge of an original world perfectly dense with being and full of transcendental potential but grounded in the tangible complexity underfoot and overhead, a world that evolved toward a saving diversity that is neither ornamental nor scenic.

One of the most striking objects recovered from the Overhill towns was a necklace, the central piece of which was a shell gorget depicting the water spider with the *tusti* bowl on its back carrying fire to the world. The spider is surrounded by eight suns, arranged in a circle that represents either time, if the eight suns are one sun moving, or space, if they represent a double division of the quadripartite world, a solar compass. Each sun is inscribed with circles and a center. The body of the spider, spread against all this circularity, and the diamond-shape octagon of the *tusti* bowl either hold the circle of suns in place or are held in place by them. Seen from a distance, the gorget looks like a seven-spoked wheel. Ten smaller disks, inscribed with rattlesnakes, were used to form the necklace from which the gorget was suspended.

This was a valued piece and a powerful one, embodying as it did the image of the origin and evolution of culture. The fire the animals acquired eventually came into man's hands, already tamed, and became, like the sun, a moving center. And the basket the water spider wove to carry that ancestral fire foreshadowed the series of vessels that improved over time, like projectile points, enabling man to emerge more confidently from his surroundings. The bowl that carried fire became the baskets that carried jerked meat and wild herbs as well as implements from hunting camp to hunting camp and, when horticulture blossomed into agriculture, the storage vessels for the surplus foodstuffs that encouraged man to travel less and make permanent homes to center his hunts. Eventually, the fire in the hollow tree on the island becomes the council fire that is carried once a year from red-clay hearth to red-clay hearth by medicine men who recount the story of the first fire so that no one forgets where all this started. In this way a fundamental reverence is carried through time.

The woven bowl on the spider's back is simultaneously an image of those first reed baskets and crude steatite bowls and a trace of nature's original gift. It is a reminder that all things come from nature and that man was shaped as surely as nature shaped its other forms of life, blackening ravens and snakes, sooting the faces of owls, refining the bodies of spiders.

But this high regard for fire, "which they adore as theire god," neither foreshadowed Western monotheism, which came to be used to underwrite the destruction of nature—"let them have dominion . . ."—nor blew up into the sun worship that flourished at Cahokia, near present-day St. Louis, which came north with Mayan agriculture and was used among the Mississippian peoples to establish larger, more stratified societies where wealth was more important than behavior. For whatever reasons, precontact Cherokee beliefs remained scaled to intelligent coexistence with nature and underwrote a culture balanced between fields of crops and the far-flung long hunt, between communal dances and ritual war. Such a culture was capable of imposing wonderful taboos—that, for example, the most dangerous animals—the wolf, the rattlesnake, the panther—should not be killed—and was also capable of remembering that a being humble as a water spider had carried fire, that its tiny silk bowl had held the gift of the Thunders.

I once watched a Cherokee make fire with a bow drill and fireboard—what is sometimes vaguely and absurdly referred to as rubbing two sticks together. This was as solemn an act as I have ever witnessed, and I try to remember it every time I light a fire in what's left of the backcountry.

The man's fire kit was kept in brain-tanned deerskin supple as the skins admired by de Soto's men. The polished hide was laid out on the ground, like an island. A bow fitted with a short length of deer sinew, still quick with a deer's quickness, was looped once or twice around a wooden drill. The firemaker pressed down on the drill with a small block of wood, sawing the bow rapidly until the charred drill tip produced a wisp of smoke from the depression in the fireboard. When the firemaker saw a coal glow, just a quarter-inch square of hardwood flaked off from the fireboard, he laid the drill aside and dropped the hot red flake into the mouse nest of tinder he had prepared, without which the burning coal would be as useless as the fire on the island. He held the small *tusti* bowl of shavings up and blew on the coal until the tinder burst into flames in his upraised hand.

Hard to say, now, whether fire-making is a practical or a spiritual art. Will West Long, who as a young boy had served as James Mooney's interpreter, "insisted that the fire on the hearth had an intensely spiritual nature" but "was human in thought, consciousness, intent, emotions, etc., and was in fact an old woman who was a grandmother in kin terms. She was a member of the family and the household. Proper treatment of the fire was essential to the well-being of the family, good family life, mannerly and proper conduct, and many rules about the conduct of the hearth contributed to the health, strength, and magical power of the old woman."

So through the centuries, the Cherokee tended fire rather than worshipped it. They brought it into their council houses and left it burning within their most sacred burial mounds. This was to follow the example of the animals that kept their own council fires burning inside the mountains.

In Cherokee culture, the gift of the Thunders glowed everywhere. The Cherokee understood that the fire that lit their way and warmed them on earth was related to the fire in the sun and the fiery leaves in the trees as well to the lightninglike stoop of a falcon and the lightninglike strike of a rattlesnake. The yellow fire in the eye of the panther and the dark fire in the belly of the bear were not lost on them. There was, in fact, a fire in every living thing.

Fire was part of all cures. The hands of the medicine man that rubbed away disease were first warmed over fire. Burning coals were dropped into medicinals. Rocks were heated for healing steam. Unprofaned, fire did not send disease; the so-called fire diseases were cured, not caused, by fire. These included an owlish sensitivity to firelight or sunlight, a shyness in the vision caused by looking at rattlesnakes. Fire could ward off diseases sent by cold-blooded creatures as well as protect a patient from the sting of frostbite or the mental cold brought by the Blue Man who dwelt in the North Land where troubles were stored. Properly invoked, fire removed pain. Figuratively, kinship was extended to fire, which was addressed as grandparent. With proper care and skill, the future could be divined from flames. Hunters stirred the coals of their campfires, looking for trails and signs of game the night before a hunt, and when they returned fed the fire the livers of slain deer.

When needed most, fire is addressed as the Ancient White One and is thought to be related to the white medicine in the sun, the apportioner of all things, the moving fire in the sky. After a death, the loved ones of the deceased are "taken to water"—brought to the river—and the fire is addressed in this guise. At the water's edge, death is acknowledged as the release of the soul from the protecting grasp of fire. The living are consoled that the fire has been left in the hearth for them so that they may live on.

Throughout these strangely shaped mountains the Cherokee respectfully tended Ancient Red and Ancient White, the flames at night and the ashes in the morning, and carried fire from place to place when they moved their towns, whose bright names they also carried about the landscape in ways that confuse historians and make old maps difficult to understand.

The Cherokee had no Great Spirit until Europeans coaxed one from them. The creation of the earth was attributed to a water beetle, an earth diver who brings a daub of mud up from the Archean depths:

> When all was water, the animals were above in Galun'lati, beyond the arch; but it was very much crowded, and they were wanting more room. They wondered what was below the water, and at last Dayuni'si, "Beaver's Grandchild," the little Water-beetle, offered to go and see if it could learn. It darted in every direction over the surface of the water, but could find no firm place to rest. Then it dived to the bottom and came up with some soft mud, which began to grow and spread on every side until it became the island which we call the earth. It was afterward fastened to the sky with four cords, but no one remembers who did this.

As in the myth of the first fire, a nonheroic being accomplishes a great task. Insects are busy in the Cherokee scheme of things, as they are in nature. But the earth diver does not so much create the earth as bring it to light. In Cherokee narrative, there is a principle of growth and movement within nature, which helps itself along with the aid of the creatures and landforms at hand—a biogenesis that, over time, accounts for what is found in the world and supports a cosmology derived from intent regard for the real as well as for the traces of ancient metamorphosis.

The earth grows of its own accord, surrounded by the primordial, Cryptozoic sea and according to some elemental law, an inherent tendency toward individual survival as well as diversity and interdependence. Nature is not, as in Genesis, constructed as a static end product—entire and in place once and for all—an object to be handed over to man, conceived of as a garden-bred creature already detached, linguistically and psychologically, from plants and animals. Nature evolves as both subject and object, wildly expressing itself as granite and sandstone, pine and oak, water beetle and wolf. "Man," Cherokee lore reminds us, "came after the plants and animals." And he came out of the original wilderness, hunting to exhaustion and sleeping on guard for thousands of years, articulating the hopes of the former and the fears of the latter until he achieved some rational mastery over both.

But that wild, antagonistic kinship between man and nature is never far from the surface of Cherokee myth and is embedded in their sacred formulas, the language of which was strange and, in part, uninterpretable even to James Mooney's wizened informants. And the polysynthetic murmur of contemporary Cherokee is still laced with the cries of hawks and the grunts of rutting deer as well as the clipped *tch*s of snowbirds and the emphatic barking of squirrels. Art and nature never came apart in the Cherokee mind. Cherokee dancers still wheel and stomp, whistling and grunting, *tch*ing and barking, as they celebrate the opportunities of each season. Given the frequency of onomatopoeia among Cherokee animal names, it almost seems that they named themselves, that, in the beginning, words came from nature, like wild forage, and that even grammar, like dance and song, was fashioned out of the rhythms of the hunt and the feast, of mating and sleeping, as well as the obligations of kinship and the demands of the council. As elsewhere in North America, the earth was the humble center of creation. A luminous spirituality was embedded in the mud the water beetle brought to light as well as in the air that dried it and the water that lapped it, and in whatever fire made the light against which creation first shone. Man no more than the gods had anything to do with it.

In the middle of the eighteenth century, the Moravians spread from Pennsylvania into western North Carolina, settling on a 100,000-acre land grant on the upper Yadkin River, near the historic boundary of the Catawba and the Cherokee. They took it upon themselves to convert the Cherokee, who, whatever they thought, did not think like them: "We believe it is the Lord's purpose to confer a blessing on the Cherokee." The blessing had to await the end of the French and Indian War, in which the Cherokee, despite some martial success, ended up on the losing side.

In 1765 the Moravian Lutheran John Hammerer found the Cherokee of the Lower Towns, in what is now upstate South Carolina, melting away before his eyes from war, disease, and alcohol. Although his task was to change them, Hammerer seems momentarily respectful of the Cherokee as he found the tribe: "They love strangers among them and are hospitable, but poor. However, a man who does not know their language is subject to many inconveniences." Hammerer also noted, with some trepidation, that the heart of the Cherokee nation was over the Blue Ridge and the Nantahalas, where the "natural ferociousness of the Over Hills" was still untamed along the banks of the Tennessee River. The heart of the Cherokee nation remained as difficult and inscrutable as the "craggy mountains and bad roads" that protected it for a little while longer from colonial encroachment.

But the Moravians were eager to try the intransigent souls of the Overhills, and a decade later they collared the Cherokee chief Attakullaculla, who was being led by Colonel Richard Henderson to the sellout at Sycamore Shoals in January of 1775. The so-called Little Carpenter was asked through an interpreter "whether they wished one of our Brethren to come among them to tell them of their Creator and Saviour?"

As a young man, Attakullaculla had been with the first group of Cherokee to visit England. He had seen British might and wealth firsthand. He knew what his kinsmen were up against in the woods of eastern North America, and he had spent his career as chief skillfully negotiating the survival of his culture against impossible odds. His response to the Moravian request was pointedly oblique: "the answer was that if any one would come and teach a school for children they would be glad." The Cherokee had been quick to see the value of literacy and education, but the chief made no mention of wanting to be imposed upon by another man's god. Of course, war intervened again, but after the British and Americans made peace in 1783, twelve years after Henry Timberlake had ventured into the Overhill towns and watched the Eagle Dance at Citico, the Brethren sent an envoy into what they assumed would be the cultural vacuum that follows defeat in war.

That envoy, Brother Martin Schneider, is not the villain of the piece. Nor are the Moravians, who did much good among the Cherokee. Schneider was by all accounts a brave and pious man, but cloaked in the true believer's self-righteousness, he seemed not to know what he would be asking of the Cherokee, who sent no medicine men to Salem to inculcate the Moravians.

A shoemaker by trade, Schneider volunteered for the task. Originally he was to accompany a Colonel Martin Armstrong, who would represent the interests of the North Carolina government, whose land bordered much of what was left of Cherokee territory. At the last minute, Armstrong withdrew from the proposed trip, leaving the devout twenty-seven-year-old Schneider to travel alone. The Moravian elders tried to dissuade him but eventually let him go with their blessing to ascertain the feasibility of establishing a mission among the Overhills.

Schneider left Salem, near present-day Winston-Salem, North Carolina, in late December, crossing the Blue Ridge, alone on horseback like William Bartram, in a blizzard. He then followed the route that Timberlake and others had taken to the Cherokee, a path that followed the North Fork of the Holston River from southwestern Virginia into what is now Tennessee, and then to the well-known ford over the French Broad River downstream of its confluence with the Nolichucky. Schneider's journal reveals that he traveled with prudence and skill, worshipped his God with humility as he went, and carried the psychological burden of his loneliness and homesickness with dignity. He refers to that same "Wilderness" the Puritans had railed against more strenuously a century before, a heathenish tangle of projected European arrogance and fear.

When the weather was forgiving, Schneider admired the relatively unspoiled, partly settled country that surrounded him, but he could not help but see it, ultimately, as *unused*: "All Waters even the greatest Rivers on this Side the blue Mountains are very clear, & have stone or Gravel Bottom. They are often broad, but very shallow, & have generally good Fords. The Country from Flour Gap hitherto is very hilly, on which account the most of the Plantations lie between two Mountains, & are very narrow & long. But the Wood is [even] on the highest Mountains very thick and good, & the Land in the Valleys is very fertile. Often I wished we had but one of their many Limestone Hills in our Neighbourhood. The People make here scarce any use of it."

Along with ancient Indian mounds, he encountered the vicious Indian haters of the Tennessee country and recognized their overt racism for what it was: "these People would rather like to extirpate them altogether, & take their Land themselves; they scarce look upon them as human creatures, which I often could perceive in their Conversations."

On the third of January 1784, Schneider reached the Tennessee River across from Citico and was taken under the wing of a Colonel Martin, who was wintering with the Cherokee. The Moravian encountered Martin "creeping out of an Indian Hothouse," obviously fairly well acculturated and comfortable with native ways. And, like James Mooney, Martin was thought well enough of to have been given a Cherokee name, no slight gesture on the part of the tribe. The next day they traveled downriver to Chota and passed Toqua on their way to the mouth of the Tellico River, where Schneider observed the ruins of Tomotley among apple and peach orchards grown wild, the town burned in retaliation for the destruction of nearby Fort Loudoun during the French and Indian War.

On the fifth, Martin and Schneider held a council with the Cherokee, possibly at Toqua or Chota. With Old Tassel presiding, Schneider presented the proposal for establishing a Moravian mission among the Overhills, which he assured those present would be a purely religious venture unattached to trade or land concessions.

After two hours of deliberation, Old Tassel gave Schneider a respectful, lengthy reply:

> The Head Chief said then, he would answer after some Time; & after 2 Hours he got up & said: He knew & could remember it very well that their Father (The King of England) had long ago sent once 2 Men to them as Preachers, but one of them died, & the other had not stayed long, because War had broke out in the Country, which he was very sorry for. Secondly, that he believed that this Man (viz. I) was a Wayer* that is a great Man, who was sent by still greater Wayers to tell them of Utajah (God) that great Man who dwells above. 3rdly That he was very glad, that again such an Offer was made to them, that they might hear & be instructed concerning him, & all the present Chiefs whom he had asked about it, were of the same Opinion. But he could give no positive Answer, till all Chiefs and Hunters were at Home; (the most of them were upon the Beaver Hunt) but when they returned he would call them all together to a great Meeting to hear their Mind, & at the next Treaty on Long Island, they would tell their Resolution.

Which was to say no. Colonel Martin told Brother Schneider that this was a more favorable answer than he had a right to expect.

Old Tassel's measured speech to the Moravian missionary is a rare recorded instance of a Native American solemnly and patiently resisting be-

* Perhaps *ada'wehi,* medicine man.

ing colonized by foreign ideas. Western metaphysics would wait on the beaver hunt. With the destruction of Colonel William Christian's punitive raid of 1776 still in evidence all around them, I think it safe to assume that Old Tassel was using the absence of the tribe's headmen as a diplomatic way of excusing himself and his people from any further destructive invasion of their lifeways, at least for a little while longer. Another winter and spring with the old ways. Schneider was a good man with good intentions, but Old Tassel seemed to know where good intentions sometimes led. The restraint packed into his speech is mountainous. Unlike the would-be missionary, the Cherokee chief demonstrated respect for two systems of belief where Brother Schneider saw only one. The Moravian left this meeting without having understood what had happened and, full of enthusiasm about the prospects, began to plan to return to Citico.

As if to underscore the native resistance in Old Tassel's reply, the Tennessee River flowed too hard and high for Schneider to be able to cross and make his way back to Salem. The great river formed by the mountains forced the well-meaning man to stay among the Cherokee for a few more days. He noted some interesting surface details about their way of life, but Old Tassel's point never hit home: "I thought much upon my Return, & waited very anxiously that the River might fall because I wished to be again in Salem at the next Comn. Meanwhile I recommended these poor blind Heathen diligently to our Savr.; & visited them often in their Houses, tho' I could not speak with any of them."

Killing time, Schneider saw the preparations for the Woman's Dance at Chota, an important event that lasted four evenings but about which he was not particularly curious. Colonel Martin tried to draw him into the local culture and told him about the Charity dances held twice a year to which the better off among the tribe contributed skins to ease the lot of the poor. But Schneider's work was done, and he had little interest in such things. The icy torrents of the Tennessee River held him captive in what seemed to him a "dark Country" until he was taken over to the north bank in a canoe and set on his way to Salem, where preparations would be made for the salvation of the "poor Cherokees."

The Cherokee sky was made of stone, the same stuff that comprised the mountains underfoot. James Mooney noted that *Galun'lati*, the Cherokee name for the sky arch, was mistaken by missionaries as the equivalent of *heaven*. But the highest place in the Cherokee mind—*Gulkwa'gine*

Di'galun'latiyun—was not metaphysical in the Western sense. The stone sky arch was part of the real world, seven hand-breadths overhead, where the sun reposed at noon and above which hawks and eagles flew.

Galun'lati confirmed that all things were earthly, which was not to suggest that man was the measure of all things. Far from it. The mountainous horizon forms an imperfect circle. A man could only see so far. When he journeyed, he carried the circular horizon with him. But he was not a center, and the world only seemed to move along with his steps. The universe had four quarters, four directions to seek, four fates for any venture. However lost a man might be, no journey was aimless.

The world was ordered to fit the way men look about them. A man standing in one place could look before him, or to his left or right, or turn and look behind him. The sun gave an objective order to these four possibilities, establishing the poles of the quadripartite universe. To the east lay the Red Land, where there was victory and success; to the north, the Blue Land, where there was trouble; to the south was Walhala, the White Mountain, which harbored peace; and to the west was the Darkening Land, black with death and defeat. Four was naturally a sacred number.

The Cherokee knew, of course, that a man's mind extended beyond what he could see. The mountains and rivers do not disappear during sleep. The hunting grounds do not vanish in summer or the council house when you are on the long hunt. The hunter must imagine game, the lover a promising response, the warrior victory. Parents imagine the lives of their children, elders the souls of their ancestors.

Still, there had been great changes since the Wild Boys drove *Kana'ti* and *Selu* from their home and started history. Beyond the four dimensions, there were rumors about strange places that could no longer be found. And it was known that there were many animals that no longer existed, some much larger and more ferocious than the creatures men knew—great hawks and wolves and panthers. There was a time when the sun was closer to the earth and it was almost too hot for men to survive. And there was a time when it was terribly cold and life was very different. Finally there were dreams, a country the Cherokee took seriously.

In this way, the quadripartite universe easily extended itself from the four lands that a man could see when standing in one place. In fact, four implied seven, the other sacred number. The fifth direction was the place where you stood in the middle world, from which you located yourself in the realm of plants, trees, and the four-footed animals. There was also the hidden lower world—the realm of snakes and fish—and the world above—the realm of birds.

To invoke *Galun'lati* without making the reference local—where the sun will begin to set, where that hawk is flying—"is understood to mean directly overhead, but far above everything of earth." There beings dwelt that might be red, white, or brown and toward whom medicinal and other invocations could be made. *Galun'lati* added metaphorical height and spiritual depth to the quadripartite universe, but in the end the Cherokee sky was tangible and finite.

As far as it can be determined, the Cherokee were not deists or zootheists, pantheists or polytheists. They did not worship the sun, the Thunders, the animals, or the ancestors of the animals that lived in *Galun'lati*. They did not even worship the plants that provided them their only medicine. They seemed to revere the lay of the land and the life of things, generously conceived, as seriously and unsentimentally as the hunter regards his game.

The Cherokee world was dense with an extraordinary range of significant being, visible and invisible. Animals, real and mythic, had transcendental powers. The elements were revered as governing forces, especially the sun, fire, and water. Inanimate objects were personified. There were strange person-gods in the world, drawn out of nature—the Red Man, the Thunder Boys, Slanting Eyes, the Red-Headed Woman—as well as invisible beings drawn out of air—the *De'tsata*, the Little People, for example, and the *Nunne'hi*, the Immortals.

All this kept the mind, body, and spirit of man on edge, helping him and thwarting him by turns, but for the Cherokee the unknown was figured in terms of the known; the real was illuminated, not denigrated, by the unreal. Spirit was a quality of matter, not the other way around, as was the Western habit of thinking. The diversity of the Cherokee imagination matched the diversity of their chosen landscape. Anything might be addressed in prayer—a spider, a rock, a ginseng plant. Cherokee metaphor never descended into metaphysics. No Cherokee ever railed against the earth or feared the woods the way the Puritans did. Groping beyond the taxonomy of Western religions, John Wesley Powell fashioned the term *hecastotheism*—"the worship of all things tangible"—for their intense regard for the found world.

Europe had its heavenly spheres and its orders of angels; the stone sky of the Cherokee was inhabited by forces and beings retired from earthly existence, thunderous powers rolling hollow, Precambrian rumbles though clouds and waterfalls and whitewater, as well as strange animal beings that seem not like the Platonic forms of things but like shaggy, extinct shapes from the Mesozoic. *Galun'lati* sounds, in fact, more like a paleontologist's heaven, or the heaven of a depth psychologist of Jungian persuasion, a realm where the "great progenitors" of present-day animals lived, "above the arch of the firmament," and were still accessible in dreams and stories.

The philosophic horizons of the Cherokee did not translate into Western terms, no more than their social and political forms fit European preconceptions. Most of what the Cherokee thought—most of what North America thought for 30,000 years—will never be known except insofar as we can still trace it in the landscape and weather and in the few documents that have some truth in them. Much was lost to misunderstanding or disregard. Mooney notes, for example, that *ada'wehi,* a human or nonhuman agent with supernatural powers, often became the "angel" of the Christian Bible, and that *asgi'na,* a word that designated a human or animal ghost, was taken to mean "devil." These agents and that polarity did not exist. Good and evil were not so easily divided and assigned to another world.

The formal, ritualistic language of the Cherokee medicine men, obscure to many Cherokee, was subject to even more misinterpretation by Europeans. According to Mooney and his successor Frans Olbrechts, misconceptions easily cascaded, obliterating, intentionally or not, the original lineaments of native ideas.

They report, to take the most important case, that there were no distinct words for sun or moon in the everyday discourse of traditional Cherokee. As in many cultures, the names of sacred entities are often secret or taboo. A word for "luminary" covered both cases and forced the speaker toward respectful circumlocution and the figurative language favored by ritual. The sun was referred to as "the luminary that is (that lives) in the daytime" and the moon as "the luminary that is (that lives) in the nighttime." In ritualistic language the sun was addressed as *Unelanun'hi,* "the apportioner," a figurative expression for its role in marking time.

> Since this [*Unelanun'hi*] has always been looked upon as their most powerful spirit by the Cherokee, the missionaries have read into his name the meaning of "Great Spirit," "Creator," and hence the verb stem . . . is now gradually acquiring the meaning of "to create," a concept absolutely foreign to its primary meaning. It is now well-nigh impossible to gain a clear conception of the part which this spirit must

have played in Cherokee religion. Only a very few of the older people can shed any light on his true nature. Some who have been mission-ized to some extent identify this spirit with the God of the Christians; others, even if they do not go quite so far, have absolutely forgotten that [*Unelanun'hi*] is identical with the sun, and have even no idea of the sex of this spirit. Although this spirit was not considered responsi-ble for the origin of things . . . , yet he must once have had the reputation of a most eminent spirit, if not of the preeminent deity. When such important tribal or ritualistic events take place as the ball game, or the search for medicine, he is always invoked in a very hum-ble and propitiating way. He and the Fire (they are still by a few of the oldest informants felt to be one and the same person) are the only spirits to which prayers, in the true meaning of the term, are ever offered; of them things are asked, while other spirits are merely com-manded to do things.

In a ritual cure, the sun might be addressed as follows:

Sharply! Ha, now thou hast come to listen to me, on high in the center thou art staying, thou (who) hast apportioned (the things) for me. Ha, now indeed thou hast given me permission (to use) the white medicine. . . .

Clearly an invocation to a powerful, very nearly otherworldly spirit, but not a prayer in any Western sense.

Sixty years before Mooney, the linguist John Pickering noted the diffi-culty of translating Christian terms—specifically Christian metaphysical re-lationships—into the earthbound language of the Cherokee. The grammar of the language naturally resisted abstractions based on assumptions for-eign to the culture. Pickering noted, for example, that "it is impossible to translate into their language this scriptural expression, *The Father, Son and Holy Ghost,*" because *father* and *son* could not be carried by a sen-tence without what he called the *"Inseperable [sic] Pronouns"* related to the web of kinship relations apart from which the words ceased to func-tion for a Cherokee.

Linguistically, there could be no Father or Son in the Christian sense. Conversely, Cherokee abstractions failed to translate into English, when they were sought out at all. The earliest record of the language are word lists of the names of those things that were of value to the interlocutors.

Interesting as the names of plants and animals are, those lists are poor in imaginative and philosophical concepts that might tell us something about precontact Cherokee thought. Among what he considered "abstractions"—concepts as opposed to nouns functioning as the names of things—Pickering listed no surprises: hardness, falsehood, depth, height, peace, war, silence or stillness as well as life, anger, love, truth, and death, the latter grouping not as free-standing concepts but as qualities attributed to a particular person. Thomas Say's word list of 1823 attributes the principal Christian concepts to the Cherokee lexicon—*God, devil, heaven, hell*—which indicate conversion to new ways. William Gerard DeBrahm, the engineer who designed Fort Loudoun and who published an important Cherokee vocabulary in 1773, noted that the Cherokee were forced, because of a limited vocabulary of English words, to reduce their thoughts and blunt their ideas: "The Indians have clear Ideas, which for want of sufficient Words they can only communicate by paraphrasing, and thereby they deliver their Intentions and Sentiments very plain."

This makes it all the more remarkable that, more than a century after DeBrahm, James Mooney found evidence of the linguistic and literary depths of the precontact Cherokee mind, material that extended well beyond the literal and that revealed the intellectual and imaginative depth of rituals frequently treated as merely quaint practices. He found the imaginative and spiritual core of the Cherokee mind entwined in what he named sacred formulas, dense verbal guides to the edge of the mythopoeic frontier of what was thinkable, the luminous realm to which John Wesley Powell's term *hecastotheism* alluded.

Mooney understood the sacred formulas to be "laudatory rhapsodies instead of prayers," a literary-religious genre unique to the Cherokee. As spoken in Cherokee, they made use of a peculiar verb form that "implies that the subject has just come and is now performing the action, and that he came for that purpose," a singular linguistic form that would suggest an act of supplication except that the verb stems were assertive or imperative, expressing a peculiar tone of demanding entreaty by means of unique accent. Through these strange prayers, the petitioner declares what he asks for.

What Mooney describes sounds much like what language philosophers call performatives or speech acts, instances where language is used as much to *do* something as to say something. In any event, some critical, unique use of language is at stake in the formulas, which are usually pronounced by a medicine man on behalf of the petitioner. This proxy speech act, very emphatic and figuratively complex, is nearly hushed as breath itself: "the words used are uttered in such a low tone of voice as to be unintelligible even to the one for whose benefit the formula is repeated." As performance, this is language at the threshold of silence. In substance, the formulas approach literal and figurative extremes. In some cases, it appears, the petitioner memorized the formula, to use, on his own, at the proper place and time.

So the Cherokee deer hunter, camped alone in the woods, prays by command to the wind, and to the river, and to the fire the night before the hunt in a condition of practical enchantment:

> Give me the wind. Give me the breeze. Yu! O Great Terrestrial Hunter, I come to the edge of your spittle where you repose. Let your stomach cover itself; let it be covered with leaves. Let it cover itself at a single bend, and may you never be satisfied.
>
> And you, O Ancient Red, may you hover above my breast while I sleep. Now let good (dreams?) develop; let my experiences be propitious. Ha! Now let my little trails be directed, as they lie down in various directions (?). Let the leaves be covered with the clotted blood, and may it never cease to be so. You two (the Water and the Fire) shall bury it in your stomachs. Yu!

The hunter addresses tangible gods—the wind that keeps his scent from the prey, the leaf-covered river that carries the life of the year through the woods, the small fire that warms his body and spirit, and the ashes of that fire with which he marks his breast, for every hunter knows he is hunted also by the fall of leaves and the flow of time out of the mountains at the end of the year. And in what might seem to be unintelligible exclamations—radical phonemes beyond the explanatory categories of contemporary linguistics—we find the warning snorts and grunts of *Odocoileus virginianus*—the plosive Yu! Ha! Yu!—which every hunter of white-tailed deer will easily recognize. The language of the prey figures into the hunter's prayer, as well it might. And what a gracious gesture—how clever and open-minded to acknowledge the language of another species in your most serious discourse.

This is the genre of Emerson's primary forms, though Emerson might not have recognized it, language strange as sunlit cliffs along a quiet river bend. These are words dark as groves of mossy hemlock, soft as creek speech, as intriguing as a woman's laughter, clear as a child's face, lonely as a man's heart when he is on the long hunt. This is prayer full of the rich detritus of this life—a fistful of leaves and mast, soil and stones—and not of the vain, self-serving expectation of another one. Hard enough for the hunter to purify himself for the next day's hunt, make himself worthy of the game he pursues.

To his enduring credit, Mooney knew he did not know what he had found when he stumbled on the sacred formulas, and he offered only approximations of their form and meaning, shaping them enough to make them intelligible to Western eyes but leaving their essential strangeness intact. Unlike many early translators of Native American thought, who tried to fit what they heard into Western habits of mind, Mooney did his best not to shift his strange material out of its original context. He was extremely sensitive to the problem of translation: The formulas "were full of archaic and figurative expressions, many of which are unintelligible to the common people, and some of which even the shamans themselves are now unable to explain. These archaic forms, like the old words used by our poets, lend a peculiar beauty which can hardly be rendered in a translation. . . . it must be distinctly understood that the translations are intended only as free renderings of the spirit of the originals."

The difference between the missionary and the anthropologist is profound. Despite the Irish Catholic Mooney's own beliefs, he left the Cherokee material to breathe its own air and recognized "the opposing forces of Christianity and shamanism" for what they were, a tragic clash of cultures. He had found a "living faith" that was "losing ground" to a better-armed faith, and he noted with sadness that the caretakers of Cherokee tradition would soon be "without honor in their country" and then gone forever. Eventually the Western drive for monoculture would cut down these ideas and images as surely as it would the old-growth forests where they had evolved.

The earliest myths of most cultures effortlessly intuit the proper scale of things—the breadth of the universe and the depth of time—and recognize that everything of value on this earth derives from nature and is often, by way of a test perhaps, a two-edged sword—like fire or rivers, like gold to hoard or atoms to split. There is in Cherokee thought, as in other North American cosmologies, an acceptance of the deep time that caught Christian Europe by surprise in the nineteenth century and that still frightens or confuses people who need dogma to organize their thoughts and protect them from their fears, people for whom the strangely feathered edges of time and space are unsettling rather than interesting.

But Holocene spacecraft confirm the intuitions of the ancients—that the earth is an island surrounded by a great ocean and that it is beautiful, limited, and fragile; that its moving horizon leads the eye and mind to the instructive enigmas of life's adaptations, the intriguing scrimshaw of evolution figured in the grain of rotting logs or the bedding planes of sandstone, ramified in the corollas of supernovas or the rocky trickle of mountain streams, expressed in the branching of a deer's antlers or the pudgy fan of a wolf's paw. Viewed from *Galun'lati,* seven hand-breadths in space, the earth looks, in fact, like paradise.

For the Cherokee, the sacred implied a geography rather than a metaphysics. The topography of Cherokee mythology is, for the most part, recognizable, a realm of mountains, rivers, and forests that lead character and narrative toward the ends of the earth.

There is, for example, a myth that recounts a journey to the sunrise, an exploration through the known world by seven restless young men. They had "made up their minds to find the place where the Sun lives and see what the Sun is like." Outfitting themselves like hunters or warriors, they set out to the east and watched their familiarity with the world fade as they traveled: "At first they met tribes they knew[,] then they came to tribes they had only heard about, and a last to others of which they had never heard." Human customs devolved the farther they got from their homeland. They encountered root eaters and acorn eaters and a barbarous tribe that buried living women with their deceased husbands.

Eventually the seven young men came to the foot of *Galun'lati,* where the sky vault reached the ground. "They found that the sky was an arch or vault of solid rock hung above the earth and was always swinging up and down, so that when it went up there was an open place like a door between the sky and the ground, and when it swung back the door was shut. The Sun came out of this door from the east and climbed along on the inside of the arch. It had a human figure, but was too bright for them to see clearly and too hot to come very near."

Their adventure was to pass through to the other side of *Galun'lati,* at the place where the sun rose in the morning, entering the inner dome of the sky vault. But the first young Cherokee to try was crushed by the rock vault as it swung shut behind the sun, and the other six were afraid to repeat the attempt. They seemed to be at an edge where men did not belong. One implication of the story is that they were brave to have journeyed so far, to have risked seeing so much, but although they were naturally venturesome, like the Wild Boys, they were as a group not reckless.* They had reached the limit of things and of their own resourcefulness. "As they were now at the end of the world they turned around and started back again, but they had traveled so far they were old men when they reached home."

Beyond explaining the origins of taboos, Cherokee myths contain nothing didactic. The values encouraged by their stories speak for themselves. Their narratives conflate recognizable hopes and fears about the world, ramifying that keen sense of the tangible into both the wondrous and the terrible, the inviting and the threatening, establishing an imaginative order at the center of which was a psychological realism that embodied considerable courage as well as an intellectual clarity—a frankness of consciousness you meet only in highly developed cultures that are still firmly attached to their roots.

Some myths foreshadow the ethical values of traditional Cherokee life, but many explore the strange border between the known and the unknown, between the present and the deep past, and do so without denying the obscure, confusing magic at the interface of those realms, particularly the magic of subconscious memory, individual and tribal, which for the Cherokee was not a symbolic realm. Their myths take place during long periods of time foreshortened into timeless moments and occupy a space laid out in nonrational dimensions that intrigued rather than frightened the Cherokee mind. Their literature is dense with an overdetermined sense of the known world—of what even civilized man confronts in nature—and assays at every opportunity the possibilities of metamorphosis that had clearly brought both man and nature out of the unfathomable past.

The beautiful myth about the death of the daughter of the sun, for example, seems to contain traces of a consciousness of great climatic change, something very like the Pleistocene cycles of hypsithermals, glacial maximums, great rains, and rising oceans. Such long-term events elude the perspective of a single lifetime, or even of many generations, and can persist in human memory only as part of strange tales in which great, unexplained changes in the conditions of life are routine and where cause and effect are figured in emblematic relations or symbolic actions that compress an enormous chronology into a single narrative.

---

* To this day, Cherokee culture is known for valuing consensus rather than individualism in matters relating to the welfare of the people.

The Cherokee story about man's antagonistic dependency on the sun seems woven around the difficult life of harsher times, but even the most bizarre strategies of survival—appeals to extreme magic—connect with recognizable features of the natural world and with the cultural life of the historic Cherokee. The common redbird—the cardinal—and the darkest mythic serpent of the Cherokee—the *Ukte'na*—easily occupy the same narrative space.

According to this tale, there was a time when the Sun was antagonistic to man. When visiting her daughter at noon, "she sent down such sultry rays that there was a great fever and the people died by the hundreds, until everyone had lost some friend and there was fear that no one would be left." The Little Men* came to the aid of humankind and changed two men into snakes, the spreading adder (hog-nose snake) and the copperhead, and sent them to kill the Sun, as desperate and irrational a desire as man could have. The spreading adder puffs itself up and spits ineffectually, the way it actually does in its bluffing attack, but does not strike. The copperhead slinks off unaccountably, in keeping with its cautious nature, apparently intimidated by the near presence of the Sun. Members of the tribe continue to die from the terrible heat. Something is wrong with the world, and the first level of magic cannot cope with it.

The Little Men then change another man into the great *Ukte'na,* a monstrous serpent, and another into the first rattlesnake, and send them out against the Sun. Unlike the shy copperhead, the rattlesnake is eager for the heroic task and outstrips the powerful, ungainly *Ukte'na:* "They made the Uktena very large, with horns on his head, and everyone thought he would be sure to do the work, but the Rattlesnake was so quick and eager that he got ahead and coiled up just outside the house, and when the Sun's daughter opened the door to look out for her mother, he sprang up and bit her and she fell dead in the doorway."

Both the rattlesnake and the *Ukte'na* depart, the latter full of so violent and dangerous a rage against mankind for being drawn into this dissatisfying misadventure that the serpent is banished to *Galun'lati.* The rattlesnake, chastened by its mistake, becomes ever after slow to strike and never strikes at humans except as a last resort. The rattlesnake becomes as revered by the Cherokee as the *Ukte'na* was feared: "Since then we pray to the rattlesnake and do not kill him, because he is kind and never tries to bite if we do not disturb him."

---

* Another name for the Wild Boys.

The Sun, outraged at her daughter's death, ceases her rounds and darkness descends on the world. The Little Men advise that seven men with seven sourwood rods be sent to "Tsusgina'i, the Ghost country, in Usunhi'yi, the Darkening land in the west" in order to bring back the daughter of the sun. The daughter is retrieved from the circle of the dancing ghosts in *Tsusgina'i* by means of the power of the seven sourwood rods. She is carried toward the country of the Cherokee in a box that is not to be opened along the way. But the daughter of the Sun begs to be released throughout the journey, complaining that she is hungry and thirsty and, finally, in need of air. Forgetting the enabling magic of their journey and thinking she might really be dying, the men opened the lid of the box. A redbird, the cardinal, flies off into the underbrush giving its characteristic cry for the first time: *"kwish! kwish! kwish!"* When they reach the settlements, not only is the box empty and the task a failure, but it is no longer possible to bring the dead back from the ghost country.

The Sun grieved so much at this second loss of her daughter that there was a flood upon the earth from her tears. After a long period of intense heat and then a time of troubling darkness and cold, "the people were afraid the world would be drowned." Since the Little Men kept urging them to use magic they could not master, the Cherokee held council and decided to try to harmonize their relations with the Sun by means more familiar to them: "They danced before the Sun and sang their best songs." The Sun resisted the music of the Cherokee until the drummer changed the song, catching her off guard so that she lifted her head and smiled. Charmed by art, nature relented, or so it seems in this story. The Sun returned to her proper place, seven hand-breaths overhead, climate reverted to manageable patterns, and the world became habitable again. The long-standing troubles were over, even though terrible consequences reverberated forever: The dead were lost to the circle of dancing ghosts in *Usunhi'yi* and the dreaded *Ukte'na* somehow managed to escape from the sky arch to make the dark places of the earth—deep river bends and mountain passes—even more troubling.

The wildness of nature was the constant that tied myth and reality together and that gave such stories a suprarational sense that carried them easily from one generation to another until the pressures of acculturation encouraged their repression. What we now know about precontact native thought in North America transcends many of the dichotomies of Western thought, especially that the observations of science and the intuitions of religion present an either/or view of the world. As long as the spiritual is understood to derive from the material and the earth is understood to be a source if not a center, then stories often passed off as primitive or quaint will take on their rightful authority.

The Cherokee, like the Greeks, understood not only tragedy in human affairs—their native stoicism had long prepared them for the contact—but they intuited the tragic underpinnings of time and space itself, which do not underwrite the myth of history as material progress. For reasons of survival, the Cherokee cultivated intense relationships with earth, air, water, and fire. They well understood the radical otherness in these things—distinct from their usefulness—and they accepted the antagonistic gulf between man and nature as spiritually instructive. The bends in a river and the wild break of the horizon as well as the largely secret lives of animals were clearly part of a great nonhuman narrative. The most important stories that could be told about the earth had nothing to do with the affairs of men. There might be order in a man's heart—if he was purified for the hunt or for the ballplay, for love or war—and there might be order in the clan, in the tribe, and even among tribes. But man would never be in control of the earth. The more he used it, the more it would escape him. This psychological acceptance and intellectual recognition of man's true condition led to practical reverence and values that ran very deep as well as to an artful, imaginative, nonideological appreciation of the universe. The farthest and nearest things as well as the beginning and the end of life were mysteries. Birth and death themselves were striking in their solemn strangeness. Cherokee theory left that strangeness intact.

Before birth, the soul of an unborn infant was coaxed along the white thread of being by means of one of the most beautiful of the sacred formulas:

> Sharply! Ha, now the white thread has come down. The soul has been examined; such-and-such are his names. The soul of the small human being has been examined, where it is growing. Either presently, or at noon, or right away thou willst come and be born to her. He will be born to her. He has been examined.
>
> Sharply! from above thou hast caused the white threads to come down. The soul has become examined. Such-and-such are his names. His soul has become examined. . . . In the first upper (world)* the white seats have been let down, and the white cloth has come to rest

---

* *Galun'lati* is composed of seven realms.

on them. The soul has come to rest upon the white thread. The soul has been lifted up as far as the first upper world, the place to where it has been raised.

This haunting invocation, which urges or follows the soul to earth, is repeated for the second, third, fourth, fifth, and sixth upper worlds.

In the seventh upper (world) the white seats have been let down and the white cloth has come to rest upon them. The soul has come to rest upon the white thread. At the seventh upper (world), finally the soul will appear in all splendor. Sharply.

These words take effect only by the side of a river—"going to water"—to which the pregnant woman is brought before dawn, the time of day when rivers are thought to awaken. If the first stanza of the invocation is left off, a petitioner may use this formula of the thread of being at the proper bend of a river to invoke long life, to cure disease, and for revenge and love.

If the seven stages of entrance into life along those white threads are obscure, so are the four stages of the soul's departure, or dissolution, in death. According to Will West Long, the death of a person's four souls took as long as a year. The anthropologist John Witthoft recorded the revered Cherokee's understanding of this elaborate process:

The soul of conscious life left the body immediately at death and continued its personal life, sometimes remaining nearby for a time, often seen as a ghost, harmless and powerless. Will believed that this soul eventually followed the "trail of Kanati" to the western land of the dead, but insisted that no one had any knowledge of that land or situation. Some people believed that this soul went into the river and followed the river up to a spring-head when it went down into an underworld. . . .

This soul is located in the head, immediately under the front fontanelle. The magic of scalping and of the ritual treatment of scalps is directed against this soul. This soul is conscious, self-conscious, has personality, memory, continuity after death, and is unitary. . . . Will called this and the other three souls "Askina," and also used the word for a ghost. This is one of the puzzling cognates to northern Iroquoian, where the word (phonetically identical!) is a rare and nearly obsolete root. It means "the soul of the bones," and is thus also used as a term for the substance of deer antler. "The soul of the bones" is also a fundamental concept in northeastern Algonkian. . . .

. . . Askina is not imaginary; we can find it in the early vocabularies, in place-names which we recorded early, and in modern ritual texts for Mohawk, Huron, Cayuga, etc.

Note that the use of Askina in the New Testament [i.e., in Cherokee translations of the New Testament] is very different, and probably based on an error by Elias Boudinot, etc. Cherokee seems to have no primary root or any root that could be used for "devil" or "evil". . . .

When the animating soul of conscious life leaves the body at the moment of death, stopping all life processes, the other souls begin to die. That of the liver is gradually diffused back into nature as a life-force and it takes a week for all of it to disappear from the body, if death has been normal. . . .

The third soul, that of the circulation, is located in the heart, and blood is its secretion. This soul is nonindividual and quantitative; it takes a month to die, its substance gradually diffusing back into nature as a life force. . . .

The fourth soul is located in the bones, and I don't understand its secretions. It takes a year to die, its essence gradually returning to nature, contributing its material to the growth of crystals in the ground, especially to the quartz crystals used in divination and conjuring. . . . Will said that the grave should be tended, weeded, etc., for a year after death, but was neglected and forgotten after that, because there was nothing of any significance left in the grave. All mourning ended a year after death, because the processes of separation of the dead from the world of the living were completed.

So the Cherokee soul succeeded in its highest task—reintegrating itself with the earth.

Beyond the ends of the earth figured in the myths were the borders of cultural consciousness marked by the densest figures of the sacred formulas, figures that teased a strange order out of the surrounding chaos. In these sacred formulas, the quadripartite universe was extended toward the seven points of the Cherokee imagination, until it vanished in the unknown. The most extreme formulas seem to be attempts to catch the wild powers of the universe *in media res,* in the hope of harnessing them momentarily for a particular human purpose—a cure or favor.

For example, the Cherokee medicine man invokes a whirlwind to distribute a patient's deadly fever and chills into the landscape, using a formula that traces a topography of cure by means of an enchanted language that leaves no part of the surrounding mountains untouched.

> Listen! O now you have drawn near to hearken, O Little Whirlwind, O ada'wehi, in the leafy shelter of the lower mountain, there you repose. O ada'wehi, you can never fail in anything. Ha! Now rise up. A very small portion [of the disease] remains. You have come to sweep it away into the small swamp on the upland. You have laid down your paths near the swamp. It is ordained that you shall scatter it as in play, so that it shall utterly disappear. By you it must be scattered. So shall there be relief.
>
> Listen! O now again you have drawn near to hearken, O Whirlwind, surpassingly great. In the leafy shelter of the great mountain there you repose. O Great Whirlwind, arise quickly. A very small part [of the disease] remains. You have come to sweep the intruder into the great swamp on the upland. You have laid down your paths toward the great swamp. You shall scatter it as in play so that it shall utterly disappear. And now relief has come. All is done. Yu!

The whirlwind is a tangible if invisible force, an unseen moving form that is perceptible only in its effects, in the swirling column of leaves and soil picked up in its path. The surrounding landscape bears the burden of the cure, and here the object of this invocation seems to be not a being but a place, the world itself. There may well be a metaphysical wish lurking in this prayer, but no Western religion retains so much reality, or depends so much on the real, as does this invocation of the whirlwind. Western metaphysics, based as it is on an absurd split between mind and body, cannot sustain such a figure or keep intact the vital relation between nature and culture, much less nurture the fabulous nesting of regard embodied in this attempt to cure a person's deadly chills and fever.

Nominally, all the sacred formulas were part of medicine, but the Cherokee broadly conceived medicine as a pharmacology of the body's spirit intimately related to the surrounding landscape, the weather, and the life of plants and animals. The ecology of mind and body was an extension of the ecology of the natural world. James Mooney, like William Bartram, began his work among the Indians by collecting medicinal herbs and trying to learn their uses. That interest led the Cherokee to trust both men. But for Mooney "it soon became evident that the application of the medicine was not the whole, and in fact was rather the subordinate, part of the treatment, which was always accompanied by certain ceremonies and 'words.' From the workers employed at the time no definite idea could be obtained as to the character of these words."

The cure for disease was as much a function of language as of medicinals; the formulas had to be verbalized properly and acted out by a Cherokee medicine man, or woman, who invoked the powers of the quadripartite universe by an art and language that sanctioned and activated the cure's medical prescription. Herbs, bark, and roots were powerless—and meaningless—outside this context. Typically, the fully extended landscape of the Cherokee imagination had to be invoked:

> Now then! Ha, now thou hast come to listen, Red Raven; away from here in the direction of the Sun Land thou art staying; quickly thou hast arisen, facing us. Nothing ever escapes thy (sight).
>
> It is merely what has become a ghost that has put the important thing under him. It is merely what has become an animal ghost that has put the important thing under him. But this is the very thing thou eatest. Thou hast once more come to take it away as thou goest along. The trails lie stretched for thee under the very earth, away toward the Night Land. Thou hast gone and put it in between (a crevice) in the forests of the Night Land, where moss grows. Who cares what happens to it! Relief has been caused.
>
> Now then! Ha, now thou too hast come to listen, Blue Raven. Thou art staying on high, in the direction of the Cold Land. The powerful wizard, what (is there) thou ever failest in? The important thing, which he has put under him, is the very thing thou eatest. Only a likeness of it will be left, when thou will have passed. (And) not for a night (only, but forever). Relief indeed has been caused.

So a hunter with cramped, twitching muscles and bad dreams is brought back into nature's good graces by means of the extreme forms of Raven, which in its ordinary guise typically follows hunters, men and wolves, in order to feast on discarded viscera.

The patient is scratched with a saw brier between the four recitations of the formula. Scarification with thorny plants, or with snake teeth or animal bones, is a common part of many cures. The medicine man holds a bowl with a decoction of the prescribed plants—common everlasting and little vetch—which he brings down to the patient in a slow spiral that imitates a descending raven. While doing this, the medicine man imitates the raven's harsh, guttural cry. In fact, the formulas are full of wild language. A short song to cure headache consists of little more than wolf howls—"wa'ya wa'ya wa'ya wa'ya du!"—perhaps because the wolf was the animal with a mind most like man's.

The formulas reflect a complex poetic field of meaningfulness that extends the tangible world toward its most extreme horizons and appeals to the extraordinary beings presumed to dwell at those margins: great dogs, terrapins, ravens, owls appearing in their red, blue, white, or black guise, depending on the quarter of the universe where they resided. The formulas represent the entanglement of nature and consciousness in the precontact Cherokee mind, a stunning distribution of the idea of the sacred, a radical imaginative and philosophic extension of thought and feeling that seems predicated on the idea of balancing opposing, barely knowable forces. The formulas are simultaneously literary and religious, though it is hard to see a distinction between the secular and nonsecular in this discourse. Taken all together, they seem part of an imaginative ecology of mind, body, and spirit in the context of which such distinctions are meaningless.

Mooney notes that some parts of the formulas were songs or alternated between a sung melody and a recitation. Verbally they depend much on repetition, particularly the medicine man's assertion of his own powers and the redirection of address to all four corners of the world. The words are accompanied by fixed gestures—rubbing or blowing medicine on the patient—the physical enactment of cure that focuses what is being said. The formulas operate at two verbal extremes, being simultaneously full of direct, almost rude addresses to the strange powers that reside at the four corners of the earth and circumlocutions that avoid naming the disease at issue or crediting it with any power. Medicinals are carefully related to cures by their physical appearance—the doctrine of signatures well known to herbalists and folklorists worldwide—or by their associated place in the landscape. The end result is an extraordinary mix of the real and the unreal, the ordinary and the extraordinary, the common and the rare.

Mooney took careful note of "numerous archaic and figurative expressions" that only the shamans were able to interpret as well as critical moments in the formulas and accompanying rituals that were beyond even their esoteric knowledge. Such moments were literary bedrock, language on the edge of tribal consciousness. For example, the formula for bringing a man back from the brink of death required a strange invocation that was full of uninterpretable material. This formula for what Mooney called apoplexy—a sudden, often fatal attack like a stroke or heart attack—is one of the most difficult that he collected:

> the formula contains a number of expressions which the medicine man himself . . . could not explain, as he in turn had obtained it from his grandfather. In fact, he was completely in the dark as to the meaning of the formula, and when pressed for an explanation became sullen and asserted that he recited the formula as it had been handed down to him, and that it was not for him to question its authority. The same difficulty was experienced in connection with formulas obtained from other medicine men, and goes to show the antiquity of the formulas, while it also proves how much of the sacred knowledge has been lost. As [Ayunini] was born about 1830, his grandfather was probably a boy when Adair wrote his account of the Cherokee and the other southern tribes in 1775.

The formulas for war, hunting, love, and revenge make more recognizable connections between the petitioner and the object of their wish while deftly establishing the psychological depth of each pursuit. Few war formulas survived to Mooney's time, since the Cherokee medicine men did not save formulas for which there was no longer a use. But the following had been kept alive during Cherokee service in the Civil War and was used for sending men off to war:

> Hayi! Yu! Listen! Now instantly we have lifted up the red war club. Quickly his soul [the enemy's] shall be without motion. There under the earth, where the black war clubs shall be moving about like ball sticks in the game, there his soul shall be, never to reappear. We cause it to be so. He shall never go and lift up the war club. We cause it to be so. There under the earth the black war club (and) the black fog have come together as one for their covering. It shall never move about (i.e. the black fog shall never be lifted from them). We cause it to be so.
>
> Instantly shall their souls be moving about there in the seventh heaven. Their souls shall never break in two. So shall it be. Quickly

we have moved them (their souls) on high for them, where they shall be going about in peace. You (?) have shielded yourselves (?) with the red war club. Their souls shall never be knocked about. Cause it to be so. There on high their souls shall be going about. Let them shield themselves with the white war whoop. Instantly (grant that) they shall never become blue. Yu!

With the awful destruction of woods and game in the nineteenth century, hunting formulas, like war formulas, fell largely into disuse. But Mooney rescued a few from oblivion, and so we have access to the bird hunter praying over the ashes of his fire in the morning:

Listen! O Ancient White, where you dwell in peace I have come to rest. Now let your spirit arise. Let it (the game brought down) be buried in your stomach, and may your appetite never be satisfied. The red hickories have tied themselves together. The clotted blood is your recompense.

O Ancient White, * * * accept the clotted blood (?)

O Ancient White, put me in the successful hunting trail. Hang the mangled things upon me. Let me come along the successful trail with them doubled up (under my belt). It (the road) is clothed with the mangled things.

O Ancient white, O Kanati, support me continually, that I may never become blue. Listen!

And in a brief formula perfectly suited to its accompanying action, the hunter silently declaims as he nocks an arrow, draws and releases—

Instantly the Red Selagwu'tsi strike you in the very center of your soul—instantly. Yu!

—the last syllable following the arrow toward its target.

And the suitor, blue with love and preparing himself for the dance, sends his thoughts with equal directness toward the object of his desire:

Listen! O, now instantly, you have drawn near to hearken. O Age'yagu'ga. You have come to put your red spittle upon my body. My name is (Gatigwanasti.) The blue had affected me. You have come and clothed me with a red dress. She is of the (Deer) clan. She has become blue. You have directed her paths straight to where I have my feet, and I shall feel exultant. Listen!

Beyond war, hunting and love, revenge could be invoked with terrible hatred:

> Listen! Now I have come to step over your soul. You are of the (Wolf) clan. Your name is (Ayun'ini). Your spittle I have put at rest under the earth. Your soul I have put at rest under the earth. I have come to cover you over with the black rock. I have come to cover you over with the black cloth. I have come to cover you with the black slabs, never to reappear. Toward the black coffin of the upland in the Darkening Land your paths shall stretch out. So shall it be for you. The clay of the upland has come (to cover you.) (?) Instantly the black clay has lodged there where it is at rest at the black houses in the Darkening Land. With the black coffin and with the black slabs I have come to cover you. Now your soul has faded away. It has become blue. When darkness comes your spirit shall grow less and dwindle away, never to reappear. Listen!

The practice of these formulas, which in the twentieth century was reduced to minor forms of conjuring, lasted longest in its most serious guises in the Wolf and Twister clans. James Mooney's principal informant, Ayun'ini, was a member of the Wolf Clan. In the 1950s, a medicine man of the Twister Clan tried to explain the source of the strange-mindedness embodied in the formulas, and of course his explanation was itself strange: " 'the minds in our clan are clear and we have more secret words; our minds are half way between hard and soft and everything we know stays. . . . the Wolf Clan is in between too.' When asked what he would do if he were sick and couldn't cure himself, he said that he would go to someone in the Wolf Clan."

Beyond the known was the unknown. Beyond familiar emotions and cultural practices and the normal tension between men and animals, there was an inexplicable, mythic violence in nature, a wildness beyond the instructive wildness of living creatures, something monstrous, a dark reification of all that inanimate weight of nature that leaned against man's being—the silent ocean of surrounding mountains, the dark forests full of uncanny surprises, the twisting rivers that rose and fell, the uncertain weather breaking against the reassuring seasons.

There was *Untsaiyi'*, Brass, a monstrous gambler whose great stone gaming wheel scarred the landscape of the Cherokee River. Thunder dressed his third son, Lightning, in snakes and sent him out with his brothers, the Thunder boys, to challenge the troublesome changeling. Lightning won all the monster's buckskin and beadwork, all his eagle feathers and ornaments, but Brass escaped with his life. They pursued him through the world, east to the great water over which the sun rose, then north to the edge of the world there and then west, from where they had come, to "the edge of the great water where the sun goes down." "But Brass never died," we are told, "and cannot die until the end of the world." The Sons of Thunder left him tied by grapevines to a pole set in the western ocean, guarded by crows who chase away the beavers who try to gnaw at the grapevines to free him.

There were cannibal spirits that lived at the bottom of deep rivers and hunted among the living at dawn, replacing their victims with a dying shade or an image of their living selves that withered in seven days. There were the *Nunne'hi,* the Immortals, who kept town houses within the bald mountains that stood out along the high peaks. They loved music and dancing, and the sound of their drums tantalized hunters. At critical times the *Nunne'hi* appeared as warriors to help the Cherokee in battle. There were also the *Yun'wi Tsunsdi',* the Little People, who animated the woods and often helped wanderers and lost hunters; the *Yun'wi Ama'yine'hi,* the Water-dwellers to whom fishermen pray; the mischievous *De'tsata* and the dangerous *Atsil'dihye'gi,* the Fire-carrier, about which little is known.

There were strange events whose significance transcended the centuries, elemental lessons like the doomed marriage of the North with the daughter of the South or the recruitment of the Ice Man, who lived in the North, to extinguish a great fire. There were the *Tsundige'wi,* a tribe of little people driven to extinction by great flocks of migrating birds. There was the man who married Thunder's sister, the hunter who attended a council of the bears inside *Kuwa'hi,* and the unhappy boy who became an *Ukte'na.* There was Tsulkalu', Long Slanting Eyes, who took a human wife to live in *Tsunebun'yi.* There was much trading of being, particularly the metamorphosis of men into animals, and much adventure.

And there were the magic forms of things—a rare woods snake with blue eyes that had supernatural powers—as well as fully drawn mythic beasts that took nature out of itself. Chief among these were the *Dakwa'*, a great fish that troubled certain places on the Cherokee River; a monstrous red leech that lived at *Tlanusi'yi*, the confluence of the Hiwassee and Valley rivers; and numerous man-eating serpents that were the bane of hunters: the *Uksu'hi*, the *Ustu'tli* that lived on Cohutta Mountain and that drew hunters by imitating the alarm bleat of a fawn, and the *Uwtsun'ta* that haunted *Nun'daye'li,* the wildest place the Nantahala River. The farther into the wild one got, the wilder the forms that nature took.

Counterbalancing the most dangerous serpent, the *Ukte'na*, was the most dangerous bird, the *Tla'nunwa*, a mythic hawk that nested on the great cliffs opposite Citico on the Cherokee River. The two completed a dark polarity of sky and water, one lurking, one hovering about the borders of the middle world where man lived. But worst of all was *Utlun'ta*, Spear-Finger, and the most dreaded *Nun'yunu'wi*, Stone Coat, who brought death into the world.

Stone Coat was a cannibalistic monster made of rock who could assume human form or make himself invisible. Before Stone Coat came among the Cherokee, there had never been a death in the tribe. His first victim was perhaps the greatest shock the people ever felt: "Such a sorrowful event caused deep sorrow in the village, for this was the first time that anyone had died." They did not know what to do—whom or what to fear. They needed a wisdom they did not have and nearly turned on one another in confusion. But they held council. Finally a medicine man dictated that the monster be waylaid along a mountain path by seven menstruating women. Tricked into violation of taboo, Stone Coat, who had brought death into the world, was undone. His dying is as significant a moment in Cherokee myth as the acquisition of fire and the Wild Boys' release of the animals from *Kana'ti*'s cave:

Stone Coat then, knowing he was about to die, said, "Cause as many of the people as can possibly come to gather about this place. Build a fire . . . around me and burn me up." It was done as he commanded and the Cherokee came from distances to witness the sacrifice. When they lighted the fire Stone Coat began to talk to them, telling them that while he was burning and the smoke and smell of his burning flesh arose toward the sky, there would issue forth a series of songs. These, he told them, were his offering to the people to aid them in all branches of life. As the songs came forth, he commanded, they were to learn them and teach them to their children, to be used forever by the Cherokee.

The dying Stone Coat also told them that if they had tried to kill him by force in the beginning they would have failed because it was ordained that they should not have relief until they had learned what suffering was. Knowing the depths of suffering and the joy of relief, he said, would make them value the songs they were now to learn and the medicine they were to gain by his death and sacrifice. He said, "You kill me so I leave disease in the world behind me. But my songs will cure that." He also told them that besides leaving with them the magic songs for dances in fulfillment of their social life, and the song formulas, he would leave them a quantity of powerful medicines in the form of pieces of stone forming his stone coat, which would be found in the ashes after the fire had consumed his body.

Then they burned his body and watched him all night. He kept on singing different songs all the time he was burning, until he died, when he became silent. Then as his spirit arose to the sky in the morning, the singing still came forth and could be heard until out of hearing in the highness. And the people, gathered around the sacrifice, learned all the songs. Some they employed for dancing when they were all together and others were used by people alone for hunting, for war, and other purposes, as medicine.

After the ascent of Stone Coat's spirit they examined the ashes and found pieces of stone all broken up by the heat of the fire. These were the particles of his stone coat. All the men gathered up the pieces. And as each took a piece of the stone he decided what line of life he would follow. Some decided to be bear hunters, some deer hunters, some buffalo hunters, some fishermen; others chose to be handsome for women. And whatever pursuit was chosen and followed became the life calling of the people and their descendants, with the songs and medicine for each purpose in life.

So for the Cherokee stone-clad death was the mother of beauty and sanctioned life's purposes, communal and individual. And however hard death might be on man's consciousness, his heart could be lifted by the songs he learned to sing for relief from suffering. Stone Coat left the Cherokee an important version of the tragic view. They could not have survived the contact without it.

. . .

Ya'nu-u'natawasti'yi: "Where the bears wash." The wild head of Ravens Fork.

The most sacred river in these mountains uncoils from its source. Like much else here, the circular river is real and metaphorical, another distinction that, before the contact, probably did not mark a difference. You can see the round river on a map, hooked like an inverted question mark around a massive exposure of basement rock on which grows the largest known red spruce in the world, an unusually shaped flow that, after a dozen miles, brings the river near its source, like a snake sliding past its own tail. Then the rocky water settles on a direction out of the mountains.

If there were panthers left in the Cherokee Mountains, they would live above the circular river, denned in dry caves feathered with spruce boughs, the pungency of which wakes the sandstone-colored cats from their drowsing and that their young must assume is the brilliant odor of air. Above the cave mouths would be daunting cliffs where peregrine falcons nested among rare avens, whose unseen blooms soften the windswept rockfaces every spring. Presumably the falcons scream, wheeling with delight, whenever panthers are born.

The same Stone Coat who brought death into the world told the Old Ones that the Cherokee eventually would be invaded from the East by powerful white men. Along with the hunting songs and medicinal formulas, he gave them a strange dance as a ritual means for warding off the contact and then, since it was inevitable, for protecting the people from its effects. This dance came to be known as the Booger, or Bogey, Dance, or the dance of masks.

Variants of this tradition show up among other eastern tribes. John Lawson, who heard wolves howling along the blackwater rivers of coastal Carolina, saw a version of the dance among the Waxsaw in 1700:

> Presently in came fine Men dress'd up with Feathers, their Faces being covered with Vizards made of Gourds; round their Ancles and Knees, were hung Bells of several sorts, having Wooden Falchions in their Hands, (such as Stage-Fencers commonly use;) in this Dress they danced about an Hour, shewing many strange Gestures, and brandishing their Wooden Weapons, as if they were going to fight each other; oftentimes walking very nimbly round the Room, without

making the least Noise with their Bells, (a thing I much admired at;) again, turning their Bodies, Arms and Legs, into such frightful Postures, that you would have guess'd they had been quite raving mad: at last, they cut two or three high Capers, and left the Room. In their stead, came in a parcel of Women and Girls, to the Number of Thirty odd; every one taking place according to her Degree of Stature, the tallest leading the Dance and the least of all being plac'd last; with these they made a circular Dance, like a Ring, representing the Shape of the Fire they danced about: Many of these had great Horse-Bells around their Legs, and small Hawk Bells about their Necks. They had Musicians, who were two Old Men, one of whom beat a Drum, while the other rattled with a Gourd, that had corn in it, to make a Noise withal: To these Instruments, they both sung a mournful Ditty; the Burthen of their Song was, in Remembrance of their former Greatness, and Numbers of their Nation, the famous Exploits of their Renowned Ancestors, and all Actions of Moment that had (in former Days) been perform'd by their Forefathers.

Lawson relates that the Waxsaw women danced themselves into a frenzy for six hours.

Communal dancing was among the most important of the Cherokee rituals. The year's dancing was tied to the seasons, as if the lives of men and women were driven, like the lives of animals and plants, by the weather. John Norton was one of many colonial visitors who observed the beauty and social importance of Cherokee dance. Visiting Cherokee in 1809, he noted: "They preserve the original dances in great purity: these are the Buffaloe dance, in which some imitate the movements of that animal, others those of its hunters: The Bear dance, the Turkey dance, and many more named after different animals, which are similar imitations. There are also other dances which are not thus distinguished, but which are imitative of life and its transactions."

Even though the Cherokee lived in the light and open air of villages and fields, their dances were, at heart, forest dances—the circling of men and women about a fire near a river. For centuries densely forested mountains towered around Cherokee dancers, who chased the darkness with light, the silence with music, the stillness with motion. The dances were in part a tribute to plants and animals, to wind and rock, and in part a graceful regression back into vegetative and animalistic postures, a moving concession to origins, a wild fusion of hope and fear at the edge of nature. The dances of the Cherokee—the wild steps and the wild drumming, the rattles and feathers—were the principal art of men and women living keenly with, not against, the natural world.

But the historical trauma of the contact worked its way into Cherokee art. Lawson noted the tragic recitation of tribal fate in the dance he witnessed. The Cherokee, too, remember the European invasion and occupation of North America with a dance that is a disruption of the idea of dancing, a deliberately destructive parody of their most graceful art. Every other Cherokee dance is a celebration of social success—in planting, friendship, love, war, hunting—and communal amity. But the Booger Dance reflects a painful consciousness of the profound negation brought on by the contact, and its enactment is a troubling performance out of sync with all other Cherokee ceremonial.

The most detailed account of the Cherokee Booger Dance comes from anthropologists Frank Speck and Leonard Broom, who witnessed performances in the 1930s at the traditionalist Big Cove community that Mooney had visited a generation before. Their principal informant was the much-respected Will West Long, Mooney's translator. Although the Stone Coat legend implied that this dance tradition is much older than the European contact, Speck and Broom suggested that, in the form they witnessed, "it might even be possible to relate the Booger Dance to the expedition of De Soto, 1540–1542, and Pardo, 1565–1567." It was, in any case, "a record of the anxieties of a people."

The dance was at once a recognition and a symbolic displacement of violence, greed, and sexual aggression—a dramatization of an incomprehensible invasion. The Boogers are given obscene names, and all the movements of the dance are permeated with a grotesque sexual farce that seemed to be both an amusing and a disturbing form of black comedy to the Cherokee audience. By all accounts, the dance is an anxious pantomime and painful to watch, funny in the way that *Waiting for Godot* or *Endgame* is funny. A dark and powerful art, the Booger Dance was held at night and only in winter, when it could have no ill effects on crops. Pregnant women were forbidden to attend performances. No other feasts were held in conjunction with it.

Speck and Broom noted that "consciousness of dramatic gesture," one of the great hallmarks of Cherokee dance, "reaches its peak in the performance of the Booger Dance" and that the communal grace, rhythm, and regularity of traditional Cherokee dances are deliberately disrupted in this strange antidance. The Booger Dance is preceded by a pleasant round of traditional social or animal dances, which are interrupted by the arrival of masked strangers.

The Boogers stagger drunkenly or swagger violently into the performance. They are clothed in rags of European cloth, or wrapped in tattered quilts and sheets, each with some sign of his nationality. They shout and whisper nonsense in imitation of European languages. Their masks are comic perversions of traditional clan or animal masks made from natural materials—wasp nests, gourds, or buckeye painted with pokeberry juice and bloodroot or stained with black walnut and sumac or marked with charcoal. These are not so much masks as antimasks, the violent faces of history.

In a parody of the contact, the Boogers reenact the disruption of Cherokee life both within the dance and within the council house where the dance takes place, since the maskers interact with the audience, deliberately ruining the art form in the act of performance. This mockery of the invaders, who parade around with mock phalluses grabbing for "girls and gold," is an uneasy form of comedy, for the drunken, armed Boogers are powerful and dominate the proceedings. They act out madness, violence, greed, and sexual aggression, not only toward the other actors in the dance pantomime but toward the audience. Nothing contains this tragicomic action; the dance drama spills out of itself in what for Cherokee culture is a terrible, deconstructive moment when Cherokee art is turned against itself in an attempt to achieve tribal catharsis in the face of historical change.

Eventually the maskers settle down enough to be approached. Like de Soto's men, they are asked where are they are from, where they are going, and what they want. They answer in strange languages that are interpreted for the audience. Their answers are always the same: They are from a "distant land," are going north or south, and have come for girls and fighting, the lust and violence that drive the whole performance. They are, for a short time, placated with a dance.

The maskers then reveal their obscene names in whispers, and taking their names for cues, each dances "awkward and grotesque steps as if he were a white man trying to imitate Indian dancing." They do this four times—perhaps a profanation of the quadripartite universe or a mockery of the four-part rituals attached to many of the sacred formulas. Every move they make confirms and profanes sacred gestures. Each masker indulges in an exhibitionism that is both humorous and offensive to the audience.

After watching the white men give a grotesque parody of their principal art, the Cherokee offer to dance one of their most sacred winter dances, the Bear or Eagle Dance—an attempt to reassert the sacred. Speck and Broom interpreted the performance of the Eagle Dance in this corrosive context as a "symbol of the submission of the Indians to the will of the invader, the gratification of his carnal demands." I think it was rather a final test of the strangers' depravity and uneducability. The critical moment in the counterdance comes with the entrance of Cherokee women clothed in traditional dress into the Eagle Dance—the spell-binding moment John Lawson noted at length. The women do not dance to gratify the invaders but to invoke traditional, naturalistic powers against these terrible events. When those powers for some unknowable reason fail to appear, the Cherokee women dance as Lawson had seen the Waxsaw women dance, as a tragic witness to the old sacred things. Speck and Broom noted the dancers' serenity, even when surrounded by sexual farce and threats of violence: "The women proceed serenely and the Boogers do not insist upon touching them during the dance movement. The dance continues—a Cherokee analogue of Aristophanes' *Lysistrata*—circling around the corn mortar in the center of the room until the song is ended."

But witnessing truth and beauty does not forestall history. The Boogers leave the stage area, break into the audience again, and try to drag women and girls outside into the dark. The Eagle Dance has not cured them. Although the women's graceful turn in the sacred dance reasserts Cherokee values, there is no cure for history in art.

Ravens Fork, the circular river, flows toward *Kitu'hwa,* the most sacred place in the Cherokee Mountains. Here "where the bears wash," the seasons walk through the woods as best they can. Great red spruce grow out of basement rock half as old as the earth, the lives of animals appear and disappear. The land here is at rest, beautifully unused for the moment. A small four-log fire might still bring vision here, if not visions, and sleep might bring dreams that lead, like streamheads, through rocky doors underground into the heart of the mountains where all the old things are, we must believe, preserved—Red Raven, Blue Dog, the Whirlwind, Thunder, Ancient Red, and Ancient White.

Prodding a fire in the backcountry, it's the new myths, not the old ones, that seem most strange—that nature can be destroyed without consequence, that material wealth in a finite world is inexhaustible, that life does not need space, that the clichés of consumer culture and the palaver of the Chamber of Commerce will see us very much further into the future, that America will continue to exist once North America has been destroyed.

I prefer the flinty fragments of the backcountry under the old stone arch of sky—the howl of red wolf on the air, running water unfurling over bedrock in a quiet place, rotting logs in old growth, a water spider with a strange tuft upon its back. What was it the old ones said?

"Man came after the animals and plants."

In what is left of the backcountry, it's the new myths, not the ancient ones, that seem most strange.

Islands

*The earth is a great island floating in a sea of water,
and suspended at each of the four cardinal points by
a cord hanging down from the sky vault, which is of
solid rock. When the world grows old and worn out,
the people will die and the cords will break and let
the earth sink down into the ocean, and all will be
water again. The Indians are afraid of this.*

—James Mooney, "Myths of the Cherokee"

The Cherokee mind tends to spatialize time. This is not surprising in people who do not keep a written history, a practice that makes the cyclical appear to be linear. Among other things, this habit of mind keeps the past at hand in only its most useful forms, which is perhaps at the heart of what is called good medicine.

I'm facing *Duni'skwalgun'i,* an ancient word rooted in rock.

Trivial names have no power, and this is clearly a powerful place. Mooney notes: *"Duni'skwalgun'i*—the double peak known as the Chimney Tops, in the Great Smoky mountains about the head of Deep creek, in Swain County, North Carolina. On the north side is the pass known as Indian gap. The name signifies a 'forked antler,' from *uskwalgu,* antler, but indicates that the antler is attached in place, as though the deer itself were concealed below."

So a great deer breathes here, concealed in this mountain pass, which may explain the fog wreathed on these slopes in early spring. *Uskwalgu. Duni'skwalgun'i.* Such words seem made of fractured rock, each edgy syllable taken directly from nature, just as the name of the wolf derived from the broken sound that rises and cracks on the air above where wolves have gathered. An unseen wolf can make itself suddenly present by howling its name. The stone deer comes into view silently, like a deer you are hunting, a telltale part of it exposed by the same slow time that uncovered these mountains, the complete form of the animal visible only to those who understand the connotations of the shapes of things and who are able to see the antlers wreathed in these chill mists. There is either a great stone animal here or a mountain of flesh and bone. Perhaps both—in the old time, words and things were fused. In mythology, as in geology, form derives from metamorphosis.

This is to try to think like running water, a logic as hard to follow as a Cherokee walking cross country in these woods. But the great stone antlers clearly center everything around them, and, as Mooney's etymology suggests, there is more here than meets the eye. I'm not Cherokee, and I have to think about these things before I can see them. But I knew from the start that those dark rock spires above the West Prong of the Little Pigeon River weren't chimneys, as they are now called, that they were, like wolves, the shape of something wild.

From the north, they are the broken and worn nubs of antlers only, a pronounced notch at the end of a ridge that comes to an abrupt end. The right beam has a small basal tine, the left is acorned and stumplike. Perhaps this is to look for the wrong thing, to be too literal. The burr of each antler is hidden in vegetation, the mountainous deer itself camouflaged by forest. Ravens hang in the air like eyes. The deer faces west, following the river at its feet toward *Usunhi'yi,* the Darkening Land, "where it is always getting dark, as at twilight." A broad-shouldered mountain hunts behind it. *Kana'ti.*

Hunter and hunted are made of the same stuff. The hunter would have the advantage in the morning, with the light behind him. In the evening, he would be blinded by the setting sun. The hunter is skillful and patient, but the prevailing wind in this mountain pass favors the deer, which is characteristically wary. Their virtues are balanced and the gap between them never narrows.

That a great deer is buried up to its stone eyes here—its nostrils filled with mountain laurel, flanks sheathed in spruce, belly tickled by hemlock, sandstone hocks and hoofs wet in the river—does not surprise me. It would be odd if the earth were empty.

As you scan this abrupt horizon, two images repeatedly meet the eye: the upward sweep of conifers, the sloping boughs of which reiterate the steep pitch of the mountainsides, and the spills of massive wedge failures sloughing rock in great piles, as if the mountains were shedding skin.

Nowhere in the Cherokee mountains is the relief of the landscape so pronounced. The relation of earth and sky is as precipitous here as falcon flight. The great mass of the southern Appalachian summit rises around *Duni'skwalgun'i,* a colloquy of 6,000-foot ridges mantled in red spruce and Fraser fir, the latter a crowning anomaly in a landscape full of botanical mysteries, a southern endemic that appears in only the most boreal conditions, a colder thing than spruce even.

A dark pelage of now-blighted Fraser fir was once the strongest sign of the accomplishment of the earth here, present to remind you, even from a distance, that the effect of mountains was to sort things out, to narrow and heighten the world to rare expressions of place. Full of the drama of making his way up the bare, glaciated flanks of Katahdin in 1846, Thoreau exclaimed that "the tops of mountains are among the unfinished parts of the globe." But here in the southern Appalachians, which in our time do not reach above treeline, the work seems done. The spirit of this place resides not so much in the romantic sweep of the horizon as in the fine grain of things underfoot, the variety and tenacity of life rooted in rock withdrawing beneath it.

The dominance of summit evergreens is one of the visual pleasures of fall, during which the shape and extent of their occupation of the mountains above 4,000 feet slowly becomes distinct. They save the highest peaks from the barren, grizzled look of the lower slopes and, from a distance, seem to wax healthier through winter, as if they thickened in the cold like fur, emerging in their best hues after the first snowfall when an alpine ground light darkens them.

The vertical tension in this landscape is most pronounced in the dead of winter, when those dark conifers wait in an empty, hoar-frosted realm ripped by bitter summit winds. Most birds and mammals have scattered to better places. Deciduous forms of plant life have retreated within themselves. But spruce and fir play by rougher rules. Conifers are well past their evolutionary prime, but the old habits that allowed them to thrive in the Permian, when the Appalachians were forming, still serve them well in the Holocene. On difficult terrain and in difficult weather, their sturdy seeds and armored cones—a hardy, patient reproductive mechanism—are well suited to wait out harsh conditions that keep the deciduous trees of the lower slopes at bay. So the spruce and struggling fir wait out winter, wind-bent and desiccated, until the short, hard season falls apart in spring and they emerge, haggard as bears.

In Cherokee thought, the primary test of creation was constancy—wakefulness through the night for animals, wakefulness through winter for plants. The most ancient Cherokee understood what ecologists now call deep time and that life was sculpted into the most fantastic shapes by the most fundamental conditions. Darkness and cold, night and winter, were the great challenges:

> When the animals and plants were first made—we do not know by whom—they were told to watch and keep awake for seven nights, just as young men now fast and keep awake when they pray to their medicine. They tried to do this, and nearly all were awake through the first night, but the next night several dropped off to sleep, and the third night others were asleep, and then others, until, on the seventh night, of all the animals only the owl, the panther, and one or two more were still awake. To these were given the power to see and to go about in the dark, and to make prey of the birds and animals which must sleep at night. Of the trees only the cedar, the pine, the spruce, the holly, and the laurel were awake to the end, and to them it was given to be always green and to be greatest for medicine.

And so the significance of evergreens, which shelter life and encourage the spirit through all conditions, was recognized as the equal of predation. A stand of spruce or fir was as powerful in its own way as a panther or wolf. That the highest, most difficult places in these mountains should be the home of such things was not surprising.

Some things are best seen from a distance. But if you come here, come in winter or, like now, at the ragged, leading edge of spring, when rotting snow is piled in circles around the hemlock and spruce while the buds of hardwoods are ready to explode and the first bloodroot rise out of the hoar-frosted soil. Keep your eye on such things. Ignore the road, the parking lot, the signs that tell you nothing. If there is noise around you, pretend it is the sound of crows.

Wash your face in the Little Pigeon River above where the trail crosses and understand that men and women have made ablutions here for 10,000 years, that this was the way from the north across the mountains toward *Kitu'hwa* in war and peace, that this place was known to the Shawnee and the Iroquois and the Lenape in the days when men thought nothing of walking from the Great Lakes to the Gulf of Mexico. Dug into that silver water, your forearms will ache with the cold of all the winters here; you will feel in the bones of your hands what the roots of spruce and fir feel, what the fractured surface of the Anakeesta outcrops feel when nothing is here except the bear and the raven, the wolf and the owl.

Walk in the woods where you can, slowly and irregularly, like an animal. Pretend you are a bear. Stop often. Flip stones; move logs aside. Tilt your head to hear. Growl and sniff the air. Unfocus your eyes to see. Let your thoughts melt toward metaphor. Stop thinking in words. Embrace the old taxonomy, savoring what is animate and inanimate, what is flexible and stiff, what is long and what is short, what is liquid and solid, what is round or unlike anything else. Enjoy the broadness of life so organized— the sanity of the tangible—and mark its details well. There is very little left of the original world, and the possibility of preserving what remains has passed. Nothing has escaped the contact. If the old Cherokee had not buried time itself here—had not seen and saved the great animals that live inside these mountains waiting for this troublesome interglacial to end— we would have nothing to look at and think about.

An overused, badly eroded trail climbs steeply to *Duni'skwalgun'i*, where at first you will see only crows wheeling in confusion over the rock, a weird cacophony that is part of things here. Wait. Spend time. The crows will depart. Moments, minutes—take anything you can get—sometimes a full hour of silence and solitude will appear miraculously, like sunlight on a chilly day.

Find an angle of repose in the rock, some commodious wrinkle of Pangea smoothed by a quarter of a billion years of rain. Sleep. Slip into that fitful daytime dream state that wakes you with your own unease when your consciousness dives into the rock underneath you. Let it go—the earth diver in your mind. Dream dreams. See what you can find.

When you can't keep yourself from waking—it's too cold, or too warm—stand up and look around you, try to see what the great stone deer sees.

Late March hammers at winter with gusts that thrum this foot-worn peninsula of rock, a copperous outcrop fragmented into great scales tilted at an ancient angle of impact. This is Anakeesta, a Cherokee word of uncertain meaning,* now the designation for this dark embodiment of metamorphosed slates and siltstones that you see also to the north and

* Possibly "place of fir."

west, where worn canines and carnassials of this violently folded rock stand out against the sandstone mass of the Unakas.

As the toothy Anakeesta ridges fall apart before your eyes, slowly crumbling as they shred clouds, ravens hang in the air below you, their broad wings beating, as if to warm the unsupportive air, their stony voices full of discontent. The flight play of ravens is serious, the exercise of war birds. When the sun has warmed *Duni'skwalgun'i,* the ravens swing back and forth across weak thermals, pitched down for speed, primaries spread so each can wheel at will, not sleekly like a falcon but abruptly with a violent change of heart, a warrior's deliberate exchange of balance for momentum in an unexpected direction. When two ravens close, for practice, they beat each other with their wings, falling together until one breaks off. Attacks in flight are frank and bold, the attackers giving themselves away with joyous cries as they dive to count coup on the ruffled necks of their comrades. This is the play of wolves taken to the air, and after you have watched the ravens of *Duni'skwalgun'i,* you will understand why, among the Cherokee, the great black bird is the highest rank of warrior, above even the wolf.

The gusting wind that buffets ravens doesn't ruffle anything else. The dwarf heaths of the outcrop have been pruned by winter into rigid thickets that have no more give in them than the rocks to which they cling. The waxy vanes of the *Ericaceae* gather sunlight so intently they do not flinch in the wind. The stout presence of Catawba rhododendron, perhaps the hardiest of the heaths, an indigenous picket in these high rocky places, is far more interesting *in extremis* than in bloom, when its prissy suburban flowers draw crowds. The thick-leaved evergreen takes whatever ground the conifers and hardwoods leave it, and so marks out difficult places and grows with difficulty, an austere talent that allows it to thrive between rock and air. It becomes as difficult as its terrain and marks the most impenetrable places in these mountains. This beautiful creature is all root and branch, twisted by every ray of sunlight that has come near it, bark shredded by the wind into the fringes of the war shirt. Over centuries, it will make soil underneath itself, aided by wedges of ice that worry the rock apart every winter and by the maze of mosses and lichens that occupy the shade beneath its whorled leaves.

On sunny days, mayflies rise with such enthusiasm out of the chill water of the Little Pigeon River, 2,000 feet below, that they end up lost on this mountainside. Anakeesta is laced with iron sulfide that gives it a rusty sheen which attracts the wayward insects. I've seen them dance over this outcrop at midday, egg-tipped abdomens extended down toward the still flows of rippled rock, which they misperceive as moving water. I've never seen a mayfly release its egg sack to the rock, but once attracted to it, they cannot easily break away, so they rise and fall persistently over the still red river, probing gingerly beneath them, lost in the internal logic of their art, mesmerized by the mountain.

Beyond the rusty rock underfoot, the lost genius of these mayflies, and the sturdy guard of the *Ericaceae,* the larger world lies around you, folded and eroded, an intercalation of sea sediments and odd, igneous intrusions propped against basement rock half as old as the earth. The entire landscape is stressed by faults that break against the grain of the longer inclinations of synclines and anticlines that take you back beyond "waves of mountains"—uncanny trope—to seas themselves.

Like language and earth, myth and science are roughly congruent here; the map of one may be laid upon the map of the other, and the resulting patterns are mutually illuminating. The relief of facts is especially deepened by those myths that compress a view of nature that extends beyond its usefulness to man, a breadth of perspective that was and remains barely comprehensible in Western terms, a radical appreciation of the nature of things.

Long ago there seems to have been not a paradise where man had dominion but a brief period when man was a modest, promising part of things. In this way of thinking, man walked not with gods but with animals. He did not rule creation, he was instructed by it. The Cherokee remember this:

> In the old days the beasts, birds, fishes, insects, and plants could all talk, and they and the people lived together in peace and friendship. But as time went on the people increased so rapidly that their settlements spread over the whole earth, and the poor animals found themselves beginning to be cramped for room. This was bad enough, but to make it worse Man invented bows, knives, blowguns, spears, and hooks, and began to slaughter the larger animals, birds, and fishes for their flesh or their skins, while the smaller creatures, such as the frogs and worms were crushed and trodden upon without thought, out of pure carelessness or contempt. So the animals resolved to consult upon measures for their common safety.

No Western tradition takes nature's view of man in this way.

Just to the south of *Duni'skwalgun'i,* along the highest spruce-darkened ridge of the Unakas, an extraordinary series of councils was held in that time before time where the Cherokee anchor their most important truths. Each species of animal met to deliberate on the problem of man. The town houses of the animals reverberated with their complaints against humankind. The bears counciled first in their town house within *Kuwa'hi,* the Mulberry Place. Bears are a powerful anomaly to the Cherokee. They are the *Ani'-Tsa'guhi,* profoundly transformed beings, an entire clan that left its human nature behind for the grace and ease of forest life. In the Cherokee account of the origin of the bear, one of the most beautiful of North American tales, their voluntary metamorphosis is deeply troubling to the clans left behind, and their final passage into the woods, during which their bodies change before the eyes of their countrymen, leaves an unsettling image and an uncanny trace in the tribe's mind. There are few, if any other, places in literature where we see the narrative origin of a species, in this case, "a drove of bears going into the woods" for the very first time.

Before the transformation, messengers are sent to stop this valued clan, but the *Ani'-Tsa'guhi* would not give in to this final appeal, so intent were they on the pleasures and adventure of another nature. But they did feel the pull of their comradeship and stopped long enough to leave an extraordinary legacy: " 'We are going where there is always plenty to eat. Hereafter we shall be called *yanu* (bears), and when you yourselves are hungry come into the woods and call us and we shall come to give you our own flesh. You need not be afraid to kill us, for we shall live always.' Then they taught the messengers the songs with which to call them, and the bear hunters have these songs still," simple and plaintive melodies, one of the treasures of Amerind art.

But by the time of the great councils, bears had seen enough of man from an animal's perspective to be willing to wage war against him, as clear a sign as any of a tragic rift in things. At first the bears propose to take up human weapons. They fashion a bow out of locust in the Cherokee manner and sacrifice one of their number to make a bowstring out of bear's gut. But their claws spoiled the release of the arrow, and when it was proposed to trim them, they stopped themselves, realizing that man's weaponry was leading them off against their nature, back into the realm that they had left. So, caught between two natures, the bears broke council undecided about what to do.

The other animals then met in their respective town houses inside the mountains, and it was the deer—"the principal dependency of the Chero-kee," in James Mooney's fine phrase—that first devised disease as a means of urging men toward moderation or of taking revenge on them for their destructiveness. Each disease had something specific to do with man's rela-tionship with the natural world and, therefore, while harmful to man, was also intended to be instructive. Deer resolved to inflict rheumatism on hunters who did not observe the proper rituals; snakes and fish then con-spired to bedevil men with troubling dreams; and every animal except one (the ground squirrel or chipmunk) declared man guilty in turn and set an ailment in his way: "They began then to devise and name so many new diseases, one after another, that had not their invention at last failed them, no one of the human race would have been able to survive." So disease entered the world and man's mortality suddenly became a mark both of his tie to nature and his disturbing distance from it.

This antagonism toward man within nature is counterbalanced by the unexplained sympathy of the plant world—perhaps the most important assumption of the Cherokee worldview. When the animal kingdom invents the diseases by means of which it sought to limit man's longevity and numbers, "each Tree, Shrub, and Herb, down even to the Grasses and Mosses, agreed to furnish a cure for some one of the diseases named, and each said: 'I shall appear to help Man when he calls upon me in his need.' Thus came medicine; and the plants, every one of which has its use if we only knew it, furnish the remedy to counteract the evil wrought by the revengeful animals. Even weeds were made for some good purpose, which we must find out for ourselves."

Thus was established a fundamental polarity within nature that was structured around what was, in Western terms, man's existential guilt about the inherent destructiveness of his presence in the world. Few cul-tures find constructive ways of entertaining this guilt—an extension of the spiritual problem of the hunter. Those that do, like the Cherokee, find it leads to unexpected avenues of spiritual growth and development.

In the Cherokee mind, the problem of man must be worked out in nature. There is no heaven and hell, no lost paradise—or wilderness—to seek, much less a gift of dominion over inexhaustible wealth. Man never walked with gods. Man might make himself better or worse—might be purified for hunting or war or marriage—but he never presumed to be redeemed or saved forever. There was merely the possibility that where life was respectful of life, where rational limits were accepted both out of self-interest and, to those who understood such things, for their transcendental

value, life would fulfill its potential, practical and spiritual. Where reckless-
ness, greed, and shortsightedness took hold, there disaster would lurk.
What else could come of such things? To protect itself, nature cloaked its
usefulness in the mysteries toward which science and art grope along parallel paths, with the implicit warning that to destroy any form of life—wolf
or weed—was to destroy the potential cure for some malady of mind or
matter. Destroying the unknown creates confusion.

So there is more here than meets the eye. The radical otherness embedded in *Duni'skwalgun'i* hangs on against the myth of dominion and consumption that has brought an overcrowded world within sight of the great
stone deer, a world where mountains are named after men rather than the
other way round, where there are too many roads and too many trails
even, and where the last wild lands are swallowed up by commerce and
idle curiosity, everything treated as if part of some passing entertainment.

"Nature," Emerson warned, "never became a toy to a wise spirit." But
here at *Duni'skwalgun'i* crowds troop up the trail through much of year to
see not the wild, cutting edge of myth but the quaint chimneys advertised
on postcards and brochures. The change in poetic is revealing and not an
innocent revision: a shift from the wild to the domestic, from the found to
the man-made, from the indigenous to the foreign, the strange to the familiar, and the spiritual to the material—a telling part of the reductive metamorphosis—now nearly complete—that seeks to tame every acre of North
America and so diffuse the difficult beauty and the instructive guilt embedded in this land.

The timeless otherness of this great stone deer and the "integrity of the
manifold objects" that surround it—the ravens and the heaths, the hemlock, spruce and fir, the red rock and the silver river below—are a challenge and a rebuke to the dull project that would erase the true meaning of
this place the way it tried to erase the Overhill towns. There are powers
here, the spirit of the old stone hunt still in the air. But they cannot keep
the encroaching world at bay—the busy road below and the ugly metasta-
sis in the horizon at Gatlinburg, which both embodies and symbolizes everything that is wrong beyond the natural horizon.

At this ragged edge of winter and spring, a groggy, bearish season I
dearly love, it takes all day for daylight to fade. I like that, too, the uncertain play of light on all this folded space, each migrant bird testing the
reality of the season for itself, moving through sunlight and shadow, skep-
tically gleaning the most hopeful places, each windblown call a moment
in the life of some wren or warbler evolved to make fleeting use of the

temporary convolutions of eternity raised here. The shape of the land will be the last to go. In a landscape where nothing is sacred, nothing is safe.

For now, for what it's worth, the sun still sets toward the Overhill towns, where I imagine men still fletch arrowwood shafts with the tail feathers of wild turkeys and women darken their hair to the color of a raven's wing with the juice of pokeberries while children are schooled in practical reverence by the variety and completeness of the life around them. Just before dark the children are put to sleep to the reassuring, twilit calls of owls, their dreams to be guided by the murmuring river and perhaps by the howling of wolves, their spirits stirred by the unearthly cries of panthers.

The trail to what is now broadly called Indian Gap climbs between the stone hunter and the stone deer through that dark forest left here by the last ice age. In early spring, red spruce shed snow all day along that steep trail, part of a fitful purification of northern things in spring sunlight. The wintering junco have already flown north and the darker southern variety moved back upslope. All year these active birds remind me of winter. The earliest long-distance migrants are also in the woods—sturdy grosbeaks and dainty warblers—island-hopping mountaintops north, braving a volatile season.

These shaggy, evergreen woods look like bear country, like the trailing edge of Michigan or Maine, and in early April bear are in the air, a distinct funk against the sweet odor of spruce. You think *skunk* at first, but the odor is flatter than skunk, without that pungent edge, and maybe you find an icy log recently rolled over, or a clump of chewed squawroot, or a hairy anal plug left rudely in the trail.

That trail climbs along a bold creek stocked, by nature, with wild trout thin and sluggish, like the bear, from winter. Slender green arcs hold in cushions of still water, flickering slowly, slightly more animate than the riverbed but far less lively than the river itself. Everything except that roaring creek is slow, even the wind gently bending the spruce, running sunlight through their boughs, and since the path is steep I climb slowly, backpack laden with all the things I need for this uncertain season. My breath plumes in the cold when I stop to peel off a layer of clothes. As I wait to catch that breath, rotted snow tumbles from the top of a spruce, creating an avalanche in the air that flushes birds out of its lower branches. The woods are a checkerboard of sun and shadow.

The stream divides and disappears as I ascend, branching through the woods, tracing every curl and joint of contour with casual precision, a kind of momentary finality in each spill. *Ela-Kana'ti tsulda'histu*—great terrestrial hunter. Along some stretches, the shallow flow slides over the trail, or the trail slips under the creek for a hundred yards, and the idea of a path in the woods becomes transparent. Wolves and ravens may have taught men how to hunt and fight. Ridges and rivers taught him where to walk.

The true head of a river is hard to fix, and there is no point in searching for such a thing, since every watercourse ends—or begins—as a dendrite grown into the cortex of silent rock at the head of a watershed, icy trickles ramified like the shallow, searching roots of spruce and fir beyond any pattern a man on foot can comprehend and lost, finally, underground, murmuring in duff and stone.

The ecological compression created by the abrupt rise of mountains works to create not a monoculture but great diversity loosely organized around a unifying theme. Particularly in its lower reaches, red spruce dominates without excluding, and the effect is a showcase of eastern forest life. Without seeming to give ground, spruce share the canopy not only with hemlock, which darken the watercourses until they reach their limit, but with yellow and sweet birch, sugar and red maples, as well as beech, black cherry, and the oaks—largely a cabinetmaker's woods. Striped maple and sassafras, dogwood and serviceberry and such persist until the terrain or an invisible thermocline fends them off. At higher altitudes, the infrequent mountain maple and the beautiful mountain ash establish themselves among the windthrows of fallen evergreens. All along American holly as well as the ubiquitous rhododendron and laurel play that evergreen theme in minor chords, which is underscored by the richness of lichen, moss, and fern life that mirrors at ground level the dark, full canopy overhead.

The diversity of this forest is apparent even before leaf-in sharpens the distinctions among the northern hardwoods that accompany the evergreens. For every variety of deciduous tree there seems to be a dozen wildflowers on the sodden forest floor, clenched in the shade and flared in the sunlight—*Claytonia* and trout lilies, hepatica and innumerable violets, bloodroot and mayapple—a disheveled, opportunistic bloom, the small forest that thrives in the brief season before the deciduous canopy closes overhead and divides that sunlight so thoroughly, leaf to leaf and branch to branch, that little reaches the ground. No flowers bloom under the shade of the spruce, which encourages an evergreen reflection of the dominant tree, exotic groves of clubmosses towering a few inches over the needle litter, images of a Jurassic landscape still on view.

This is the diversity of the southern Appalachian cove forest rarefied by altitude and still well planted with northern species that, like the resident junco, never went back north. The rising slopes alongside the trail winnow these cold-hardy trees from the temperate mix of the cove forest below, and as you head the upper reaches of streams into the harsher summit world, you see how every tree and shrub has been selected over time for its place in this landscape.

Unless you look for it, you won't see the change to full-blown spruce forest until you've crossed a threshold you cannot find underfoot, however many times you backtrack down the trail or explore cross-country searching for the exact edge of it. There is a shifting order in any intact forest, a continuum of continuity and change that adds up, grossly perceived, to a sudden shift of gestalt—the higher loading of evergreen perhaps, a denser use of space as spruce close ranks, a darkening in the understory in which a changed diversity lurks, a new shape of canopy, and, despite your constant ascent, a loss of sky. At some point, the sensation of walking through woods changes to the feeling of being in a forest. Get on this trail before the crowds destroy the sound and silence of things here, and it will seem dreamlike, the way the Maine woods suddenly appear in Tennessee.

At 5,000 feet or so, where red spruce is in its glory, hemlocks have disappeared, along with most of the northern hardwoods and all but the hardiest shrubs. Except for spruce you see only yellow birch and beech, the former small and wiry, the latter prop-rooted on rocks and stumps, taking any chance at growth. Here and there, clusters of Fraser fir struggle to restore the species. Fern colonize edges of mossy boulder fields, which channel water to their roots. Indescribable lichens make soil out of bedrock and air, and, wherever a dusting of soil covers rock, colonies of moss thrive that, in turn, nurse herbs and tree seedlings. The branches of mature trees are hung with beards of usnea that live, like birds, off the air. Snags are stacked with shelves of blackened polyphores that look more ancient than the dead wood on which they feed. This forest is soaked with sounds mellowed by its mossy acoustics—a distant surf of wind immediately overhead, a deeper percussion from woodpeckers hammering on the whitened spires of dead spruce, a hollower chill in owl calls. Red squirrels clamber in northern tones and fuss in alarm all year like farmers, as if winter were always approaching.

Spruce can thrive on thin mountain soils, and in the right exposures will form pure stands where spruce, spruce snags, and moss-covered spruce logs are the only forms that catch your eye. In such places you don't miss the apparent loss of botanical variety for the perfect beauty and the blue-green fullness of such a boreal place. But if you have hiked up through the transition, you sense that the idea of a spruce forest has been schooled on the lower slopes and that the pressure of all those hardwoods just out of view has brought out the best in this ancient evergreen.

Wherever a confluence of ridges shelve across widely spaced contour lines, spruce flats invite cross-country travel. The soil is deeper in such places, the trees larger, the landscape more unified. It takes some effort to walk off against the grain of things, especially with a backpack, but off-trail the linear illusion of travel is lost and the woods confront you without an edge or center. Every line of sight is tangent to something just out of view. You can't walk far in a straight line, but you can always take another few steps—over a thatch of logs, around a spill of boulders, through fuzzy, chest-high conifers—roughly pursuing a heading over uneven ground.

Old-growth spruce harbors rare sensations, unusual ratios of light and space, sounds and odors for which we have little language. Boulder fields of frost-cracked rock steam in the late-morning sunlight, creating shifting mists that hide solitary deer, or the illusion of solitary deer, against a background of tangled windthrows. Ruffed grouse drum from all directions, using the spruce logs dulcimer makers covet for sounding boards, identifying themselves with that unmistakable sound that, reverberating though all that standing timber, cannot—unless you are a grouse—be traced back to its point of origin. These are not mystical impressions. This is how complex and beautiful the world can be.

Kinglets and nuthatches move studiously through the spruce canopy, gleaning seeds and keeping some sort of irregular time in the woods with nasal *aant*s and *peent*s that break against the long, haunting melody of the winter wren. While I watch the canopy, my heavy, off-balance footsteps tear through thick mats of ground moss, releasing a scent of soil rich as the odor of coffee rising from a newly opened can.

The forest floor is littered with the birth and death of things. In fact, the virtue of a climax forest is to provide conditions for the proper intimacy of life and death, the commonplace continuity in nature that harbors eternity, if the theme needs a name, without promising immortality. A red spruce grows here for three centuries, stands dead for fifty years, falls and then rots for another hundred. The faint, log-shape hump of moldered wood in front of me, on which birch and beech and new spruce compete for time in time, takes me back to de Soto, who—although he passed within sight of these mountains—could not see this forest much less *that* seedling for the gold in his eye, or takes me back to the last Cherokee to hunt game or medicine here before the great disturbance that has made the common life of things rare and nature so generally endangered and reduced that we keep it in parks. And, of course, this old-growth red spruce is rare. In fact, most of what survives in North America surrounds me here, and I'm not sure whether I'm enriched or impoverished.

Picea rubens ranges from southern Ontario, New Brunswick, and the Canadian maritimes to the southern Appalachian summit region. In the north, it is part of lowland forests as well as a mountain dweller, and may grow down to sea level at the extreme of its range, where it persists in the cold fogs along the south shore of Chaleur Bay, across from Gaspé, and around the Bay of Fundy on out onto Nova Scotia as well as Prince Edward and Cape Breton islands. North of these places black spruce takes hold all the way to treeline and tundra.

The continuous northern distribution of red spruce spills from Canada across the St. Lawrence over northern New York and New England south to northeastern Connecticut. South of the Adirondacks and New England, *Picea rubens* survives only in an archipelago anchored in New York's Catskills and Pennsylvania's Poconos and then arcs southwest in increasingly smaller upland refuges across central Pennsylvania, where it is naturally rare, on into the Alleghenies of eastern West Virginia and the southern Appalachians proper. Islands of red spruce appear again in substantial stands on the highest mountains of western Virginia, western North Carolina, and eastern Tennessee.

Like many northern species of plants and animals, red spruce are restricted to higher and higher elevations the farther south they appear, rough evidence of the climatic correspondence between latitude and elevation known to botanists as the Appalachian extension. You see this peninsula of northern forms in the distribution maps in field guides for mammals, birds, reptiles, insects as well as the trees, shrubs, mosses, and herbs that comprise their habitat—innumerable life-forms that follow the southern Appalachians into latitudes where they could not survive were it not for the rise of mountains. In fact, the biological diversity of eastern North America peaks here in the Cherokee Mountains, where northern and southern life-forms are juxtaposed. Where they reach high enough, the Black Mountains, the Unakas, the Balsams, and the southern Blue Ridge provide niches for a flourishing of many forms of life equally at home a thousand miles to the north while simultaneously providing unique ground for southern endemics and establishing the northern limit of many southern, even semitropical forms of plant and animal life.

In effect, the southern Appalachians are a palimpsest of life distributed and redistributed by the tides of glacial advance and retreat and the cycles of warming and cooling within glacials and interglacials, the same forces that cast meanders into the Little Tennessee River and built its terraces and floodplain. Those inviting changes drew Paleo-Indians east from the Mississippi Valley and eventually brought the Cherokee to where their imagination fit the landscape as perfectly as the tips of a vulture's wings fit these fluted slopes. Roughly speaking, paleobotany confirms mythology. Time embellishes space.

By noon, sunlight has warmed the spruce and fir, if not the air beneath them. The same breeze that carries their bittersweet scent moves blocks of colder air about, and the feel of the day changes from moment to moment. The terrain has stumped me at a woody cliff I can get neither up nor around with my awkward frame pack, which teeters and catches vegetation whenever I try to scale steep ground. I'm only a few hundred yards below a more forgiving contour that would take me to the Appalachian Trail, but I have to negotiate a longer way to it—down and around and up.

The spring seep through this shadowed cliff face is still largely frozen in place and there are several inches of snow along its base. Scuffed deer tracks and gray, furry curls of fox scat show this *is* the way down toward where the ridge can be traversed into the next watershed. In a few hundred yards the rocky seam becomes a streamhead I can't find on the map. A smooth rock face catches sunlight where the cliff angles to start a river on its way. The ice sheathing melts from the sun-warmed rock out, so that water staggers in viscid blobs behind the frozen pane, river molecules stirring. A fine moss assays the silver base of the icicles that fringe an overhang painted with a fluorescent yellow lichen barely palpable to my fingertips. Diminutive, translucent thrice-cut ferns, a cell or two thick, nod from the wet rock alongside single sprigs of laurel that look like rare herbs. The cliff turns here, bending its layers of sandstone into a horseshoe-shape enclave at the center of which a shallow bowl of ice water just barely spills over the stream's first stone lip.

I step into the cold, sunlit sound of trickling water.

Propped against my pack, I lunch on cheddar and chocolate and an orange, watching a river form out of stone and ice and sun. The cliff of stacked sandstone I had been following has turned downslope and crumbled underneath itself, becoming a bed for the creek it created. There is more flow in the first hundred yards below me than melting snow and ice account for, and I assume that this ridge is supercharged with water and that the mountain underneath me is pumping hard. Although the creek starts in shallow depressions in bedrock steps that don't concede much to the idea of running water, before long a thin cascade forms, linking small pools lined with cobbles and stone and fine gravel—the pecking order of long-term erosion—and below that the familiar riffle-pool-riffle grammar of a mountain stream takes hold.

That first bowl of water is as clear as air in April or October. I would need a microscope to find life in it, and perhaps even then the slide would show what I see—nothing. To the naked eye it is a principle, an element, a primary form like a spruce needle or a wren.

Some mineral in the sandstone gives off an odor as piercing as chlorine but sweeter, as if the resins of spruce and fir had gotten into it. In this dense, vivid world, everything seems filtered, clarified to its essence and then metamorphosed—sandstone blown away, grain by grain, in the same breeze that winnows seeds from the spruce, this numbing creek water distilled by sunlight from the rock that forms its bed, the rock in turn scoured and sorted by the creek freed here. Perhaps it is the thin blue light of an April day, that temperate gleam of spring sunlight glowing from the stone arch of sky. An indigenous clarity surrounds life here. The qualities of earth and water and air overlap. The idea of order in spruce-fir is clear—one element purifies another—and the random thoughts of mountains—sandstone cliffs wrinkled into creek beds, the fox and deer whose tracks I followed, the mossy icicles and translucent ferns, the healthy spruce and the dead fir—are worth close inspection.

Overhead, a red squirrel in its gray phase, which I mistake at first for a flying squirrel, barks alarm. Northern flying squirrels can be found here, but they are rare as saw-whet owls, rose-breasted grosbeaks, mountain cranberry, and paper birch, small groves of which are tucked away, here and there, chalky apparitions stranded this far south, waiting for the next glacial. Red squirrels are common enough, but squirrels, red and gray, are a fine animal in the wild and, along with the crow, one of the most vocally complex creatures you can encounter. The one I'm watching chirrups and chatters in a beech tree, turning about in different display positions, violently quivering its hind quarters and jerking its tail, which only reaches to the nape of its neck. Ears up, expressive koala-face hardened well beyond its cute, cartoonish qualities, its intent bark throws a serious circle of alarm into the woods.

The ground is littered with cuttings and cones, some open with only a seed or two still hung inside, others still wrapped tight, the scales unsprung. The closed cones are fine as basketry or snakeskin—symmetrical and waterproof, strong and light—image and embodiment of a perfect vessel. The small, winged seeds within them look like trout alevin—eyed tails—the start of something. Those tiny, quarter-inch-long seeds, far more compact than maple keys, are designed to helicopter long distances on summit winds. In their own way, trees are migratory. Many are broadcast far beyond conditions hospitable to germination and become food for mammals and birds. Enough remain at the foot of mature spruce to ensure recruitment within the forest.

Spruce don't bear cones until they enter the canopy and their crowns thicken in direct sunlight. Trees can mature in as few as fifteen years, but in a healthy stand, where gaps develop slowly, a spruce may serve a prolonged apprenticeship in the midcanopy shade, waiting up to fifty years for the opportunity to propagate. Once given the chance, they are prolific and can bear seeds for two or three centuries. The spruce grow large and healthy on this northern exposure, casting a communal shadow across the rocky slope. There are trees too thick for my arms to reach around, stolid old giants with the dark rough hide of older spruce, a deeply furrowed bark, a rind of scaly cork half turned to stone.

The idea of red spruce does not reach its limit in the southern Appalachians. The mountains are not nearly high enough to exhaust the species' tolerance of cold and harsh conditions. Long before spruce would become thinned and dwarfed by altitude, the Fraser fir appears, crowding spruce out entirely on the highest peaks. And although spruce are now encroaching on the domain of the blighted firs, the dead ranks of the firs still hold the highest places.

The Cherokee were correct about the character of conifers. Conifers evolved to pioneer difficult ground, which is why the spruce and fir are here in the first place. Eighteen thousand years before the present, during the harsh climate of the most recent glacial maximum, the entire world below me would have been a hardy mix of conifers—spruce and fir as well as jack pine and larch, the latter two no longer present. Where I am now would have been above treeline, wind-swept boulder fields and tundra. This arrangement persisted for 5,000 or 6,000 years. By 10,000 years ago, by which time man had hunted into the region, spruce and fir were established associates. As postglacial climate warming began to peak 8,000 years ago, the spruce-fir forests of the southern Appalachians separated from the northern spruce-fir complex somewhere near the thirty-eighth parallel and then fragmented, broken apart by the steep relief of the southern mountains, which frequently dipped down below the altitude the trees required. The southern spruce-fir forest receded to a natural minimum during the warming, which lasted until 4,000 years ago. At the same time many of the more boreal forms of plant life were extirpated and the forest was pruned to something like its current mix of species. During the subsequent cooling trend the spruce-fir assemblage then expanded in favorable locales and remains in those few places where it was preserved.

Spruce and fir grew well together, competing through their shared advantages and complementing one another with reciprocal characteristics that seemed to ensure the maximum use of the terrain and changing climate. Left undisturbed, spruce live twice as long as fir—two centuries as opposed to one on average—but fir grows more quickly and often outcompetes spruce for the gaps that open as part of the natural regime of regeneration in old-growth forest. Where gaps are large, both conifers are apt to lose ground to mountain ash, pin cherry, and yellow birch, ambitious hardwood understudies waiting in the wings.

The undisturbed spruce-fir association was a tight weave of reciprocal characteristics that underwrote the long-term stability of a forest that has adapted to the roller coaster of Holocene weather. The larger, longer-growing spruce produced bumper crops of seeds less frequently than the Fraser fir. Fir seedlings outgrew spruce seedlings and, with deeper-reaching roots, were less susceptible to drought. A fir sapling also had the advantage of a faster growth rate than a spruce sapling when the opening created by a windthrow suddenly showered it with sunlight, releasing its pent-up growth potential. In many ways, fir got a faster start.

But spruce was more shade tolerant and could outlast fir during a long period of suppression beneath a canopy that didn't open. And, once given the edge, spruce grew larger and lived longer, holding a coveted position in the canopy well beyond the endurance of a given fir. The smaller fir died sooner, losing its place in the canopy more quickly. In turn, fir regenerated faster and, being more prolific, produced more candidates to try the canopy again as soon as another opportunity presented itself.

Between the two species, which shelter more than 150 less obvious forms of life, these rough slopes were well used. The competition between spruce and fir more resembled a dance—a graceful give-and-take—than a race. The survival of the fittest has a music to it far more complex and subtle than the sweaty, dog-eat-dog metaphors it is usually summoned to support. Because of the blight, that old order is gone, but its seeds are still here, practicing, as it were, until the genes of a fir seedling somewhere on these slopes mutates a resistance to the bark-boring insect that kills the young trees off before they reach maturity. With all the standing dead firs, this spruce-fir realm is not the dark forest it should be—not as cool and moist—and because the openings in the canopy encourage a thick growth of hip-high seedlings, it does not have the open look at ground level it once had. But the dense nursery of spruce and fir is impressive and encouraging.

This off-trail walking is a constant detour, but that's really the goal, and I have all afternoon to loop a few miles through this old growth that compresses so much time in so little space. The point is to lay the day out along these slopes and leave it there. Twenty yards down the creek bed, I stop, then stutter-step and stop again, which flushes a grouse out of partridgeberry still scarlet with winter cold. The sound and sight of flushing game always seem detached and create the impression that two things are happening at once, a perceptual diversion that saves many a grouse in the fall, when a hunter is apt to shoot the sound rather than the bird making it. There's a soft flutter and buzz from nearly underfoot, then a moment when the bird is freeze-framed with its tail fanned down for short takeoff lift until the clear, static image is suddenly replaced by a tawny blur veering out of sight before it seems possible, given the slow, nondirectional commotion of the flush.

In half a mile I leave the creek and log-hop through spruce-fir toward a saddle in the next ridge south, descend this to a dry seam where a deliciously cold stream of air is trapped, and then traverse a dry, open slope until I pick up a well-maintained trail that will take me to the summit ridge. There is deer and bear sign all along, but the creaking pack or the scent of me drives game out of sight, and all the way to camp I walk in that empty circle that often surrounds a walker in the woods.

Designated campsites are one of the necessary evils of an overcrowded backcountry, a problem exacerbated by the Appalachian Trail, which funnels crowds along the Appalachian summit. I would rather have slept by the sandstone horseshoe and its nameless stream, learned something about the woods there, dreamed some spruce-fir dreams with my head on the ground, but the Mt. Collins shelter—which offers a rodent-infested wooden bunk screened by chain-link fencing—will have to do. This site is so overused, the Park Service has had to plant several Port-a-Sans out back. In front of the shelter, there is an enormous fire ring littered with half-burned trash and impossible firewood—charred log ends and stumps and branches of green wood ripped from living trees—evidence of the panic fires of winter campers who did not know what a winter night was like here at 6,000 feet.

It is already early evening by the time I hang my pack from one of the ropes in the shelter, where mice are a greater threat than bears. What had become a warm afternoon cools quickly as I stretch my legs and walk about, enjoying the buoyancy of my relative weightlessness. My calves feel pleasantly knotty and my thighs strong from walking, ridged in the long, taut muscles with which the mountains reward you. A flow of birdcalls picks up briefly as the last long rays of daylight tint the midcanopy and then taper off with the waning light. A grizzled deer appears at the edge of camp, an antlerless summit buck, browsing and watching—head down, head up, half step, turn, turn, head down. When I move, it crashes off.

Evening cools quickly, raising my hunger. The drumming of grouse, intermittent all day from every quarter, ceases as light and warmth slide off the slopes. The spruce darken. The wrens and warblers disappear, folding their wings, I suspect, inside the windproof conifer seedlings. A wintry sunset puts a purple glow behind the ranks of trees that line the ridge crests to the west and north. *Gadalu'tsi.* Fringe standing erect.

I cook a simple meal on a gas stove and then make a small fire ring within the large one. Gathering night wood, I come on northern things in the twilight—moosewood and reindeer lichen, Zen gardens of shining club moss amid which I find the thin fingers of its Arctic form poking through splits in tattered skeins of birch bark. A northwest wind with a promise of changing weather in it produces a light rain of spruce needles and rattles the stunted hardwoods, twisted crones of pin cherry and yellow birch.

I build a small, four-log fire—practical acknowledgment of the quadripartite universe—using, as I like to do, yellow flames of birch bark for tinder. One thing lights another. Form flows. The Cherokee loved the magic that gracefully crossed boundaries as much as they loved the polarity that clarified the things of this world.

In the backcountry, history disappears and the old world returns at night, coaxed by firelight and, tonight, a cold arc of moon pulsing so hard I can see the remainder of the dark sphere hidden in the sky.

Daylong days and a midnight sun might be a welcome sign in the Arctic, a transcendental visitation at the ends of the earth, but we'd go mad here in the crowded middle latitudes if the sun never set. Things dance at night in our slender woods, what's left to dance in what woods are left. After the fire settles into itself, squaring the circle of stones, I walk out from camp, make night rounds like a bear to see where I am.

The campsite is set on a plateau just below and to the north of the summit ridge, a few miles east of *Kuwa'hi,* where the bears held their council. At night, the myths matter. It's a half mile farther along the spur trail to the main ridge. Spruce-fir looks strong at night, filled in with nameless shades of darkness and unlit sounds. Screech owls whinny back and forth through the wind-tossed spruce.

Despite the wild, pathless way I came here, there's a road on the summit, a strange-looking thing at night—man's answer to the stars here, I suppose, a strip of asphalt leading to a parking lot and a battery of rest rooms. Across the road, there's a vantage south into North Carolina and that broad recessional of mountains people drive up here by the millions to see every year. Somewhere out there in the dark below me the Tuckasegee and Oconaluftee rivers come together at *Kitu'hwa* and flow on toward where the Little Tennessee dies in Fontana Lake.

As I watch the varieties of darkness recede toward the horizon, a small hawk—a Cooper's or merlin—slices improbably fast from behind me and high overhead. Just a gray silhouette gone over the ridge in the same moment it arrives, distinct despite its speed, a visitation followed by the quick-cutting sound of wings from out of sight below me as it banks to trace the canopy.

The raptor reminds me of Thoreau's boreal, hawklike intelligence, the form his mind and heart assume near the end of *Walden,* when he becomes the hawk he watches and what is literal and figurative in his mind and heart and writing merge perfectly, the way form and function glow together in nature. Unlike his mentor Emerson, for whom nature was a philosophical constant, Thoreau always kept an eye on history, politics, and commerce, which tempered his Romanticism and chased his love of nature with foreboding. In the end, Thoreau was nearly a modernist, much closer in spirit to Twain and Faulkner than to Wordsworth or Longfellow. In *The Maine Woods,* he gives us a glimpse of the terrible logging of old-growth white pine in northern Maine and climbing Katahdin seems a bit desperate to touch primal things before they were lost forever.

Still, Thoreau waxed Romantic when he got the chance—you feel good in the open air and want to howl a little—and, deep in a backcountry that still led somewhere—the wildest place he would ever be—Thoreau celebrated, for all of us, "pure Nature . . . vast and drear and inhuman . . . savage and awful, though beautiful. . . . the unhandseled globe. . . . the fresh and natural surface of the planet Earth, as it was made forever and ever"—something to which we no longer have access. The ambitions of Romanticism have long since collapsed around us, and its largest themes are unsupported by the fragments of the world we have left ourselves. If anything, nature is more exquisite at this point in history than any other, but the poignancy of our moments in what is left of the American woods does not preserve anything or augur well.

A quarter mile from camp I can smell the thin smoke from my fire, borne on that northwest breeze, and I follow my nose back through the woods. From the shadows, I watch that fire—gift of the Thunders—and the circle of light it throws around my empty camp—the shape of ceremonial, circumference of the dance. I half expect to see myself step into the glow, hunker down, and poke the flames. I half expect to see the old dancers.

I think of the virtues of the animals that became the founding spirits for the Cherokee clans. I think of the autumn dance of whitetails in rut and the delicate way bears walk. I think of the stillness of trout, of the silver of moving water. I think of the masks that animals wear that became the masks of those dancers, of the way men learned to drum on hollow logs like grouse, to pipe like wood thrush, to weave like spiders, to fashion baskets light as spruce cones, to scream in battle like ravens, to hunt like wolves.

I think of the wolves crossing paths with me on the head of Panther Creek and the howling I heard on Anthony Ridge. I think of the veery piping on Whistling Branch, the waterfowl flushing away from me on Citico Creek, the rain beating on my canoe as I tried to sleep and dream above Chota on the haunted, polluted shores of Tellico Lake, the strangely silent geese in the fog upriver of Chota. I think of the saw-whet owl, which I have never heard, and of the flying squirrel, which I have never seen, and of all the things I have never seen but hope to see.

Today it was bloodroot pushing through the icy filaments of hoar-frosted soil, that wall of ice where a river started, the rough elephant skin of centuries-old spruce, the blighted Fraser firs with crowds of seedlings at their feet, the red squirrel and the grouse, the mossy ground, the trail, the road. The sandstone cliff, the creek, the earthy air.

I feed the small fire for a few hours hunched in the glow and bundled against the stiffening wind, hoping that all this spruce and its attendant Arctic forms would tease green sheets of borealis from the black horizon.

Something makes a half circuit of the camp in those same shadows from which I watched the fire, walking slowly, not a browsing gait but the soft, halting rustle of a watching tread, staying downwind—curious or worried to see what is here. A fox, a deer, a bear. Then windy silence until a horned owl begins to mark sidereal time from the vantage of a dead fir.

By midnight a raven's wing of sky is taut with stars and this summit is clearly the bottom of something.

Watch the fire die, feeling a cold night close in. Feel a wolfish wind pick up, focusing that cold and rattling the cage where I will sleep. Spread the remaining coals with a stick and watch them fade quickly, one by one, red to black. Remember the water spider carrying a lit coal across the water from one island to another in a woven bowl upon its back. Envision the shell gorget they found at Citico, the image of that water spider surrounded by suns and rattlesnakes.

I wish I had been here a thousand years ago.

By now the wolves must know they are on an island.

Cold foggy morning. The stone arch of sky dissolved around the stars last night and descended, leaving hard frost and granite air. I'm half awakened by light and cold. Coccooned in a winter bag, I try to hold onto my fading sleep, watching masts of spruce drift through clouds as the mountains lean into the wind and the long bedrock keel underneath me slices toward the mouth of Baffin Bay. Only my face feels the stinging air. Visibility is maybe twenty yards. I might be anywhere. Perhaps I'll walk up a moose today, or move through caribou, hear loons instead of ruffed grouse, cross paths with gray wolves rather than red.

By the beginning of this second spring of wolves, in March of 1994, *Canis rufus* must have figured out that it was, in effect, living on an island formed by the preserved uplands of the Great Smoky Mountains National Park and that fifteen miles north or south of the southern Appalachian summit wolf country was a problematic, Balkanized affair that made no more sense to the mind of a wolf than the first treaty maps did to the Cherokee. Nonetheless, in addition to the inexorable inroads of development, there were more than a million and a half acres of national forest lands beyond the national park—the Cherokee to the north, Pisgah to the east, Nanatahala to the south, and the Cherokee again to the southwest—that were, from the perspective of a wolf, suitable ground to roam. The U.S. Forest Service had not agreed to accept red wolves on their lands, though they were considering this complex and controversial possibility. The legal boundaries of the red wolf restoration were still the boundaries of the Great Smoky Mountains National Park.

The original Tremont male had probed beyond those legal limits when it crossed the Little Tennessee River at the Cheaoh Dam, where Chris Lucash and Barron Crawford twice retrieved it. The Tremont female had stayed on the island of mountains, thoroughly exploring the Smoky Mountain backcountry, running the summit and zigzagging the cove forests. The adopted Tremont young had spilled out of wolf country at the first opportunity. Both generations of the Cades Cove wolves, content with their game-rich valley and secure in their well-defined home turf and social structure, had little inclination to roam too far for too long.

Only one wolf from those first two wild litters of April 1993 remained at large during the winter that had just ended, the surviving female pup from the original Tremont pair, 593F, which came to be known to the few people aware of her existence as the Tellico Plains wolf. Like her male littermate, 592M, which had explored north beyond the national park boundaries the previous autumn without creating much of a stir, 593F traveled widely to the southwest from November of 1993 to March of 1994, temporarily extending the de facto boundaries of wolf country far beyond even the Tremont male's ambitious forays.

In mid-November of 1993, the seven-month-old wolf took off on her own, apparently following the wolf-scented summit west over Gregory Bald and then down to the Little Tennessee River, as her father had done twice the year before. Then she either crossed the river at the Cheaoh Dam and ran the rugged Slickrock-Citico Wilderness west, or—more likely—she followed the river downstream through the same stretch of the valley of the Overhills I had floated in October.

Lucash had detailed the trek, or what he knew of it, on the map that hung in the hallway outside his mobile-home office in Cades Cove.

"We lost contact with her for a couple of days because of bad weather. Then she got over the mountains, down to the river and across somewhere, and the next thing we knew she's down around Tellico Plains."

This put her farther out of the national park than any wolf had been, forty miles, beeline, from the Tremont pen, where her only surviving litter mate, 592M, was being held for the winter along with her elder sibling 525M.

Lucash didn't want to set out traps for the wolf with the woods of eastern Tennessee full of hunting dogs, so he kept close tabs on the Tellico Plains wolf. During that time she drifted farther southwest toward Madisonville, Tennessee, a rural area roughly halfway between Knoxville and Chattanooga. Interstate 75, ten miles to the west, was presumed to be sort of a firebreak on the wolf's movement in that direction. To the east, 593F had 300,000 acres of the Cherokee National Forest for escape habitat and seemed to set up operations for a while somewhere between the Tellico and Hiwassee rivers.

All this extracurricular travel would have been alarming if the wolf had been making headlines along the way. But the travel of the Tellico Plains wolf was not at all like the carousing of the Tremont pups—scavengers of meat scraps and chickens who set off dogs and porch lights. Her course was more like the purposeful scouting expeditions of the Tremont male. But unlike her father, the wild-born 593F never reached the end of the psychological tether that had pulled 357M up short in the Yellow Creeks. Although 593F was often in the vicinity of settlements and towns, crossed roads and at least one state highway, no one reported seeing her, nor were there complaints about missing livestock—which were all around for the taking—or harassment of backyard pets or animals.

Needless to say, Fish and Wildlife followed the wolf's movements carefully.

"She kept us busy. We spent a lot of time on the ground tracking her. Then we'd lose her and I'd fly, just to get her again, and we'd try to keep up with her on the ground again. At one point she got as far as Athens."

Although Lucash often was exasperated by the difficulty of keeping track of 593F, he seemed impressed and pleased by her flawless behavior while she was on the lam.

"She wasn't like the other wolves. Nobody was seeing her. Nobody was complaining. She was avoiding residences, avoiding dogs, avoiding roads, traveling at night. Nobody knew a thing about her until we started notifying people, to get permission to trap her. We didn't want her out of the park, but she was exactly the kind of animal we wanted."

And even after word got out that a wolf was roaming the area, there were no complaints or problems.

Disturbing no one and nothing, the Tellico Plains wolf enjoyed the first full winter a wild-born wolf had assayed in these mountains in memory, a secret winter at large between the old stomping grounds of the Cherokee and the Creek, in the shadow of Chattanooga and Knoxville, one small step for *Canis rufus* and a giant leap for predator restoration everywhere. Nocturnal, secretive, and self-sufficient, 593F established her own territory—hunting, sleeping, traveling at will for three and a half months, crisscrossing the old Overhill country within sight of the twenty-first century.

After waiting the hunting season out, Lucash, Crawford, and John Weller, a new assistant from the Horn Island, Mississippi, facility, discovered that 593F was wilier than any other wolf or coyote with which they had dealt. In fact, they never were able to lure her into a trap, and they spent more nights than they care to remember sleeping in their trucks.

"When we started trying to set traps on her in mid-February, she was already trap smart. She just was avoiding everything and we were after her for a long time. We had traps right on her at least ten times, when we'd locate her in a woodlot we could get to, but she just didn't come near them. She just knew what was going on. We'd weather the traps two, three, four days before we baited them, let them get rained on, and still she wouldn't go near them."

In March 593F started drifting back toward the national park and was east of Madisonville again on the far side of Tellico Lake. Lucash and his crew accidentally flushed her from a woodlot one night and realized that maybe they could flush her and dart her if they couldn't get her to put a paw in a one of their padded leg holds. They kept on setting traps but also kept the dart rifle loaded and handy in case they walked her up again.

"So we tried it a couple of times and we ran her back and forth and she eventually holed up in a big pile of downed wood. There was a treetop on top of a brushpile and it was thick. I mean, there was only one way in and one way out. John was tracking her and Barron and I had dart guns. We came in from three sides and she just held tight and tried to hide. I had to crawl into to where she was, a jungle gym of limbs. I shot her from six feet away through the branches. That's how we finally got our hands on her."

During her four-month run, the Tellico Plains wolf had staked out a forty-square-mile territory and had gotten fifty miles from that rock ledge where she had been born. In a larger world, she could have been left alone forever. In any event, the wild-born Tellico Plains wolf proved that U.S. Fish and Wildlife had, in fact, put healthy wild wolves back into the southern Appalachians and that, judging from her behavior, the survival instincts of *Canis rufus gregoryi* were intact. When uninfluenced by undue contact with humans, the red wolf was no more a nuisance or a threat than bobcat or bear. 593F was also proof that an immature red wolf without a family or cohorts could survive its first winter, that the instincts for hunting and exploration, although improved by intergenerational example, were still present in the animals that had come through the captive breeding program. She was also proof that the original southern Appalachian wolf could readapt to a terribly fragmented landscape and that, even in the presence of livestock, the wolf—an exemplary predator rather than a scavenger—preferred wild prey.

Thoreau wrote that in *wildness,* not in *wilderness,* was the preservation of the world, a distinction we need now to hang a little hope on, since no true wilderness remains. In the winter of 1993, the Tremont male got halfway home toward wildness, laying down a trail out of the mountains, across the big river, to the edge of a world that is now nothing *but* edge. That edge confused it—the dogs, the human voices and odors, the manthings—because to the rational mind of a wild animal, an edge without a center, without a deep-forest interior, does not make sense. To the nose and mind of a wolf, the contemporary world must seem oddly contaminated and thin, as if it were two-dimensional. In any event, the Tremont male's wild instincts gave out twice in the same place. It seemed caught between the two roles it had in Cherokee mythology—its role as man's original companion, an ally against impending chaos of history, and its role as man's competitor, avatar of the radical otherness of wild nature.

Then in the winter of 1994 his daughter, the well-born and wild-born Tellico Plains wolf, trotted off, extending and improving her father's journey, having understood, in whatever way wolves figure out the puzzle of possibilities left to them, where the secret interiors in this landscape were, the places where she might be a wolf. It is not too much to say that 593F reestablished wildness in the Cherokee Mountains, put a gleaming edge back in the woods of North Carolina and eastern Tennessee for a season before being hauled back to the national park in the back of Lucash's Bronco.

The travel of the pen-born juveniles during the winter of 1993–1994 was equally revealing. That same December, while the Tellico Plains wolf was at large to the southwest, 525M, the eighteen-month-old male offspring of the dead Tremont adults, took off toward the northeast, probably running the spruce-fir summit and then down into the Gatlinburg-Newport area. But 525M succumbed to the temptations of a salvage cattle operation outside of Newport, Tennessee, apparently scavenging carcasses from a burial pit for diseased animals. He was trapped in mid-December and then put back in the Tremont pen until a mate could be found for him in the breeding program.

The telemetry data and anecdotal information, though not a basis for scientific interpretation of red wolf behavior, seemed to indicate degrees of wildness unfolding from generation to generation. The less contact a given wolf had with humans to begin with, the less contact it would seek out or tolerate. The best wolves tolerated none and sought only hunting territory and mates. The fundamental distinction—embodied in the Cherokee myth about the wolf's original displacement into the wild by its domestic counterpart, the dog—held up quite well. The wild wolf was the wolf that was not there. The problem wolf was not a wolf. But the wilder wolves, like many a lover of the backcountry, were clearly looking for a world that wasn't there anymore. In any event, the second and third generation of Smoky Mountain wolves had learned to move circumspectly once they came down out of the forested island.

Walking west through a thinning fog, I can feel the Appalachian Trail rise underfoot, backpack following me reluctantly, the creak of it odd in the moody, monochrome silence. It's still cold, but I'm warm with breakfast and walking. This is the finest stretch of the southern Appalachian summit, a long walk above 6,000 feet.

In the old order of things, before the blight, Fraser fir crowded out the spruce on the highest peaks of the Smokies and the Black mountains. Red spruce are now encroaching on the former terrain of the fir, but for the most part you walk through a ghost forest of dead trees. What once was fir forest, a realm of shade and moisture, is now a bright, unnatural expanse. Ranks of whitened fir snags, bleak as bones, reflect the summit light they once absorbed and put to better use. The ecosystem supported by Fraser fir has unraveled. Odd, rare forms of life have declined or disappeared since the 1960s, when the blight moved in—spiders, mosses, and liverworts congenial with or adapted specifically to the bark of Fraser fir. Ground mosses and their dependent species, like the spruce-fir moss spider, are threatened by a loss of shade and moisture. Without the windbreak of fir, surrounding spruce are more subject to windthrow. But there is a canopy at your knees, thickly-sown fir seedlings that share the same predicament as American chestnut. They sprout, seem about to thrive, and then die off before they mature.

The trail continues to rise, but the promise of a truly alpine forest is never fulfilled. Despite the boreal look of the stunted trees and exotic, northern ground cover and the strange life of the rock outcrops at this altitude, the mountains cannot reach treeline. In the fog, I imagine krummholtz and tundra, but I can't get to it here. The southern Appalachian summit reaches only an implied conclusion.

I pass below Clingman's Dome, beneficiary of the parking lot at the end of that asphalt road I visited in the dark last night, the disenchanting reward that greets Appalachian Trail hikers after their first 200 miles of rugged foot travel. I do not know who Clingman was, but I know of no one, except perhaps Oconostota or Dragging Canoe, who deserves to be remembered in such a way here. This is *Kuwa'hi,* highest point in the Cherokee mountains, where the bears counciled. The fog is just as well. It has kept the cars and crowds away. An asphalt trail leads from the parking lot to a concrete observation tower somewhere above me. Strange redundancy—a tower on top of a mountain. On a clear day you can see Dollywood.

The fog burns off as I make a pleasant descent along the Appalachian Trail through fir snags and seedlings, mountain ash, beech, and yellow birch along the rocky spine of the summit. The high-altitude hardwoods loosen the grip of the conifers, which taper off steadily in a few miles until spruce and fir remain only in isolated clumps and the entire evergreen theme from mosses and ground pines to old-growth spruce disappears in favor of the more open and spare deciduous understory. There is a healthy-looking stand of spruce in a little swale between the shelter at Double Spring Gap and the one at Siler's Bald, a half-dozen thick-boughed trees standing together like The Burghers of Calais. Then you leave the spruce-fir world behind. Through the Narrows, the summit itself is just a worked edge of ankle-turning bedrock that offers long, panoramic vistas into the jigsaw of interlocking watersheds to the north and south—a deeply dissected landscape. Stream sounds carry up on the sun-warmed air where they mix with the breeze that luffs the close-growing vegetation. Animals are scarce along the narrow summit, which is more a realm of sky than earth. For long stretches, the trail is bordered only by air. Even birds are mostly below you.

Beyond the tortuous Narrows, the trail climbs to Siler's Bald, another old mountain grazing ground. At the near edge of the bald I came on a backpacker who was taking a standing rest from his load, pack at his feet, looking down the pleasant vee of the Hazel Creek drainage. He nodded when I stopped to share the view, which required no conversation.

When I got around to asking him where he was going, he said

"Maine." On the Appalachian Trail, this is the classic through-hiker punchline that celebrates in a word the grandness of their design. A short-haul backpacker like myself will tell you where he is making camp that night, five or ten miles down the trail.

But this young man wasn't making the usual quip. He said it flatly, as if that were the straight answer to the question. He didn't seem to enjoy the frontier humor, or sense the broad pleasure of declaring, in Tennessee, that he was walking to Maine.

He looked roughed up, the way most through-hikers do, but he also had that narrow, confused look I used to see in the eyes of college students when I taught. You would see that look in only the best and worst students, as if the muscles of the face were involuntarily contracted around a question that wasn't being asked. The unasked question led to either great success or great failure.

"Maine," as he called it, was about all this hiker had. I eyed his under-sized backpack and meager array of gear—Appalachian Trail hikers are notoriously laden with the latest—and while I prodded him in desultory conversation, it became clear he was walking 2,000 miles along the wild spine of eastern North America on the thinnest of forethought. I told him what I knew of the route and offered to jot down some notes for him on his maps—good places to go off the trail to get supplies and so forth. But he had no maps and was literally just following the white blazes from Georgia to Maine, trusting to the trail itself.

It turned out he had just dropped out of college, victim of the vertigo of freshman year, and I might have passed him off as a burned-out escapist, but he had walked more than 200 miles from Georgia across difficult terrain in a volatile season. He had crossed the Blue Ridge and the Nantahalas, was halfway across the Unakas, and had far more title to a spot in the trail that day than I did. He may not have heard of Bartram and Adair and Timberlake, but he had crossed paths with all of them in the Cherokee Mountains, shared with them some fatigue and bad weather and loneliness and had rare glimpses of the primal beauty of the world. Despite his meager outfit and absurd lack of planning, he had made it to this point, and that travail alone had given him some authority, which may be what he felt he lacked when he left school for the trailhead at Springer Mountain.

He'd go back to college, he said, after he had gotten to Maine, but I don't think he was sure about that.

I told him he should read Thoreau's book about the Maine woods, especially the section on Katahdin. He either didn't understand why I brought up Katahdin or didn't like getting a reading assignment. He nodded, cutting me off.

"Thoreau was a great writer," he declared, as if he wanted to make it clear that was not something he had learned in school but was something he had decided to believe on his own. He had read some of *Walden* and "Civil Disobedience," perhaps, enough to sense that this Thoreau had been an outsider and a lonely traveler who had come through, that he lived above clichés and confusion and demagoguery, and proudly paid a stiff price to look his troubling country in the eye.

"He was a good citizen," I answered, trying to hang something on his tone, but politics was on my mind, not his, and the young man looked at me as if I had said something deliberately obscure, like one of his teachers. He didn't need a lecture. He needed to be going to Maine.

While he packed up to leave, I tried to retrieve myself by telling him about the wolf restoration, the most glamorous thing I knew.

He took the news lightly but seemed to value the word.

"Wolves," he said aloud to himself in the same measured, satisfied way he had said "Thoreau."

"Wolves . . . wolves are good." As if he had decided then and there and quickly added wolves to his small kit.

I told him again they were *red* wolves and that he might have crossed paths with them near Gregory Bald, but he didn't encourage more of a spiel from me.

"Wolves," he said again aloud to himself, as if he liked the heft of the word, the well-shaped sound of it in his mind. He was at least 1,800 miles from whatever was going to bring his life into focus, but he knew good nouns and names when he heard them. Like Thoreau, the idea of wolves would travel with him.

He slung his backpack lightly up, hitching it easily on his shoulders. And then he told me his name, which struck me as an odd thing to do. Not as if he were introducing himself—he didn't stick out his hand in that officious way young men sometimes have—but as if he were just declaring his name, carving it on the air since I had forced him to waste time there. A healthy, modest boast, I thought, and I was glad to learn his name.

I didn't know if this traveler was on the brink of great success or great failure, but I silently wished him one or the other in the narrow country before him, and I was sorry he had not been left a wider, wilder world through which to walk.

III

TIME IN A FOREST

> *I wonder which was more frightened among old tribes—those bursting out of their darkness of woods upon all the space of light, or those from the open tiptoeing into the forests.*
>
> —D. H. Lawrence, *Sons and Lovers*

Old Growth

> To preserve wild animals implies generally the cre-
> ation of a forest for them to dwell in or resort to. So
> it is with man. . . . The civilized nations—Greece,
> Rome, England—have been sustained by the primi-
> tive forests which anciently rotted where they stand.
> They survive as long as the soil is not exhausted.
>
> —Henry Thoreau, "Walking"

When a Cherokee dreamed of snakes, he was treated for snakebite upon awakening. In these forested mountains, mind and body were as intimate as night and day, and a decoction of heartleaf and snake tongue—hepatica and walking fern—might protect the dreamer from the missteps of his waking life. This dreaming was not symbolic but an unadorned intrusion of the real. The rattlesnake in the mind was the rattlesnake beside the path, a being with a spirit independent of human confusion. Such was indigenous respect for the thing itself, a habit of mind that leaned toward observation of the other rather than projection of the self.

This is old growth in early May, a few odd days in woods that never felt an ax, the rarest kind of place in North America, a fragment of true forest. Such sacred groves would be in these mountains, which fended off history as long as they could, hid red wolves and red men as well as ancient trees and soils with their attendant life, intact places where creation progressed as it was inclined to before the great disturbance.

The Cherokee, like all native easterners, were first and foremost forest people, and their thoughts were forest thoughts. The green thought in a green shade was not a literary invention. The forest was the source of their deepest beliefs and best medicine. But the power of native medicines did not come solely from the chemical properties of plants. Cure came, in part, from the places where plants grew. All the grubbing of ginseng and other medicinals profit the modern-day plant hunters and pseudoshamans nothing. Their prizes are as inert as the pills and potions sold in health food stores. I've seen the plant hunters in the woods, tearing herbs from their native soils, throwing them in cardboard boxes, or at trailheads furtively shoving garbage bags of plants into the trunks of their cars, hoping to get a little magic and money from the woods. But the business of roots and herbs was a philosophic enterprise, part of a way of life in situ. There once was a topography to the way people thought and behaved. The possibility of a cure for something that had gone wrong—for being lost in mind or body—was a gift of place.

The place that mattered most, that was the most powerful, the wildest place, was the deep forest interior, where nothing had been changed by man.

In the southern Appalachians, the way into old growth is always the same: an interstate, to a state highway, to a two-lane blacktop that leads past smaller and smaller towns; then a dirt road to a trailhead at an old logging road—overgrown, you hope—off which a faint path leads you toward the stream you've been listening to since you hit the logging road and from which you can take your bearings, using that stream as a wandering baseline. A half mile up this watercourse you strike the trace of an old trail used by hunters and the few people who know what's hidden on the slopes ahead.

A trail descended from a logging road makes for suspiciously easy walking. Even after such a road has become overgrown and offers only an inviting footpath, you can tell its origins from the odd consistency in its grade and the way it glides along an unnatural contour. That's how the machines got in the garden and the logs got out. But the fragment of trail I'm on now jags through the woods as if it had a more intimate relationship with the terrain, unwinding footfall by footfall along a narrow bevel of least resistance through the tangled vegetation and around sudden brows of rock without altering anything in its path. Unless you adjust your pace to match the jagged surface of real ground, this path will turn your ankle and run the toe of a boot into the constant variation underfoot. A trace of ancient trial and error, a true trail makes choices that are sometimes hard to fathom, thoughtfully looping downslope to avoid a windthrow that disappeared a century ago but jamming you against the tree that fell last winter. It's the narrow, winding path of predator and prey, the way of hunters and warriors, lovers and medicine men. A rare thing now, a true trail, a trail that leads somewhere.

If you set out in the dark, daylight arrives twice at your feet, suffusing at first, unaccountably, from the woods around you, often in a gray mist of ground fog, breath of that nearby stream exhaled into the woods, and then, hours later, falling from overhead, brightly as light through the apex of a cathedral window. This time of day between the first and second light is, like the hours of dusk when night is visibly in the air, a time to observe your misperceptions, glints in the middle distance of that old doubleness of things, subjects and objects as elusive as drumming grouse moving about the morning woods like the Wild Boys, leading you on.

From a rise in the trail I see smoke simmer from a small clearing given over to wildflowers and Christmas fern and bordered by spicebush and serviceberry. But the smoke is strange, rising and then falling again, as if I were watching a short loop of film. Half awake, I lean on my walking stick and watch the smoking old field as I listen to the thoughtful song of a yellow-throated vireo high overhead and wonder about what I am seeing.

So that first kind of morning light hovers in spiderwebs strung between the taller ferns, a thousand smoky auras trapped in globes of dew beaded on silken threads, each array pulsing in a slight breeze I hadn't noticed and reifying, as a forest often does, a fragile interface of fact and impression.

Old growth, of course, is rare, but some survives even on national forest land, hidden both from the appetite of lumber companies and the prurience of hiking guides. The best places are always uphill, toward the great spine of mountains, but the ascent is easy, a stiff walk only if you are in a hurry, effortless if you are not. Off-trail, your pace is dictated by terrain and vegetation and by the way the mood of forest features directs your mind along. I'm drawn to the rock outcrops strewn through every watershed like wreckage from a crash, jagged chest-high shelves of wet stone sheathed in cushion moss that sprout forests of tiny hemlock nurslings that shade the moss that make soil for their roots, a minor symbiosis, another dancing loop. In the woods, life thrives on coexistence.

As I get deeper into the trackless woods, I keep a bold creek on my left and pick my way through ranks of second growth—or third or fourth or fifth, for all I know—impressive if you've never seen the old places or don't spend much time in any woods. But even after fifty years, a reforested clear-cut is still more clear-cut than forest. Managed forests are woodlots.

The root of *forest*—from the Latin *foris,* for "out of doors," and associated with *silvam,* "the outside wood"—takes us back toward Western notions of wildness and wilderness. But in English the word was severed from its roots in the Middle Ages as the original forests of the British Isles were cut down for the pastures and deer parks that profited and amused the nobility. Once that dark, tangled place beyond the pale, forests became merely an extension of culture, still out of doors but no longer an outside wood in the primitive sense that was either threatening or inviting, depending on your cast of mind.

The word devolved back toward its original meaning with the European settlement of North America, where neither Puritan nor Cavalier found the king's tidy woods, cleared for hunting on horseback, but rather the impenetrable forest of the Iroquois and Cherokee, the old wild place of European nightmares, a tangle full of wolves that might devour one's livestock and heathens who might not worship one's god. Here was a continent half covered with a forest as hard to interpret as to exploit, the dark outside wood again. So the word *forest* glowed red from the settlers' writings until that forest, too, was cut down and the natural life within it, as well as the cultures that lived astride it, was destroyed. And then the word was tame again.

The older sense of the word is perhaps a trace of a fundamental distinction between what is inside culture and outside of it—that frame of untamed nature that has disappeared, except when, at night, we look into the starlit blackness overhead. Tangled in the etymology of the word *forest* is the trace of a fundamental continuum that degenerated into an apparent antithesis once the Industrial Revolution reduced nature to raw material and then consumer culture turned it into a toy. Lurking beyond the unmarked word *outside* is the keener word *other,* which suggests that a true forest is strange and dangerous, something to be feared and destroyed, not just for profit but also for ideological reasons, for the narrow peace of mind that thrives on monoculture—the consciousness that hated those old tangled woods, and all those tangled languages, and those fabulous people who were different, a consciousness still very much with us.

Needless to say, most of the forest that originally covered the southern Appalachians was destroyed, along with the rest of the eastern forests. The fragments left standing survived by accident or isolated acts of prudence. The paucity of such places is a measure of something lacking in man. The rarity of old growth is unnatural.

The tack I'm on takes me through a tract of fifty-year-old pole timber that contrasts sharply with what's up ahead. I come this way deliberately. If I were blindfolded, I could feel the edge I'm looking for and tell you exactly where the old woods start. There is a threshold beyond which the synesthesia unique to intact forests takes hold. There is nothing like it in the world.

Even blindfolded, I would feel light become an object tangible as the bulky trees that draw the darkness of the forest floor upward, as if compensating for the intruding rays from overhead. I would hear the woody, mellow silence that supports the reciprocal sounds of wind and birdsong between the gusts and notes of which I would hear the shape of randomly well-used space. I would smell time in last century's peaty rot and in this year's first new leaves. Walking across the soft, uneven ground, I would feel even older time roll underfoot as deeply furrowed waves of never-disturbed soil crested in foot-thick mats of sphagnum moss and broke over the faded forms of pre-Columbian hemlocks and tulip poplars ghosting underneath. Standing in the deep pit at the base of a tree recently crashed out of the canopy, I might, still blindfolded, find an arrowhead just by digging with my fingers in the cache of dirt and stone unearthed from the centuries by its upturned roots, testing with my fingertips for the unmistakable scallop of a worked edge.

In old growth, I'd be overwhelmed before I'd taken the blindfold off.

Entering a true forest from second growth is as dramatic an experience as walking into a cathedral from a city street and having one kind of space immediately replace another. The faint trail winds and rises through an old clear-cut, the floor of which is dry and brown and empty in those places where it isn't a monoculture of mountain laurel. But the edge is abrupt, inspiring or heartbreaking, depending on which way you are going. Once you've brought the nave into view, you see how the most refined aesthetics of high culture came from the woods. Shafts of light drop from a height into the unsettling darkness around you as if through high-arching stained glass. You expect music, and once you are another hundred steps farther on that music—variations on the theme of natural silence—rises from all quarters as ground never torn to hell by a skidder operation rolls and buckles into a forested watershed that towers and leans over itself, a place large and intimate as a church.

The depth of field alone will stop you in your tracks, from groves of tiny orange spores periscoped out of the mossy banks aside the trail to the open crowns of 200-foot poplars that check the sky. You start walking like a deer, holding your breath and hanging your steps, turning your head from side to side to find a focal point in this rare glimpse of a complete world, hoping something flushes out of the busy stillness.

The trail, deeply grooved but not eroded, brings you nearly eye level with the thick roots of the big trees that are the most obvious sign of time here. They emerge from mounds of soil tapered up to their flared bases—poplar and hemlock the size of small redwoods, finely chiseled mountain silverbell the size of hemlock and poplar; outsize red maples and sugar maples; yellow birch and buckeye, their tightly wound wood concealing their years; enormous papaw and basswood; smooth-bark magnolia and elegantly prop-rooted beech. All arranged according to some calculus of soil and aspect and centuries of weather. Biomass, in the jargon of ecologists. More life than thought can handle.

More death, too, arrayed in rotting trees strewn about the slopes like seeds and occupying as much space as the standing wood. But it is not the fallen giants, so rare to see, that really draw the eye. It's the faint impression of a log beached in the mossy earth and about to disappear forever that tells you time moves slowly here, but moves, that the woods are made of wood and that this century's saplings are rooted in last autumn's fertile detritus and the faint, fading life of the last millennium.

The phrase *old growth* is recent. An ecological term with some poetry in it, it is nearly an oxymoron in a consumer culture that thrives on waste, except in nature, where it won't do to let trees fall and rot in this way, no more than oil can be left under Arctic tundra or coal in mountains, no more than marshes or beaches can be let alone for the life and pleasures they encourage. The earth must be *used,* we are told, in order to be valuable. No matter that this idea is demented and that the wasteful practices it encourages doom us to progressive impoverishment. Call this philosophy utilitarianism, the movement that rebuilt the devastated American woods in the twentieth century only to cut them down again under the Solomon's baby rubric of "multiple use." Call it "wise use," a slick, corporate-sponsored movement that seeks to destroy what little is left of North America behind a smoke screen of conservative sophistry. Or call it conservatism, which seeks to conserve nothing. The idea goes back to the Puritan Cotton Mather, one of those pious Europeans unhinged by the original American forest. "What is not useful is vicious," the bright-eyed believer declared. Is this true?

Old growth is life and death come round. Not in some textbook cycle, but joined at the hip, dancer and the dance. This is not the swift, unforgiving relation of predator and prey laid out around me. This is older—some strange, formal enfolding of senescence and conception, a beautiful loop worked out a long time ago, ancient as tides, inscrutable as smoke rising and falling in place from an oldfield.

Off-trail, my footsteps disappear behind me, lost on the resilient ground moss encouraged by the shade of the hemlocks and other evergreens. Even before leaf-in, these woods are dark, as if the shadow of the earth itself were being cast up into the midstory above which gnatcatchers enjoy a light that never reaches the ground. Beyond the constant and constantly disappearing birds, there is not much animal life to see—a gray squirrel flaring in freeze-framed poses along a branch back toward the trunk of a tree. Red squirrels in hemlocks, jabbering like monkeys. Bands of diminutive woodpeckers, jabbering like squirrels.

March trashed the woods with windthrows, a rough cull of what made it through the winter but wasn't fit this year for spring. A giant hemlock with a tragic flaw lies across my way, chest high to me. The woods around it look bombed, the wounds of the splintered trees so fresh I look for the tail end of the sound of the crash. But the reverberations are all visible, not aural. Birds still seem shy of the place and flow around it, tentatively gleaning the interesting edges of the new opening.

A spiked stump fifteen feet tall reveals a shattered twist within the exposed base of the tree that must trace an old weakness, an embedded lightning scar from a century or two ago that was the tree's Achilles' heel, an old incision from the Thunders. At any rate, there is no rot in the exposed heartwood and cambium, which on close inspection are only faintly weathered, and what's left of the base of the tree looks solid, even shorn of the thick, corky bark that lies in chunks all around.

It looks as if a hand reached down and snapped the tree like a yarrow stalk. A hemlock this size, its boughs loaded with ice, needs to be structurally perfect to survive a strong, sudden wind. This one wasn't. The tree dropped at 290 degrees, a bearing that implicates a storm from the Gulf reaching inland. Measured roughly against my walking stick, a hand-carved shaft of hickory I've notched for the task, the hemlock is three foot four inches in diameter about twenty feet up the trunk. In these fertile cove forests, where they are often codominant with poplars, hemlocks grow rapidly, but I think it's safe to guess that this tree was at least 200 years old and possibly as much as a century older. Four-hundred fifty-year-old hemlock have been cored in these mountains, and somewhere in North America there is a 900-year-old specimen, an unimaginable shaman in the age of industrial logging. So what blocks the path takes me another way, at least back to Jefferson and Bartram, and since I'm going nowhere in particular this impasse is a find.

The fallen tree is broad enough to walk on, and I pace it off as best I can, making my way with difficulty though its picket of upper branches, which are so far from the roots of the disaster that they are still green with life. The trunk measures roughly 130 feet. Add the base and the tip, the latter broken off no doubt in that first gigantic bounce, and you have a 175-foot hemlock, as fine an expression of time and space as you could want to see, sage light-gatherer and shade-giver, mute woody figure and ground, old connector between earth and sky.

There is more space in old-growth forest than it seems, given the completeness with which life occupies the ground. Two-foot-thick silverbells and a five-inch yellow birch were destroyed when the hemlock fell. Another silverbell, scarred and shorn of branches on one side but left standing, will probably die in place, quickly become a snag. The top half of the hemlock came down in a cushion of rhododendron, itself probably a century old, which simply gave way around it and is now hung with hemlock cones and the tender, lime-green growth of the big tree's upper branches. It will take a spring and summer for it to finish dying on the ground. In the meantime, the fragrance of hemlock sap is rich on the air.

There may be tragic flaws in wood, but there are no tragedies in nature. Nothing benefits midcanopy aspirants and the forest floor like a canopy opening. There are at least thirty hemlock saplings ready to thrive in the newly available sunlight, most probably offspring of this parent tree and now released for growth by its demise. The largest of these are twenty feet tall, eight or ten inches in diameter at breast height. The midcanopy hardwoods, a prudent mix of the ubiquitous red maple and a sprinkling of dogwood, sassafras, and yellowwood, witch hazel and sourwood, umbrella tree and magnolia and papaw, all of which will slowly grow faster until the young hemlocks or a poplar shade them out again. Sprawling rhododendron, graceful viburnums, and other opportunistic shrubs will expand their holdings. Perennial herbs—mayapple, the trilliums, hepatica, and violets—are already thriving in the boon of sunlight while the club mosses and ferns that needed the hemlock's moist, cool shade die back in that same light, retreating and redirecting themselves underground, migrating en masse toward the younger evergreens. The fungi waiting under the leaf litter will puzzle out the new conditions as they have been doing for millions of years. Squirrels will gnaw the last crop of tiny hemlock cones.

Birds will glean their gnawings. Voles and deer mice will hunt the thriving log as if it were a godsend, trailed by hungry kingsnakes and copperheads. If I could wait here long enough, the static scene would move and the extraordinary patience and intelligence in nature would unfold.

And the hemlock itself, already well colonized by mosses and lichens drawn to the bark of the living tree, will support another century or two of life, at least—drawing borers and decomposers, yeoman of life on earth, while it slowly softens into a nursery log. Left alone, fifty years from now it may well harbor more species of plant life on and around it than you could find in the thin, struggling forests of the Old World, where wood is never wasted in this way. And for a few centuries, it will lie here for people to walk around or sit on, a worthy object for their curiosity or study—a useless, vicious thing.

As you walk through old growth, the mind ships so much detail it founders on all this reciprocity of life and death, a fullness replete with instructive vanishing points. Old growth is life tapered at both ends, but never severed from the place where it appeared and disappeared.

Here in early May, wind and sunlight contend for mood, as if the seasons were changing hands overhead, late winter and early spring both toying with the greening canopy of poplars, the branches of which click and clatter when a strong breeze passes. A hawk scoots before the wind, flushing small bands of dun-colored birds out of the furled poplars and into the shelter of the hemlocks, where they organize themselves with rills, chirps, chips, as well as three- and four-note piped phrases distinct to the ear as leaf shapes are to the eye, not the long, passionate songs of mid-May but perfunctory locator calls.

Like bears and wolves, the passerines have a life of their own, which even binoculars don't help much to penetrate. Given the choice, many prefer old growth, not just for the vertical range of forage but for the relatively safe edges of inconspicuous forest openings and the variety of nesting sites—not the bomb sites of clear-cuts but the modest natural openings time leaves in a forest. If I stay still, those gray specks of life still avoiding the long-gone Cooper's hawk will drift down into the midcanopy, where buds as well as last year's seeds await and I can twist blackburnian warblers, wood pewees, wrens, and kinglets into focus and work at matching language and tribe until they notice me, the threat below, and fly off.

Full sunlight creates the illusion that there are many paths where there are none, that there are straight lines in a world of curved green space, an openness within the closure of the woods. I follow an avenue of light through dog-hobble and fetterbush alongside a mossy boulder field minced into a hundred possible snake den openings. As I walk along, banging my walking stick on the rocks, I remember the disheartening sight I once had of a dozen slack-bodied timber rattlers lying out, black and brown piles of arm-thick coils, soaking up sunlight like Mesozoic wildflowers. Their black and yellow bands of woodland camouflage rippled faintly as they warmed themselves, slowly uncoiling from their stolid winter conscious-ness and preparing for summer nights rewound in hollow stumps or sliding alongside fallen trees, heat-seeking small mammals, and birds' eggs, ready to strike with that lightninglike quickness they get from soaking in the sun.

I angle off the boulder field toward the stream that drains this slope, a deep but narrow watercourse that runs hard and clear all year, one of those wonderful flows so deeply rooted in its watershed that it seems com-pletely detached from the weather. That hard, clear flow thrums around quivering trout, ice age refugees stuck in the mountains, left behind by time like red spruce and Fraser fir. And not just trout, but wild brook trout, *Salvelinus fontinalis,* stream-born fish native to these mountains, dis-tinct and unreal as flying squirrels.

I stop the overflow of forest detail by sitting still and watching the trout, which spook at my approach but soon fan out again once I am seated. For all their beauty and antiquity they are shackled to a simple hunger that ends up feeding many a kingfisher, raccoon, and water snake. Scaled to place, mature fish here are five or six inches long, survival food at best. Their value is in their presence, olive arcs of salmonid DNA living and dying for the most part unseen.

Like most animals, they are extraordinarily wary in one plane only and are easily deceived. If I break off quarter-inch bits of yellow leaf stems and flick them into a feeding lane the trout rise each time, white mouths taking and rejecting my crude Yellow Sally over and over until frustration triggers a suspicion so slow to form it would be useless to them if I really was fishing.

I continue on rounds I've made before, skirting the head of the boulder field, cruising through a dark grove of hemlock large as the shattered tree I measured. Then over an indistinct ridge and across a broad, open slope toward a dry creek bed through hemlock and poplar and their cove forest associates, a now-unusual uneven-age diversity that brings me here every season, year after year.

I can't describe it. The southern Appalachian cove forest looks like a diorama a bear would imagine, prone to sudden silence and darkness even at midday when a passing cloud can plunge the woods into a green gloom that I assume suits the shaggy mind of *Ursus americanus,* so harried a being now, and unsettles me even though I'm seeking both the bear and the gloom.

In that unsettling midafternoon darkness, a forest moves around you the way tundra or desert or ocean moves, in that slow spin of intact landscapes that must be the mind's eye tracking the rotation of the earth against the sky at the horizon, or some circuit at the base of the cerebellum enjoying the elliptical ride around the sun, a dim apprehension of the angles and motions that gave rise to such an enthralling accident of earth, air, water, and light, the wild music of some deep-space cellist bowing the spare phrases that move the earth through solar winds that eventually stir the tiny flowers of oak and maple overhead, rustle the leaves of serviceberry and ironwood around me, and lift the head of the bear I've never seen here to the man-scent in the woods.

Perhaps the uncluttered brains of animals are still tuned to that fundamental starlit music, subconsciously feel the careening underfoot and step with it. Perhaps it is some fabulous sidereal awareness that enables a 400-pound black bear to shuffle through dry leaves or walk through thick brush with perfect, unaccountable silence. I suspect the bear whose plump scat and well-clawed boundary trees are so obvious here has seen me and, beyond disappointment at the rare intrusion, has not been much interested in the sight.

There's an odd log near where I sit to wait out my ursine secret sharer. Unlike the bear, it's always here. I've come to call it "the bear" in my field notes, which would be endlessly confusing to someone who perused them not knowing that one day I shifted the name of one thing onto another to see what would happen, that a mythic switch had been made. But in a myth, the strange log would do well for an absent bear and, who knows, perhaps in old growth bears hide themselves from men as logs or stumps. Perhaps the old woods are as strange as they look. I'm fairly certain that aboriginal myths derived from watching rather than adventure—from staring into fire and water and woods, all places where metamorphosis is the norm.

The log is odd in several ways. First, it's a log and not a tree, not a timbered log but an eight- or ten-foot chunk of one of the old forest giants, three feet or so in diameter, the rest of which is gone. There is not the slightest sign of the original tree. No rotted trunk. No stump or root cluster. From this point in time, the log is an unaccountable object. In this realm where everything is interconnected, this big splinter seems detached from everything around it, like deep-space debris on the forest floor.

Its bark shed long ago, the log is smooth and bare. There is not a thread of moss or a single fan of lichen on it, as if there were something in the wood that held the decomposers off, some persistent resin that hardened the idea of it. It has that airy color, that winter gray of weathered chestnut, and looks, big as it is, as if you could pick it up.

The problem of this log, or chunk of tree, is that it hasn't aged. It shows no sign of rot. If it is chestnut, it would be dead at least fifty years, fifty summers and winters here. But it looks more polished than weathered, as if someone had been sanding and oiling it to raise the grain, which is tight as the wood on a well-fitted cask. The thing has refused to let go, as if time itself had gotten too tightly knotted in the wood, like a memory. As if *this* were the spirit of the place and not the living trees and dense shrubs, the passing birds or the resident trout or anything else you could name here. A bearish thing.

The log is alive with patterns, and the patterns look as if they were emerging rather than disappearing. The grain flows boldly around the knots branches left, the exposed wood drawing fresh designs out of the heartwood. Those whorled eyes damn near pulse, the sapwood still at work burning into the cambium with hot intention, writing. The wood is hard and tight as soapstone, more firmly patterned in death than in life, as if it were growing on the other side of things now, still using what we call time to its advantage, expressing some inanimate desire in the pattern it holds out to view where no one ever sees it, not as if it were frozen in time but as if time were frozen in it.

The word *old* loses much from Cherokee, which had many terms for the way in which things persevere in time. The first observers of Native American languages noticed this, as if it were important: " 'the word *old* is employed by us in the most general sense. We say in our languages, *an old man, an old horse, an old basket,* &c. The Indians, on the contrary, vary their expressions, when speaking of a thing that has life and of one that has not; for the latter, instead of the word *old,* they use terms which convey the idea, that the thing *has lasted long,* that it has been used, worn out, &c.' This appears to be also the case with the *Cherokee.*"

In 1831 the linguist John Pickering reported *utysanyhi* as a markedly respectful adjective for the man who *"has passed the middle age."* To be old was to have grown. The word *akayvlike* was used in speaking of an older woman, as if the sexes had a different experience of time, a fact worth embodying in language. The female adjective was used to cover the case of mixed company, an expression perhaps of Cherokee matriarchy. Another word was used to designate old animals, male and female, and still a different word to designate old things—old garments, bows, and trees.

Pickering's fragmented information gives out here, oddly lumping inanimate, man-made objects with animate, living beings, which probably was not the case. The linguistic world of the Cherokee was dense with observant, respectful connotations. I suspect a bow, a man-made thing that wore out, did not age linguistically in the same sense that a tree—which grew and died and rotted—aged, and that whatever special word was used to modify the striking antiquity of these trees in the depth of the forest has been lost, a word that implied the complex implication we grope for with the phrase *old growth*. In any event, the time embodied in these enormous trees would not have been a quality lost on the mind of a forest people who sought to maintain a keen awareness of the interdependence of nature and culture, a people who had, for example, different words to refer to a log depending on how far away it was from the speaker, or for a mountain in general and a mountain in place. Which suggests that in Cherokee, even nouns for inanimate objects shifted thoughtfully with a change in perspective, the way things do, a mobility and precision of usage that gives the language considerable depth.

Lovers of forests are easily ridiculed by pragmatists. But in old growth you do feel as if you have gotten to the bottom of something, as if the trunks of the large trees were roots, or cords that hang the forest from the sky in the manner of the Cherokee creation myth. Wood, I have read, is a botanically conservative substance, an evolutionary idea for a living being supported in part by its own dead cells, cells that change considerably through distinct stages after death in order to continue to serve the living tree. An idea that has not changed much over time, wood is an animate way to outdo bone and rock for flexible, architectural strength. Looking at the deeply furrowed bark of these old trees, it is not hard to see where the idea of fluted columns came from, the idea of graceful, monumental support. And the basic structure of a tree, a lamination of dead and living cells cooperating easily across that daunting boundary—heartwood, to xylem, to cambium, to bark—mirrors the forest itself, where life and death are joined cell to cell, figure and ground. Even so, the large old trees that survived history here are hard to fathom, the depth of old growth elusive. There is not much language for it.

The largest poplar here must be twenty or twenty-five feet around and may well be the oldest living thing I have encountered in these woods. I know for a fact that poplar this size core out to 300 or 400 years of age. But after a few centuries, the superficially distinct rings of annual growth cross a threshold and enter the realm of a history permanently obscure and hidden from us. The heartwood of a tree this size may well be rooted in the discovery and the contact.

This tree is dying, engaged in that primordial shift of phase or state that is the principal drama here. Its crown came down long ago, along with the upper third of its trunk. Loss of access to the canopy must have shifted its growth into its unusually heavy and awkward lower branches. Only one of those branches is leafing this spring. An outsize seedling, two feet in diameter, grows alongside the old giant, heading eagerly for the canopy gap left long ago by its parent. The two trees have grown so long together they seem fused at the base. Much bark has shed from the larger tree. Six-inch-thick slabs litter the base. The tender green leaves issuing from the one healthy branch seem absurd, as if this were taking growth—or life—too far. There's no proportion left in the great tree, no beauty, nothing to admire except the ungainly fact of it. The trunk is studded with enormous boles. Even the woodpecker holes look ancient, glazed with time, signs of life from another world. A cavity large enough for a bear to use in winter has formed from an old scar near the base. A fine, dry moss covers the lower trunk, which also hosts complex colonies of ferns and trillium. The base of the tree seems to have enlarged into a pedestal to support its weight, bulging out from the normal slope characteristic of what passes elsewhere for large poplars.

No less acute observer than the twenty-two-year-old Charles Darwin, his subconscious already drifting toward the Galapagos, had difficulty describing old growth when he arrived on the coast of South America in the spring of 1832 and encountered "what has been so long my ambition, virgin forest uncut by man & tenanted by wild beasts." In fact, if you follow the voyage of H.M.S. *Beagle* through Darwin's correspondence, where his feelings are closer to the surface than in *The Voyage of the Beagle,* it seems as if it were only "after having in real earnest strolled in the forests of the new world"—that he began, five months into a five-year journey, to believe in the possibilities of his travel and glimpsed the enormity of the task that lay before him, that of being a naturalist in a new world.

But he found it hard to get a purchase on the complexity of the tropical rain forest of the uncharted Brazilian interior. England and Europe had nothing but glorified woodlots for a thousand years. Darwin is not being falsely modest when he writes to his sister Caroline: "The scenery here chiefly owes its charms to the individual forms of the Vegetation: when this is united to lofty hills & a bold outline, I am quite sure the incapability of justly praising it, will be almost distressing. . . . I am generally at a loss either how to begin or end a sentence." And he is not being melodramatic when he writes to his mentor Henslow: "It is positively distressing, to walk in the glorious forest, amidst such treasures, & feel they are all thrown away upon one." Darwin sounds more like his self-employed American contemporary Thoreau than Her Majesty's Naturalist when he extols the virtue of simply "wandering in the sublime forests" and encourages his sisters to skip the dry, scientific parts of Humboldt for the Romantic, descriptive moments that inspired him.

After three months exploring the forests inland from Rio de Janiero, Darwin was still grappling with the impact of undisturbed old growth: "I well know the glories of a Brazilian forest.—Commonly I ride some few miles, put my horse & start by some track into the impenetrable—mass of vegetation.—Whilst seated on a tree, & eating my luncheon in the sublime solitude of the forest, the pleasure I experience is unspeakable." In the richness of species, the complex relations among livings things (he wrote enthusiastically to Henslow about the bewildering abundance of parasitic plants), and the completeness with which undisturbed vegetation occupied the land, Darwin found a life's work: "if I gain no other end I shall never want an object of employment & amusement for the rest of my life." He noted with satisfaction that he "could sit for hours together & find every minute fresh objects of admiration."

Of course, Darwin's admiration led him far, and it was, in the end, New World nature that led the Old World to its finest idea, the symphonic notion of evolution—that great orchestration of continuity and change occurring over a shocking span of time—the idea that simultaneously opened nature to modern appreciation and verified the intuitions of Paleo-Indians, that the earth was ancient and complex and to be revered for its own sake. At one time, after all, the entire planet was a new world.

Even after the *Beagle* left the tropics and Darwin witnessed new wonders, he could not get the forest out of his mind. Again to Henslow: "At this present minute we are at anchor in the mouth of the river [the Rio Plata]: & such a strange scene as it is.—Every thing is in flames,—the sky with lightning,—the water with luminous particles, & even the very masts are pointed with a blue flame,—I expect great interest in scouring over the plains of M Video, yet I look back with regret to the Tropics, that magic line to all Naturalists.—The delight of sitting on a decaying trunk amidst the quiet gloom of the forest is unspeakable & never to be forgotten."

So there is some precedent for sitting on a log in a true forest and enjoying the humbling fact that there is more life than language here.

The snowfall that night was so soft it didn't wake me, a silent drift of large wet flakes, unexpected but not unusual. When it snows in the backcountry, you have the odd feeling that it has snowed everywhere. Actually the reverse is usually true, and it may well be just the mountains underfoot that dawn found whitened this morning. One of the pleasures of backcountry travel is that your news goes unreported in Knoxville and Asheville and Atlanta. You've slipped the noose of traffic and the grinding dullness of the manufactured world of which the Chamber of Commerce is so proud. The mountains can distill unpredicted local weather out of any passing front. Throughout spring and fall, surprise is the rule. I carry a winter sleeping bag, and gaiters, gloves, and balaclava through the middle of May.

But no dense cold greets me when I unzip the tent door and stick my face into the world, no trackless, snow-bound forest. Just a film of wet snow and an unseasonal light that, judging by the pale-blue sky, will be gone by noon. What Darwin called "the quiet gloom of the forest" clarifies in this Arctic light, a soft glare that unveils the permanent darkness in these woods.

A better snow would invite extended tracking and lead me on toward what I haven't seen—more white-tailed deer than I thought were around, but more deer mice than deer, as well as squirrels and raccoons and owls, all of whose overlapping activities were scrawled on last night's thin snow in a palimpsest of wing tips and tails, talons and claws. But no impress of a bear's foot, because the bear of the place is not some tent-sniffing campground bear. And no stark fan of a wolf's paw, because there are no longer any wolves in the woods.

A year ago spring was full of wolves. The Cades Cove and Tremont females were denned up and giving birth to those first two litters of wildborn wolves—*Canis rufus*'s promising, unpredictable Generation-X. But by the end of April 1994, there were no free-ranging red wolves in the southern Appalachians. Wolf country was empty again.

I had met with Chris Lucash in Cades Cove before this old-growth cruise, expecting him and his crew to be caught up in the excitement of locating wolf dens and inspecting litters. I assumed they had been following the swollen females in tightening circles all month until the mothers-to-be started nipping at their belly fur and chose their dens. Instead I found that Fish and Wildlife had circled its wagons and that the wolf restoration had contracted back into its holding pens. The red wolf was back in captivity, watching the world through the chain-link grid. There would be no wild-born wolves in the spring of 1994.

The lockup was no fault of *Canis rufus*. In fact, the wolves had confirmed the theory of the restoration. If wildness in biological terms was successful readaptation, most of the wolves had succeeded in becoming wild. Which is to say they hunted and ate, howled and slept, traveled and bred. The beauty of such wildness was that it caused no problems. Beyond occasional sightings and the accretion of telemetry coordinates, the fine grain of their lives and the soft flow of their intent consciousness was the wolves' secret to keep. And as the theory predicted, degrees of wildness unfolded from generation to generation. Readaptation was a process, an endless self-education. Tame wolves were a nuisance; wild wolves caused no trouble. In the ideal restoration wolves would be everywhere and no one would ever see them.

The role of captive-born wolves might prove to be temporary—perhaps they were only delivery vehicles—but give wild-born red wolves enough time and space and they will reintegrate themselves into their native country as well as foxes, bears, and bobcats. By the end of the winter of 1994, it was clear that the red wolf was capable of escaping into a future that restored it, as far as was possible, to its past. Fish and Wildlife had succeeded.

But the wolves had been returned to a fallen world, and in the spring of 1994, Chris Lucash was poised at an important juncture when events forced him to deal with limitations not in the wolves but in the world to which they had been returned—the wildness that was not there. The pleasure and excitement as well as the value of having another crop of heavy-lidded pups tumbling in the leaf litter had to be forgone while problems were solved.

By the spring of 1994, the well-traveled Tremont group had eroded into fragments, undone by natural and unnatural causes: the adult female dead in a wolf fight the previous June, one pup killed by a coyote in August, the big male dead of antifreeze poisoning in October. The disorderly adopted juveniles had been shipped out on dishonorable discharges. The remaining

Tremont wolves—the release juvenile, 525M, and the surviving wild-born pups of 1993, 592M and 593F—no longer had a social structure around them.

The Cades Cove wolves were also coming up against the limitations of the conditions of their release. Because of their visibility to park visitors, these wolves had become the first family of Smoky Mountain wolves and must have resembled, in appearance and behavior, the last such family of red wolves to inhabit this place when the first white settlers arrived in the early nineteenth century and started killing them off. In fact, their release was designed to re-create the problem of that historical moment.

The Cades Cove adults had gotten through the winter of 1994 undeterred by the wholesale death of their wild-born offspring, the blast of parvo virus that wiped out four pups in the summer of 1993. However strong their emotional bonds and however keen their social sense, wolves don't mourn—death must come on the animal mind like weather. But the loss of the generation of 1993 left a gap in the family order and, perhaps, in the developing hierarchy of the pack. As far as anyone knew, the family *was* the pack for *Canis rufus*. Those four pups would have been in training during their first fall and winter. The movements and behavior of all the adults would have been affected by their presence. Although inexperienced, the wild-born young would have been wily, skittish creatures, less inclined to cross roads in daylight or to show themselves in pastures, less tolerant of the scent of humans and man-made things, another improvement in the wildness Fish and Wildlife was trying to cultivate or conjure. Despite the burden they would have imposed, they might have led their elders back toward invisibility, taught them something about pure wildness in exchange for being fed and nurtured and tutored on the hunt.

Although there was no year class to tend to in the winter of 1994, the juveniles were getting older and the home range in the cove was strained. Wolf country, too, was becoming crowded. One male juvenile was still submissive around its parents and tended to rendezvous with them more frequently than its more independent siblings, approaching the adult wolves with its ears back, tail down, and ready to respond quickly to the dominance displays that kept peace in the family. But by the middle of their second winter, the other three Cades Cove juveniles were getting restless. Their parents' home range was starting to bind, and they were beginning to itch for territory and mates of their own. Wolves, like everything else, need room to grow.

In late January one of the male juveniles, 538M, took off on an extended trek, following the summit ridge northeast up through spruce-fir country and then down to the Pigeon River, which curves west through the mountains on its way to meet the French Broad. 538M undoubtedly crossed this beautiful, polluted watercourse and its accompanying inter-state where the Appalachian Trail crosses them, perhaps using the foot-bridge that carries hikers over the booming traffic and tainted whitewater, and then moved up into the Cherokee National Forest, where it was recap-tured on Rag Mountain, nearly fifty miles from Cades Cove. Although the wolf had caused no trouble during its travel, it had reached a double dead end: The Cherokee National Forest was off-limits, and there was no poten-tial wolf mate out there. The restless wolf was brought back to Cades Cove and held in an acclimation pen for breeding and rerelease.

Meanwhile, in the cove, a natural splitting of the original family pack seemed to be under way, an interesting, never-before-witnessed process. The other two juveniles stayed within the cove but developed more inde-pendent patterns of travel and their own rendezvous sites. While his cohort 538M was on the road, two-year-old 539M apparently decided to build onto the home place rather than strike out for new territory. The young male established an independent home range in the foothills west of but adjacent to Cades Cove. Since 539M was ready to begin a life of his own, Fish and Wildlife recaptured him in February with the intention of breed-ing him in captivity with female 467F, a wolf born at the Smoky Moun-tains facility in 1991.

The lone female juvenile, 541F, also had been frequenting the western end of the cove, not a problem in itself, but she was seen several times in the company of a male coyote. During the Smoky Mountains reintroduc-tion, Fish and Wildlife observed two kinds of interaction between red wolves and coyotes—virulent antagonism on the part of adult wolves and, in the absence of the adults' example, a willingness on the part of the juvenile wolves, male and female, to consort with *Canis latrans*. That pos-sibility could undo the whole purpose of the southern Appalachian project. One of the last things Fish and Wildlife needed was hybridization between its red wolves and coyotes. That would defeat the quest for genetic restora-tion; in addition, it indirectly raised the nagging question of the red wolf's origins and taxonomic status.

In November of 1993, for example, a small coyote was observed fol-lowing 539M, which showed no concern at the coyote's proximity, into a woodlot where the family was holing up. The adult wolves were not so tolerant and challenged the coyote immediately, chasing it at full tilt out of the woodlot, keeping after it for more than a mile. The juvenile joined in this chase, apparently relearning something it had forgotten—that coyotes and wolves are ecological competitors.

But left to their own devices, unmated juvenile red wolves without territory of their own apparently abandon the wolf's antipathy to its canid cousin. When 541F, the two-year-old Cades Cove female, was seen traveling with a coyote for several weeks in late March, just after breeding season, she was captured and placed in a holding pen with the Tremont juvenile 525M, captive since its excursion to the cattle burial pit outside of Newport, Tennessee, the previous December.

In the spring of 1994, Lucash was feeling the pinch—the need for wolves with mostly wild experience for future releases and the need for an expanded territory. These two needs were related at several levels and were, in at least one way, contradictory. Wild-born or wild-raised wolves would ensure less man-wolf interaction, but wild wolves probably would travel more, as the younger generations of his wolves were doing. But given room to move and mating choices, they would steer clear of humans and coyotes.

In a sense, the land Lucash needed was in Wyoming. The afternoon I stopped to talk with him at his Cades Cove trailer heaven, he and his crew were meeting with visiting Fish and Wildlife officials from the gray wolf project that was taking shape at Yellowstone National Park. Lucash didn't invite me to sit in on this powwow, but he pulled up to my spot in the nearby drive-in campground that evening proffering a cold beer and an update on what had been a hectic season.

I had bug-covered topo maps spread out in the glare of a Coleman lantern on the campsite picnic table, and I showed him the routes of my old-growth cruises, which would take me, like the newest generation of wolves, beyond the confines of the Smoky Mountains into the Pisgah and Nantahala National forests. As he filled me in, it became clear that the unflappable Lucash was frustrated by the fact that his own project was chuffing to a stop while the Yellowstone wolf restoration, headed by Mike Phillips, his former boss at Alligator River, was gathering steam and attention.

The familiar gray wolf, *Canis lupus,* had of course been exterminated in the American West with the same vigor as had the red wolf in the Southeast. In fact, in 1914 the U.S. Congress provided the funds to complete the extirpation of wolves from Yellowstone National Park, forty-two years after the park had been established by Congress as a sanctuary for American wildlife. Thirty years after that feat was accomplished, Aldo Leopold, wolf hunter turned advocate of predator restoration, was recommending that wolves be returned to Yellowstone. Leopold's change of heart and mind was the beginning of a great turn in American consciousness, the kind of advancement in natural sympathy for which Henry Thoreau had hoped. After nearly another three decades, passage of the Endangered Species Act in 1973 simultaneously saved *Canis rufus* from extinction and created the legal framework for wolf restoration east and west.

When the relatively unheralded red wolf project began at the Alligator River Wildlife Refuge on the coast of North Carolina in 1987, the controversial Yellowstone plan was still hung up in Congress, where the western ranching industry held considerable sway. But by the fall of 1992, when the Cades Cove and Tremont wolves were released in the Great Smoky Mountains, Congress had finally appropriated funds for the Environmental Impact Statement for Yellowstone, making a gray wolf release all but inevitable there and in Idaho. By the spring of 1994, the final Yellowstone EIS had been issued and was on its way to the desk of Secretary of the Interior Bruce Babbitt, who was eager to sign it.

Lucash knew as well as I did that considerably more glamour attached to wolves in the West than in the East, an old differential that operated on many levels. There were a thousand people who knew of Lewis and Clark for every one who had heard of William Bartram. California redwoods and the foggy old-growth forest of the Pacific Northwest were common knowledge. Even most southerners were unaware of the spectacular groves of old-growth hardwoods tucked away in the southern Appalachian backcountry. For years the red wolf restoration proceeded at Alligator River, Bull Island, Horn Island, and in the Great Smoky Mountains with little fanfare and not much publicity. The scientific literature took full note of Fish and Wildlife's extraordinary accomplishment with red wolf restoration in the eastern United States. Internationally, the red wolf project was considered "a model for carnivore re-introductions," "the first time that any carnivore extinct in the wild had been returned to a portion of its former range." But the possibility of heavyset gray wolves silhouetted against the familiar backdrop of Yellowstone's smoky landscape was network news. The anomalous, little-known red wolf carving out a niche for itself in the eastern woods was, as it had been since Bartram's day, a sidelight.

In both the short and long run, I had always thought the red wolf's lack of cachet was an advantage. A plan in the early 1980s to restore red wolves to middle Tennessee and Kentucky blew up in Fish and Wildlife's face, in part because of too much of the wrong kind of publicity. Nothing protected predators more than anonymity. Let the national media do the call of the wild thing out in Montana and Wyoming and Idaho, where photographers could more easily contrive an illusion of wilderness and great space. The red wolf had learned to live off what land was left to it in the East. That unobtrusive adaptability was the key to its future.

As we talked, it was clear that, at least for the moment, the growing hoopla surrounding the Yellowstone releases was getting to Lucash. Pushy wildlife photographers for the national magazines on their way to spend a month in Yellowstone would stop to spend a half day in Cades Cove, expecting his crew to flush a wolf or two in front of their lenses. Jaded freelance journalists drifted through the Smokies for a one-time look-see at the red wolf operation before heading west, having already decided that the gray wolf was the real story. The fact that Fish and Wildlife had restored breeding wolves to eastern Tennessee and western North Carolina— within howling distance of the whitewater venue for the 1996 summer Olympics—never seemed to sink into the public mind. In April 1994, when his own program was running up against its inevitable limitations and seemed to be losing its luster, Lucash was salivating at the thought of having the 8 or 9 million acres his Yellowstone counterpart had to play with.

In the Great Smoky Mountains, it was cattle—great devourers of space—that brought the red wolf program to a halt in the spring of 1994, and, of course, it was cattle and other livestock that had sent *Canis rufus* to the brink of extinction in the first place. But Fish and Wildlife had chosen Cades Cove as the first release point in part because it offered, in Lucash's words, "a worst-case scenario" for wolf-livestock interaction, the belly of the beast from the point of view of wolf restoration. From day one, the Cades Cove wolves had been tempted by a calving herd of 200 to 250 breeding black Angus as well as another 100 to 200 heifers and older calves. If you wanted to prove that wolf restoration could *not* succeed, this was the place to do it. Without denying that cattle could be a powerful attraction for wolves, Fish and Wildlife wanted to demonstrate once and for all that, with proper management on both sides, wolves and livestock could coexist with a reasonable minimum of trouble. Moreover, they were prepared to provide compensation for whatever depredation occurred.

In retrospect, the really surprising thing was how little interaction there had been. The wolves did not barrel out of the acclimation pens and gleefully tear into all that passive cow flesh. Since the restoration began in October 1992, no healthy adult cow had been bothered by the wolves. Seven calves were presumed to be taken by wolves in the first fourteen months of the restoration. Although coyotes may have been the culprits in some of these cases, compensation was made. All of these losses occurred outside the two protective calving corrals Fish and Wildlife had devised. All of the calves taken by wolves were newborns, less than a week old, but reimbursement was made on the expected average weaned weight of 450 pounds, more than adequate compensation.

By and large, the Cades Cove wolves confirmed what was already known. Well-known wolf researcher David Mech had been arguing for years, on the basis of studies in the United States and Canada, that "unless wolves learn to take livestock or to recognize livestock as a legitimate prey, they don't seem to know how to handle it. . . . They seem to prefer to hunt the prey they traditionally have been hunting." With wolves and cattle living side by side in Cades Cove for nineteen months, no healthy adult cow or heifer was attacked by wolves and only four newborn calves were taken under what could be considered normal circumstances. No calves, not even the defenseless slippery newborns, were taken when the protective corral system was in place. *None.* Part of wildness was a preference for wild food.

Extreme weather was a factor in wolf predation on calves in both the spring of 1993 and 1994. One of the earliest observations about eastern wolves seemed to correlate aberrant behavior with the stress and chaos of bad winter weather. Colonial naturalist Mark Catesby had noted in 1731 that wolves that normally fled from the sight of a single man sometimes became emboldened in bad weather. The two serious breaches in the normal behavior pattern of the Cades Cove wolves were attributable to two bouts of severe weather—a blizzard in March of 1993 and heavy rains and catastrophic flooding in the early spring of 1994. It didn't help matters that the worst weather in the Smokies coincided with the calving season of late winter and early spring, the most tempting time of year for wolves to turn their attention to the cattle pastures.

Three newborns were lost during the blizzard of 1993, when the stockowner Rex Caughron could not get to his pregnant animals to move them to safety. But the change in behavior brought on by that blizzard was not permanent; the wolves soon returned to their normal prey and left cattle and calves alone. During the rest of 1993, the first full year of wolves, there was no further interaction between wolves and livestock.

But in the spring of 1994, bad weather again caused problems. Rex Caughron's cows began dropping calves in January, three to four weeks earlier than the year before. The fifteen or twenty calves born that month caught Fish and Wildlife off guard, and they had trouble keeping up with the way the pregnant cows were being shifted from pasture to pasture. But they had the two secure calving corrals. As long as births took place in a corral, or mothers and newborns were moved quickly to them, the calves were safe. Since there were coyotes at large with or without the wolf program, this was wise practice anyway. The corral worked well to keep the wolves—and coyotes—away from the vulnerable calves. Only one calf was lost before the flood damage, and compensation was paid for that animal.

Torrential rains and subsequent flooding in March damaged a good deal of pasture fencing and destroyed the two corrals. Without them, Caughron went back to the old method of pasturing even pregnant animals. In open pastures cows are surprisingly well able to fend off wolves, or at least to discourage them from wasting energy in fruitless assaults. Passive as they are, grazing animals, like the browsing white-tailed deer, have the defenses afforded by numbers, alertness, and spatial arrangement. So even without the secure birthing corral and with eighty calves on hand, only one calf was reported missing by the beginning of April. Fish and Wildlife paid for the missing calf even though they were unsure whether wolves or coyotes were responsible.

A dry summer left Caughron with little hay on hand, and he did not want to overgraze. But some pastures were more secure than others. He was soon using pastures overseen by the hilly woodlots where the wolves like to hole up, woody islands that the wolves used as staging areas for hunting pasture game. Lucash foresaw what was likely to happen, but cooperation between the grazing operation and the restoration apparently broke down during a difficult season. Pregnant cows often go off by themselves, giving up the buffer of open pasture and the safety of numbers. When cows started dropping calves in the lee of stumps and dead trees, often near the edges of the woodlots where the wolves cooled their heels, Lucash had a waking nightmare on his hands.

Lucash laid all this out for me between gusts of canned sitcom laughter from the motor home next door.

"Rex started losing calves at the rate of a calf a day. Things went from bad to worse fast."

Soon there were six calves missing, presumed to be taken by wolves, and Lucash finally convinced the stockowner to move the remaining animals back to more secure pastures. But the Cades Cove wolves were completely sidetracked from their wild ways by this bonanza of easy meat, and they became bolder and smarter about cutting themselves in for a share of the livestock operation. One Sunday in April Caughron—whose father had been one of the last ranchers in the cove before it became part of the national park—watched wolves kill a calf right in front of him and then suffered the indignity of the once-circumspect Cades Cove wolves boldly taking another from the herd from within what had previously been a secure corral. Once again Caughron was reimbursed for his losses, but Lucash had a family of wolves on his hands that had gone off the rails.

A wolf's Achilles' heel is that it does not forget anything it learns, even habits that get it into trouble. The oldest Cherokee myths and the earliest settler's anecdotes confirmed that wild as they were at heart, wolves could be drawn to the fire and that, once there, could be hard to drive away. Colonial explorer John Lawson described an encounter with what was very likely a red wolf in piedmont Carolina in 1709: "After we had supp'd, and all lay down to sleep, there came a Wolf close to the Fire-side, where we lay. My Spaniel soon discover'd him, at which, one of our Company fir'd a Gun at the Beast; but, I believe, there was a Mistake in the loading of it, for it did him no Harm. The Wolf stay'd till he had almost loaded again, but the Bitch making a great Noise, at last left us and went aside. We had no sooner laid down, but he approach'd us again, yet was more shy, so that we could not get a Shot at him."

Once the wolves started raiding corrals, it didn't take Lucash long to realize that the Cades Cove wolves, showcase animals for so long, were irretrievably focused on the calves, as incurably attached to the wrong thing as the wolf Lawson had observed.

"We could keep paying for the calves, but we couldn't let the behavior go on. The wolves had learned to defeat the fences and take calves out of corrals and pastures. They were lost."

After a year and a half of independence, the Cades Cove wolves had been tamed, corrupted beyond repair. Wild wolves had become marauding wolves, wolves ruined at the settlement edge.

Lucash reluctantly pulled the plug on what had been his most successful animals, and, for the time being, the most interesting animal in the southern Appalachians was displaced by the least interesting animal. By the time my topo maps were pockmarked with a second round of beers, the significance of the narrative was sinking in and I was shocked by the news that there were no wolves at large. Lucash, who wasn't paid to worry about narrative continuity, shrugged the hiatus off as easily as he had shrugged off the deaths of the Tremont wolves.

"It's not that big a deal. We can always get wolves to make it in the cove. Once things cool down and we straighten out the breeding and grazing operation, we'll be back where we were."

On April 17, 1994—the project's low point—the original Cades Cove adult pair, 341M and 378F, were recaptured after a successful run of nearly eighteen months. On April 21 Tremont wild-born 592M and 593F were shipped out to Alligator River for breeding and rerelease, a reward for their pioneering efforts in the Smokies. The Tremont juvenile, 525M, was already in captivity, as were the Cades Cove juveniles, the traveler 538M and the coyote-prone 539M and 541F. Three days later, on April 24, the only other cove juvenile, the submissive 537M, was captured. For the first time in a year and a half there were no free-ranging red wolves in the southern Appalachians.

Of course, as soon as the wolves were penned up, coyotes flowed back into Cades Cove.

It didn't surprise me that the wildness of the red wolf, which Fish and Wildlife had proved was intact, had led straight to the missing wildness in the world. I wouldn't want to argue the point on the floor of Congress or before a meeting of the Chamber of Commerce, but you can entertain the notion that a world that is uninteresting to wolves will one day very soon be uninteresting to human beings. The same tragedy that befell wildlife in North America awaits man. We are all becoming creatures of the edge.

I felt penned up in spirit after getting the disappointing news from Lucash. After a year and a half of doggedly pursuing the idea of wolves in these mountains, I was lean and footsore enough to be realistic in my expectations, but *wolf,* like *forest,* led me from what was left of nature in the present to a larger sense of what these mountains had been like in the past. But I could still track the life of an Appalachian spring unsanctioned by wolves. Certainly a snow-lit May morning in the southern Appalachians is worth seeing for its own sake. I had known that from the beginning. Sleeping under the thick silence of old growth is as good as hearing wolves howl. And waking up in a true forest—like awakening on a beach or in a desert or on the edge of a swamp—is one true measure of a morning.

There were still many forms of wildness to pursue. The snow in the branches of the hemlocks hung a glare in their dark, oriental forms and reopened their wintry structure. Understory evergreens reasserted themselves in winter guise—rhododendron leaves curled in the cold, galax shone ruddy on the snow—but the forest floor was a study in contradictions. Colonies of bright new ferns were laid low. Snow buried violets. Ice encased forests of tiny ground pine, which looked like miniature spruce at treeline. Empty seedheads of rattlesnake plantain still standing from last fall, a few tiny brown globes hung stubbornly in their husks, looked more in season than the clenched hepatica and *Claytonia* that barely rose above the snow. Yesterday's insect hum was stilled. Staghorn beetles stood at snowy cave mouths. At soil level this was a blizzard.

The unreal light dissipated as I cooked breakfast, and the oncoming season quickly reasserted itself. Wrens and creepers reified in the sunlight, the former silently picking through brush like wood rats, the latter spiraling up snow-dusted tree trunks. The cold hammering of a woodpecker on a frozen maple accompanied my pumping up the gas stove. Juncos came to coffee, which I drank while walking around to keep warm. When sunlight stirred insects to life, a pair of grayish-blue gnatcatchers careened around the open canopy, sometimes spinning down to the understory like falling leaves. Glossy brown woodthrush swung in and out of view at ground level. Something like a catbird that was not a catbird cried from out of view, and the air was soon filled with a half-dozen other voices I did not know. Grouse puttered in the distance from all directions like small chain saws starting up to clear the woods of broken limbs.

If the extremes of summer and winter determine the absolute limit of what can afford to live in the southern Appalachians, the way the weather backtracks some nights in spring and fall determines what will thrive in a given year. The extraordinary mix of northern and southern species underwrites the healthy profusion of life the eye grossly perceives in these woods. There is more of everything in old growth, and this southern Appalachian cove forest was one of the finest, most variegated forms of old growth. In such a densely settled place, something thrives in every hour of weather, the way people do in small, prosperous cities, and it is not unusual to find a maidenhair fern—which I might track north to the Canadian Arctic—growing at the base of a magnolia—which I could pursue beyond the equator.

If red wolves lead us back to the middle Pleistocene, this beautiful orchestration of life takes us a bit further, into the Tertiary. Stanley Cain, who studied southern Appalachian old growth in the 1930s and 1940s, declared them "the finest example of temperate Tertiary forests to be found anywhere in the world, except probably in Eastern Asia. . . . a botanist familiar with the modern flora of the cove hardwood forests of the Smokies would find himself 'at home' among the temperate forests of the Miocene and later Tertiary, could he be transported back in time."

Odd that the botanist Cain should be led by this great gathering of trees to speak, without apparent contradiction, of being at home in a strange place, of being one with the other, the double-edged sensation Freud identified as the heart of experience of the uncanny. Cain suggests that undisturbed nature does in fact take us back in time, that our encounters with what used to be called the sublime are not illusory, not escapism or psychological fantasy, but rather a good close reading of traces of our original relation to a found world—the realm of animals and plants, weather and landforms. The escapist illusion is that we are not dependent on and related to such things.

After breaking camp, I leave old growth behind because there is no more of it through which to walk. And the truth is, had I not gone in circles for a day, I could have traversed it in an hour. But unless you are starved for *any* bit of nature, there aren't many such places worth dwelling on or in—places where you can soak up the size of trees so large they jump a category in the mind, and walk slowly over soft, uneven ground casually inspecting the heartening variety in the forms of things, the hidden interplay of life among root, rock and soil, the flow of light and sound that weave such fabulous space out of such a long stretch of time.

Old growth would not have been preferred habitat for red wolves, but it was where wildness was nurtured in all its forms. Old growth sanctioned the lives of wolves and rivers and their kin, the *i'nage'hi*—those who dwelled in wilderness. Myth and history overlapped in the deep forest interior, where indigenous cultures kept contact with unused nature. All the important stories were entangled with the darkest part of the woods.

By the time I was a mile from where I had camped, the hemlocks were shedding snow, darkening as their branches closed, and the whitened ground around me browned as if the earth were baking. I moved off up the steaming slope, picking my way through the disappointing ranks of second growth I soon encountered, a fledgling, even-aged woods as yet unschooled and unsorted by time. In three or four centuries it will be an interesting place, if it is left alone, which is unlikely.

Not long after James Mooney had taken stock of Cherokee mythology on the Qualla Boundary in western North Carolina, two government foresters cruised the 10,000-square-mile southern Appalachian summit region in order to inventory its natural resources, particularly its standing timber. In 1900 and 1901 H. B. Ayres and W. W. Ashe had the enviable task of doing the fieldwork for a detailed report on "forest conditions" for the Geological Survey of North Carolina, the Bureau of Forestry of the U.S. Department of Agriculture, and the United States Geological Survey of the Department of the Interior. Their report, *The Southern Appalachian Forests,* was published by the U.S. Geological Survey in 1905 and remains, along with Mooney's work, one of the most important books on the region.

The foresters examined "10,000 square miles between New River Gap in Virginia and Hiwassee River in western North Carolina and northern Georgia, having an approximate length of 190 miles and varying width of 35 to 65 miles." This "choppy sea" of mountains—even foresters couldn't resist the oceanic metaphor—was the heart of the old Cherokee country that Mooney had delineated. By the standards of precontact Cherokee culture, the Appalachian summit region was overrun in 1900; by today's standards, it was barely settled: 318,000 people, 440 miles of railroad, 50 miles of tramway, 5,000 miles of wagon road, "much of which is bad, and, during the frequent rains, impassable." Surrounding this wonderful lack of development was "a vast extent of forest, principally hard wood, consisting of 137 species of trees." Add 174 species of shrubs as well as uncounted varieties of herbs, forbs, grasses, plants, lichens, mosses, ferns, and fungi. Then restock such woods with the full variety of its original wildlife and imagine a backcountry trek through such a place.

The richest watersheds contained as many as 100 tree species and their attendant shrub and plant communities. Of the northwestern slope of the Unakas, Ayres and Ashe reported:

> 92 per cent is wooded. . . . In the coves . . . the soil is fertile. . . . As a rule the earth is fairly well covered and thus protected from erosion. . . . In this region streams heading in unbroken forest are notably clear and show little fluctuation, while those from cleared lands are muddy and inconstant. While present erosion is limited, there is evidence that it would be very great if large areas of the earth were uncovered. . . . the forest of this great mountain side is practically unbroken. . . . Over 100 species of trees grow here, an unusually large number for one locality. Northern and southern trees are close neighbors, and all may be seen between elevations of 1,500 to 6,700 feet.

In 1900 this diversity existed in watershed after watershed of intact forest—not isolated groves of old growth with a few large trees on show like exotic zoo animals, but mile after mile of continuous and continuously varied old growth, one of the most biologically diverse places on earth. Ayres and Ashe had come to the Cherokee Mountains at a critical time in the natural and economic history of the region. Although 80 percent of the country they surveyed had been damaged by fire—often only in the understory—most of it was intact "original forest," Ayres and Ashe's term for old growth. There were a few small mills operating along the bigger rivers, but for the most part the lower slopes had been only selectively cut for the most valuable species and the upper slopes were pristine, still the dark province of the Tertiary and of Cherokee mythology. Six decades after the removal, the forests of "the real people" were still standing.

Wildlife, however, had suffered the fate of the Cherokee. "The once abundant game is gone," Ayres and Ashe reported, "trout have been dynamited, deer hunted, and turkey, quail, and pheasants [i.e., grouse] slaughtered until game is nearly exterminated. . . . The reestablishment of beaver on the numerous sources of these streams would go far toward steadying the flow and preventing floods." No mention is made of wolves, bears, or mountain lions.

Ayres and Ashe, who were working for Gifford Pinchot and the fledgling national Forest Service, did their work with a divided consciousness. They were on a timber cruise, not a biological survey. The contradictory founding task of the U.S. Forest Service was inscribed between the lines of their report. Although they were ultimately tallying up the millions of board-feet of valuable lumber "wasting away" on the stump, they well understood the fragile, interdependent ecosystem before them, particularly the relation between deep, undisturbed soil, clear flowing mountain streams, and the fabulous diversity of plant, shrub, and tree life in the southern Appalachians:

> One can hardly travel a quarter of a mile in an undisturbed portion of the forests without finding pure, cool water. These waters filter through moss and leaves a short distance, then follow the clean, stony bed of the brook down the mountains. . . . Springs are frequent and many of them especially in the wooded region are pure, cool, perpetual. In general the streams from the forested portions of the mountains are suitable for all uses, but those from pastures and clearings, and especially those that follow roads, are impure. . . . Variation in

stream flow has been notably increased by the clearing away of the forest near the sources of the streams.

Ayres and Ashe identified "fires, lumbering, and clearing of lands for farming" as the principal threats to an "original forest . . . wonderful in the extent, density, size, and quality of its timber trees, and the variety of their species." Fires, which became more of a problem as timbering progressed up the mountain slopes, permanently reduced forest diversity and health by destroying soils and promoting erosion: "Under such conditions a forest cannot reproduce itself."

In Ayres and Ashe's view, the only ecologically acceptable lumbering was select cutting, which preserved "the continuity of the forest" and did not destroy the soil, ruin streams, or change the fundamental diversity of the forests—a complex, dynamic balance that could not be "managed" any more than the life of an ocean can be managed. Mechanized clear-cutting and indiscriminate bark peeling were economically counterproductive in the long run and ecologically disastrous. But in 1900 the handwriting was on the wall: "In many places the mountain forests surviving the fires have been protected by the difficulty of access. In recent years, however, the advancing price of lumber has stimulated lumbering. . . . The lumberman is increasing his activities at a rapid rate and is yearly going farther into the forests."

Clearing mountain slopes for grazing and agriculture was equally short-sighted and ruinous. In the absence of tree root systems, dense moss mats, forest floor plant communities, and the deep shade afforded heat-sensitive humus from the layered shade of understory, midcanopy, and canopy trees, cleared lands rapidly became worthless. Much of the "improved" land Ayres and Ashe inspected had already been abandoned. Most of the region, they insisted, "should forever remain in forest."

Even before large-scale clear-cutting and the development of rural lands for industry and tourism, the region was being degraded by short-sighted exploitation:

this system of progressive exhaustion and abandonment of the land has led to great and widespread erosion, by which thousands of acres are now gullied and as worthless as the "bad lands" of the West. . . . Over the more elevated portion of the Appalachian Mountain region erosion is so rapid that the slow-growing hard-wood forests do not readily regain their footing. . . . The effect of exposing mountain

lands to the full power of rain, running water, and frost is not generally appreciated. During heavy rains the earth of freshly burned or
freshly plowed land is rapidly washed away. The streams from such
lands are often more than half earth, and the amount of soil thus
eroded every year is enormous.

Ayres and Ashe did not see the worst of what was to happen to the
original southern Appalachian forest, when the narrow-gauge railroads
were run to the ridge lines and the mountains were stripped bare in a few
decades, exacerbating all the problems they had already identified. From
the old black-and-white photographs of the period, the land looks as if a
foreign invader had destroyed it for spite.

I kept the dominant stream of the place within earshot and continued
uphill, intending to cross over into the adjacent watershed to the southwest
and descend its watercourse until I intersected the logging road along
which I had hiked in. Off-trail, I keep track of myself like a hunter, by
staying aware of my relation to the stream and ridge that define the watershed I'm in. But in the field orienteering is an art, not a science. Not every
creek you jump across shows as a blue line on the map, and some of the
map's blue lines have run dry in the world. And in the southern Appalachians, laurel slicks or rhododendron-choked slopes tend to push you off
your intended route in the way that a gusting crosswind affects a pilot.
After two or three miles you may not be exactly where you think you are,
which in good weather is one of the pleasures of walking cross-country.

By late afternoon I knew I was not where I thought I was. The stream I
had followed back down the mountain doglegged off in the wrong direction. At the top arc of my circle, I had inadvertently crossed two ridges,
not one, and was in the wrong watershed, a not uncommon mistake since
the heads of these small mountain streams are adjacent and not distinct.

So I was lost. Not grandly lost, which is impossible now, but I was not
where I had planned to be. Of course, since I didn't have to be anywhere in
particular, it was hard to create an emergency out of the disorientation. I
don't much care for wandering aimlessly in the woods, but I could enjoy
the haphazardness in my walking, and I rather liked design that unfolded
retrospectively. By my best guess I was six or seven miles from last night's
camp and now maybe twelve from the trailhead where my truck was
parked. So I made camp where I was, which meant I was home for the
night and so not lost.

This odd day had never found its center. There wasn't a speck of snow left in the woods, but gusts of cold air still blew out of nowhere, as if autumn were approaching the greening woods. A clear, cobalt blue sky promised a cold night.

There's a moment toward evening, before dusk begins, when what is foreign and familiar in the woods is perfectly joined. If I ignore my high-tech gear and just watch the woods, I can see the doubleness of my own being reflected in the life of things around me—that I am this strange animal that is not an animal and that these woods are my home and not my home.

Once I've made a ring of stones and laid a four-log fire, I'm beyond being lost or found. A tiny creek slurs beyond the flames, the light of which enlivens the tattered bark of the yellow birch around me and the smooth skin of young maples. Flaring firelight mimics daylight, then damps itself to coals; night begins. Darkness arranges itself in the woods in degrees of obscurity. Animals move, rustle, then still themselves while inanimate things quicken as life redistributes itself through the forms at its disposal. The brow of jutting bedrock I use for a kitchen changes shape at will. Trees loom, a kind of nightly old growth takes shape in these hard-used woods. Except for the odd clink of my things, history backs off. I think again how difficult it would be on the eye and mind if the sun never set, if all these rhythms set in motion 8 or 12 billion years ago didn't impinge on us, offering instruction once every day with its own version of nonreturning curves inscribed in the simplest, oldest things we have not yet begun to understand—the variety of leaf shapes and tree bark, the secret lives of animals, the presence of weather and land in the back of our minds, all the things that simultaneously gather around and shrink from a man in a forest, all the things that do not answer well to narrow uses.

I assume the complexity of language was prompted by the complexity of nature. Perhaps the tangle of synapses in our brains has more than a passing similarity to the understory and canopy out of which man emerged. Our words and thoughts are undergrowth. "In the woods," Emerson rebuked the Puritans, "we return to reason and faith." Even people who are at first uneasy in the woods come to sense that the tangled place that seems so foreign is somehow familiar. Home and not home. Literally *unheimlich*, uncanny. Perhaps the people who hate or fear the big woods are ashamed we came, frightened and unsure of ourselves, out of the dark, that life beyond their tame lawns—the ritual rectangle that keeps the forests and wolves and Indians at bay down to the present day—that life beneath the thin crust of consumer toys and entertainments is so *strange,* so *formidable,* still largely rooted in the Cryptozoic, in the oceans and beyond the stars, hidden from us and happily alien to us. Perhaps they are too proud to acknowledge their past as blue-green algae, their kinship to creodont and miacid.

Thoreau's wish for posterity was that by walking into nature, anywhere in America, any child or woman or man would be able to "find himself in a new country," would be able to climb "over the prostrate stems of primitive forest-trees" as I had been doing, partly for the physical pleasure and spiritual joy of the effort but also to remind themselves that "hope and the future are not in lawns and cultivated fields, not in towns and cities." I am pleased but surprised that what is left of the deep woods—"the raw material of life"—is not more crowded than I find it, that more people are not out traversing the last best places secretly hoping to get lost.

Ernest Fenollosa, the sinologist rescued for our contemplation by the poet Ezra Pound, conjectured that "in Chinese the meaning 'to be lost in the forest' relates to a state of non-existence" in the same way that the Sanskrit-English roots for "to be lost" and "perish" overlap. As if in the deep woods you are in danger not so much of being physically lost—a superficial worry—but of being so lost once—so unplaced—that you ceased to be, slipped into the inanimate sense of being that affords a tree or a boulder its well-weathered self-possession and that makes us regard such things, when we spend time among them, as being more than meets the eye.

Wild life and wild places seem to animate the appeal of this otherness, bring it closer to us, put a face on it—a bear or wolf or deer's face—so that we begin to see our old selves in the mirror wearing the old masks. Perhaps that is why the Cherokee have so many stories about the metamorphosis of men into animals, so many tales of shared being or of men getting lost without loss. Perhaps the primal forest fear was not that we wouldn't find our way home but that, like the *Ani'-Tsa'guhi,* the bear people, we wouldn't want to, that we would lose the desire to be human in favor of some old, uncanny allegiance with the bear and the owl, choose to dwell in the dark outside wood where spring and winter weave the double-wall vessel of the year, that one day we would look over our shoulder one last time before loping off on the long hunt with raven and wolf.

Crossing Paths

Long ago, long before the Cherokee were driven from their homes in 1838, the people on Valley river and Hiwassee heard voices of invisible spirits in the air calling and warning them of wars and misfortunes which the future held in store, and inviting them to come and live with the Nunne'hi, the Immortals, in their homes under the mountains and under the waters. For days the voices hung in the air. . . .

—James Mooney, "Myths of the Cherokee"

The road to Sand Creek and Wounded Knee, indeed perhaps the road to My Lai, comes up from Charleston through the Blue Ridge in northern Georgia. It fords this river just upstream of Russell's field, a floodplain well seeded with pottery shards and trade beads where there once was a Cherokee town, one of those places that slips through the uncertain language of the old accounts—Chatuga, Chatugee, Chattogee, Chattooga—English struggling with *Tsatu'gi*, a Cherokee word of Creek origin conjectured to mean " 'he drank by sips' or 'he has crossed the stream and come out upon the other side,' " pragmatic and poetic renderings of some event associated with this ford.

Part of the floodplain has been opened as neatly as if an operation was in progress, the fine alluvial soil dug out in neat meter squares arranged to expose a rectangle of yellow subsoil beneath the black plow zone. The slick clay surface of the subsoil reveals the placement of the wooden posts of the last town house at Chattooga Town, a circular structure supported by a quadripartite frame, squared circle of the Cherokee, dwelling place of a sacred fire. Each meter of soil removed is placed in a numbered bucket and then taken off to be sluiced and sifted, as if it contained something valuable.

A hearth has been exposed inside the circle of posts, a raised ring of glazed red clay that contained this settlement's council fires. Even off to the side in the excavated rectangle, the hearth is clearly a center. The ruddy clay contrasts sharply with the black and yellow soils. The red daub eye makes a strong image in the field of rye and vetch grown wild. Although Chattooga was neither a large nor an important town in the historical record of events, you could infer the entire Cherokee world, pragmatic and imaginative, from what has been unearthed here: the hearth, the arrangement of the town house postholes, the smaller outlines of summer and winter homes, the placement of the settlement on a fertile floodplain protected by a steep, forested ridge at a pronounced bend in a river. Chattooga was one of the Lower towns, the southeasternmost extension of the Cherokee in colonial times, a humble gateway to history.

That history is as hard as the rampart of Blue Ridge basement rock that casts cold shadows across Russell's field even on a bright June morning, as beautiful as the blue and yellow sound of the Chattooga soughing over the stones of its well-worn bed, as enigmatic as white-tailed deer watching archaeologists move quietly about their excavation.

For six years Gerald Schroedl has overseen a painstaking unearthing of Chattooga Town every summer in order to study the silent past through the mute clarity of its artifacts. Schroedl did his doctoral research on the association of bison remains with archaeological sites in his home state of Washington but came east to teach at the University of Tennessee in Knoxville. He was starting his career when the proposed Tellico Dam prompted the huge salvage archaeology operation on the Cherokee Overhill towns in the 1970s. The term *salvage archaeology,* most archaeologists will concede off the record, is an oxymoron posing as a euphemism.

Schroedl oversaw the excavation of Chota, where the Cherokee celebrated great victories against the British in the autumn of 1760. He was there when they uncovered the grave of Oconostota and studied the superb town house at nearby Tomotley where Ostenaco had entertained Henry Timberlake in December of 1761, when the British officer came with the peace terms that formally ended the bitter Cherokee war. Schroedl knew the archaeological riches and the spiritual significance of the Overhill towns as well as anyone. And he knew how much history and prehistory was lost to the future when the valley of the lower Little Tennessee River was inundated.

As lean and grizzled as any true digger, Schroedl looks and talks like he's been through the fire of practicing archaeology in a world given over to reservoirs, highways, and shopping malls. He is dead serious in a friendly western way, laconic and loquacious by turns, a flat-out realist with a romantic gleam in his eyes. When I met him in May of 1994, with the red wolves penned up 100 miles away in the Smokies, Schroedl and his students seemed to be doing something important at Chattooga Town, something that made up for the bulldozers and noise and hurry imposed on the Overhill digs by TVA's bureaucratic itch to close the gates on a dam its own research showed was unnecessary and that replaced the sacred places of an ancient culture with a polluted reservoir that benefited only real estate developers and tour boat operators.

The Chattooga Town site is especially valuable because most of the Lower towns were also inundated by reservoirs. It is ironic how many Cherokee towns have been erased by killing the rivers that watered their fields and sustained their philosophical relationship to the land. The largest, Keowee and Toxaway, were lost to archaeology like the Overhills, destroyed when the Keowee River and Little Rivers were dammed in the 1960s. A proposal to dam the upper Chattooga, famous for its world-class whitewater, was abandoned under pressure in the 1960s and the river and a narrow corridor saved by the National Wild and Scenic Rivers Act, a farseeing piece of federal legislation that inadvertently protected this non-descript field.

There are no bulldozers or backhoes at the Chattooga Town dig, no bobcats like Schroedl had at Chota, no black diesel smoke in the air. No machine in the garden this time. It's quiet here. This is earth-moving on a finer scale. Schroedl's students stop often to file the edges of their masonry trowels. Then, on hands and knees, they resume gently scraping the yellow soil of the town house floor, keeping an eye out for postholes and artifacts or for some unexpected oddity that might be an important piece of the past coming to light. You can hear the river above their filing and scraping, buttery bass notes of smooth rock and purling water behind the bite of shovels and the creak of wheelbarrows. Occasionally deer drift out of the surrounding woods to browse in the field. After the sun breaks above the cool bulk of Chattooga Ridge, red-tailed hawks get up on thermals. By midday war parties of billowing, sunlit thunderheads appear silently in the sky, violent and beautiful.

Shovels and wheelbarrows pass for heavy equipment here. The only disruption in the air comes from a gasoline-powered generator tucked away in a corridor of sycamore and alder that cling to the riverbank. The generator powers a pump that draws water from the river for the sluice boxes where objects emerge—mostly pottery shards and glass trade beads, the latter barely larger than the grains of soil washed away through the mesh. Hard to believe the red and blue beads once had so much power. There was a dark magic in all those trade goods. Most of the shards have the cross-checked ridges of the complicated stamped tradition, archaeological jargon for a slight but distinct embellishment paddled onto the red clay vessels that dates them as the work of historic Cherokee.

Schroedl runs an archaeological field school at the site. A few dozen students and some volunteers trade their labor for course credit or just for the experience. Beyond the trowel and shovel work, there is the sifting and tagging of artifacts, surveying and preliminary site interpretation as well as exposure to some of the most sophisticated tools of modern archaeology—proton magnetometry and ground-penetrating radar. Mostly its a matter of carefully digging in the earth to see what's hidden there—discovering the discovery, as Henry Thoreau would have it.

"This is the way it should be done."

Schroedl takes great pride in practicing minimally invasive archaeology here, a slow form of excavation that leaves the site intact at the end of each season for study the next. In his six years of work he has explored only the uppermost layer of occupation—the historic Cherokee town that was abandoned in the 1730s. He has deciphered the posthole patterns for four or five town houses and can date the village back at least to 1670, the year Charleston was founded and the beginning of continuous contact between the British and the Cherokee.

For Schroedl, the upper level of the site is a way to study the contact. When the last town house burned, the conflagration sealed the floor and the contents of the building, capturing an image of Lower town life and leaving Schroedl a palimpsest of artifacts to read and interpret. He has himself a little Pompeii on the upper Chattooga River.

The artifacts recovered from the site reveal the shifting economy and changing lifeways of Cherokee culture in the 1730s. But there is something enigmatic in the assemblage that emerged at Chattooga. There were neither many of the stone tools of precontact Cherokee technology nor many trade goods of European origin. Chattooga Town, undoubtedly like many other Cherokee villages, was suspended between two worlds in the early eighteenth century. The village's last economic venture seems to have been the manufacture of large quantities of stone pipes, a long-standing

Cherokee art, using European iron tools—an attempt to cope with the swirling changes of history.

Beyond the current excavation, time drops off precipitously around Chattooga Town. Forest Service test pits on both sides of the river and on a ridge above the town site have yielded pre-Cherokee ceramics and a Woodland period hearth as well as late Archaic projectile points—beautiful palm-size Savannah River specimens and smaller, older Palmer points that date to 9,000 years before the present. The place has always been a crossroads.

A century before Schroedl and his students started sifting soil here, James Mooney's work among the eastern Cherokee was interrupted by the Ghost Dance revival among western tribes, a widespread resurgence of Native American spirit among the Arapaho, Cheyenne, Kiowa, Apache, Caddo, Wichita, and Sioux that made Indian agents uneasy from the Dakotas to the desert Southwest. Rather than continue his work in North Carolina among the Cherokee in the fall of 1890, Mooney got director John Wesley Powell's permission to travel west to study the religious significance of the movement for the Bureau of American Ethnology. He was en route to the Indian Territory when the massacre at Wounded Knee occurred on the Pine Ridge Reservation of the Sioux on December 29, 1890.

By the time Mooney visited the site where Big Foot's Minniconjous clashed with the Seventh Cavalry, the mass grave had been fenced with wire by the survivors and the crude fence posts smeared with red medicine paint, to mark what was sacred there. Mooney, who knew the details of Native American history well and who wrote an incisive historical essay on the Cherokee, immediately understood what kind of place Wounded Knee was and what he called "the sickening meaning of such affairs as the Chivington massacre in Colorado and the Custer fight on the Washita, where the newspaper reports merely that 'the enemy was surprised and the Indian camp destroyed.' " He left a troubling afterimage of what had happened there:

> On New Year's day of 1891, three days after the battle, a detachment of troops was sent out to Wounded Knee to gather up and bury the Indian dead and to bring in the wounded who might be still alive on the field. In the meantime there had been a heavy snowstorm, culminating in a blizzard. The bodies of the slaughtered men, women, and children were found lying about under the snow, frozen stiff and covered with blood. . . . Almost all the dead warriors were found lying

near where the fight began, about Big Foot's tipi, but the bodies of the women and children were found scattered along for 2 miles from the scene of the encounter, showing that they had been killed while trying to escape.

Mooney included an invaluable account of the Wounded Knee incident as part of his study of the Ghost Dance revival. Though he drew no explicit connections, he well understood the relation of the massacre of the Sioux to the long history of the Cherokee and to the violent contradictions on which nations are built. Those contradictions have a history; some of it lies here, in the mountains around Chattooga Town at the foot of the Cherokee country.

Misunderstandings that arose between the Cherokee and the British during the French and Indian War flared into hostilities that led to a British declaration of war against the Cherokee in November of 1759. One consequence of this antagonism between the former allies was the Cherokee siege of Fort Loudoun, the British outpost among the Overhill Cherokee, along with six months of vicious border fighting along the eastern frontier. This conflict eventually drew more British into the interior. And when they came, they came not only to do battle with warriors but to destroy the people on a scale the Cherokee had not foreseen. They passed this site, fording the river where a nondescript highway bridge now spans it, on their way into the Cherokee mountains.

In the mid-eighteenth century, the southern colonies were neither manned nor equipped well enough to fight the Cherokee, who were well led by proven warriors, well organized in relatively small bands, and well motivated. The Cherokee knew the ground they fought on and fought for it as if it were their own. Despite another smallpox epidemic in 1760, the Cherokee nation could still put an effective fighting force in the field, particularly when they could contrive to fight at close quarters. The Cherokee did not have to be taught guerrilla warfare, which they had been practicing for thousands of years. Although they had quickly learned to use cheap trade guns and smooth-bore military muskets, they had not given up the art of making the heavy war bow. The British knew not to take the nation lightly.

In February of 1760 Lord Amherst, the commander-in-chief of the British forces in North America, dispatched 1,300 army regulars from New York to Charleston, twelve companies of highlanders and a battalion of Royal Scots, seasoned men who had fought in the backcountry of western

Pennsylvania and northern New York as well as against the French and their native allies in Canada. Amherst beefed this contingent up with light infantry and grenadiers. The force was commanded by Colonel Archibald Montgomery, who, on arrival in the Carolinas, augmented the British army regulars with 350 colonial rangers and provincials, a handful of civilian guides, as well as 40 or 50 Catawba scouts who relished Cherokee scalps for reasons of their own.

Mooney summarized the invasion of the Cherokee Lower towns in what is now upstate South Carolina:

> In June, 1760, a strong force of over 1,600 men, under Colonel Montgomery, started to reduce the Cherokee towns and relieve the beleaguered garrison. Crossing the Indian frontier, Montgomery quickly drove the enemy from about Fort Prince George and then, rapidly advancing, surprised Little Keowee, killing every man of the defenders, and destroyed in succession every one of the Lower Cherokee towns, burning them to the ground, cutting down the cornfields and orchards, killing and taking more than a hundred of their men, and driving the whole population into the mountains before him.

After Little Keowee, Estatoe was put to the torch: "A pretty town of two hundred houses, it was well supplied with corn, ammunition, bearskins, and plunder from the English settlements. The troops looted and burned every house and killed a dozen persons who had lingered. From Estatoe the army hurried to give Qualareetchee, Conasatchee, and Toxaway the same treatment." Montgomery wrote to Amherst that the Lower Cherokee had been "effectually corrected."

He then demanded the surrender of the Middle and Valley towns—the Cherokee settlements west of the Blue Ridge Mountains along various headwaters of the Tennessee River, which led in turn to the Overhills and Fort Loudoun. In the absence of a reply, Montgomery unhitched his wagons, had his men fashion makeshift pack saddles out of bearskins, reloaded his equipage onto mules and horses, and marched reluctantly into the mountains on the well-worn but narrow paths of the deerskin trade.

On June 23, 1760, the British left Fort Prince George, which stood among the ruins of the still-smoldering Lower towns. Their last fortified outpost behind them, they crossed the Keowee River and took the well-known trail toward the Middle Settlements. The next day they forded the Chattooga River here, turned downstream for a few miles, and then ascended War Woman's Creek, alongside which they made camp. The trail then curled north into the heavily forested Blue Ridge Mountains through what is now called Rabun Gap and down into the upper watershed of the Little Tennessee River along which the Middle Settlements of the Cherokee were strung.

Sixteen hundred redcoats marching in column across the Blue Ridge on a well-known path could hardly be a surprise. Six hundred Cherokee warriors from the Lower and Middle towns led by Seroweh and Tistoe, the Wolf of Keowee, waited for the British in dense woods along the river between Etchoe and Nikwasi. With the sacred mound and fire of Nikwasi a few miles downstream, the Cherokee engaged Montgomery's forces while they were making their way downriver through close country on June 27. At Tessuntee Old Town the Cherokee inflicted heavy casualties as well as doubts that, after another day of skirmishing, forced the British back over the mountains to the relative safety of Fort Prince George, where they unloaded many wounded from their packhorses.

By all accounts, the Scottish highlanders were impressed with the southern Indians. The Scots would not have known that the Cherokee warriors were inspired by the proximity of the mound of Nikwasi, under which the Immortals lived. They would not have known that those Immortals, the *Nunne'hi,* dressed as Overhill warriors, had once before come to the aid of the Cherokee of the Middle Settlements to repel an invasion from the southeast at the place where the Cherokee chose to engage them. To foes of the Cherokee, the *Nunne'hi* were invisible and seemed to be an angry force coming out of the rocks and trees and the darkly folded landscape.

Although he would not have been impressed by the legend of the *Nunne'hi* or even understood its psychological value to a Cherokee warrior, Montgomery was intimidated by the steep, strangely shaped mountains that seemed to swallow his long thin line of troops in a maw of vegetation. Morning came late in the mountains and evening early. All the extra dark favored the natives. He was exaggerating from real fear when he reported that his troops had assayed "passes the most dangerous man ever had to penetrate." From the safety of Fort Prince George he sent word to his superior in New York that "we had done so much as you intended" though he admitted " 'tis impossible for this detachment to extirpate them."

In fact, it was this defeat of the British below Etchoe that emboldened the Overhill Cherokee to force the issue at Fort Loudoun, whose garrison was starved into surrender by August, the British commanders agreeing to terms at Chota on August 7. Loss of this fort, which had been intended in part as a deterrent against French incursions upcountry from the lower Mississippi Valley, was news in New Orleans and Paris as well as in New York and London.

On August 9, 1760, the British flag at Fort Loudoun came down and the bedraggled garrison marched out according to the agreed-upon terms. They were to be allowed to return on foot to Fort Prince George, armed with enough shot and powder to get them home. That night the British camped along Ball Play Creek, a few miles upriver from the fort. After a secret council, the most adamant of the Overhill warriors attacked them at reveille, killing twenty-five soldiers. This equalled the number of Cherokee hostages the British had executed at Fort Prince George in the winter of 1759, an event that had intensified the Cherokee War. The attack on the British at Ball Play Creek, although a breach of the terms of capitulation, has come to be seen as an assertion of Cherokee law, a tribal enforcement of blood vengeance that in the mind of the more adamant Cherokee warriors took precedence in this case. In the Cherokee mind, this was justice being done, and—except for Dragging Canoe's heroic resistance during and after the American Revolution—was one of the last great assertions of Cherokee sovereignty.

Colonial newspapers throughout the East offered lurid accounts of the affair, which, given the anger of the Cherokee, were perhaps not inaccurate: "Vengeful warriors scalped Demere while he was yet alive and made him get up and dance before he died. The survivors became captives of those Indians who had seized them and led them away. Some were beaten in the face with raw scalps to hasten their movement. Parading the captives through each of the river towns, the warriors herded them into the chunky yards near the town house, and flailing them with switches and clubs, made them dance."

The feasting and hunting during the autumn of 1760 was joyous—a release of rage that echoed off the walls of the Unakas and ran down the chattering, leaf-choked Cherokee River from Talassee to Tuskegee. Even the angry warriors of Citico, whose men had been murdered by Virginians when the British and Cherokee were allies against the French, were satisfied. The Cherokee invited the French and even the hated Creek to celebrate with them and witness what their warriors had done against the king's men. David Corkran, who details this period of Cherokee history, recounts the singular moment: "At Chota on September 1 they [a small band of Creeks] saw a sight no southern Indian had seen since

D'Artaguette's defeat by the Chickasaws twenty years before: two hundred white soldiers dancing as captives of red men." For a few months even the Cherokee of the Middle Settlements and the Valley Towns were incited to take up the hatchet and scalping knife. But a hard winter soon descended on the tribe, which had not had trade with the whites for two years, and by spring the Cherokee were ready for peace.

In retrospect, the summer and autumn of 1760 proved to be the high point of Cherokee military success against the European invasion of their country. The fighting skills of the Cherokee were as keen as those of the Apalachee, who had harassed de Soto three centuries before, but the defeat of Montgomery's forces at Tessuntee Old Town, where Cherokee warriors had driven the best troops the British had from the field, the capture and destruction of Fort Loudoun, and the bold reassertion of Cherokee law at Ball Play Creek led only to an escalation of the force applied against them. While the Cherokee celebrated at Chota that autumn and made their captives dance around the council fire, Carolina raised the bounty on Cherokee scalps to £50 and a 350-ton troop ship was loaded with arms and reinforcements in New York. Three days before Christmas 1760, the *Brotherly Love* set sail for Charleston.

Chattooga Town was spared this violence. The town had apparently removed itself from history twenty-five or thirty years before Montgomery's men forded the Chattooga River here. Since his objective had been to burn all the Lower towns, he would not have failed to mention its destruction as one of his accomplishments.

By the British census of 1721, Chattooga was one of the smaller Lower towns, with ninety inhabitants representing perhaps ten or fifteen families spread out over 100 acres along the river upstream and downstream of the council house. By contrast, Toxaway—one of the towns burned by Montgomery—had 500 or 600 people. But Chattooga had a name and a council house and a council fire and was well situated for agriculture, hunting, and trade. The trader George Chicken had visited the town in 1715 and makes mention of the head man of Chattooga in his diary. Sir Alexander Cuming, self-appointed diplomat for the British Crown, had spent the night of August 5, 1730, here. The town disappears from written records after that, although it persists as a place-name, "Chattogee," on T. Kitchin's "A New Map of the Cherokee Nation" of 1760.

For reasons unknown, Chattooga Town was burned and abandoned in the mid-1730s—by hostile Creek, perhaps, or by its own disease-ravaged inhabitants, who moved away en masse to merge with another town or dispersed by families to clan relations in other towns. Its name reappears elsewhere. In any event, the town's last council house was burned, its roof and timbers collapsed over its hearth, which remained hidden for two and a half centuries until the patience of archaeology discovered it. The site would have been an overgrown field when Montgomery passed here, coming and going, in 1760 and when his successor came the following year to avenge the battle of Etchoe and the events at Fort Loudoun and Ball Play Creek.

In the spring of 1761 a well-ordered and well-supplied column of 2,600 men led by Colonel James Grant, one of Montgomery's subordinates on the 1760 expedition, made its way up from Charleston along the same trading paths Montgomery had traveled into the Cherokee country. Grant was inclined to make peace, but the crown needed to regain prestige, and the commercial interests in Charleston thought that a little warfare would be good for business. One of Grant's captains, Christopher French, kept a journal.

A two-mile-long column unwound from Charleston on March 20, struggling with heavy rains and the swollen creeks that fed the Saluda River. French notes odd events. One night they felt what they thought was a slight earthquake. At Fort Ninety-Six, 200 miles from Charleston, their cattle were harassed by the wolves that fell in behind their supply train. At night they watched their Indian mercenaries—some Seneca brought from New York as well as Chickasaw and Catawba dredged from the streets of Charleston—dance whatever makeshift war dances such compromised warriors could devise. The dancing increased as they approached the mountains. At Black Rock Creek, they killed a "large Rattle snake & a water snake which had another in it almost as large as itself." They noted "Great abundance of Deer every Place we came to, in so much that they came amongst us, & were sometimes affrighted from the grounds where we encamp'd." They also moved bears, turkeys, and grouse, but like de Soto's men were unable to kill any and, despite their compasses, got lost in the woods when they tried to hunt. They feared Cherokee snipers the whole way upcountry, but they liked the land they saw. The rivers, which rose and fell with the rain, were always troublesome, but the floodplains were fertile, the old fields and fired grasslands affording good pasturage. The towering forests that leaned over them were like nothing they had ever seen.

As the British approached the foothills of the Blue Ridge, the large piedmont rivers split into smaller and smaller tributaries draining narrower and darker valleys. Finally they encountered the ruined Lower towns, Montgomery's work from the year before. French notes that at Fort Prince George, once again the final staging area for the push across the mountains, they were "a little alarm'd one Night by a vast howling of Wolves," a howling in which their own Indian allies happily joined.

The British left Fort Prince George before dawn on the seventh of June, equipped, Grant himself noted, like shock troops, "without tents or baggage except bearskins, blankets and liquor." They traveled with nearly the same number of horses as de Soto and went the way Montgomery had gone: "We march'd about five, & at about 2 Miles distance we reach'd Ocunnih Mountain which is extremely high & about four Miles over, the prospect from it behind us was very extensive. The ascent was very tedious and troublesome." Then Grant's column crossed the Chattooga. "On our march & not far from Chatughi River which is Eleven Miles from our last Encampment we pass'd another Hill down which there was a pretty little Riverlet, with abundance of water-falls. We after cross'd the afore mentioned River which is Rapid & pretty broad, it reach'd to the middle. We next came to a place call'd the War Woman Creek which is very rapid & reach'd to the Knee. Here the Country is very strong, having vast high Mountains which command the Road all around."

The column then turned north into that strong country and, after a fatiguing uphill march of fifteen miles, encamped at Tuckareetchee Old Town, as had Montgomery's men. The next day they followed the narrow passage down the pristine headwaters of the Little Tennessee River toward the Middle towns with "orders to put every soul to Death."

Their Catawba scouts encountered scattered Cherokee as soon as they entered the dark folds of the mountains. On June 9 they destroyed Sticoa Old Town and another town nearby it and later in the day Estatoe Old Town. On the tenth the Cherokee fired on the head of the column as it moved down the upper Little Tennessee River. Although the attack was made not far from the ground where Montgomery had been defeated, this time the British were able to deploy in a better situation than Montgomery's men had managed. Both a frontal assault and an attack on the British supply train failed. After inflicting serious but not crippling casualties on the British for three hours, the Cherokee retired, rebuffed as much in spirit as in body. They later revealed that the "young Warrior of Estatoe" and several other headmen had been killed in the assault. Most of the warriors of the Cherokee nation had been thrown into the battle, and their casualties (twenty to thirty dead) as well as their failure to drive back the British unnerved them. The survivors said "they saw Fire flash from" British eyes as well as from their guns.

The British pressed on down the Little Tennessee with the Cherokee only skirmishing against them. They reached Echoi, which they "tore to pieces & set Fire to." Then Tasse was torched and they forded the river and continued downstream to Nikwasi, where they turned the town house into a field hospital. On the eleventh the British licked their wounds. They buried their dead indoors or dumped them into the river to keep them out of Indian hands and spare them the postmortem indignity of scalping, a practice indulged in by both sides in such fighting. On the twelfth they burned the cornfields surrounding Nikwasi and whatever buildings they were not using themselves. On the thirteenth Neowee and Canuga, newly settled by the refugees from the Lower towns, were burned. Montgomery had driven the people of the Lower towns to the Middle Settlements. Grant drove both populations over the rugged passes to the Overhills.

For the most part, the British burned ghost towns and killed, or had their Indians kill, the few civilian stragglers who remained. When given the opportunity, they were as brutal as the Spanish had been more than a century before. Grant notes pointless murders matter-of-factly: "a poor miserable squaw was brought in from Tassee and put to death. . . . an old man was found in the town and put to death."

Amid this dizzying violence, French and his colleagues remained aware of the beauty of their surroundings: "The prospect from some of the Hills [is] pleasant, though not very extensive, occasioned by a circumstance extraordinary enough & perhaps not to be parralled [sic]—viz. That go to the highest Mountain you can see yet when on the top of it you see others still higher. This we experienced every Day's March."

On the fourteenth of June they reached Watoga. "Here we halted pull'd up all the Corn, cut down the fruit Trees, & burn'd the Houses, in number about Fifty. We then continued our march to Ayoree, 1 mile, where we encamp'd & began to destroy the Corn immediatly." On the fifteenth they destroyed fields and crops and on the sixteenth they reached Cowee, largest of the Valley towns and, like Nikwasi, one with a mound and a sacred fire that remain to this day. "This is plesantly situated upon the River. We halted & destroy'd a great quantity of Corn, & cut down fruit Trees."

The British used Cowee as a base camp and once again turned a council house into a field hospital. Some of their dead from upstream met them. They fished bodies out of the river. Determined "to demolish every eatable thing in the country," Grant reduced his men's rations so that he could extend his supplies and reach every town within his army's grasp. A detachment of 1,600 men was sent on the path over the Cowee Mountains to the Out towns along the Tuckasegee River:

> We march'd again through the strongest country ever I saw, anything we had yet pass'd being nothing to comparison with this. It began by descending Stickowe Mountain which was so very steep & made so slipery by some Rain which fell, that it was nearly as difficult to get down as up, from here our March was, either through deep Vallies, render'd in some places almost dark by Trees or upon the sides of immense Mountains with steep precipices on one side, & the remaining part of the mountain a great height above, & the path so narrow as to render it very Dangerous to a Traveller who has nothing to consult but his Safety, whereas we expected to be attack'd every minute. In short it was the most fatigueing march that ever was made. We reach'd some straggly Houses, however without accident at one o'Clock, here we halted 'till about ½ past three in which Time we destroy'd some Fields of Corn & burn'd the Houses, we then proceeded & reach'd Stickowee about five, This Town stands pleasently situated upon the north branch of the Tanasee which here takes it's name from the Town.

From the sixteenth to the twenty-eighth of June they destroyed the string of Out towns—Usinah, Coweechee, Burning Town, Stickoee, Conutory, Tuckoreechee, Tessantee, and Elajoy—along with their stores and fields. The few civilians who were rounded up were routinely tortured and put to death. Most had fled. The Seneca, Catawba, and Chickasaw were set free to perpetrate atrocities for reasons of tribal vengeance or personal blood lust. The latter were credited with killing the principal man of *Kitu'hwa*, the most sacred town of the Cherokee, which was burned on June 27. When the work was done, Cowee was destroyed on July 2 and Grant's troops, most of whom had worn out their shoes, shuffled back upriver.

The Cherokee continued guerrilla warfare against the British as they returned up the valley of the Little Tennessee through the burned fields and towns of the Middle Settlements. Small war parties were able to get inside the army's guards to do some killing and scalping of their own or at least count coup to save face for the people. But even the most war-prone leaders knew they could not fight a standing battle against such a large show of regular army strength, discipline, and firepower.

The success of Grant's mission was cause for much self-congratulation among the British. The tables had been turned from the year before. The embarrassing Cherokee War was over. Grant boasted in his journal that he had driven "5,000 people including men, women and children . . . into the woods and mountains to starve. They have nothing left. . . ." Veterans of the march across the Alleghenies in western Pennsylvania on the way to the fighting at Fort Pitt insisted that the march over the Cowee Mountains was the hardest the British had done in North America. Colonel Grant repeated James Adair's fib that the Cherokee Mountains were more rugged than the Alps, which like Adair he claimed to have seen. Mooney notes that Grant was credited with pushing "the frontier seventy miles westward" in three weeks of ethnic cleansing.

Before leaving the valley of the Little Tennessee, the Chickasaw left a war token in the path as a final insult to the ruined Cherokee, but no man, white or red, Grant noted, was willing to fight Cherokee warriors in the mountains: "when these Cherokees get into the mountains none of the other Indians can come near them." The hungry column retraced its steps over the Blue Ridge, most of the men tired and tattered. They followed the path back down to War Woman Creek and recrossed the Chattooga River here, reaching the Keowee River opposite Fort Prince George on the ninth of July.

On the twenty-first the Cherokee sent an old man to the fort with a flag of truce, a string of white beads, and an offer to straighten the Path. The war chiefs Oconostota and Standing Turkey had "gone hunting" and left diplomats like Attakullaculla free to engage in Long Talks, make peace, and negotiate its price. Despite the decisive display of force by the British, this took time. Attakullaculla was not willing to give away the rights of his people and the British were still not eager to march against the Overhills, who had not been touched by Grant's punitive raid. And the Mankiller of ruined Nikwasi remained adamant about the right of the Cherokee to defend their country and retain their sovereignty over it. The Cherokee were not broken, but Grant's army had conquered its own fears about campaigning in the mountains, a campaign the Americans would remember.

For weeks both the Cherokee and the British talked out of both sides of their mouths. Neither was free to acknowledge, given the fiction surrounding such negotiations, what the ultimate goal of colonization was. The expeditions of Montgomery and Grant had been the Cherokee's first experience of a systematic attempt to exterminate them. The implications of the contact had never been more clear. Sir Alexander Cuming, who had passed through Chattooga Town in 1730, had warned an assembly of warriors in the town house at Keowee that if they failed to cooperate with the British, "they would become no People," a threat of negation that was now more than rhetorical. More than half the towns and stores of their nation had been destroyed. They faced a hard winter, and a harder history was at their door.

What passed for peace after such events was finally arranged, but the country remained unsettled. As summer gave over to autumn, Christopher French had less and less of historic or military importance to record in his journal. Near the end of September he notes, apropos of nothing in particular or perhaps of the general unease, that "we have had Wolves in greatest numbers howling about our Camp during this month than any Time heretofore." Finally some temporary rapprochement was achieved, and the British eagerly left Fort Prince George before bad weather set in and trapped them in the mountains along with their victims.

Atahi'ta, "*the place* where they shouted."

In these mountains the past is another country wreathed in a fog of violence and beauty, the intriguing double helix of American history: Montgomery. Grant. Christopher French. Thousands of soldiers following orders. Warlike Ostenaco and Oconostota. Outraged Seroweh and Tistoe, the Wolf of Keowee. The wolves of Keowee themselves howling around Fort Prince George. Long-suffering Attakullaculla, always in the middle, and all the nameless refugees from the Lower, Middle, and Out towns, three-quarters of a great nation displaced into a mountain winter.

Fourteen years after the Grant expedition, the Quaker botanist William Bartram forded the Chattooga River below the Chattooga Town site and made his own way into the strong country of the Cherokee. Like Montgomery and Grant, like de Soto for that matter, Bartram traveled in spring. He departed from Charleston on April 22, 1775, and reached Fort Prince George, by way of newly founded Augusta on the Savannah River, sometime in the middle of May. Although much of Bartram's account is taken up with invaluable lists of the plant and tree species he observed as he rode along, his mind, like the mind of the Cherokee, seems evenly divided between history and nature.

Approaching Fort Prince George, Bartram observes the ruins of the

Lower towns. Except for the small Cherokee village called Sugar Town by the whites, there was little left: "this fertile vale within the remembrance of some old traders with whom I conversed, was one continued settlement, the swelling sides of the adjoining hills were then covered with habitations, and the rich level grounds beneath lying on the river, were cultivated and planted, which now exhibit a very different spectacle, humiliating indeed to the present generation, the posterity and feeble remains of the once potent and renowned Cherokees." Bartram notes the idle "posts or pillars of their habitations" that archaeologists now seek. Near the fort he rides past the ruins of Keowee, more of Montgomery's work, commenting only that there are "no Indian habitations at present."

Spring was well advanced along the coast and in the piedmont when Bartram had started out, but the season recedes as he travels upcountry, the early blooms of the forest floor waning as he moves north and then reblooming as time catches up with him. Like Christopher French, Bartram notes the stunning size of the old-growth forests through which he passes, but he is equally impressed by the quality and changing character of those forests, the great variety in terrain and vegetation.

Because relations with the Cherokee are still unsettled, Bartram waits at Fort Prince George for an Indian guide to accompany him and give him a measure of safety. But, anxious to be gone when the flowering of plants and trees aids his identification of species, he leaves Fort Prince George alone on May 19 and proceeds northwest across the Keowee and Little Rivers. The trading path to the Middle Settlements switchbacks against the grain of the Blue Ridge, leading Bartram over a buckled sequence of narrow mountains separated by cold, fast-flowing streams, the tight folds of valley and ridge that unnerved Montgomery and made Grant nervous. But Bartram, unarmed, looks about with curiosity rather than guilt. He admires a flowering locust as would Emerson or Thoreau, as a thing of natural beauty and philosophic import: "a singular pleasing wildness and freedom in its manner of growth."

At the base of Oconee Mountain Bartram passes more native ruins, although he doesn't distinguish between recent and ancient calamities. Mounds intrigue him. He knows the precontact North American past is a deep mystery, that although the East is being rapidly settled and changed, the essence of the landscape has been ignored all along. After his ascent he stops to admire the recessional of green and blue ridges to the southeast and, alone in a dangerous but beautiful country, tries to find metaphors for the land around him. The mountainous wilderness appears "regularly undulated as the great ocean after a tempest; the undulations gradually depressing, yet perfectly regular, as the squamae of fish or imbrications of tile on a roof"—European figures for the American landscape, each an awkward fit, as if the land belonged to another language. Bartram notes that mountains and sky are indistinguishable at the horizon, that where there is great space one thing merges into another.

Then he abandons metaphor for a short burst of Romantic rhetoric full of psychological if not geographic truth: the "magnificent landscape" is "infinitely varied, without bound." In William Bartram's hands—as in Thoreau's—this assertion is an expression of intellectual and spiritual awe. Eventually the idea will become a debased conceit of politics and commerce—that there is infinite wealth and space at Bartram's feet. This pernicious idea traveled behind the supply trains of Montgomery and Grant, following the wolves that followed their beef cattle. In fact, the idea—a hallucination caused by greed—traveled with de Soto during his incursion into the southern Appalachians.

But on that spring day in 1775 William Bartram was admiring something more than potential wealth from the summit of Oconee Mountain, something real and immaterial. About to descend into the Cherokee country, he was on the edge of the sacred. To the botanist, tangible proof of that was a new species flowering around him—*Rhododendron catawbiense*—Catawba rhododendron, a southern Appalachian endemic that thrives on steep slopes where it often alternates with mountain laurel, the two giving an oddly floral edge to rocky windswept outcrops.

Bartram then descends a winding road through what he kept insisting was incomparable forest. Proceeding toward the Chattooga River, he notes how delicate southern plant species associate with hardy northern stock and details, in a rush of English and botanical Latin, how much latitude is compressed on the rich uplands through which he passes:

> where grew many plants and trees common in Pennsylvania, New-York and even Canada, as Pinus strobus, Pin. sylvestris, Pin. abies, Acer saccharinum, Acer striatum, s. Pennsylvanicum, Populus trimula, Betula nigra, Juglans alba, &c. but what seems remarkable, the yellow Jessamine, (Bignonia sempervirens) which is killed by a very slight frost in the open air in Pennsylvania, here on the summits of the Cherokee mountains associates with the Canadian vegetables, and appears roving with them in perfect bloom and gaeity; as likewise Halesia

diptera, and Hal. tetraptera, mountain Stewartia, Styrax, Ptelea, and AEsculus pavia, but all these bear our hardest frosts in Pennsylvania.

The Cherokee mountains proved to be an uncanny place for Bartram, a native Pennsylvanian, a place where he found himself home and not home, where one form of life merged into another in ways both Thoreau and Darwin would help to unravel, a place where land was finely wrought and naturally well used. Anticipating Emerson, the American woods deepened both his reason and his faith.

Continuing northwest, he passes through "magnificent high forests" pocked with natural meadows and more native ruins and then through a gap in Chattooga Ridge that points him toward the river here. He describes land we will never see whole again:

> The surface of the land now for three or four miles is level, yet uneven, occasioned by natural mounds or rocky knobs, but covered with a good staple of rich earth, which affords forests of timber trees and shrubs. After this, gently descending again, I travelled some miles over a varied situation of ground, exhibiting views of grand forests, dark detached groves, vales and meadows, as heretofore, and producing the like vegetable and other works of nature; the meadows affording exuberant pasturage for cattle, and the bases of the encircling hills, flowering plants, and fruitful strawberry beds: observed frequently ruins of the habitations of villages of the ancients.

He crosses the Chattooga—"a delightful river, the main branch of the Tugilo"—fording it, apparently, below Chattooga Town, above the main river's confluence with War Woman Creek. Like Montgomery and Grant, Bartram follows the trading path up this watercourse through what is now called Rabun Gap and then north over the modest ridge that separates, in effect, the Atlantic Ocean from the Gulf of Mexico.

From the upper reaches of the Little Tennessee River in northern Georgia, Bartram's mind takes in the whole, still-vast Cherokee country from one corner of the eastern continental divide

> which separates the waters of Savanna river from those of the Tanase or great main branch of the Cherokee river, which running rapidly a North-West course thro' the mountains, is joined from the North-East

by the Holstein, thence taking a West course yet amongst the mountains receiving into it from either hand many large rivers, leaves the mountains immediately after being joined by a large river from the East, becomes a mighty river by the name of Hogehege, thence meanders many hundred miles through a vast country consisting of forests, meadows, groves, expansive savannas, fields and swelling hills, most fertile and delightful, flows into the beautiful Ohio, and in conjunction with its transparent waters, becomes tributary to the sovereign Mississippi.

Which is to take the long view of the Cherokee country and concede the requirements of grammar to the lay of the land and its rivers. Bartram gave the name Mount Magnolia to the summit of this crossing, but the name did not stick. Neither did his name stick to the new species he described from a specimen there—the beautiful mountain magnolia that came to be named after the Scottish botanist John Fraser.

It was this crossing of the Blue Ridge from South Carolina into Georgia and then on into the valley of the Little Tennessee River in western North Carolina that, Bartram tells us, "wholly engaged" his imagination in the land around him. You can still feel in his writing an enormous appetite for animated detail, driven by an ambition that is neither literary nor scientific. Although William Bartram's descriptions often stay within the conventions of eighteenth-century nature writing, his prose at times verges on a modern, abstract apperception of the native significance of what he sees—the luminousness of nature Europe had forgotten in its itch for commerce, that otherness beyond both art and science that Emerson, Thoreau, Whitman, and Dickinson, among a very few others, would recognize as the transcendental gleam in things, basis of the sacredness of mountains, rivers, and forests. The European mind, dizzy with conquest, had forgotten that the sacred was, like gold, hidden in nature, embodied in thunder and thundering waterfalls, in the odd shapes of mountains, and in the lives of animals, birds, and trees. A new species of rhododendron and magnolia were more than natural facts. The land before Bartram needed no development.

Bartram was well weathered by the time he reached the Cherokee country. He did not wear his piety on his sleeve, and he practiced science as if the facts mattered as much as his faith. It is not surprising that his prose takes on the bloom of a new species—a view of land and wildlife displaced sharply toward the strange sacredness of Native American consciousness.

In the rocks and air, in the enormous tulip poplars and hemlock that towered over him, in the twisted rhododendron and laurel through which he pushed and in the open faces of bloodroot and hepatica at his feet Bartram began to see the odd connections, juxtapositions, and metamorphoses that underwrote the wild geometry of the Cherokee mind.

Bartram was ahead of and behind his time, and descending the headwaters of the Tanase, he struggled toward that uncanny psychological threshold you seek in the wild among wild things:

> I perceived at some distance before me, on my right hand, a level plain supporting a grand high forest and groves; the nearer I approach my steps are the more accelerated from the flattering prospect opening to view; I now enter upon the verge of the dark forest, charming solitude! as I advanced through the animating shades, observed on the farther grassy verge a shady grove, thither I directed my steps; on approaching these shades, between the stately columns of the superb forest trees, presented to view, rushing from rocky precipices under the shade of the pensile hills, the unparalleled cascade of Falling Creek, rolling and leaping off the rocks, which uniting below, spread a broad, glittering sheet of crystal waters, over a vast convex elevation of plain, smooth rocks, and are immediately received by a spacious bason, where, trembling in the centre through hurry and agitation, they gently subside, encircling the painted still verge, from whence gliding swiftly, they soon form a delightful little river, which continuing to flow more moderately, is restrained for a moment, gently undulating in a little lake, they then pass on rapidly to a high perpendicular steep of rocks, from whence these delightful waters are hurried down with irresistible rapidity.

The Cherokee and Creek, I suspect, had a word or two to describe this forested cascade—a noun for the brow of bedrock and its basins, a verb for the shape of the falling water in the air. In Cherokee, the verb undoubtedly would have been an onomatopoeia and conveyed the sound as well as the significance of the way the land spoke here. Perhaps stories would have been attached to the place. The thunders, after all, were said to frequent waterfalls.

Bartram's psychological and philosophical need to bring a cascade of language to the land here is as important as the scene he conveys, which should not be dismissed, or accepted, as merely picturesque description.

His writing is simultaneously beautiful and labored, as all such writing is—the wording of the world. But in the end, it's as if the English language were being shorn here at these falls, broken against referents it could not manage because English was a language based on dichotomies foreign to the wholeness of this landscape. Here English is being purified, brought down to earth, partly because of Bartram's writing and partly in spite of it. Like all good travelers, Bartram writes himself into a kind of linguistic homelessness and leaves the best language he has pooled, reforming itself, swirling in bedrock basins.

So William Bartram stops, humbled, before one of a thousand such cascades in these mountains—every hiker knows how common they are—and sits down on a mossy rock to observe and think and search for words. In the Cherokee Mountains Bartram is very near to Muir and Thoreau, to the young Darwin in Brazil, and to a very few other writers of European ancestry who have approached moments of native consciousness in North America, who have shown such high regard for the details of place and risked enough of themselves to give us permanent access to their informing spirit.

From the mountainous divide between the Chattooga and the Little Tennessee rivers, Bartram continues his "lonesome pilgrimage" down through a rugged country that eases as the latter river grows, fed from every creek-lined crease in the mountains, broadening its floodplain to suit its needs. He weathers a thunderstorm and then finds an Indian cabin that seems a good place to spend the night. He turns his horse out in a meadow, gathers wood for a fire, and sups on biscuit and dried beef while his clothes dry. An ordinary evening in the backcountry. He watches night come in clear, calm and cool.

The next day he passes Sticoe, which Grant had burned, and then crosses the Tanase for the first time, a baptism of sorts in at the head of the beautiful Vale of Cowee. Downstream Bartram observes "on each side of the road many vast heaps of these stones, Indian graves undoubtedly"—the Cherokee dead from the pitched battle against Grant fourteen years before.

Approaching the Middle Settlements, the trading path becomes a spacious, well-beaten road that leads Bartram, as it had led Grant, from town to town. Many had been rebuilt. Bartram passes Echoi and then Nikwasi. At Whatoga, he is perceived to be a peaceful man, his intent interest in plants taken as proof of his intelligence and culture. He is not only treated well but is solemnly brought within the quadripartite universe by the headman of Whatoga, who Bartram tells us has the piercing, fiery eye of an eagle:

> My venerable host gracefully and with an air of respect, led me into an airy, cool apartment, where being seated on cabins, his women brought in a refreshing repast, consisting of sodden vension, hot corn cakes, &c. with a pleasant cooling liquor made of hommony well boiled, mixed afterwards with milk; this is served up either before or after eating in a large bowl, with a very large spoon or ladle to sup it with.
>
> After partaking of this simple but healthy and liberal collation and the dishes cleared off, Tobacoo and pipes were brought, and the chief filling one of them, whose stem, about four feet long, was sheathed in a beautiful speckled snake skin, and adorned with feathers and strings of wampum, lights it and smoaks a few whiffs, puffing the smoak first towards the sun, then to the four cardinal points and lastly over my breast.

Few white men have been so honored.

Finally he reaches Cowee, which sprawls across the river: "one of the most charming natural mountainous landscapes perhaps any where to be seen; ridges of hills rising grand and sublimely one above and beyond another, some boldly and majestically advancing into the verdant plain, their feet bathed with the silver flood of the Tanase, whilst others far distant, veiled in bleu mists, sublimely mount aloft, with yet greater majesty lift up their pompous crests and overlook vast regions."

Even the Shawnee, bitter enemies of the Cherokee, considered the region around Cowee "a good country." Mooney conjectured that the English name derived from *Ani'-Kawi'*, place of the Deer Clan. A Shawnee captive who once admired it advised them to never let it go. Bartram compares it to the Roman fields of Pharsalia and the Greek Vale of Tempe. The Cherokee lost it by treaty in 1819, when they lost *Tsiya'hi*—Cades Cove— and everything north of the Tennessee River.

The white trader at Cowee advises Bartram not to venture alone to the Overhills. But after spending a few days exploring around Cowee, waiting in vain for a native guide, the eager botanist follows Iotla Creek up into the Nantahalas, "being determined at all events to cross the Jore mountain, said to be the highest land in the Cherokee country." A steep, winding path leads him to Wayah Bald, a wolf place.

From Wayah Bald, the quadripartite universe is laid out for Bartram as it had been on Oconee mountain: "I beheld with rapture and astonishment, a sublimely awful scene of power and magnificence, a world of mountains piled upon mountains." Once again the horizon suggests endless variety and scope and pushes Bartram to the brink of Thoreau's Romanticism: "an expansive prospect, exhibiting scenes of mountainous landscape, Westward vast and varied, perhaps not to be exceeded any where." But Bartram has ridden up into cold mountain air, and the life around him turns through finite cycles. He notes that the yellow jasmine, which was past bloom down in Charleston, was just beginning to open on the upper slopes of the Nantahalas. And history is also on the horizon. From Wayah Bald, the short arc of the Cowee Mountains, which had impressed Grant's men when they crossed them on their way to burn the Valley towns, stands out distinctly to the east with the Vale of Cowee at their feet.

The centerless recessional of ridgelines and river valleys that Bartram admired still fills the horizon in all directions with that uncanny fusion of randomness and order that underwrites wild landscapes—the natural shape of the world buckled into view, back of some great beast, roof of the underworld. The ridges seem like the worked edges of an ongoing creation, coruscations of the earth's mantle pressure-flaked into sharp scallops that cut the air. Like the valley of the Little Tennessee, the scene at Wayah Bald is still something to see.

Every traveler who has ever been here admires the view and tries to take the measure of it. There is a reason why we do not have language adequate to such places, which pour over the eyes as if you were lying on the bottom of a river. Failure to perceive the mystery of a place is a failure to perceive its value. The rational mind tends to define one known in terms of another known, a sane and sensible way to proceed. But wildness—that thrilling, sacred energy in nature—transcends analogy, like a wolf, or a wolf howl, or the strange silence that trails the howling. The early European observers, all of whom had a dangerous ocean crossing in the back of their minds, couldn't help but see oceans of mountains in such places, but that trope is frozen and fails both water and rock. In an odd moment, the land nudged Bartram's language another notch toward the spirit of an indigenous awareness, which encourages nouns to be animated by unfamiliar predicates without explanation. Perhaps his consciousness was relaxed by fatigue: "the towering mountains seem continually in motion as I pass along." The motion of the true traveler and the stillness of wild landscape are one.

Bartram descends the rugged west flank of the Nantahalas, which puts shattered fragments of the mountains constantly in his way. He passes here through Wayah Gap and then follows the trail west, crossing the once-wild Nantahala River near where it is now dammed. Not far from the ford, surrounded by old-growth hemlock, he encounters Attakullaculla and his retinue on their way to Charleston from the Overhill towns. Bartram recognizes the well-known Cherokee chief, whose distinct features and small stature give him away.

Attakullaculla has had a strange life. He was the youngest of the noble savages that Sir Alexander Cuming took to London in the summer of 1730 to gain favor with the king. Wearing court dress, he had his portrait painted and sat in a box at Sadler's Wells. He had been at Windsor Castle, had been to the Tower of London and Canterbury Cathedral and even Bedlam to see the lunatics. This forest person sat through a medieval mystery play and a drawing room comedy, strange things for a young man born on an island in the French Broad River to witness. He told his guide and interpreter in London: "They are welcome to look upon me as a strange creature. They see but one, and in return they give me an opportunity to look upon thousands." Attakullaculla must have had odd dreams some nights at Chota, which became his home, nights when the sound of the Tanase became the sound of the Thames and he was taken away again. We'll never know what faces haunted him most—the politicians or the priests, the passersby in London or the lunatics at Bedlam.

The sixty-year-old Cherokee was as widely traveled in the Old World as the restless Quaker was in the New. But there alongside the Nantahala, Attakullaculla was in his own country, and William Bartram steps from the path, leaving the way open as a sign of respect. The Cherokee chief approaches the botanist with a smile on his face and, clapping his right hand on his own breast and then extending the same hand to the white man, announces his name: "I am Ata-cul-culla."

The red man is pleased when Bartram, who is no flatterer, tells him that he knows who he is—"the great Ata-cul-culla." Bartram adds that he "was of the tribe of white men, of Pennsylvania, who esteem themselves brothers and friends to the red men, but particularly so to the Cherokees." Which was to say he was a Quaker, not an Englishman or an American, but a Friend. When Bartram informs Attakullaculla that he has traveled from

Charleston, the Cherokee asks after John Stuart, superintendent of Indian Affairs, whose life the Cherokee chief saved from the summary executions at Ball Play Creek after the capture of Fort Loudoun.

This is an odd moment alongside the brawling Nantahala. Attakullaculla had been at Sycamore Shoals in March, where for reasons still unclear he had acceded to the infamous Henderson Purchase. Cherokee rights to what eventually became Kentucky were sold to a land-speculating judge for a song. This was the low point of Attakullaculla's career. He was on his way to civilized Charleston, with its many churches and bustling wharfs, "the place of lies" to the Cherokee. But Bartram was more interested in plants than politics. They were like the dog and the wolf swapping places in the Cherokee myth—the Indian probing the contours of the new culture, the white man looking for the old wild things. Attakullaculla tells the plant hunter that he is "welcome in their country as a friend and brother," a sentiment to which his party gives assent. They shake hands in farewell and the Cherokee proceed on their way, apparently following the same path that Bartram had taken from Cowee.

When Bartram crosses paths with Attakullaculla, he is on the verge of reaching a lifelong goal, a goal that many other colonial naturalists and explorers—Mark Catesby and John Lawson among them—had in vain. More than 500 miles from Philadelphia, more than 200 miles from Charleston, the Blue Ridge and Nantahalas behind him, he has made the longest and hardest part of his journey. "I yet persisting in my intentions of visiting the Overhill towns continued on; leaving the great forest I mounted the high hills."

He climbs out of the Nantahala watershed between the Valley River Mountains and the Snowbird Mountains, and follows Junaluska Creek to the Valley River fifteen miles above its confluence with the Hiwassee. Bartram must have spent that night somewhere along Junaluska Creek, only thirty miles from Talassee, the nearest Overhill town, by way of the trail along the Cheoah River, which would have taken him to the Tanase. Only one or two days of travel remain.

But next day Bartram's mind turns, and for the only time in his writing, he tells us he finds the surrounding vegetation uninteresting. A man who was interested in everything around him has gone blind with other preoccupations: "descending them again on the other side and so on repeatedly for several miles, without observing any variation in the natural productions since passing the Jore." Repetition has never bothered him before; in fact, his prose revels in it.

The meeting with Attakullaculla apparently reminded him of the yet-unsettled treaty negotiations between the British and the Cherokee. Attakullaculla's presence at Chota would have assured Bartram's safety. Perhaps he had been counting on it. But now perhaps hotter heads were making talks around the council fires. Perhaps the Citicos were angry again. Bartram probably wished that the Cherokee chief had spared him a guide or some tangible token of protection. He was a truly brave and intelligent adventurer, but he seems to have felt the tether stretching too far there along Junaluska Creek. Unnerved, I think, by the smoke of history, Bartram gives up his great ambition without comment. You can easily miss the moment in his narrative. A day or two from Talassee—gateway to Citico, Chota, and Tomotley—Bartram turns around on the path and follows Attakullaculla's steps back toward Cowee and Fort Prince George and Charleston.

A year after Bartram crossed and recrossed Wayah Bald, four military expeditions were sent against the Cherokee, who sided with the British in the crown's dispute with the American settlers. Armies came from four directions, a dark and bloody eruption of the quadripartite world against them that fatally weakened the Cherokee hold on their homeland.

From the southwest, Colonel Samuel Jack and a few hundred Georgians burned towns on the headwaters of the Chattahoochee and Tugalo rivers in July of 1776. From the southeast came Colonel Andrew Williamson with 1,860 South Carolinians who marched on the remnant Lower towns and destroyed them as Montgomery had done.

From the east, General Griffith Rutherford and 2,400 North Carolinians destroyed the Out and Middle towns, reenacting Grant's accomplishment. Then the combined forces of Williamson and Rutherford moved on to destroy the western settlements along the Hiwassee and Valley rivers: "Every town upon Oconaluftee, Tuckasegee, and the upper part of Little Tennessee, and on Hiwassee to below the junction of the Valley river—thirty-six towns in all—was destroyed in turn. . . . the Cherokee made but poor resistance, and fled with their women and children into the fastnesses of the Great Smoky mountains, leaving their desolated fields and smoking towns behind them."

As Mooney and others describe it, "the merciless character of this old border warfare" became routine:

> As the army advanced every house in every settlement met was burned—ninety houses in one settlement alone—and detachments

were sent into the fields to destroy the corn, of which the smallest town was estimated to have two hundred acres, besides potatoes, beans, and orchards of peach trees. The stores of dressed deerskins and other valuables were carried off. Everything was swept clean, and the Indians who were not killed or taken were driven, homeless refugees, into the dark recesses of Nantahala or painfully made their way across to the Overhill towns in Tennessee.

"In addition to the ordinary destruction of war," Mooney writes, "—the burning of towns, the wasting of fruitful fields, and the killing of the defenders—we find that every Indian warrior killed was scalped, when opportunity permitted; women as well as men, were shot down and afterward 'helped to their end'; and prisoners taken were put up at auction as slaves when not killed on the spot."

Finally, from the northeast, Colonel William Christian led 2,000 Virginians down the Holston River toward the Overhill settlements on the Little Tennessee, which he reached in November. The deserted Overhill towns were destroyed by Christian's men, one by one, excepting the peace town, Chota, which would be needed as a site for diplomatic negotiations.

The effect upon the Cherokee of this irruption of more than six thousand armed enemies into their territory was well nigh paralyzing. More than fifty of their towns had been burned, their orchards cut down, their fields wasted, their cattle and horses killed or driven off, their stores of buckskin and other personal property plundered. Hundreds of their people had been killed or had died of starvation and exposure, others were prisoners in the hands of the Americans, and some had been sold into slavery. Those who had escaped were fugitives in the mountains, living upon acorns, chestnuts, and wild game.

You can visualize the movement of armies well from Wayah Bald, which overlooks *Atahi'ta*, Wayah Gap, "the place where they shouted," where the natural cry of the wolf and the unnatural cries of history came together as they had outside the palisades of Fort Prince George, when wolves and Indians howled in unison as Grant's troops prepared for their march. Cherokee warriors, male and female, put up a fight against Rutherford at *Atahi'ta*, inflicting heavy casualties before retreating in the face of impossible odds.

The odds never improved. By 1838, despite their rapid acculturation to white ways, the charade of treaty-making with the Americans came to an end when Winfield Scott and federal and state soldiers escorted the bulk of the Cherokee to Oklahoma, in winter at bayonet point, the same tool of nation building that Mooney had seen evidence of at Wounded Knee. Many Cherokee were marched out of northern Georgia—where the gold de Soto had been looking for was finally discovered—over the same mountain roads that Bartram and Attakullaculla had traveled. Many died in internment camps in western North Carolina and east Tennessee. The Trail of Tears wove itself out of many paths around Wayah Bald, following creeks to rivers, all of which flowed into the Tanase, along whose sacred banks the men, women, and children of the nation were massed before being herded west.

The drumming of the *Nunne'hi,* which once was heard frequently from Wayah Bald, is said to have stopped just before the removal.

Tsunda'nilti'yi: *where they* demanded the debt from him.

I'm back in old growth, underneath the closed canopy of late June, camped alongside the trail William Bartram would have taken to Talassee.

If you kept on where Bartram stopped, headed for the Overhills, you would descend Junaluska Creek a few miles down to the Valley River. Then you would follow the river upstream five miles until it petered out below the pronounced gap between the Snowbird and Cheoah mountains. Pass through the gap, traveling northwest, and you will quickly come on Tulula Creek, which at some point downstream below Bear Creek becomes the Cheaoh River.

Of course, now there are roads along these rivers—some so wide and well paved they are disheartening—as well as towns and tracts of houses sprawling across a unique landscape in familiar patterns. The surrounding forests have been clear-cut many times since Bartram's day and have lost much of their former grandeur. The Cheoah, like the Valley and Hiwassee, the Nantahala and the Little Tennessee, has a dam across it that backs up a bulging aneurysm of still water that passes for a lake. Upstream of so-called Lake Santeetlah, the Cheoah flows the way it will, gathering creeks from the hem of the solemn Snowbirds and Cheoahs, listening to many voices and speaking in one, shuttling creek water into the green and white weave of a river. The original trail along the Cheoah to the Overhills was well used and led to the war paths that headed north toward the Shawnee and the Iroquois. James Mooney noted that there were many rock cairns along the river from the passage of warriors, each cairn with an unknown story attached to it.

All the strong-minded creeks grow silent at Lake Santeetlah, which like Fontana Lake and all the others in this region has no natural shoreline, since it is raised and lowered for power generation and flood control. Of course, flooding and soil erosion are greatly exacerbated by the clear-cutting practiced on the surrounding slopes as well as by the road building and development. What passes for forests now are badly diced up with the well-graded logging roads threaded like termite tunnels throughout the southern Appalachians. But in late June the mountains are green with life and Santeetlah Lake is full of spring runoff and looks natural enough. From the west, Little Snowbird, Snowbird, Little Buffalo, and Santeetlah creeks stall in inviting fingers of green water stirred by bream and mallards.

Not far up Santeetlah Creek, Little Santeetlah winds back toward the summit ridge of the Unicoi. I have backpacked up Little Santeetlah Creek a few miles and made camp on a small triangular flat hung above a thin spill of water that feeds a swirling pool of Little Santeetlah. Each watercourse has a distinct sound. At the foot of camp the two blend into a theme for old growth scored for water and rock, one bright and one dark. Because of the dense rhododendron cover, I cannot quite see the Little Santeetlah from where I've pitched my tent.

Beyond the circle of green—a sphere really given the height of the canopy—lies the largest tract of virgin old-growth cove forest left in the southern Appalachians. I'd be happy to argue that the fall of Little Santeetlah Creek from the Unicoi summit to its union with big Santeetlah a few miles downstream is the most beautiful flow of water left in this world. The stream's basin of old growth hums like a great earthy drum, years of maple and oak, ash and hickory laminated into the sounding boards of standing and fallen timber rooted in or rotting on deep black soil.

Everything here leans toward running water—cinnamon fern spilling out of the shadows, solitary ladyslippers blooming late in rare sunlit niches—handfuls of sunlight fallen through the canopy like shattered glass, warrior bands of ghostly Indian pipe, the ubiquitous laurel and rhododendron—rock-lover and soil-lover—common sassafras and serviceberry—settler's trees—and, of course, the sturdy poplar and hemlock—pillars of the canopy—and exotic magnolias and papaws crisscrossing the understory.

The Cherokee do not recognize the name Santeetlah, but they have a name for this particular spot of ground where I am camped. A simple but enduring anecdote is associated with the place. Mooney recounts it: "TSUNDA'NILTI'YI: 'Where they demanded the debt from him,' a fine camping ground, on the north side of Little Santeetlah creek, about half-way up, west from Robbinsville, Graham county. Here a hunter once killed a deer, which the others of the party demanded in payment of a debt due them."

I have come here partly because of the beauty of this old-growth forest and the creek it inspires, partly because William Bartram would most likely have taken this way to the Overhills, and partly because of this spare, suggestive anecdote about obligation and repayment, as fine and useful a fable for meditation as anything in the *Analects* or in *The Greek Anthology*. I am also celebrating the return of wolves.

As Lucash promised, the hiatus in the red wolf restoration was brief. While I was getting lost in the Pisgah National Forest in May, sixteen red wolves were born in holding pens at Great Smoky Mountains National Park. Although this captive denning and birthing was a step back for the animals, psychologically and socially, it did keep the clan expanding genetically and gave Fish and Wildlife new wolves with which to work, sixteen variations on the theme of *Canis rufus gregoryi*.

The day after the last Cades Cove wolf was pulled from the field on April 25, 468F gave birth to a bumper crop of eight pups in the Tremont pen. After weaning, two of these pups were moved to another adult pair to keep 468F's litter to a manageable size. A week later the retired Cades Cove female, 378F, whelped three pups at the Cades Cove facility. On May 10 541F gave birth to a litter of five in another Cades Cove pen.

With no wolves in the wild, Lucash, Crawford, and Weller put away the radio-tracking gear and went back to tending wolves by hand, once again trying to manage their animals without domesticating them. The flash floods of March had damaged the roads and washed out some trails in the Abrams Creek and Little River drainages. This made getting around difficult, which was a blessing in disguise. The wolves saw even less of Lucash's crew than they otherwise would have.

It is not uncommon for one or two pups in a litter to die during the first few weeks after whelping, especially with large litters. Although the newborns were vaccinated twice in June, each of the three litters lost a pup from unknown causes during the month. In each case, the carcasses were consumed by the parents.

By the end of June 1994 the new Tremont group was ready for release. 468F and 451M had been paired in January and moved into the backcountry Tremont pen on Thunderhead Branch. They were both captive-born animals, one with and one without experience in the wild.

In fact, 468F was from the first litter of captive-born red wolves to be born in the Smokies back in 1991. She hadn't missed a turn of season in these mountains since she had been born and if it was true, as some researchers thought, that at acclimation sites wolves took in the night sky, and learned it, she had as good an idea of where she was as any red wolf in the world. Moreover, 468F had been at large during the experimental release of 1991, when Lucash was testing the waters and getting the bugs out of his tracking and retrieval operation. She did well as a free-ranging juvenile the year she ran free. But like a Mercury astronaut who did not make it into the Apollo program, she was back in a pen with her littermates when another family of wolves was chosen for the so-called permanent release of October 1992.

468F's mate, three-year-old 451M, was another story.

"We're taking a risk with him," Lucash admitted when I visited with him on my way to the Chattooga Town dig. The wolf he had wanted to breed with 468F had died suddenly from an intestinal infection that had led to a ruptured lower intestine. 451M was the backup. There was nothing wrong with him, but Lucash preferred wild-born wolves from Alligator River, or at least wolves with some experience in the wild. His first choice, 373M, had been born on Horn Island and had some freedom there, but 451M was born at the Audubon Zoological Gardens in New Orleans and had spent his entire life in captivity. He was more wild card than wild wolf.

Despite his doubts about 451M, Lucash was relieved to be getting back into the wolf-tracking business. He planned to soft-release the animals near the end of the month, when the pups would be about six weeks old. The release of wolves with a litter this young was something new, but it closely simulated a wild-born grouping. By now there were wolves in wolf country again, circling the Thunderhead drainage.

I am trying to close a few circles of my own. I'm following Bartram, in spirit, from Junaluska Creek to the Tanase, up Little Santeetlah and down Slickrock Creek to Calderwood Lake, the most solemn of the stillwater impoundments of the Little Tennessee River that I descended last autumn. From there, where Bartram would have turned downstream toward Talassee at present-day town of Calderwood, I'll take the trail upriver toward the mouth of the Cheoah below the Cheoah Dam and then follow the river back upstream to Little Santeetlah. Along the way I'll pass where the original Tremont male slipped into the Yellow Creek Mountains—where they still talk about him and, although he is dead, claim to keep seeing him. On my way up the Cheoah I will pass the warrior cairns about which Mooney wrote.

The trail to *Tsunda'nilti'yi* is a true trail, a well-carved footpath woven along the north slope of Little Santeetlah, hung a hundred feet or so above the creek to take advantage of drier ground, looping up small coves to cross the cold hard-flowing little tribs that purl from the surrounding slopes. The narrow path is worn down to bedrock and tree roots in many places, a true way that opens and closes softly as you pass along, greenbrier and Virginia creeper reaching for your ankles, laurel and rhododendron tapping you on the shoulders.

I have more names for things in May than June, when most forest floor plants are past flowering and, as Bartram knew, identification becomes more difficult. The complex flowerheads of galax are still coming in, blooming from bottom to top like the forest itself; some late laurel still hold out branchfuls of those delicate pink bowls that gather light like porcelain; here and there a few Indian cucumber root hold up the nodding starlike flower evolved to serve that species. But it is mostly just *forest* to me now and will be until berrying in autumn, the green word serving as the name for all this overlapping, unnamable life.

But I have just spent the day with a botanist and a forester, and I know the life around me is not, in fact, unnamable. This morning I was hiking off-trail lower down in the cove, thinking I was getting closer with every step to the heart of this green darkness, when I heard an odd popping sound. Not the two-cycle drumming of grouse or the percussion of a woodpecker, but a mellow *ping*ing that reverberated like sonar through the woods.

I followed the sound to a young woman who was counting tree rings in the middle of nowhere. Although she seemed disappointed that the noise that preceded me through the dense vegetation had not turned out to be a bear or something interesting, she was nonplussed and greeted me in a friendly way, as did her partner, a stocky, dark-haired man with some Cherokee in his square face and black eyes. He had what I assumed was a tree corer in hand. The two of them were, apparently, uncorking the woods.

His accent was Appalachian, mellow and woody, full of syllables displaced toward natural sounds; hers was not quite English and not quite Australian—the clipped consonants and rising, slightly drawn out vowels of a New Zealander, it turned out, an urbane-sounding country speech.

They were standing within a grid of surveyor's tape looking at the pencil-thin core of wood they had just extracted from a large chestnut oak.

I introduced myself and explained, as best I could, what I was doing—day hiking from my campsite on Little Santeetlah, following passable terrain and keeping general track of myself with a map and compass. They were one month into a survey of the plant communities of the Joyce Kilmer–Slickrock Wilderness. Given that this was one of the most botanically diverse areas of North America, I was surprised such a survey had not been done long ago. But it hadn't, and they didn't mind my attaching myself to their work. I paid them with the latest news on the red wolf restoration, about which they were glad to hear. Students of old growth, they were in the wildness business themselves.

Claire Newell was doing research for her doctoral dissertation for the University of North Carolina at Chapel Hill. Dale Holder, a native of nearby Stecoah, was a Forest Service technician who had been lent to Newell's project. Using topographic maps and aerial photos, Newell had preselected a hundred sites that represented the full range of botanical variety in and around the Horse Cove Basin, the 3,000 acres of old growth drained by Little Santeetlah Creek. Aspect, slope, altitude, bedrock type, and soil cover as well as the generally observable nature of the land and vegetation were all taken into consideration. Each day she and Holder would shoulder their packs, hike into a site that offered some unique or representative set of variables, and set up shop.

Shop was a twenty- by fifty-meter rectangle marked out into ten- by ten-meter modules. A pair of metal conduits that anchored the ends of the center line made the site reusable for future studies. Like Gerald Schroedl, Claire Newell wanted to begin what she hoped would be an ongoing study. It took them maybe half an hour to lay out their standardized sampling plot. Then all they had to do was record every species of herbaceous and woody plant—flowers, vines, ferns, shrubs, and trees—and quantify them in various measures.

We were up on a south-facing slope, at about 3,000 feet, inside the pristine, unlogged basin drained by Little Santeetlah. This particular plot took in a slab of moist, colluvial slope, where boulders that had weathered out of the exposed bedrock a thousand feet above us had come to rest. The frost action of the severe winters here during the glacial advances farther north had most likely chewed them up and sent them rolling. But by now they were so well covered with moss and vegetation that the boulders seemed more plant than rocklike. Despite the rough appearance of the site—it was very difficult to walk around—the rich soil beneath and between the bedrock float supported a dense understory and a complex array of large old trees.

"It's quite simple, really," Claire Newell explained. "I record everything I see."

Which she proceeded to do as I followed her around the first module. She stooped among that dense vegetation, picking her way along, turning over leaves, inspecting the hairs on leaf stems, the way twigs jointed, grazing a bit as botanists tend to do, using taste and odor to pick apart subspecies, confirm first impressions or raise doubts about what she's got in hand. On her hands and knees Newell nosed around plants, shrubs, and the difficult hardwood seedlings, writing everything down on a clipboard as she cooed in Latin, for her benefit, and in English, for mine, turning the orchestral forest into a clear score of notes: blueberry, blackberry, laurel, greenbrier, red maple, black gum, sassafras, striped maple, black oak, scarlet oak, locust, white hickory, wintergreen, rattlesnake plantain, violets, sourwood, white oak, white pine, grape, flame azalea, buckberry, black cherry, tulip poplar, false Solomon's seal as well as chestnuts larger than any I had seen and, of course, the eared leaves of *Magnolia fraseri,* William Bartram's magnolia in all but name. This was Bartram's work she and Dale Holder were doing; here were Bartram's travels.

As Newell recorded plant and shrub species, taking account of their relative density and mapping the ways they overlapped, her partner did the trees. Holder identifies them like a forester, by bark and shape, eyeing the wood on the stump as if it were an animal frozen in front of him for a moment and checking the leaves only to confirm what he sees in the wood. This helps him to discern hybrids, which are not unusual in old growth, where nature has so many cards to play and where there are significant genetic differences within the same species. At one point he called his partner over to examine a tree with the bark of black oak and the leaves of red, a trump of diversity. To Claire Newell's Latin, Dale Holder adds many local names for things, some cases that differentiate variants in which science is uninterested—some maples will give you prettier gunstocks than others—and cases where local usage lumps together what taxonomists have split apart—the hickory of an ax handle is just as good from mockernut as pignut; either will stand up against stove wood.

In any event, between the two of them, Newell and Holder could identify nearly every plant and tree within one of their sampling sites, and it only takes an hour or two for them to attach the names of as many as 130 species to the life of a plot the size of an Olympic swimming pool. This was botanical diversity equal to what Ayres and Ashe had reported, and this was the only intact watershed of its size left in the southern Appalachians.

Thirty years after Ayres and Ashe had made their timber cruise, James Agee came to the Tennessee Valley to report on the region for *Fortune* magazine. Agee, who was hardly likely to sing the praises of growth and development without irony and sly ambiguity, noted that "nature had set the stage for something of a Utopia" in the southern Appalachians. "And if you believed only the Chambers of Commerce . . . you might believe that 2,000,000 people haven't done so badly." Agee reported that 7 billion board-feet of lumber were being cut each year out of the forests along the old Cherokee River and that "you could paint the whole valley" with fine figures of how much temporary wealth the land produced. But he saw the devastation behind the numbers, and he came to the same conclusion, in the same words, as had the foresters Ayres and Ashe: "But here is the other side of the picture: careless fires and unregulated cutting have ruined and are ruining great stands of timber on watersheds where trees should have stood forever." All the problems Ayres and Ashe had predicted had come to pass: "whole communities have been and are being pauperized, abandoned. When the forests are no more, where the farms are steep, where the land is light, where copper fumes wander, vast acreages of farmland are rapidly being totally laid waste by erosion. The waste land descends unimpeded into the river slowly but surely to choke the channels and to fill in great natural reservoirs that cannot be replaced." It seems a miracle but was, in fact, largely an accident that this one watershed was saved to study and enjoy.

Despite their complementary expertise, there were a few plants that neither Newell nor Holder could identify. These they collected for identification later. Each evening, Newell pressed leaves and leaflets between damp felt pages as Bartram had done, perhaps the truest kind of book you could create out of these woods. In addition to the plant life, they noted bryophytes and fungi as well as they could, estimated the amount of woody debris, and took into account anything else that contributed to the facts of life in the sampling site. They cored representative trees for their age and took soil samples from each module for chemical analysis. The bird life around us was subtle but overwhelming, and ornithologists have confirmed an equivalent diversity in that realm, as have entomologists and anyone else with a specialty designed to map some aspect of the diverse life of this rare, extraordinary place. Such woods are full of distractions—wild turkey and grouse and the pileated woodpeckers that seem to function like sentinels. At one site Dale Holder found bear hair on a bed of shield fern and at another a one-button timber rattler, which he carefully picked up and moved out of harm's way.

Lunch was full of conjecture. Since American chestnut dominated much of the cove until the 1930s, unlogged does not mean undisturbed here. Even though this was old-growth, virgin forest, it was particularly dynamic old growth, with chestnut replacement under way and the ultimate pecking order of canopy and midcanopy species as yet undecided.

Claire Newell was surprised at the amount of red maple, which she assumes will eventually lose out to the oaks slowly aspiring to the canopy. Holder was particularly good at seeing the forest that is not there, and Newell frequently prompted him to interpret the site to account for the situation of the larger, older trees. In his mind's eye, he can see the old chestnut forest, the demise of which was revealed by most of the tree cores he extracted from the oaks, whose widened growth rings reveal release about sixty years ago.

Chestnuts were a broad-crowned tree and took much of the sunlight for themselves. Their death was a boon to every other species. Even where the big old trees have rotted into the soil, you can see the circles they occupied. The old people of Graham and Cherokee counties remember the forest as having an open understory because of the shade of the chestnuts, which helps to explain the early records of travelers riding without complaint on horseback through such woods. Oleta Nelms, who greets visitors to the famous grove of enormous yellow poplars at the foot of the Joyce Kilmer forest, remembers that chestnut forest from her youth and is proud to tell you that the chestnuts were in bloom—a stunning white—the year she married: "The woods had a different look, a richer shine, a glistening color when the chestnuts got old and spread their crowns. You could just walk through the woods underneath them. When they died, the limbs fell off the trees, then the bark fell off and the wind rocked them down and the tulip trees and hemlocks grew so large as they are now."

Every ecologist I have ever talked to has come to the same conclusion: despite the fact that we have few naturally functioning forests left, we really don't know what a forest is. But tonight at *Tsunda'nilti'yi,* I have a few more words for the things around me and a better understanding of the way this forest moved through time. And knowing a bit more, I have a deeper sense of the unknown here and a sharper sense of loss.

I gather a very little wood for a symbolic fire and, after eating, listen to the stream sounds shift register in the dark and watch the firelight briefly illuminate a weathered eye in a poplar log. The gray wood flows around the worn stob of a branch weathered down to a knot that pushes the grain around itself like a boulder deflecting the flow of a river. Sounds and odors arise from the woods the way they do at night. The old tree melts in the dim red light of the coals, burns smokelessly, loops back through time.

Once a fire is lit, you tend to take stock. It seemed to me I was doing pretty well. I was a writer exploring my chosen country. There were seven red wolves at large—not within howling distance, but somewhere out there in this herd of mountains. A hundred miles to the southeast, Gerald Schroedl's students were filing the edges of their trowels for tomorrow's search for the past at Chattooga Town. And Claire Newell, farther from home than Bartram even, was pressing the day's plant specimens in a large book of felt leaves. Tomorrow she and Dale Holder would be somewhere in this watershed, setting up their plots and walking respectfully around bear beds and rattlesnakes while they identified trees and plants, calling out the names in the same botanical Latin William Bartram had used 200 years ago. And there were 3,000 acres of old growth around me, as undisturbed a place as I could find.

But on the trail yesterday, I could hear the explosions from yet another road being blasted through the so-called wilderness, fragmenting the finest forest left in the southern Appalachians into smaller, less luminous pieces. And not that long ago there had been tens of millions of acres of such woods, escape habitat for the otherness in nature—wolf, bear, mountain lion, as well as Stone Coat and the raven-mockers who brought death to the edge of the old settlements, the Wild Boys, the Thunders, *Kana'ti,* and *Selu.* The larger, wilder forest that is now gone had a darker center and a brighter edge and a civilization nestled up to it, a culture laid down in towns along rivers that purified the souls and imaginations of people who refused to kill the eagle, the rattlesnake, or the wolf. Whitman wonders, in *Song of Myself,* whether "the flowing savage" was waiting for civilization, as the Europeans assumed, or already past it.

The Chinese ideogram *chuan-chu,* which expresses "the general abstract notions of vanishing, defect, want, negation," is constructed from the images of "a multitude of men, acting upon a forest, felling the trees," which suggests that the destruction of nature is not an unfortunate byproduct of culture but its most deep-seated, secret, self-destructive goal. That, slowly but surely, we seek our negation and call it progress.

I eye the embers of my small fire, mesmerized like an animal, and listen to stream-drawn moonlight turning the leaves of the old trees through the short bright night, watch shapes from the Tertiary sway in the shadows overhead. Tonight I am as rich with old growth as anyone in eastern North America. And I am not sure which is more remarkable: that so little is left or that anything at all remains.

Ataga'hi

Westward from the headwaters of Oconaluftee River, in the wildest depths of the Great Smoky Mountains, which form the line between North Carolina and Tennessee, is the enchanted lake of Ataga'hi, "Gall place." Although all the Cherokee know that it is there, no one has ever seen it, for the way is so difficult that only the animals know how to reach it. Should a stray hunter come near the place he would know of it by the whirring sound of the thousands of wild ducks flying about the lake, but on reaching the spot he would find only a dry flat, without bird or animal or blade of grass, unless he had first sharpened his spiritual vision by prayer and fasting and an all-night vigil.

—James Mooney, "Myths of the Cherokee"

"Man is rich," Thoreau writes, "in proportion to the number of things which he can afford to let alone." In that antiphora—contrary motions come to rest in the mind of our finest countryman—a promising culture momentarily fulfilled its promise. Three centuries, from the clamber of de Soto's army to the quiet of a Concord morning, three centuries before that sentence came to the American mind, a nearly indigenous idea. Then it died back into literature, where it was preserved as rootstock, like the blighted chestnut seedlings here on the headwaters of the Cataloochee River or the hip-high Fraser firs struggling around *Kuwa'hi*, where the bears held council, fifty miles to the north. *Kuwa'hi* is not far from where *Ataga'hi* is said to be, ostensibly hidden between Miry Ridge and Thunderhead Mountain. Thunderhead overlooks the Tremont drainage and was one of the haunts of 357M, the original Tremont male. Very often, when Lucash and Crawford lost the big wolf's signal, it was exploring the folded slopes of Thunderhead, which are convoluted enough to make line-of-sight tracking impossible.

For several centuries European maps insisted that there was, in fact, a large lake in the southern Appalachians. It appears, drawn in detail, on the well-known Le Moyne map of 1591 situated among the *"Montes Apalatci, in quibus aurum argentum & aefinuenitur"*—the Appalachian Mountains, in which gold and silver are found. An enormous waterfall, which pours out of the mountains in the middle of the Cherokee country, fills the lake, agitating its surface. Despite the animated volume of water falling into it, and despite the fact that Le Moyne was very attentive in depicting rivers, the lake has no outlet to the east, and there is no apparent source for the waterfall in the west. The strange, self-contained body of water is accompanied by a legend: *"In hoc lacu Indigenae argenti granainveniunt"*—In this lake the natives find grains of silver. The lake persisted as a will-of-the-wisp on European maps into the mid-eighteenth century, after which it was given up. Of course, the sacred lake of the Cherokee had nothing to do with gold or silver, but legends change over time and in different contexts. *Ataga'hi,* the Cherokee tale suggests, will not be found by line-of-sight tracking either.

Gadalu'tsi, in late summer, passing through Robert Palmer's woods, woods for which I'm much obliged. Mooney derives Cataloochee from *gadalu'tsi,* "fringe standing erect." He took the phrase to mean "the appearance of the timber growing in streaks" on the slopes of Big Cataloochee Mountain. The streaks may be the intermingled swaths of hardwoods and evergreens, hemlocks on the lower slopes and red spruce near the summit. But I'm inclined to think that Mooney got this wrong and that the word and phrase refer to the fringelike appearance of forested ridge tops anywhere in the Cherokee Mountains.

The trail to Robert Palmer's woods is unfortunately called the Boogerman Trail. Of Robert Palmer we know only that he was shy and that, unlike his neighbors, he refused to let his woods be logged. For his reclusiveness and love of the woods Palmer was mocked as "the Booger Man"—much as some long-forgotten citizens of Concord sniggered behind Henry Thoreau's back. The mockery, which had nothing to do with the Cherokee dance, has been preserved in the thoughtless trail name, and field guides pass on the slender anecdote about Palmer without reflection. Let the record show that these fine poplar, hemlock, and northern red oak—towering over me as it is rare for trees to do now—are Robert Palmer's woods and that Robert Palmer, for all his reclusiveness, shares more with us than the sociable people who sold their trees and mocked a thoughtful albeit lonely man, another of the *inage'hi*—a dweller in wilderness. In my field notes, I refer to this way as the Palmer trail.

Palmer's woods are well above Caldwell Fork, a hard-charging tributary of the sultry Cataloochee. Palmer's Branch, a thin spring-fed rill, sunken in gravel and moss, flows slowly toward the strong fork through Palmer's homesite, an appealing wedge of land tucked into a forgotten corner of the world. The first time I came up here, my eye missed the invisible homeplace. But I felt the logs of a small bridge underfoot—an ancient, barely necessary structure well covered in moss, galax, and some thrice-cut fern. The ancient footbridge had a thin soil cover, worn in the middle by passersby. When I stopped to look around me, intrigued by a man-made object that seemed to have grown there, the old homesite suddenly revealed itself around the nearly silent flow of water at my feet.

I could see where a house would have been set among the dense summer vegetation—rooms of umbrella leaf and fetterbush, flame azalea and rhododendron; a wrap-around porch of dogwood, striped maple, and red bud; nodding baneberry and a spill of meadow rue and sorrel where the steps might be, persimmon and crabapple in the yard. Palmer's cabin would have been faced south, catching as long an arc of sunlight as possible between the raised horizon of mountains hidden beyond the foreground of forest.

Palmer's woods are not undisturbed old growth and do not have the grandeur of the Kilmer-Slickrock Wilderness. But they are all the more moving and beautiful for the ghosts of homesteads that were once carved into the forest, homesteads developed only up to a point, man and nature having worked out some sensible rapprochement in the backcountry during a brief historical moment when necessity and luxury were not so far apart. Along the quietly busy rill I find rusted metal hoops and tools—a moth-eaten shovel blade with violets growing through it, its handle long since rotted out, its throat pinned to a shaft of air; a thick-hubbed iron wheel from a logging cart or perhaps a small mill; a rusted-out washtub full of sweetfern.

Late-summer thunder follows me down the pleasantly empty trail that curves back toward Caldwell Fork. I move bear twice, catching a glimpse only of the second—a cinnamon snout in that black, dished face, one of the great forest masks, and that stocky presence which turns athletic on the run. *Ya'nu*. They appear and disappear so suddenly, I half believe bear do live underground.

The thunder brings sheets of rain that cuts the fragile September heat and quiets the insect hum I had stopped noticing until I missed it. Before I have gone a mile the rain has moved down the watershed, shafts of sunlight brighten the dripping woods, and one by one a forest collection of warblers emerges from the hemlocks—blackburnian warblers singing in the midcanopy, black-and-whites squeaking higher up, northern parulas trilling against the rising count of black-throated greens and the muffled *chep* of yellowthroats. Suite for sunshine after rain in older growth. I'm not surprised that Bartok, among others, came to the Carolina mountains to study music.

Halfway back to Caldwell Fork, toward which the Palmer trail loops, there is a fine grove of American chestnut, living and dead, caught in the rift of the infamous chestnut blight. The first time I saw these trees, there were so many young chestnuts, I assumed they were chinkapin, which has a nearly identical leaf. But among huge prostrate chestnuts, a fine array of chestnut saplings thickly occupied the slope. The fallen trees were hollowed by time and splitting up into fence rails in the sun, but there were large chestnut snags still standing, which is rare to see. Maple and magnolia, persimmon and black gum stood in waiting but deferred to the poplar and oak that had benefited most from the demise of *Castanea* here up on the isolated Cataloochee headwaters. I walked around the site, while a pileated woodpecker hammered into a damp snag, trying to find a tree that had broken through the blight and fruited.

The Palmer trail brings me back to Caldwell Fork near the remains of an old homesite, one of Robert Palmer's more substantial neighbors who has left stronger signs of his presence. The stone foundations of his house are caught between order and disorder, time being a mason willing to work in either form. These foundations are a puzzle, perhaps the remains of more than one building or the outline of a dog-trot house, with the outdoors running through the middle of it. Flat, stream-smoothed slabs of sandstone quarried from the nearby creek were the most stable building blocks here, river work come to hand to build a home with. But each odd boulder fragment and chunk of quartzite taken from the woods in haste worked against the well-hewn river rock. When no one was looking, the mountainside shrugged the whole affair apart frost heave by frost heave.

I walked the length of each foundation up and down but, since the trees on either side were equally large, could not tell which side was once walled in and which walled out. The window places had collapsed both ways, and there was as much forest in this home now as there were signs of a home in this forest. I kept an eye out for copperheads, very often the principal tenants of old rock walls, but discovered only a ring-necked snake sliding through the partridgeberry at my feet when I stopped to rest and contemplate the site—a twig-gray creature with a faint dorsal band, named for its distinct yellow neck stripe, which I saw now had thin black margins except underneath where the yellow flowed under its chin. I kept still and watched the snake move along deliberately at the base of the wall, stopping frequently, shaking its head from side to side, working the humid air over its sensors, I presume, vigorously flicking its tongue. It penciled up over a mossy rock, carefully hunting across it, and then slithered over back onto the ground, barely shifting a leaf as it threaded itself, partly visible and partly hidden, through the leaf litter.

I shucked my backpack and pitched a tent a few miles farther up Caldwell Fork at a well-used horse camp just below the crest of the Cataloochee Divide. The camp is well above Palmer's woods, but for some unknown reason three ancient poplars had been left standing nearby. I dutifully went to see them, although I am suspicious about the worth of any attraction fingered by a field guide.

Despite my skepticism, what is left of the three old trees was impressive. A sacred wood is not so easily destroyed. There is a hitching post for horse traffic and muddy paths beaten around each centuries-old specimen. Someone had carved his initials in the largest tree, but although they were still legible when I saw them, that insult was being outgrown, the tree's strange, otherworldly bark melting around that pathetic claim to fame.

A century and a half ago, Thoreau made a variety of this complaint and graciously got beyond it: "You cannot go into any field or wood, but it will seem as if every stone had been turned, and the bark on every tree ripped up. But, after all, it is much easier to discover than to see when the cover is off. It has been well said that 'the attitude of inspection is prone.' Wisdom does not inspect, but behold. We must look a long time before we can see."

So for the moment I note that beyond the great poplars—misused but imperturbable as monks—are large, well-wrought beech and hemlock, outsize rhododendron and laurel, and a forest floor full of cinnamon fern and wildflowers colonizing the root pits of fallen trees half rotted into the rich thick soil where poplar seeds simmer in the late-summer heat.

Caldwell Fork was still a bold stream here in the head of the watershed, cool to the touch even after a summer of heat, vocal during its lowest flow. There was a fine pool just above camp near where I gathered wood. Of course I stopped to watch the green water purling over a low-head dam of ledge rock on its way to the Cataloochee, the Big Pigeon, the French Broad, the Tennessee, the Mississippi. Like wolves, these headwater streams are great travelers in all seasons, equally at home among waves of mountains or mountainous waves. It is not surprising that, for the Cherokee, they were central to wisdom and purification. To treat the world as a home is common sense. Ecology is not a new science or part of some radical political agenda. It is the old order underfoot.

Dark-red rainbow trout, wild if not native, hold in the seams of the pool's invisible currents, fielding invisible insects to their left and right, making graceful sport out of some strict law of energy expenditure. Water striders ride the surface tension just out of reach, obeying laws of their own, fragile and invulnerable. A waterthrush flutters downstream and disappears into the streamside brush. Half-tame deer filter out of the woods, three of them with oddly dark coats, none of them as wary of me as they should be. Late afternoon melds into early evening. The last sun stirs small blue-gray mayflies out of the stream—*Baetis,* the pedantic fly fisherman in me insists. The trout tilt and rise to the sailing duns, coming back a bit for them. When I rise to regather my armload of wood, the trout disappear and the deer shift away uneasily. On my way back to camp, a veery bursts into song behind me.

I've pitched my tent on the margins of the ruined campsite, where the compacted soil and hacked-up trees break the mood of the creek and the woods. When I clear away years of leaf litter to make a fireplace in the rhododendron alcove where I had settled, I discover a small fire ring just where I need it, a perfect circle of stones some backpacker laid down a year or so, or five or ten, ago. The stones were chosen with care and laid out with a good eye in a perfect circle. The fist-size building blocks are chased with filigrees of moss and chinked with earth. A fine ash lay underneath the damp leaf litter, as if the last fire in it had burned out hot, but it has been long enough since the fire ring has been used for a two-leafed sprig of mountain maple to have taken hold in it. A flat keystone is built into the ring, which breaks its symmetry but serves to hold a pot and pan. I'd like the trout for dinner but don't feel up to killing anything. In fact, I feel as if I'm wearing out my welcome in these woods, as if although there's more to see—to *dis*cover—I've gone about as far as I can go.

I light a fire in the mossy ring of stones. The veery starts up again, from somewhere in the midcanopy near that trout pool. Three-note combinations, flutelike but not sweet, the melody roughed up toward jazz. The bird flirts with a cloying tune like Coltrane or Monk but quickly fragments and extends it, adding odd, unpredictable rhythms that invite and defeat expectations, making the bird's art more memorable if harder to remember.

I suppose a fire ring just outside a cave mouth is one of the oldest signs of man—a practical means for containing the transcendental shapelessness of fire, a ring of order around the appealing chaos of the flames; another domestication of the wild. A fire in the backcountry is private as well as social—a focal point of thought, memory and visions as well as the ring of conversation, council, community. Good for boiling water, too, for tea and noodles.

The veery holds forth again around eight o'clock, perhaps in some hopelessly delayed mating attempt—this is September, after all. But to my surprise his song elicits a chirping response—a high-pitched, rattling answer coming in on the end of each two or, more often, three-note, phrase, overlapping. A desultory yes, I take it, Molly Bloom's "as well him as another." Once the response becomes part of the performance, the male only occasionally returns to the "ee oh lay" that forms the base melody, trusting more boldly to improvisation each time through.

A deer snorts out of the darkness, though I don't understand how it could be surprised by my presence. Firelight catches its green eyes and a flashlight shows it to be one of the dark-coated deer. *Awi'*. I lay on a few more sticks of wood, guilty but fascinated by the way moss and lichens burn, their faint incense aromatic, medicinal. The renewed circle of light throws back the woods. The four yellow birch that supplied the tinder hold the firelight in my small camp, light also held in the pale undersides of nearby hemlock branches and rhododendron leaves. A fawn bleat from the other side of the larger campsite draws the transfixed doe away. Then the veery again, well after nine o'clock, alone.

It is impossible to catch the larger structure of the vocalization, which has such long, irregular breaks in it—silences during which the sound of the stream rises, thrumming like a bassist in the dark—that you cannot tell when the song is over. Each pause within the composition is possibly the end of the whole, which puts a peculiar, unresolved stress on each fading riff. Any bar might be the last. The song of the veery, like the howl of a wolf, is hard to savor.

Midnight. Firelight disintegrates into a city of red coals that barely illuminates the circle of rocks that contain it. The woods are gone. The veery. The deer. Strong magic, strong medicine in the *Tao* of stones and fire, like the wolf howl or the veery's song, each simultaneously a window and a mirror, a part of consciousness, a part of the world. Then fall asleep to the faint crinkling of a faded fire in the backcountry, under the canopy of a forest with roots that reach back before the contact. Then dream within earshot of the Long Man chanting.

The wolves, too, have gone as far as they can go.

While I was reaching my limits on the Cataloochee Divide at the end of the summer of 1994, the second Tremont family struggled with its freedom, succeeding and failing at being wolves. 468F ran true to form. More than a year of captivity had not undone the benefits of her earlier run in the wild. She frequented the lower part of the drainage but stayed clear of roads, sometimes traveling with her pups and sometimes stashing them in a safe place while she hunted. She was a good wolf. In late December Lucash showed me her territory on that familiar map outside his office. He spoke of her in the same glowing terms as the Overhill wolf.

"She's perfect. Nobody sees her."

As if his job was to make wild animals disappear.

Her mate, 451M, was another story, rather like the original Cades Cove male.

"We took a gamble with him and it didn't work."

For a month the wolf wasn't seen much, but then he started hanging out on roads around the end of July. The usual hazing tactics failed to push him over to the other side. The wolf was inexplicably road-bound. Lucash recaptured 451M in August, after he was observed limping along Laurel Creek Road in a dazed condition. After being looked over by the University of Tennessee veterinarian, who could find no injury to explain his strange behavior, the wolf was rereleased for another try in late September. He was a little warier of humans for a few days but eventually came back down out of the Tremont drainage and scavenged along the park roads, less wild than any adult wolf Lucash had released and, in the end, a bit of a joke to the locals, who got used to seeing the tentative, insecure animal around the outskirts of Townsend, Tennessee. When reports came back from park rangers in mid-October about 451M scavenging picnic areas and wandering down the state highway that led out of the park, Lucash brought the wolf in for good.

For the most part, the three Tremont pups—706M, 710F, 711F—followed the good example of their mother, disappeared into their own wild lives in the backcountry shunning, or ignoring, the broken behavior of their father. But they did not do well physically. When Lucash and his crew starting trapping the pups to collar them in December, the young wolves were found to be underweight. 706M weighed in at only twenty-two pounds; 710F tilted the scales at twenty-seven pounds and was heavily infested with internal parasites. Lucash was emphatic about their poor condition.

"It was like somebody had taken a big chunk out of their growth cycle."

This was perhaps due to the sparser prey populations in the backcountry and to the fact that their male parent was apparently not hunting for them. The strangely behaving 451M had tried at least once to establish a rendezvous site near a closed section of the Tremont road for the pups, but probably he had not contributed to the care and feeding of his young. 468F did what she could on her own but apparently could not keep up with the pups' demands.

Moreover, the wolves had competition, which was perhaps also due to the absence of an aggressive adult male. While trapping the wolf pups, Fish and Wildlife caught two coyotes in the Tremont drainage, animals that Lucash had to admit didn't look much different from the wolves except that they were in better physical condition. One young-of-the-year coyote, a few months older than the wolves, weighed a robust thirty pounds. The coyotes were relocated to another section of the park, and in mid-January 1995 they brought in 468F with the third pup, 711F. By March the other two pups from 468F's litter the previous year were presumed to be dead, normal attrition especially under the circumstances.

The behavior of 451M in captivity became progressively stranger, and the limited success of the second Tremont release turned out to have an identifiable cause. A victim of progressive retinal atrophy, the wolf had been slowly going blind. Wolves that exhibited odd, independent behavior—the lone wolf of Romantic literature—often had vision problems that put them at a terrible disadvantage in the wild and caused them to abandon their social role in the family or pack. The four-year-old 451M coped with life in the acclimation pen during the fall of 1994 and the winter of 1995, apparently memorizing the few trees and objects in his shrinking world. But eventually he couldn't compensate.

Lucash watched the wolf fade in captivity.

"He could run through things like he could see, but when one of us went in there, he got confused and started running into trees and other wolves. We took a close look at him and saw his pupils were always dilated, as if he couldn't get enough light, even in the day. By the time we got him to the University of Tennessee, his eyes had no sensitivity to light at all."

451M was euthanized and, since his disease was possibly genetic, Lucash put the word out to have his bloodline tested.

With the Tremont female and her three pups in the Tremont pen for the remainder of the winter of 1995, Lucash was free to plan a major expansion of the red wolf program. More than two years into the restoration, the U.S. Fish and Wildlife Service and the National Park Service remained firmly committed to the future of *Canis rufus*. The Yellowstone gray wolf restoration now overshadowed the remarkable reappearance of William Bartram's wolf in the southern Appalachians, but researchers came from as far away as South Africa to observe what had been accomplished in the Great Smoky Mountains.

In late May of 1995, I found Lucash and Crawford sorting skulls and jawbones on the picnic table between their trailers. They were taking measurements and observing tooth wear on two groups of skulls. The smaller, narrower skulls were from coyotes; the larger were red wolves. In the wolf the canid skull broadens into what wolf lovers insist is a structural wolfishness that shows in the face—a sign of the thing itself, shell of the brainy difference between a scavenger and a hunter. In practice, it could be difficult to tell the difference.

The largest skull on the table turned out to be that of the original Tremont male, his teeth well worn but still formidable, eroded into an irregular horizon, like the mountains he roamed for a time. I played Hamlet to Lucash's Yorick, and took the skull and jaws from him to admire them. These were the teeth that had flashed up at us from the bottom of the plywood box when the first Tremont wolves were being prepped for release. I set them, in my mind, down next to the skull and antlers I had stumbled on and coveted up on Ekaneetlee Branch.

The long-dead Tremont male had, it turned out, taken on a mythic life of his own. Back in September, the same week that the forensics division of Fish and Wildlife shipped the wolf's carcass back to the Smoky Mountains, Lucash had been contacted about a boy on Yellow Creek Road in Graham County, North Carolina, who had been bitten by what was thought to be a wolf. This was the community into which the Tremont male had wandered and, in effect, surrendered a few months after its first release. Lucash assured the local authorities and the folks who lived along the foot of Yellow Creek Mountain that the big wolf that had once disturbed them was long dead and that Fish and Wildlife's radio-tracking data showed that none of their wolves was in the area. Undoubtedly the boy had been bitten by a feral dog, which was, of course, unfortunate. But it was interesting, and good to hear, I thought, that the wolf was remembered so vividly as part of the place.

Lucash was more interested in the future than the past and had been planning to use 1995 to reassert the presence of *Canis rufus* in the southern Appalachians. Park Service biologists confirmed that he had a good prey base to work with, especially good reproduction in the unwanted wild boar population due to a good mast crop in the fall of 1994.

Cades Cove had not had wolves in over a year, ever since the original family there had been retired because of cattle depredations in the spring of 1994. It took until the end of the year to hammer out a new agreement among Fish and Wildlife, the Park Service, and Rex Caughron, the Cades Cove stock owner. This was time well spent, since Fish and Wildlife wanted to demonstrate that a permanent solution could be achieved and that wolves and cattle could coexist if a reasonable effort was made to keep them apart. The new permit laid the groundwork for coexistence along the same lines that worked in northern Minnesota, which had a free-ranging population of gray wolves as well as a healthy coyote population. The Park Service was erecting high-tensile electric fencing to create a secure eighty-acre calving pasture. Caughron agreed to follow well-defined husbandry practices, particularly during calving season. Fish and Wildlife agreed to keep track of the wolves, as they had been doing all along, and to work closely with the Farm Bureau on any problems that arose outside the park. It was still the case that no healthy adult cow had been attacked by red wolves.

Once the fencing was completed, two new Cades Cove adults would be released. Lucash paired a big male, 538M, one of the juveniles in the original Cades Cove family, with a female, 565F, which had been born in a research facility in Eureka, Missouri. But in April a windfall came his way—an intact family of ten wolves, called the Whitetail Pack, from Alligator River. Two adults, one juvenile female, and seven wild-born pups had taken up residence on private land, Whitetail Farms, just outside of the Alligator River National Wildlife Refuge. They were relocated to the Cades Cove acclimation pen in April. Two pups died in captivity early in May, but Lucash still had a fully developed red wolf family with considerable experience in the wild ready for release.

The Tremont group got a new adult male. At the end of January, 539M, another one of the Cades Cove juveniles, was brought back from

Alligator River, where he had been idling in a pen, to replace 451M as a mate for 468F, who had done so well during the summer and fall of 1994. This pair and 468's offspring from the spring of 1994 were released on April 17, 1995, in effect a third Tremont release. 468F knew her territory well, denned up within a week or so of release and had a litter. Fish and Wildlife left her alone until May 5, when they walked the signals to a large, cracked boulder where she had two healthy, ten-day-old pups snugged in a little hollow spot. Lucash speculated that she may have had a larger litter and either lost some at birth or, as sometimes happened, split her litter. 468F seemed both circumspect and expert in the terrain and had taken the family into a rugged section of the backcountry to den, far from the familiar release area, a very good sign that she knew where the safest part of her territory was.

Those two pups tucked away in bedrock somewhere on Defeat Ridge were the first wild-born wolves since the litters of the spring of 1993 and were the best proof of the vitality of the red wolf restoration. Lucash also was pleased that the juveniles were staying up around the den sites feasting on the yellow- and brown-striped boar piglets the adult wolves brought in for them. This third Tremont group was the most coherent family of backcountry wolves Lucash had ever tended. Thunderhead Mountain had wolves again.

Lucash had been looking for a third release site in the park since the restoration began. He had chosen the Elkmont area, the headwaters of the Little River drainage to the east of the Tremont watershed. An acclimation pen had been constructed near the Little River and stocked with a pair of wild-born wolves from Alligator River in January: a three-year old male, 504M, and a short two-year old female, 660F. 504M had been confined for heartworm treatment, but both he and his mate seemed unaffected by the handling they had received.

The Little River drainage had what appeared to be a well-established coyote population, and Fish and Wildlife formally requested "freedom to trap and remove coyotes from specific situations and areas in the Park to facilitate colonization by red wolves and reduce potential hybridization." A policy for favoring the return of a native species over the encroachment of a nonnative, migrant species was worked out during the winter. In late March Lucash's crew began trapping coyotes in the Elkmont area in order to clear a corridor for the wolf release and came up with two breeding adults and a juvenile female. The Elkmont wolves, which had not mated, were released on April 10, 1995. Much like the first Tremont pair, unencumbered by pups and faced with the southern Appalachian backcountry, they started wandering independently after three or four days. All in all, Lucash said, it would be a good spring for wolves.

But not all the news in the spring of 1995 was good. New Cavaliers and Puritans had taken over Congress, clutching a niggardly document that made no mention of American nature. Part of their plan was to return to the joyride of unregulated commerce and capitalism—the cannibalism of the Gilded Age that had stripped the American landscape bare during the latter half of the nineteenth century. While this might be fun for some, it boded ill for wild lands and wildlife.

These well-heeled revolutionaries plied a tub-thumping patriotism which was a bit vague on the details of American history, and a self-proclaimed religiosity which had a strange hint of violence in it. A hatred of diversity, cultural and natural, was in the air. The so-called Contract with America was wielded like a blunt ax toward legislation only slightly less important, in my mind, than the Constitution and the Bill of Rights— the Endangered Species Act, the Wilderness Act, the Clean Water Act, the Clean Air Act, among others.

Like most federal workers, Lucash never discussed politics, but his wolf show was brought to us by the Endangered Species Act, high on the hit list of the 104th Congress, which moved quickly to impose a moratorium on listing new species and threatened to gut the act, if not revoke it, just as it planned to gut the Environmental Protection Agency's enforcement budget. In the name of a false economy, big changes were being made. Although there was no longer any money to subsidize school lunches for disadvantaged children, there was money to subsidize the timber industry, and a Salvage Logging rider sponsored by a North Carolina congressman slipped through the legislative process and renewed the rape of the woods in wolf country. "Politics," Thoreau wrote, "is but a narrow field, and that still narrower highway yonder leads to it." The fate of forests and wolves, among much else, was once again in the hands of the narrowest interests. And somehow the impassioned budget-slashing in Washington missed the enormous subsidies routinely doled out to the resource extraction industries—timber, mining, grazing, oil, and gas—the nation's longest-standing and most intractable welfare recipients. Odd.

The controversy about the taxonomic status of the red wolf also refused to go away and, wittingly or unwittingly, resonated with attacks on the practice of protecting endangered species, a practice that cannot, I freely admit, be defended on purely economic grounds. In a continuing attempt to turn gold into base metal, Robert Wayne, along with John Gittleman, published a new assault on the red wolf in the pages of *Scientific American,* where they were reaching for a wide audience for their view of "The Problematic Red Wolf." After briefly noting the wolf's beleaguered history, Wayne and Gittleman quickly called attention to the cost of the red wolf program—$4.5 million for the next five years in their account—a factor not normally relevant to a discussion of species status. They rehashed their previous findings that they had been unable to find a distinctive red wolf code in their study of mitochondrial and nuclear DNA and that there was considerable overlap in the genetic characteristics of red wolves, gray wolves, and coyotes, a confirmation of what was already well known.

They interpreted their inability to find the red wolf in the double helix as proof that the red wolf was not what Ronald Nowak and others had said it was—a distinct species of North American wolf that antedated, in evolutionary terms, both the gray wolf and the coyote. On the strength of not having found what they were looking for, Wayne and Gittleman "deduced that the red wolf may not be a unique species" and theorized that the red wolf was a hybrid of gray wolf and coyote. Reasoning backward, they discounted Nowak's fossil evidence and the cranial measurements he had asserted could be used to distinguish among coyotes, red wolves, and gray wolves. After deconstructing the red wolf in theory—which threatened its legal status under the Endangered Species Act—Wayne and Gittleman concluded by making a halfhearted argument for its preservation anyway, because it "may be the last, albeit impure, repository of genes from a now extinct gray wolf subspecies," hardly a distinction that would cut much mustard even in front of a sympathetic congressional committee. Although they seemed only to establish that they could not prove a negative, Wayne and Gittleman felt that "the problem of classification was largely resolved by DNA testing." They accused proponents of the red wolf of being "motivated by politics," an accusation that cut both ways.

There is no question that the red wolf had become "problematic." It had not been problematic for Native Americans of the Southeast, who imitated its distinctive howl in their rituals. Under the guise of the "black wolf," it had not been problematic for William Bartram and others in the eighteenth century, who routinely distinguished a southeastern wolf, distinct in appearance and behavior from the eastern gray wolf, once thought of as a subspecies, and certainly from the coyote and the western gray wolf. But by the time John James Audubon painted what he thought was a red wolf in the middle of the nineteenth century—the result looked much like a coyote—the natural history of American canids was lost in the wholesale destruction of land and wildlife to which the political short-sightedness of the day now urged a return. Scientific and political confusion seemed perfectly entwined around this little-known animal.

Canis rufus gregoryi might have held its ground quite confidently in that wonderful drawing used for the frontispiece of Young and Goldman's 1944 *The Wolves of North America,* but by the time David Mech had published his much-respected *The Wolf: The Ecology and Behavior of an Endangered Species* in 1970, the red wolf had become "the peculiar creature of Louisiana and Texas" most known for causing "considerable confusion." At times Mech discussed the red wolf as a legitimate species but seemed inclined to accept the view of it as a hybrid of the gray wolf and coyote, the view for which Robert Wayne kept trying to come up with evidence. At an important symposium on the red wolf in 1975, Curtis Carley, U.S. Fish and Wildlife field supervisor for the federal Red Wolf Recovery Program, frankly admitted the difficulties surrounding *Canis rufus:* "We do not know what a red wolf is. . . . Our only tie to the red wolf of history is the skull collection residing in the U.S. National Museum." Those skulls had been the basis of Ronald Nowak's original study, which, despite Wayne and Gittleman's interpretation of their DNA evidence, seemed to be the only work that had gotten close to "the red wolf of history."

I spoke with Ronald Nowak after Wayne and Gittleman's article appeared in July of 1995. He was tired of the controversy and worried about its inadvertent political implications, but his views on the origin and nature of the red wolf had not changed.

"Nothing has changed in my view, really nothing at all, except that I can recognize the reasonable possibility that perhaps the red wolf and the gray wolf intergraded. But as far as the separate evolution of the red wolf, its origin in the Southeast, its uniqueness to that area . . . all of that is the same except that it may be reasonable to consider [the two wolves] maybe only distinctive racially rather than specifically, or subspecifically."

He was confused by Wayne's "absolute drive" to dismiss the red wolf, especially at a time when this played into the hands of those who wanted to terminate the red wolf program.

"The relationships among wolves worldwide are very complex, and we are still only beginning to understand many things. New genetic evidence keeps complicating matters, and genetic information is subject to interpretation."

Nowak was coauthoring a book chapter with Wayne on taxonomy and evolution that he thought might help resolve the question. He believed that, eventually, the fossil, morphological, and genetic evidence could be resolved in such a way that would vindicate his view of the uniqueness of the red wolf. He did not understand Wayne's insistence that his interpretation of the genetic evidence was the only one possible. Whatever had happened to the red wolf in history—no one disputed the historical problem of hybridization—its evolutionary role was unassailable.

"If there had been no red wolf, if we could all agree there had been no red wolf based on Wayne's evidence, we would still have to invent the red wolf because there had to be a transition, an evolutionary transition, between the little coyote-like ancestors of all modern canids and the big gray wolves. There had to be something in between. The big gray wolf that we see now in North America did not just jump out of the little coyote. It had to go through a long intermediate phase and that was the red wolf."

The story of the red wolf is important no matter where that story leads. I had known that the animal was controversial from the beginning of my interest in it and had, of necessity, taken its ambiguity to be a strength rather than a weakness. I take that ambiguity to be an instructive part of its mythic, historical, and scientific importance. What is not known about the animal is as significant as what is known; destroying the unknown creates confusion.

For whatever it was worth in the summer of 1995, I took heart in what Lucash had said, that it would be a good year for wolves. The problem of hybridization with coyotes remained a significant concern, as did the future of the Endangered Species Act, but what was left of the art of the red wolf was being practiced in what was left of the wild in the southern Appalachians. When these beautiful creatures were done with their lives in the woods, I told myself—because I was getting tired of caring about so many things on the verge of disappearance—they slipped behind the veil, safe from both politics and science, and wandered the margins of an enchanted lake. I could not do better than the old myth.

Before they learn to fly, flight is in their minds, some myth of *Archaeopteryx.* All morning they will stand at the cliff's edge and stare, as if trying to remember. For hours they preen themselves and wind-hover, until they let go of the world and suddenly there is no place on the jagged bedrock from which to follow how they twist the air.

At midday they are in the sun and the sky becomes a place where falcons were.

Toward evening, underwings gleaming, they return as scimitars, blades swept out of heaven, or as life weaving flight out of nothing—gliding, turning, soaring to stall on rising columns of air, then stooping, for practice, at the earth.

Eeseeoh. River of many cliffs. Halfway home, at Linville Gorge in North Carolina, where I often stop to watch for peregrine falcons.

Eeseeoh is a questionable tidbit I picked up from a field guide and does not look or sound like a Cherokee word. The corruption and loss of language, like the corruption and loss of land and wildlife seems inescapable. My own struggle with understanding the past was full of errors and misconceptions, no doubt. Pursuing the truth in things head-on is ill-advised. But *Eeseeoh* signifies in its garbled way something about the nature of this place—there is, in fact, a cliff-shrouded river thousands of feet below me.

Historically, the Linville River gorge was known to be a Cherokee place. The dramatic skyline of its north rim is composed of sacred shapes—now known as Hawksbill and Table Rock—which can be seen from as far away as the Black Mountains, the strangest mountains in the Cherokee landscape and where *Kana'ti's* cave is said to be. The rock expressions at Linville Gorge are best observed from a distance. Get too close to them and you will see that they are desecrated, ruined with trash and trails, hardly seen or treated for what they are. At the head of the gorge there is a spectacular fall of water over rippled ledges of granite and gneiss, an unusual breach in Blue Ridge basement rock that lets the river flow east into a rectangular plunge pool that looks very much like the drawing of the elusive lake of the Cherokee on the Le Moyne map.

The Linville River often is heavily laden with silt from the overdeveloped land upstream, but despite plans in the nineteenth century to dam the river, it still flows freely, wild and loud. There are stands of old growth in the gorge, most of which is too steep to log profitably. Wildness takes care of its own when it can. Ancient eastern hemlock and monumental tulip poplar thrive in the cliffy river mist. Claire Newell did fieldwork here the summer before I met her in the Kilmer-Slickrock Wilderness. She reminded me that André Michaux had botanized at Linville Gorge in the late eighteenth century—looking for wonders among *"les roucers de al Montagne*

Hock-bill et de Table Montagn"—and that the type description for *Pinus pungens,* table mountain pine, was made here by Michaux and honors, indirectly, the Cherokee claim to this landscape.

If the solemn, oriental eastern hemlock is my favorite forest tree, the rugged table mountain pine, a southern Appalachian endemic, is my favorite species of the edge. *Pinus pungens* thrives between rock and air, where no other tree could imagine itself. A table mountain pine grows here where I watch for falcons, with Hawksbill to the west and Table Rock itself to the east across the open space of the river gorge. Having broken through barren rim rock, the twisted pine occupies an empty place even the stunted mountain laurel nearby shun. But despite its difficult circumstances, the tree is heavily laden with clusters of its fiercely spined and tightly shut cones.

Although compared to forest hardwoods it is not an especially long-lived tree, the thick-skinned table mountain pine tends to keep hold of the difficult sites it occupies. The species' persistence in the same place from generation to generation was not lost on the Cherokee, for whom the tree was a symbol of long life and health. The tree's relationship to fire, on which it thrived, undoubtedly did not go unnoticed. The jagged conifer was shaped like lightning and loved high-elevation rock outcrops where lightning frequently struck. Fire suppressed *Pinus pungens'* few competitors and opened its brutal cones, which could stay closed for as long as a quarter of a century. The undistinguished-looking pine needed fire as much as water to survive.

Like the table mountain pine and the red wolf, the peregrine falcons for which I wait on this late-summer evening are also simultaneously part of myth and history. As an airborne predator the peregrine has no equal, not even among the eagles. Long ago, the idea of the peregrine had become the Thunderbird of the Southeastern Ceremonial Complex and had enlarged itself into the dreaded *Tla'nuwa',* the great hawk of the Cherokee imagination. If the wolf was the finest reification of the wildness of animals, the slender but ferocious peregrine falcon was the final form of what has been called the "evolutionary triumph" of flight.

Historically, however, the peregrine's fate had been much like that of the red wolf. The combined ill effects of pesticides and loss of nesting sites decimated the species in the eastern United States during the twentieth century. An extensive search of all known historical eyries in 1964 found them empty; in fact, the eastern subspecies of peregrine—the Appalachian peregrine—was extinct. Beginning in the 1970s, a closely related subspecies was reintroduced in the Appalachian and Adirondack mountains and along the Atlantic coast. Before I had even heard of the red wolf, I spent two summers watching the hacking of peregrine falcons from a cliff in the Blue Ridge Mountains of Virginia.

The release of falcons to the sky is as undramatic as the release of wolves to the earth. Young birds are trucked and carried to a suitably remote cliff site in plywood boxes, one side of which is screened so that they can acclimate themselves to their new location. The birds are fed quail and pigeons and watered by hack site attendants they never see, and who protect them from foxes and raccoons. After a few days, the screening is removed from the hack boxes and the birds emerge. Their first response to this unprecedented freedom, this strange reprieve from history, is to be stunned and cautious. For days you can observe the most agile bird on earth, the fastest animal alive, walking about apparently unaware, or unsure, of its great skills. The beautiful birds shift their scaly feet nervously on the slanting rock, looking down at it, and shuffle their wings about as if their wings were in the way. Until they fly, they must view the space before them as we do, as empty and dangerous.

The instinct to fly is no doubt inborn, but the young falcons are perhaps encouraged by the silent turkey vultures passively riding thermals rising from the valley floor and by the ravens that frequently come to play loudly in the air in front of the cliff. The flight of a raven is clearly an improvement on the flight of the vulture, but falcon flight is another thing entirely and the mockery—or the challenge—of ravens eventually becomes too much for falcons to bear.

After a day or two, the young falcons begin taking short glides into the treetops below them, getting a feel for the lift in their shapely wings, the powers of their form. They make short flights back and forth in front of the hack site, swinging farther out of view each time. After they learn to hitch rides on midday thermals, which take them to new heights and load their wings with possibilities the vultures and ravens cannot imagine, they begin to exercise the freedom of their wildness and create a fabulous order in the air no one would have imagined without them.

Like newly released wolves, the peregrines return for a few weeks to their release point, practicing the art of flight in a familiar place. I remember spending days at the hack site watching the sky—the shock of their sudden appearance from impossible angles, their balletic flight, and then the way they were suddenly gone, at first for hours, and then for days. Once they have fully explored their extraordinary maneuverability, and fitted it to hunting moths, butterflies, and birds, falcons stoop less and less frequently past the hack site and even their distant cries are heard less often. They learn to disdain the food left for them. One by one they disappear forever. In a month or so they are gone. Some wildness has disappeared back into the world and the work is done. After lingering for a few weeks, to make sure the birds are gone, the hack site attendants take the memory of falcons, visible and invisible, home with them.

The bedrock truth of Romanticism, resistant to even the most corrosive modernism, is that consciousness is our participation in the infinite. But consciousness needs found objects—the wolf, the falcon, the table mountain pine. Our only access to the infinite is through nature, where we find, coldly bordering our own mortality, all time and all space—the shifting geography of being expressed through the art of evolution. To see a falcon or a wolf, or an eastern hemlock or a table mountain pine, and suddenly understand something about yourself or your culture is not necessarily to anthropomorphize.

I saw red wolves in the backcountry once, for a minute or two. I have never seen or heard a peregrine falcon except at a hack site. Still, having seen the wolf and the falcon, I can now imagine them and pursue, from a distance, the truth and beauty I know for a fact they embody. I would not want to do without either the fact or the image, and I do not understand a culture that willfully destroys its access to such things. For whatever reason.

"Thus the animal lives unhistorically," Nietzsche writes, sounding oddly like Thoreau, "it hides nothing and coincides at all moments exactly with what it is; it is bound to be truthful at all times, unable to be anything else." It seems that we cannot escape what Albert Camus, hardly a Romantic, called the "innocence of the wolf"—a wildness some love and some hate. Whatever it is, the wildness hits close to home.

Of course, animals don't live unhistorically. The falcons banded and released those two summers in the Blue Ridge nested in Pittsburgh and New York because in the East there is more cliff space on skyscrapers than in the mountains, where tracts of homes crawl up the slopes everywhere, everyone jostling for a slightly better view of what their own presence destroys. And the red wolves of the southern Appalachians were hemmed in, as I was, by pollution and roads and the ugly boom towns of rural tourism, which also destroy their own reason for being.

But Nietzsche put his finger on the philosophical essence of wildness—a truthful, sacred being in animals that slips through history where it can and that we admire even though the history which destroys the truth and beauty we desire is our own.

I spent the better part of two summers watching falcons disappear into a hazy sky without knowing what I was doing. I took voluminous notes but couldn't write a word and find I have not much to say now. With falcons as with wolves, it was impossible to watch the transition to wildness. Any true account of it would have to be a myth. Later I understood that watching an empty sky in the hopes that a falcon would return had prepared me for a sustained, if unsuccessful, pursuit of the wildness of wolves, which in the summer of 1995 were repeating their modest themes and no longer seemed to need my prosaic curiosity, if they ever had.

During the summer of 1995, the Elkmont wolves traveled widely without disturbing anyone. The male and the female explored independently—one south, one north—assaying the world between the Big Pigeon and the Little Tennessee rivers. The female slipped through private lands outside the park much of the time, took a look at the outskirts of Knoxville and at Douglas Lake—in which the French Broad and Holston rivers die—but eventually returned on her own and was known to frequent *Duni'swkalgun'i*, the great stone antlers buried in spruce and fir. The male made a bold swim across Fontana Lake, cast his spirit as the first Tremont male had done through the Nantahala National Forest, and also returned to the park on his own. He settled in Cades Cove but, unlike the original Cades Cove wolves, who had been a great tourist attraction, he was rarely seen.

The new Tremont wolves did well in the backcountry on the slopes of Thunderhead and turned out to have a third pup, as Chris Lucash had suspected. The transplanted Whitetail pack was released in July. Although Fish and Wildlife hoped they would simply take up residence in Cades Cove, which had proved such a stable center for wolves, the adults and juveniles ranged widely and unpredictably.

In the end, it did not surprise me that politics had turned against the wolf. It is as true now as it was in Thoreau's day that one way to get to the center of American politics is to walk into the American woods and take a look at what is there and what is not there. That will tell you all you need to know about what is happening in places of power. North America was depicted as a small archipelago of islands on fifteenth- and sixteenth-century European maps, an obstacle of land between Europe and China. The islands enlarged themselves into a continent for a few centuries, and then the continent shrunk and fragmented again into an archipelago of

islands—the few fragments of forest, the few pieces of river we now contemplate. From the point of view of nature—of wild lands and wild life—
North America is still not much more than an exploited colony. One
Gilded Age replaces another. Thoreau's great question remains not only
unanswered but unasked—"To what end does the world go on and why
was America discovered?"—and the solemn Cherokee view, that history is
tragic, seems apt.

A hack site is not an eyrie, no more than an acclimation pen is a wolf
den. We have passed through the end of nature and are living the Faustian
dream.

I've never seen peregrine falcons at Linville Gorge, but when I stop
here, to savor an old edge of the Cherokee country, I watch the sky bordered by this table mountain pine and replay the flight of falcons in my
mind as I know it to be, a sight I could not have imagined if I had not seen
it, no more than I could have imagined red wolves or a rock-loving pine
tree that needed fire.

Needless to say I never got to the Cherokee Mountains, but I have
found good points of access—*Tsiya'hi, Diga'kati'yi, Tsistu'yi, Tsulunwe'i,
Ya'nu-u'natawasti'yi, Duni'skwalgun'i, Kuwa'hi, Tsatu'gi, Atahi'ta,
Tsunda'nilti'yi,* and *Gadalu'tsi.* I have accepted the fact that these points of
access are ultimately impasses to an outsider. *We must look a long time
before we can see.* But I know where rivers are hidden in lakes and where
the Overhill towns are buried. I know some of the old words and some of
the old stories, although I have probably garbled both. If I have returned
to old wounds in this landscape, that is because they have not healed well.
Among other things, I know where to find table mountain pine and where
falcons and wolves might be. Without such things, we will never again
glimpse our original being. Without the old horizons, we will go blind.

Here at Linville Gorge I watch for falcons and accept a passing raven
and its wild cries as a good sign, not a sign that I will see falcons this
evening, but a sign that I am waiting well. Across a still-wild river gorge,
sacred shapes form a horizon. That marked horizon is reassuring, and I am
reminded of the eleventh-century landscape painter Kuo Hsi's observation
that mountains are the "storehouses of the world, in which are found the
treasures of heaven and earth."

The river below me shifts register as sunlight rises up the north wall of
the gorge, which goes dark in yet another transition I cannot describe and
would not have imagined on my own. Table Rock and Hawksbill briefly

glow like fire at sunset and then turn to stone. I wonder what the proper names for them are.

Time spirals in warm gusts of wind like a falcon in the sky, like a wolf hunting on a mountainside.

Just before full dark, a peregrine stoops from high behind me, a gray visitation, improbably fast. Then the sleek bird rises back into view from the darkened canyon, opens its primaries to shed lift, and lands silently on the rock shelf thinly sheltered by the pine.

Time spirals. Like a falcon. Like a wolf.

The otherworldly peregrine leans forward as if the dark space before it suggested flight. The pine leans over the falcon.

Darker, the day moves west.

The bird is still as stone.

Pinus pungens waits for fire.

Notes

Full citations appear in the sources.

ix   epigraph: Emerson, *Selected Writings*, 10.

Prologue: No Heaven, No Hell

4   "the Cheerake mountains": *Adair's History*, 248.
5   "the whole country": Mooney, "Sacred Formulas," 333.
6   "the entire Allegheny": Mooney, "Myths," 14.
8   "wild and dusky": Thoreau, *Natural History Essays*, 127.
9   "carried a scalp": Mooney, "Sacred Formulas," 315.
    "Here prayers": Mooney, "Sacred Formulas," 312.
    "It is impossible": Mooney, "Sacred Formulas," 318.
10 "a wonderful completeness": Mooney, "Sacred Formulas," 319.
    "The language": Mooney, "Sacred Formulas," 309.
    "It is evident": Mooney, "Sacred Formulas," 318–319.
11 "who still prayed": Moses, *The Indian Man*, 174.
    "It was very impressive": Moses, *The Indian Man*, 179.

"as with other tribes": Mooney, "Myths," 231.

12   Mary Austin: "The disposition of the aboriginal poet is to arrange his words along what, for want of a better term, I have called the landscape line, the line shaped by its own inner necessities." Austin, *The American Rhythm,* 54. Austin presented free-verse translations of several of Mooney's formulas and claimed to have formulas directly from Leota Harris, a Cherokee. Austin noted the "hypnotizing murmur" of Cherokee and the difficulty of translation (n. 24).

"I don't want": Fading Voices interview with Bessie Jumper, February 17, 1987. Taped interview in Cherokee by Lois Calonehuskie and Gil Jackson; transcription by Lois Calonehuskie. Box 2, folder 3. Museum of the Cherokee. Cherokee, North Carolina. Portions of the Fading Voices interviews were published in the *Journal of Cherokee Studies* 14 (1989).

14   "The Indian": Mooney, "Myths," 98. Contemporary historians echo his observation: "Many eastern visitors noted that the frontier whites thought of Indians as little better than animals and were as ready to rid the country of them as they were to wipe out bears and wolves." McLoughlin, *Cherokee Renascence,* 48.

15   "There are some": Leopold, *A Sand County Almanac,* vii.

I. WOLF COUNTRY

17   epigraph: Mooney, "Myths," 280.

Mind on a Wolf

19   epigraph: Leopold, *A Sand County Almanac,* 129.
26   *"Dine'tlana a'nigwa"*: Mooney, "Myths," 242–248.
29   "They are good hunters": Mooney, "Myths," 280.
32   "This was John Oliver": *Sketches of the Olivers* gives both 1821 and 1818 as the Olivers' arrival date but provides more evidence for the latter. Dunn, *Cades Cove,* accepts 1818.

"Game is going": McLoughlin, *Cherokee Renascence,* 3.
33   "moving forest oratory": Corkran, *The Cherokee Frontier,* 60.
34   "We want": McLoughlin, *Cherokee Renascence,* 215.
"as long as": *Early Travels in the Tennessee Country,* 141, 138.
"barely sufficient": McLoughlin, *Cherokee Renascence,* 162.

35   "alternative for many": McLoughlin, *Cherokee Renascence,* 57.

"It appears to me": McLoughlin, *Cherokee Renascence,* 242–243.

36   "howling wilderness": *Sketches of the Olivers,* 5; Dunn, *Cades Cove,* 1–13.

Fire in the Path

45   epigraph: Arthur, *Western North Carolina,* 62.

50   "We continued": W. Bartram, *Travels,* 126–127.

"the tyger": W. Bartram, *Travels,* 5, 30.

51   "of incredible magnitude": W. Bartram, *Travels,* 126.

The Alachua: Bartram's modern editor, Francis Harper, quotes ethnographer and historian John Swanton that "the Alachua tribe was the Potano which was encountered by De Soto in 1539 and possibly by Narváez eleven years earlier. In 1565 Laudonnière's Frenchmen assisted the Utina in an attack upon these people, and the Spaniards found them difficult to subdue" *(Travels,* 368). Alachua shows as a place-name in northern Florida on the Herman Moll map of 1729–1736? from which the dust jacket detail for this book is taken.

52   The historical record: Hariot, *A Briefe and True Report,* 20; Captain John Smith, *Complete Works,* I, 155; Lawson, *A New Voyage,* 119; *Catesby's Birds,* 157.

53   "Although the red wolf": Nowak, *North American Quaternary "Canis,"* 44.

"I have been": W. Bartram, *Travels,* 177.

Darwin: Darwin uses the paradigm of wolf-deer interaction as his introductory example in "Illustrations of the Action of Natural Selection, or the Survival of the Fittest" in the fourth chapter of *The Origin of Species.*

54   Through the years: Nowak offers the clearest summary: "Goldman . . . combined the wolves of the south-central and southeastern United States into a single species, *C. rufus,* that he considered distinct from all other North American wolves. He combined the latter into the species *C. lupus.* Goldman said that *C. rufus* 'exhibits a departure from the true wolves, and in cranial and dental characters approaches the coyotes.' He listed the names of *C. rufus rufus* for the Texas subspecies, and *C. r. floridanus* for the eastern race, and he also described *C. r. gregoryi,* a new subspecies in the lower

Mississippi Valley. . . . Goldman used the vernacular 'red wolf' for the species *C. rufus,* presumably on the basis of Audubon and Bachman's description of the 'Red Texan Wolf.' This term, however, is not found in any of the early literature discussing wolves in states east of Texas. . . . this popular term seems to have been restricted to parts of Texas until Goldman introduced its use throughout the range of *C. rufus." North American Quaternary "Canis,"* 25. Francis Harper's attempt to promote Bartram's original binomial, *Canis niger,* as the scientific name for the southeastern wolf was rejected in 1957 by the International Commission on Zoological Nomenclature.

Audubon: *Quadrupeds of North America,* pl. 82.

55 "Wolves . . . seemed to disappear": Young and Goldman, *The Wolves of North America,* 27. They also note a case of gray wolves moving into an area of western Tennessee after red wolves were extirpated: "Twenty-five years since the small black wolf was exterminated, and now [c. 1895], as though dropping from the sky, comes this gray monster that none of our dogs can successfully tackle . . ." 49.

"logging has probably": Shaw, "Ecology, Behavior, and Systematics," 9–10.

"bounding along": Summers, *Annals of Southwest Virginia,* 1546. This is from an account of the backwoods career of Wilburn Waters (aka Welborn Waters), an infamous wolf hunter of southwestern Virginia.

"the great wolf": Arthur, *Western North Carolina,* 523. It is worth remembering that the first game law in North America was a wolf bounty.

56 "most of the red wolf's": Shaw, "Ecology, Behavior and Systematics," 36.

The popular outdoor press: "Some Notes on Wolves," *Forest and Stream,* February 3, 1906, 180–181. "Some Notes on Wolves," *Forest and Stream,* January 27, 1906, lists "gray, white, black, red, buffalo, timber, or woods wolves" and complicates matters further with a category, "little wolves," in which it includes "the prairie wolf, coyote, and barking wolf." Young, "It's Red but Truly All-American," 57.

57 "the native wolf": Nowak, "The Mysterious Wolf of the South," 50.
"designs . . .": W. Bartram, *Travels,* 288, 286.

58 "Early next morning": W. Bartram, *Travels,* 252. Bartram, of course, is horrified. This response to wolves has not gone out of fashion. Two hundred years later, and twenty years ago, John Shaw noted during his study of the red wolf on the Texas–Louisiana Gulf Coast that "at least four wolves were killed in the study area within one year. Three were shot . . . and the fourth was roped from horseback and clubbed." Shaw, "Ecology, Behavior, and Systematics," 44.

71 "Wolves that have": Rutter and Pimlott, *The World of the Wolf,* 127.

73 "Fossil history": Nowak, "The Red Wolf Is Not a Hybrid," 594–595. "There may never": Nowak, *North American Quaternary "Canis,"* 29–30.

74 *"Canis edwardii":* Nowak, *North American Quaternary "Canis,"* 84.

78 "Eastward I go": Thoreau, *Natural History Essays,* 105–106.

79 "I trust": Thoreau, *Natural History Essays,* 110–111.

Chalaque

85 epigraph: Williams, *In the American Grain,* 45.

Juan Ortiz: This reconstruction of de Soto's incursion through the Southeast is based on the three primary source accounts of the expedition. I have woven details, paraphrases, and quotations from the following into my narrative: "The Narrative of the Expedition of Hernando de Soto by the Gentleman of Elvas," Buckingham Smith's translation edited by Theodore H. Lewis in *Spanish Explorers in the Southern United States, 1528–1543* (1907; rpt. New York: Barnes and Noble, 1946); "The Account by a Gentleman of Elvas," translated and edited by James Alexander Robertson; Luys Hernández de Biedma's "Relation of the Island of Florida," translated and edited John E. Worth; Rodrigo Rangel's "Account of the Northern Conquest of Hernando de Soto," translated and edited John Worth in volume 1 of *The De Soto Chronicles.* I have also quoted a statement of Oviedo's from Carl Ortwin Sauer's *Sixteenth Century North America.*

98 misnomer in Old World maps: "The mountains were identified by that name at least as early as the 1560s by René Laudonnière. William P. Cumming noted that 'During the last quarter of the sixteenth century this name became the most popular designation for the southeastern area; it continued to be used by continental

geographers until well into the eighteenth century, when it appears as a kind of generic term for the Indian country back of the foreign settlements.' " Hann, *Apalachee,* 10.

"Among the Cherokee": Mooney, "The Ghost-Dance Religion," 1100.

100 According to the Cherokee: Mooney, "Myths," 239–240.
103 "lived beyond": Mooney, "Myths," 183.
107 According to the Yuchi: Lankford, *Native American Legends,* 70–72.
117 "in Wildness": Thoreau, *Natural History Essays,* 112.
118 "the wildness": Thoreau, *Natural History Essays,* 113.

II. THE CIRCULAR RIVER

119 epigraph: Mooney, "Myths," 240.

Windows

121 epigraph: *Early Travels in the Tennessee Country,* 261.
"great formative ability": Gabelentz (1852) in Krueger, "Two Early Grammars," 4, and John Pickering (1831?) in Krueger, 34.
"there are many": Pickering, quoting Heckewelder in Krueger, "Two Early Grammars," 55.
122 "The American languages": Gabelentz in Krueger, "Two Early Grammars," 8.
128 "cheap water power": Wheeler and McDonald, *TVA and the Tellico Dam,* 57.
131 "there was no": Mooney, "Myths," 324.
134 "constantly speaking": Mooney, "Myths," 547.
138 "Their towns": *Adair's History,* 238–239.
139 "They were immense": Mooney, "Myths," 315.
141 "About 100 yards": *Lieut. Henry Timberlake's Memoirs,* 63.
145 "The west half": Payne Papers, Vol. 3, p. 51.

The Constant Fire, The Old Sacred Things

147 epigraph: Mooney, "Sacred Formulas," 342.
148 "by ye fire": "Letter of Abraham Wood" (1673) in *Early Travels in the Tennessee Country,* 35.
"In the beginning": Mooney, "Myths," 240–242.

153 "insisted that the fire": Witthoft, "Cherokee Beliefs Concerning Death," 72.

154 "When all was water": Mooney, "Myths," 239.

155 "We believe": "Schneider's Report," *Early Travels in the Tennessee Country,* 245–248.

156 Nor are the Moravians: The relationship between Christianity and the Cherokee should not be oversimplified. In recent times the churches have been a strong force for preserving traditional Cherokee language and culture.

157 "All Waters": "Schneider's Report," *Early Travels in the Tennessee Country,* 253–260.

161 "is understood": Mooney, "Sacred Formulas," 359.

John Wesley Powell: Mooney attributes the term to Powell in "Sacred Formulas," 340. Powell's system for understanding indigenous spiritual ideas is summarized under "mythology" in Part I of the *Handbook of American Indians North of Mexico.*

162 Mooney notes: Mooney, "Sacred Formulas," 346 and "Myths," 507, 510. Witthoft confirms this: "Cherokee seems to have no primary root or any root that could be used for 'devil' or 'evil.' " "Cherokee Beliefs Concerning Death," 69.

They report: Mooney and Olbrechts, *Swimmer Manuscript,* 19–20.

163 "Sharply!": Mooney and Olbrechts, *Swimmer Manuscript,* 287.

John Pickering noted: Krueger, "Two Early Grammars," 44.

164 "The Indians have": *DeBrahm's Report,* 108.

"laudatory rhapsodies": Mooney, "Sacred Formulas," 344.

performatives or speech acts: The classic example is the "I do" of the marriage ceremony, which is classed as an action as well as a statement. One *does* something by pronouncing those words in the proper context. Speech in that case is a mode of action as well as a mode of expression.

165 "the words used": Mooney, "Sacred Formulas," 310.

"Give me the wind": Mooney, "Sacred Formulas," 369–370.

166 "were full of": Mooney, "Sacred Formulas," 343–344.

"the opposing forces": Mooney, "Sacred Formulas," 308–309.

167 "made up their minds": "The Journey to the Sunrise," Mooney, "Myths," 255–256. There is an important Iroquois version of this myth.

169 "she sent down": "The Daughter of the Sun," Mooney, "Myths," 252–254.

171 "Sharply!": "This is to Take People to the Water With," Mooney and Olbrechts, *Swimmer Manuscript,* 195.

172 "The soul of conscious life": Witthoft, "Cherokee Beliefs Concerning Death," 68–70. Witthoft noted the strain between the prevailing Christianity and Will West Long's attachment to the old beliefs: "Will had never been a church member, and I understood him to say that he had never been christened, despite the fact that his father was a Baptist lay preacher. He was, of course, raised by his mother. He once told me of how many of the older men had very unwillingly become Christian because of the constant pressuring from their daughters. He said he would never give in to the churches" (68).

174 "Listen!": "To Treat the Great Chill," Mooney, "Sacred Formulas," 360.

175 "it soon became": Mooney, "Sacred Formulas," 310.
   "Now then!": "This is to Scratch Them," Mooney and Olbrechts, *Swimmer Manuscript,* 206–207.

176 "wa'ya wa'ya": "This (is for) When They Have Their Heads Aching," Mooney and Olbrechts, *Swimmer Manuscript,* 188.
   "numerous archaic": Mooney, "Sacred Formulas," 309.

177 "the formula contains": Mooney and Olbrechts, *Swimmer Manuscript,* 231.
   "Hayi!": "What Those Who Have Been to War Did to Help Themselves," Mooney, "Sacred Formulas," 388.

178 "Listen!": "This is for Hunting Birds," Mooney, "Sacred Formulas," 371.
   "Instantly": "To Shoot Dwellers in the Wilderness," Mooney, "Sacred Formulas," 372.
   "Listen!": "This Tells About Going Into the Water," Mooney, "Sacred Formulas," 379.

179 "Listen!": "To Destroy Life," Mooney, "Sacred Formulas," 391.
   "the minds": Raymond Fogelson, "The Conjurer in Eastern Cherokee Society," 66.

180 "the edge of": Mooney, "Myths," 314.

181 "Such a sorrowful": Speck and Broom, *Cherokee Dance,* 14.
   "Stone Coat then": Speck and Broom, *Cherokee Dance,* 15–16.

183 "Presently": Lawson, *A New Voyage,* 38–39.

184 "They preserve": *The Journal of Major John Norton,* 70. Walker Calhoun of the Big Cove community on the Qualla Boundary has

done much to keep alive the Cherokee Dance and song tradition. He has recorded and commented on many Cherokee dances, including the Booger Dance, on the audiocassette *Where the Ravens Roost: Cherokee Traditional Songs of Walker Calhoun,* produced by the Mountain Heritage Center at Western Carolina University in Cullowhee, N.C. Will West Long was Walker Calhoun's half uncle.

185 The most detailed account: Speck and Broom, *Cherokee Dance,* 25–39.

"it might even": Speck and Broom, *Cherokee Dance,* 37.

"a record of": Speck and Broom, *Cherokee Dance,* 3.

"consciousness of": Speck and Broom, *Cherokee Dance,* 2.

187 "symbol of": Speck and Broom, *Cherokee Dance,* 34.

Islands

189 epigraph: Mooney, "Myths," 239.

"Duni'skwalgun'i": Mooney, "Myths," 516.

190 "where it is": Mooney, "Myths," 543.

191 "the tops of": Thoreau, *The Maine Woods,* 86.

192 "When the animals": Mooney, "Myths," 240.

195 "In the old": Mooney, "Myths," 250.

196 "a drove of": Mooney, "Myths," 326.

197 "They began then": Mooney, "Myths," 251–252.

198 "Nature never": Emerson, *Selected Writings,* 5.

200 a unifying theme: Botanists Peter White and Charles Cogsbill consider the red spruce to be "the unifying element" of the entire Appalachian chain. White and Cogsbill, "Spruce-Fir Forests of Eastern North America," 3.

III. TIME IN A FOREST

221 epigraph: D. H. Lawrence, *Sons and Lovers,* 239.

Old Growth

223 epigraph: Thoreau, *Natural History Essays,* 117.

228 "What is not": Matthiessen, *Wildlife in America,* 57.

234 "the word *old*": Krueger, "Two Early Grammars," 55. This is John

Pickering quoting Heckewelder's *Notes on Eliot's Indian Grammar*.

236 No less acute observer: *Correspondence of Charles Darwin, Vol. 1,* quoting from the 8 Feb.–1 March 1832 letter to R. W. Darwin; 2–6 April 1832 (to Caroline Darwin), 5 July 1832 (to Catherine Darwin), 14 July–7 Aug. 1832 (to Susan Darwin), 23 July–15 Aug. 1832 (to J. S. Henslow).

243 "a model": Moore and Smith, "The Red Wolf as a Model," 263, 265.

245 "unless wolves": Fischer, *Wolf Wars,* 63.

247 "After we had": Lawson, *A New Voyage,* 50.

249 "the finest example": Cain, "The Tertiary Character," 233. Cain's thesis has been refined to reflect a more kinetic view of botanical periods, but his essential insight remains intact.

251 H. B. Ayres and W. W. Ashe: Ayres and Ashe, *The Southern Appalachian Forests,* passim.

255 "In the woods": Emerson, *Selected Writings,* 6.

256 "find himself": Thoreau, *Natural History Essays,* 114.
   "in Chinese": Fenollosa, *The Chinese Written Character,* 15.

Crossing Paths

257 epigraph: "The Removed Townhouses," Mooney, "Myths," 335.

261 "the sickening meaning": Mooney, "The Ghost-Dance Religion," 881; 876–878.

263 "In June, 1760,": Mooney, "Myths," 43.
   "A pretty town": Corkran, *Cherokee Frontier,* 209.

264 "passes the most": Corkran, *Cherokee Frontier,* 213–214.

265 "Vengeful warriors": Corkran, *Cherokee Frontier,* 220–221.
   "At Chota": Corkran, *Cherokee Frontier,* 222.

267 Christopher French: [Captain Christopher French], "Journal of an Expedition," 275–301.

268 "without tents": "Journal of Lieut. Col. James Grant," 26.

271 "5,000 people": "Journal of Lieut. Col. James Grant," 35.

272 "they would become": "Journal of Sir Alexander Cuming (1730)," in *Early Travels in the Tennessee Country,* 132.
   He departed: William Bartram's journey to the Cherokee is frequently misdated as 1776. I follow Francis Harper's understanding of the route. *The Travels of William Bartram,* pt. 3, chaps. 2–4.

278 the wording of the world: This phrase is Stanley Cavell's, *The Senses of Walden*, 44.

281 "They are welcome": Kelly, "Notable Persons," 4.

283 "Every town": Mooney, "Myths," 49–53.

287 "TSUNDA'NILTI'YI": Mooney, "Myths," 410.

292 "nature had set": Agee, "Tennessee Valley Authority," 5–6.

294 "the general abstract": Wieger, *Chinese Characters*, 36. The idea that some Chinese ideographs can be traced back to pictures of things or actions, a belief of Ezra Pound's and Ernest Fenollosa's, comes in and out of favor among scholars. Wieger's etymology may currently be out of step with academic scholarship, but his example intrigues me. It must point back toward something.

Ataga'hi

297 epigraph: Mooney, "Myths," 321.

"Man is rich": Thoreau, *Walden*, 74.

298 *"Montes Apalatci"*: Le Moyne de Morgues (Jacques) *Floridae Americanae Provinciae Recens & exactimissima descriptio,* in Goss, *The Mapping of North America*, 44.

301 "You cannot go": Thoreau, *Natural History Essays*, 28–29. Thoreau seems to be describing the young Darwin: "The true man of science will know nature better by his finer organization; he will smell, taste, see, hear, feel, better than other men. His will be a deeper and finer experience. We do not learn by inference and deduction and the application of mathematics to philosophy, but by direct intercourse and sympathy." Science depends, Thoreau concludes, on possessing "a more perfect Indian wisdom."

309 "Politics," Thoreau wrote: Thoreau, *Natural History Essays*, 101.

In a continuing attempt: Wayne and Gittleman, "The Problematic Red Wolf," 36–39.

311 "the peculiar creature": Mech, *The Wolf*, 347, 22.

"We do not know": Klinghammer (ed.), *The Behavior and Ecology of Wolves*, 529.

313 *"les roucers"*: "Portions of the Journal of André Michaux," 112.

316 "the innocence": Camus, *Notebooks 1935–1942*, 71.

318 "storehouses": Kuo Hsi, *An Essay on Landscape Painting*, 43.

Sources

Adair's History of the American Indians [1775], ed. Samuel Cole Williams. New York: Promontory Press, 1930.

Agee, James. "Tennessee Valley Authority." In *James Agee: Selected Journalism,* ed. Paul Ashdown. Knoxville: University of Tennessee Press, 1985.

Arthur, John Preston. *Western North Carolina: A History (From 1730 to 1913).* Raleigh, N.C.: The Edward Buncombe Chapter of the Daughters of the American Revolution of Asheville, N.C., 1914.

[Audubon, John James.] *Quadrupeds of North America.* Vol. 5 of *The Complete Audubon.* Kent, Volair Books for the National Audubon Society, 1979.

Austin, Mary. *The American Rhythm: Studies and Reëxpressions of Amerindian Songs,* enlarged ed. New York: Houghton Mifflin Company, 1930.

Ayres, H. B., and W. W. Ashe. *The Southern Appalachian Forests.* Dept. of the Interior, U.S. Geological Survey Professional Paper No. 37. Washington, D.C.: Government Printing Office, 1905.

Bartram, William. "Travels in Georgia and Florida, 1773–74: A Report to Dr. John Fothergill." Annotated by Francis Harper. *Transactions of the American Philosophical Society,* new series 33, pt. 2 (1943).

[———.] *The Travels of William Bartram.* Naturalist's ed., ed. Francis Harper. New Haven, CT: Yale University Press, 1958.

Basso, Keith. "The Western Apache Classificatory Verb System: A Formal Analysis." *Southwestern Journal of Anthropology* 24 (1968).

"Bessie Jumper Interview." *Journal of Cherokee Studies* 14 (1989).

Cain, Stanley. "The Tertiary Character of the Cove Hardwood Forests of the Great Smoky Mountains National Park." *Bulletin of the Torrey Botanical Club* 70, no. 3 (1943).

Camus, Albert. *Notebooks 1935–1942.* Translated by Philip Thody. New York: Harcourt Brace Jovanovich, 1963.

Catesby's Birds of Colonial America, ed. Alan Feduccia. Chapel Hill: University of North Carolina Press, 1985.

Cavell, Stanley. *The Senses of Walden.* San Francisco: North Point Press, 1981.

Chapman, Jefferson. *Tellico Archaeology: 12,000 Years of Native American History.* Report of Investigations No. 43, Department of Anthropology, University of Tennessee/Publications in Anthropology No. 41, Tennessee Valley Authority (1985).

Chapman, Jefferson, et al. "Man-Land Interaction: 10,000 Years of American Indian Impact on Native Ecosystems in the Lower Little Tennessee River Valley, Eastern Tennessee." *Southeastern Archaeology* 1/2 (Winter 1982).

Corkran, David. *The Cherokee Frontier: Conflict and Survival, 1740–62.* Norman: University of Oklahoma, 1961.

Crawford, Barron. "Coyotes in Great Smoky Mountains National Park: Evaluation of Methods to Monitor Relative Abundance, Movement Ecology, and Habitat Use." M.A. Thesis, University of Tennessee, 1992.

Cridlebaugh, Patricia. "American Indian and Euro-American Impact Upon Holocene Vegetation in the Lower Little Tennessee River Valley, East Tennessee." Ph.D. diss., University of Tennessee, 1984.

Cumming, William. *The Southeast in Early Maps.* Chapel Hill: The University of North Carolina Press, 1958.

[Darwin, Charles.] *The Correspondence of Charles Darwin, Vol. 1: 1821–1836.* Cambridge: Cambridge University Press, 1985.

Darwin, Charles. *The Origin of Species.* New York: Macmillan, 1962.

Davidson, William, et al. "Athapaskan Classificatory Verbs." *Studies in the Athapaskan Languages,* ed. Harry Hoijer. University of California Publications in Linguistics, Vol. 28. Berkeley: University of California Press, 1963.

DeBlieu, Jan. *Meant to Be Wild: The Struggle to Save Endangered Species Through Captive Breeding.* Golden, CO: Fulcrum Publishing, 1991.

DeBrahm's Report of the General Survey in the Southern District of North America [1773], ed. Louis De Vorsey, Jr. Columbia, S.C.: University of South Carolina Press, 1971.

Delcourt, Paul. "Quaternary Alluvial Terraces of the Little Tennessee River Valley, East Tennessee." In *The 1979 Archaeological and Geological Investigations in the Tellico Reservoir,* ed. Jefferson Chapman, Report of Investigations, No. 29, Dept. of Anthropology, University of Tennessee/TVA Publications in Anthropology, No. 24 (1980).

The De Soto Chronicles: The Expedition of Hernando De Soto to North America in 1539–1543. Vol. 1, ed. Lawrence A. Clayton, Vernon James Knight, Jr., and Edward C. Moore. Tuscaloosa: University of Alabama Press, 1993.

Dowling, Thomas, et al. "Response to Wayne, Nowak, and Phillips and Henry: Use of Molecular Characters in Conservation Biology." *Conservation Biology* 6, no. 4 (1992).

Dunn, Durwood. *Cades Cove: The Life and Death of a Southern Appalachian Community.* Knoxville: University of Tennessee Press, 1988.

Early Travels in the Tennessee Country: 1540–1800, ed. Samuel Cole Williams. Johnson City, TN: The Watauga Press, 1928.

[Emerson, Ralph Waldo.] *Selected Writings of Emerson,* ed. Donald McQuade. New York: Random House, 1981.

Fading Voices interview series. 1987. Museum of the Cherokee. Cherokee, North Carolina.

Fenollosa, Ernest. *The Chinese Written Character as a Medium for Poetry,* ed. Ezra Pound. San Francisco: City Lights Books, 1936.

Fischer, Hank. *Wolf Wars.* Helena, MT: Falcon Press, 1995.

Fogelson, Raymond. "The Conjurer in Eastern Cherokee Society." *Journal of Cherokee Studies* 5, no. 2 (Fall 1980).

Gittleman, John (ed.). *Carnivore Behavior, Ecology, and Evolution.* Ithaca, NY: Cornell University Press, 1989.

Goss, John (ed.). *The Mapping of North America: Three Centuries of Map-Making 1500–1860.* Secaucus, NJ: Wellfleet Press, 1990.

Haas, Mary. "Classificatory Verbs in Muskogee." *International Journal of American Linguistics* 14 (1948).

———. *The Prehistory of Languages*. The Hague: Mouton, 1969.

Handbook of American Indians North of Mexico, Part 1, ed. Frederick Webb Hodge. Washington, D.C.: Government Printing Office, 1912. (BAE Bulletin No. 30.)

Hann, John H. *Apalachee: The Land between the Rivers*. Gainesville: University Presses of Florida, 1988.

Hariot, Thomas. *A Briefe and True Report of the New Found Land of Virginia* [1590]. New York: Dover, 1972.

Hickey, Joseph (ed.). *Peregrine Falcon Populations: Their Biology and Decline*. Madison, WI: University of Wisconsin Press, 1969.

Hudson, Charles. *The Juan Pardo Expeditions*. Washington, D.C.: Smithsonian Institution Press, 1990.

———. *The Southeastern Indians*. Knoxville: University of Tennessee Press, 1976.

"Journal of an Expedition to South Carolina." *Journal of Cherokee Studies* 2, no. 3 (Summer 1977).

"Journal of Lieut. Col. James Grant, June–July, 1761." *The Quarterly Periodical of the Florida Historical Society* 12, no. 1 (1933).

The Journal of Major John Norton 1816, ed. Carl Klinck and James Talman. Toronto: The Champlain Society, 1970.

Kelly, James. "Notable Persons in Cherokee History." *Journal of Cherokee Studies* 3, no. 1 (Winter 1978).

King, Duane. "Cherokee Classificatory Verbs." *Journal of Cherokee Studies* 3, no. 1 (1978).

———. "A Grammar and Dictionary of the Cherokee Language." Ph.D. diss., University of Georgia, 1975.

Klinghammer, Erich (ed.). *The Behavior and Ecology of Wolves*. New York & London: Garland STPM Press, 1979.

Korstian, Clarence. "Perpetuation of Spruce on Cut-Over and Burned Lands in the Higher Southern Appalachians." *Ecological Monographs,* 7 (1937).

Krueger, John. "Two Early Grammars of Cherokee." *Anthropological Linguistics* 5, no. 3 (1963). Contains John Pickering's *A Grammar of the Cherokee Language* (ca. 1831) and a translation of Hans Conon von der Gabelentz's *Kurze Grammatik der Tscherokesischen Sprache* (1852).

Kuo Hsi. *An Essay on Landscape Painting (Lin Ch'üan Kau Chin)*. Translated by Shio Sakanishi. London: John Murray, 1935.

Lankford, George. *Native American Legends.* Little Rock, AR: August House, 1987.

Lanman, Charles. *Letters from the Alleghany* [sic] *Mountains.* New York: G. P. Putnam, 1849.

Lawrence, Barbara, and William Bossert. "Multiple Character Analysis of *Canis lupus, latrans,* and *familiaris,* With a Discussion of the Relationships of *Canis niger.*" *American Zoologist* 7 (1967).

Lawrence, D. H. *Sons and Lovers.* New York: Viking, 1968.

Lawson, John. *A New Voyage to Carolina* [1709]. March of America Facsimile Series No. 35. Ann Arbor, MI: University Microfilms, 1966.

Leopold, Aldo. *"A Sand County Almanac" and "Sketches Here and There."* New York: Oxford University Press, 1987.

Lieut. Henry Timberlake's Memoirs 1756–1765, ed. Samuel Cole Williams. Marietta, GA: Continental Book Company, 1927.

Matthiessen, Peter. *Wildlife in America.* New York: Viking, 1987.

McLoughlin, William G. *Cherokee Renascence in the New Republic.* Princeton, NJ: Princeton University Press, 1986.

———. "New Angles of Vision on the Cherokee Ghost Dance Movement of 1811–1812." *American Indian Quarterly* 5 (1979).

McLoughlin, William G., et al. *The Cherokee Ghost Dance: Essays on the Southeastern Indians 1789–1861.* Mercer University Press, 1984.

Mech, L. David. *The Wolf: The Ecology and Behavior of an Endangered Species.* Garden City, N.Y.: Natural History Press, 1970.

[Melville, Herman.] *The Writings of Herman Melville,* vol. 15, *Journals.* The Northwestern-Newberry ed., ed. Howard C. Horsford and Lynn Horth. Evanston, IL: Northwestern University Press, 1989.

Mooney, James. "The Cherokee Sacred Formulas: Statement of Mr. Mooney's Researches." *Journal of Cherokee Studies* 7, no. 1 (1992).

———. "The Ghost-Dance Religion and the Sioux Outbreak of 1890." In *Fourteenth Annual Report of the Bureau of American Ethnology,* pt. 2. Washington, D.C.: Government Printing Office, 1896.

———. "Myths of the Cherokee." In *Nineteenth Annual Report of the Bureau of American Ethnology,* pt. 1. Washington, D.C.: Government Printing Office, 1898.

———. *"Myths of the Cherokee" and "Sacred Formulas of the Cherokees."* Reprint. Nashville, TN: Elder Booksellers, 1982.

———. "Sacred Formulas of the Cherokees." In *Seventh Annual Report of the Bureau of Ethnology.* Washington, D.C.: Government Printing Office, 1891.

Mooney, James, and Frans Olbrechts. *The Swimmer Manuscript: Cherokee Sacred Formulas and Medicinal Prescriptions.* Bureau of American Ethnology Bulletin 99. Washington, D.C.: Government Printing Office, 1932.

Moore, Donald, and Roland Smith. "The Red Wolf as a Model for Carnivore Re-introductions." *Symposium of the Zoological Society of London,* no. 62 (1990).

Moses, L. G. *The Indian Man: A Biography of James Mooney.* Urbana: University of Illinois Press, 1984.

Nash, Roderick. *Wilderness and the American Mind* [1967], 3rd ed. New Haven, CT: Yale University Press, 1982.

Nowak, Ronald. "The Mysterious Wolf of the South." *Natural History* 74, no. 1 (1968).

———. *North American Quaternary "Canis."* Monograph of the Museum of Natural History, University of Kansas, No. 6 (1979).

———. "The Red Wolf Is Not a Hybrid." *Conservation Biology* 6, no. 4 (December 1992).

Oosting, H. J. and W. D. Billings. "A Comparison of Virgin Spruce-Fir Forest in the Northern and Southern Appalachian System." *Ecology* 32, no. 1 (1951).

The Payne Papers. Typescript at the Museum of the Cherokee. Cherokee, North Carolina. Courtesy of the Newberry Library, Chicago, Illinois.

"Portions of the Journal of André Michaux, Botanist, written during his Travels in the United States and Canada, 1785–1796." *Proceedings of the American Philosophical Society* 36 (1889).

Runquist, Jeannette. "Analysis of the Flora and Faunal Remains from Proto-Historic North Carolina Cherokee Indian Sites." Ph.D. diss., North Carolina State University, 1979.

Rutter, Russell, and Douglas Pimlott. *The World of the Wolf.* Philadelphia: J. B. Lippincott, 1968.

Sauer, Carl Ortwin. *Sixteenth Century North America: The Land and the People as Seen by the Europeans.* Berkeley: University of California Press, 1971.

Say, Thomas. "Vocabularies of Indian Languages" [1823]. In Reuben Gold Thwaites (ed.), *Early Western Travels 1748–1846,* Vol. 17 [appended to pt. 4 of *James's Account of S. H. Long's Expedition 1819–1820*]. New York: AMS Press, 1966.

Schroedl, Gerald (ed.). *Overhill Cherokee Archaeology at Chota-Tanasee.*

University of Tennessee Department of Anthropology Report of Investigations 38/Tennessee Valley Authority Publications in Anthropology 42 (1986).

Shaw, John Harlan. "Ecology, Behavior, and Systematics of the Red Wolf *(Canis rufus)*." Ph.D. diss., Yale University, 1975.

Sketches of the Olivers: A Family History 1726 to 1966. Pinehurst, N.C.: Colonel Hugh R. and Margaret T. Oliver, 1987.

Smith, Bruce. "The Archaeology of the Southeastern United States: From Dalton to de Soto, 10,500–500 B.P." In Vol. 5 of *Advances in World Archaeology,* ed. Fred Wendorf and Angela Close. Orlando: Harcourt Brace Jovanovich/Academic Press, 1986.

Smith, Captain John. *A Map of Virginia* [1612]. In *The Complete Works of Captain John Smith (1580–1631).* 3 vols., ed. Philip L. Barbour. Chapel Hill: University of North Carolina Press, 1986.

Snyder, Gary. *A Place in Space: Ethics, Aesthetics, and Watersheds.* Washington, D.C.: Counterpoint, 1995.

"Some Notes on Wolves." *Forest and Stream.* Jan. 27, 1906; Feb. 3, 1906.

Spanish Explorers in the Southern United States, 1528–1543 [1907]. New York: Barnes and Noble, 1946.

Speck, Frank, and Leonard Broom. *Cherokee Dance and Drama* [1951]. Norman: University of Oklahoma, 1983.

Summers, Lewis Preston. *Annals of Southwest Virginia 1769–1800.* Abingdon, VA: Lewis Preston Summers, 1929.

Swanton, John. *Final Report of the United States De Soto Expedition Commission* [1939]. Introd. Jeffrey Brain; foreword William Sturtevant. Washington, D.C.: Smithsonian Institution Press, 1985.

Swanton, John. *The Indians of the Southeastern United States* [1946]. Washington, D.C.: Smithsonian Institution Press, 1979.

Thoreau, Henry David. *The Maine Woods.* New York: Harper & Row, 1987.

[———.] *The Natural History Essays.* Salt Lake City, UT: Gibbs Smith, 1980.

———. *Walden.* Salt Lake City, UT: Gibbs Smith, 1981.

Wayne, Robert. "On the Use of Morphologic and Molecular Genetic Characters to Investigate Species Status." *Conservation Biology* 6 (1992).

Wayne, Robert, and John Gittleman. "The Problematic Red Wolf." *Scientific American* 273, no. 1 (1995).

Wayne, Robert, and S. Jenks. "Mitochondrial DNA Analysis Implying Extensive Hybridization of the Endangered Red Wolf, *Canis rufus.*" *Nature* 351 (1991).

Wayne, Robert, et al. "Mitochondrial DNA Variability of the Gray Wolf: Genetic Consequences of Population Decline and Habitat Fragmentation." *Conservation Biology* 6, no. 4 (1992).

Webb, William, and Raymond Baby. *The Adena People, No. 2.* Columbus: The Ohio Historical Society, 1957.

Wheeler, William, and Michael McDonald. *TVA and the Tellico Dam, 1936–1979: A Bureaucratic Crisis in Post-Industrial America.* Knoxville: University of Tennessee Press, 1986.

White, Peter, and Charles Cogsbill. "Spruce-Fir Forests of Eastern North America." In *Ecology and Decline of Red Spruce in the Eastern United States,* ed., Christopher Eagar and Mary Beth Adams. New York: Springer-Verlag, 1992.

Wieger, L. *Chinese Characters* [1922]. New York: Dover, 1965.

Williams, William Carlos. *In the American Grain* [1925]. New York: New Directions, 1956.

Witthoft, John. "Cherokee Beliefs Concerning Death." *Journal of Cherokee Studies* 8, no. 2 (Fall 1983).

Young, Stanley. "It's Red but Truly All-American." *American Forests* 81, no. 1 (Jan. 1972).

Young, Stanley, and Edward Goldman. *The Wolves of North America* [1944]. New York: Dover Publications, 1964.

Index